MANCHESTER MEDIEVAL LITERATURE AND CULTURE

GESTA ROMANORUM

Manchester University Press

Series editors: Anke Bernau and David Matthews

Series founded by: J. J. Anderson and Gail Ashton

Advisory board: Ruth Evans, Nicola McDonald, Andrew James Johnston, Sarah Salih, Larry Scanlon and Stephanie Trigg

MANCHESTER MEDIEVAL LITERATURE AND CULTURE

The Manchester Medieval Literature and Culture series publishes new research, informed by current critical methodologies, on the literary cultures of medieval Britain (including Anglo-Norman, Anglo-Latin and Celtic writings), including post-medieval engagements with and representations of the Middle Ages (medievalism). 'Literature' is viewed in a broad and inclusive sense, embracing imaginative, historical, political, scientific, dramatic and religious writings. The series offers monographs and essay collections, as well as editions and translations of texts.

Titles Available in the Series

The Parlement of Foulys (by Geoffrey Chaucer)
D. S. Brewer (ed.)
Language and imagination in the Gawain-poems
J. J. Anderson
Water and fire: The myth of the Flood in Anglo-Saxon England
Daniel Anlezark
Greenery: Ecocritical readings of late medieval English literature
Gillian Rudd
Sanctity and pornography in medieval culture: On the verge
Bill Burgwinkle and Cary Howie
In strange countries: Middle English literature and its afterlife:
Essays in Memory of J. J. Anderson
David Matthews (ed.)
A Knight's Legacy: Mandeville and Mandevillian Lore in early modern England
Ladan Niayesh (ed.)
Rethinking the South English legendaries
Heather Blurton and Jocelyn Wogan-Browne (eds)
Between earth and heaven: Liminality and the Ascension of Christ
in Anglo-Saxon literature
Johanna Kramer
Transporting Chaucer
Helen Barr
Sanctity as literature in late medieval Britain
Eva von Contzen and Anke Bernau (eds)
Reading Robin Hood: Content, form and reception in the outlaw myth
Stephen Knight
Annotated Chaucer bibliography: 1997-2010
Mark Allen and Stephanie Amsel
Roadworks: Medieval Britain, medieval roads
Valerie Allen and Ruth Evans (eds)
Love, history and emotion in Chaucer and Shakespeare:
Troilus and Criseyde and Troilus and Cressida
Andrew James Johnston, Russell West-Pavlov and Elisabeth Kempf (eds)
The Scottish Legendary: Towards a poetics of hagiographic narration
Eva von Contzen

Gesta Romanorum

A new translation

CHRISTOPHER STACE

with an introduction by Nigel Harris

Manchester University Press

Copyright © Christopher Stace 2016

The right of Christopher Stace to be identified as the author of this work has been asserted by him in accordance with the Copyright, Designs and Patents Act 1988.

Published by Manchester University Press
Altrincham Street, Manchester M1 7JA
www.manchesteruniversitypress.co.uk

British Library Cataloguing-in-Publication Data
A catalogue record for this book is available from the British Library

ISBN 978 0 7190 9715 7 *hardback*
ISBN 978 1 5261 2726 6 *paperback*

First published by Manchester University Press in hardback 2016
This edition first published 2018

The publisher has no responsibility for the persistence or accuracy of URLs for any external or third-party internet websites referred to in this book, and does not guarantee that any content on such websites is, or will remain, accurate or appropriate.

Typeset in Monotype Imprint with Scala Sans display
by Koinonia, Manchester
Printed in Great Britain
by TJ International, Padstow

Contents

Abbreviations	xii
Introduction	xiii
Translator's preface	xxvii
List of variant readings	xxix

Gesta Romanorum, translation

1	Of love	3
2	Of compassion, and the relief of one's kin	8
3	A just verdict	10
4	Of the justice of those in judgement	11
5	Of aspiring to fidelity	12
6	Of following reason	15
7	Of the envy of the wicked towards the good	17
8	Of vainglory	19
9	Of overcoming natural malice through gentleness	22
10	Of forgetfulness	26
11	Of the poison of sin, on which we are nurtured daily	28
12	Of dissipation	30
13	Of unlawful love	33
14	Of one's duty to honour parents	37
15	Of the life of St Alexius, son of the senator Euphemianus	39
16	Of an exemplary life	45
17	Of perfection of life	48
18	All sin, however grave in predestination, is pardonable, unless subject to the hell of despair	60
19	Of the sin of pride	63
20	Of misfortune and tribulation	66
21	Of guile and conspiracy and the caution required to oppose them	70

22	Of worldly fear	73
23	Of spiritual medicine	74
24	Of the devil's enticement by means of worldly goods	75
25	Of ingratitude and the forgetting of benefits	77
26	Of humility	79
27	Of just repayment	81
28	Of the abominable cunning of old women	84
29	A noteworthy tale concerning wicked judges	87
30	Of crime and judgement	89
31	Of the harshness of death	91
32	Of good inspiration	93
33	Of boastfulness	94
34	Of the consideration of life	96
35	Of the restoration of peace and the punishment of those who disrupt it	100
36	Of the course of human life	101
37	Of lifting the mind to heaven	104
38	Of the forethought required to extinguish sin	106
39	Of the reconciliation between God and man	107
40	Of skill in the manner of examination	109
41	Of the triumph of Christ and his measureless charity	111
42	Of the lack of charity	112
43	Christ closed hell by his Passion and willing death	114
44	Of envy	115
45	How only the good will enter the kingdom of heaven	116
46	Of the seven mortal sins	118
47	Of the three kings	120
48	Of the just consequence of evil	122
49	Of the cunning delusions of the devil	124
50	Of the praise of those who judge justly	125
51	Of unjust administrators	127
52	Of fidelity	128
53	Good rulers should not be changed	129
54	Of the celestial kingdom	130
55	Of the recall of a sinful soul sent into exile to make atonement	132
56	Of the remembrance of death	138
57	Of perfection of life	141
58	Of confession	145
59	Of excessive pride, and how the proud are often brought to extreme humility: a notable tale	147

Contents

60	Of avarice and its subtle temptations	154
61	Of the necessity of foresight	157
62	Of the beauty of a faithful soul	159
63	Of the pleasures of worldly things	162
64	Of our Lord's incarnation	165
65	Of the care of the soul	167
66	Of steadfastness	169
67	Of defences which are inadmissible in extreme cases	171
68	Of proclaiming the truth until death	175
69	Of chastity	177
70	Of the compunction of a faithful soul	180
71	Of the reward of the heavenly home	182
72	Of the destruction of the ungrateful	184
73	Avarice makes many blind	187
74	Of foresight and forethought	189
75	Of the avoidance of worldly cares	191
76	Of concord	194
77	One must not covet riches	196
78	Of the constancy of mutual love	198
79	One should not make ignorant presumptions	199
80	Of the devil's cunning and the hidden judgements of God	200
81	Of the wonders of God's providence and the rise of Pope Gregory	203
82	Of the judgement of adulterers	216
83	Of the meticulous safeguarding of the soul	217
84	Of the need for continual remembrance of God's goodness	220
85	Our prayer is like sweet music before God	222
86	God has compassion on sinners who beg for divine mercy	224
87	Christ gave himself up to death for us	226
88	Of the devil's cunning, which leads many to their death	228
89	Of the threefold state of the world	229
90	Of freedom of choice	231
91	Of sloth and idleness	233
92	Christ chose to die that we might live	235
93	Of the inheritance and the joy of a faithful soul	236
94	The beautiful soul, once infected with the leprosy of sin, cannot regain its former beauty except through the deepest sighs and sorrows	237

95	Christ restored our inheritance of the heavenly kingdom	239
96	The present life is a life of pardon and grace	240
97	Of death	241
98	God can be conciliated in this life	243
99	Of Christ's valiant battle and his victory	244
100	Christ does not with justice destroy a sinner at once, but mercifully awaits his repentance	246
101	The world is steeped in evil and there is tribulation on every side	247
102	Of the transgression of the soul and its wounds	250
103	Of the need to do everything with harmony and forethought	254
104	Of the remembrance of kindnesses	258
105	Of the inconstancy of everything good and especially of right judgement	260
106	We must be on our guard against the devil lest he beguile us	262
107	Of the remembrance of death and not delighting in temporal things	265
108	Of faithfully keeping one's promise	268
109	Those the devil enriches he finally lures into hell through their avarice	271
110	Of the miraculous recall of sinners and the merciful consolation of those in distress	274
111	Of the care and vigilance we must exercise towards the flock entrusted to our care	283
112	Of the healing of the soul by the celestial physician, whereby some are cured and some not	285
113	Of the spiritual battle and our reward for victory	287
114	Of the deliverance of mankind from the abyss of hell	289
115	Of Christ's dying for our reconciliation	291
116	Of the love of God, who loves us all equally, until we disregard him through our sins	293
117	Of the obdurate, who refuse to be converted, and their punishment through their appointed judgement	295
118	Of deceit and cunning	298
119	Of all things living in this world, man is the most ungrateful for the benefits he has received	301
120	Of the subtle deceits of women	306
121	Of worldly glory and luxury, which deceives many and leads them to destruction	312

Contents

122	Of adulterous women and the blindness of prelates	314
123	Young ladies should be kept from wantonness by their parents and not left to their own inclinations	316
124	Women should not be trusted, and no secrets should be told to them, since when they are angry they cannot keep them hidden	318
125	Women not only reveal secrets, but also tell many lies	321
126	Women are never to be trusted and especially not in the keeping of secrets: an amusing example	323
127	Of the justice and equity shown by Christ, the wisest judge, in his hidden judgements	325
128	Of those who unjustly seize the goods of others: their judgement at the end will be severe	328
129	The test of true friendship	332
130	A wise man is more valuable than a strong	334
131	Of the rich, to whom it is given, and the poor, from whom what they have is taken away, and how God rewards them for all eternity with the gift of a heavenly home	336
132	Of the envious, whose wicked lives infect the good	338
133	Of spiritual friendship	340
134	Of the innocent death of Christ	341
135	Of our conscience, and how, when it is anguished, we should have recourse to God through confession and good works	343
136	A shepherd of souls must be vigilant	345
137	Of the natural goodness of Christ and the compassion he naturally shows to sinners who turn from their ways, and how Christ accepts those whom the world rejects	347
138	Those whom we cannot overcome by severity, we should win over by kindness	349
139	Of the wounds of the soul	350
140	Of the justice and equity to which we must always aspire in our present and future lives	351
141	We must always listen to sound advice and reject what is not	353
142	Of the snares with which the devil seeks to entangle us in manifold ways	355
143	Of the fear of the last judgement	359
144	Of the present state of the world	361

145	Of the way of salvation, which our Lord God revealed through his son	366
146	Princes and other grandees must be boldly rebuked for their misdeeds	368
147	Of the bane of sin that poisons the heart	370
148	Sin will be punished in one place or another	370
149	Of vainglory, which is attended by many evils	372
150	Of the dew of celestial grace	373
151	Of the sinful soul made leprous through its sins, and how it is cured	374
152	Christ delivers us from eternal peril and the assaults of demons	378
153	Of temporal tribulation, which at the last shall be turned to everlasting joy	379
154	Of the heavenly home	409
155	Of the manner of fighting against the devil through Christ's Passion	411
156	Of the cause of the destruction of Troy	416
157	Of the punishment of sinners who do not make amends for their sins in the present life	417
158	Of the soul's immortality	419
159	Of the invention of vineyards	421
160	How the devil prevents us from doing good	422
161	One must always be grateful to God for his goodness	424
162	We should be wary of cursing	426
163	Of inordinate fear	429
164	Of the perversity of the world	433
165	Another example of the perversity of the world	435
166	Of the game of chess	436
167	Of heeding good counsel	443
168	Of eternal damnation	447
169	Of the twelve laws, and how a man should live	449
170	Of calling the sinner to the way of repentance	453
171	Of excessive love and loyalty, and how truth delivers us from death	455
172	The constancy of a faithful heart	459
173	Of the burdens and troubles of the world and the joys of heaven	468
174	No-one can alter the teaching of nature; and of the punishment for ingratitude	471

175	Of the strangeness of the world and its wonders, together with an interpretation of them	474
176	Of spiritual medicine	477
177	Of persecution	479
178	Of foresight, the mother of all riches	482
179	Of gluttony and drunkenness	487
180	Of fidelity	490
181	Of adultery	493
Bibliography		494
Index		497

Abbreviations

Scripture references are to the Douai Bible. Abbreviations are as those of the New American Bible with the exception of Ecclesiastes (= Eccles) and Ecclesiasticus (= Ecclus).

Caxton   William Caxton, *The Golden Legend or Lives of the Saints*, Temple Classics series, 7 vols, London: Dent, 1900
Herrtage   *The Early English Versions of the 'Gesta Romanorum'*, EETS, 33, ed. Sidney J. H. Herrtage
G.L.   Jacobus de Voragine, *The Golden Legend*; references are to the 2nd rev. edn of Giovanni Paolo Maggioni, Florence: Sismel, 1998
F.D.M.   Valerius Maximus, *Facta et Dicta Memorabilia* (=*Factorum et dictorum memorabilium libri IX*)
H.A.T.   *Historia Apollonii Tyri*
K.   Keller (1842)
L.   anonymous edn, Lyon (1555)
Migne   J.-P. Migne, *Patrologia Latina*, 1844–55
O.I.   Gervase of Tilbury, *Otia Imperialia*, ed. F. Liebrecht, Hanover: C. Rümpler, 1856
Oest.   Oesterley (1872)
Pliny   *C. Plini Secundi naturalis historiae libri XXXVII*, ed. K. F. T. Mayhoff, Leipzig: Teubner, 1906
Roze   J.-B. M. Roze, trans., *La Légende Dorée*, Paris: Garnier-Flammarion, 1967
Ryan   William Granger Ryan, trans., *The Golden Legend*, Princeton, NJ: Princeton University Press, 1993
V.   Vulgate
Warton   Thomas Warton, *A History of English Poetry from the close of the 11th Century to the commencement of the 18th Century*, London, 1774–81; rev. edn, 1871; Vol. III, diss. iii, '*On the Gesta Romanorum*'

Introduction

Gesta Romanorum ('Deeds of the Romans') is the title conventionally given to a diverse corpus of Latin stories (or exempla),[1] many based on Classical sources, which are accompanied by edifying interpretations designed for use by preachers. The *Gesta* were extensively read and enormously influential in the later Middle Ages, and indeed well into the early modern period. They were transmitted in a very large number of manuscripts (at least 300 of which are still extant), as well as in approximately forty printed editions dating from between 1472 and 1558, and were also translated into numerous European vernaculars: we know of four German redactions, as well as versions in English, French, Czech, Polish and Russian.[2] Moreover traces of the *Gesta*'s influence can be found in the works of such celebrated authors as Boccaccio, Chaucer, Gower, Shakespeare, Hans Sachs, Lessing, Hofmannsthal and Thomas Mann.[3]

No-one knows for certain when, where or by whom the *Gesta* were first compiled. The earliest surviving dated manuscript is Innsbruck, Universitätsbibliothek, cod. lat. 310 (generally referred to as J), which was written in 1342; but there are numerous indications that this manuscript does not transmit the earliest version of the collection, and a scholarly consensus has developed that it originated around 1300. Relatively recently, Brigitte Weiske argued plausibly that traces of the *Gesta*'s influence can be found in the *Solsequium* of Hugo von Trimberg, in which case at least parts of our compilation must have been available in some form by 1284; yet in the same volume Nigel F. Palmer demonstrated that certain other stories were discernibly influenced by sections of the *Moralitates* of Robert Holcot, which is generally dated to the 1330s.[4] Such evidence is only superficially contradictory, however; rather, it serves to reinforce the reasonable assumption that, for all its elements of consistency, a collection as diverse and complex as the *Gesta* is likely to have developed gradually over a period of decades either side of 1300, rather than being attributable exclusively or in its entirety to a particular author at a particular time.

As to the *Gesta*'s place of origin, the only two credible candidates are England and the German-speaking lands – for whatever reason, there are few manuscripts or other signs of widespread reception in the Romance area. A disproportionate number of the surviving manuscripts come from South Germany or Austria, though the importance of this fact should not be overestimated given the huge overall increase in manuscript production that occurred in precisely those areas in the later Middle Ages. Of perhaps greater consequence for attempts to establish the *Gesta*'s origins are the traces of German or English that appear in several manuscripts. The *Gesta*'s editor, Hermann Oesterley, was right to urge caution in drawing conclusions from these about the origins of the work as a whole, rather than of individual copies of it; nevertheless S. J. H. Herrtage's and Brigitte Weiske's profitable analysis of Middle English terms used and simultaneously glossed in early versions of stories such as our no. 166 has suggested that these may well have been composed by a native English speaker writing for a Continental audience.[5]

As suggested above, it is impossible to ascribe the *Gesta Romanorum* to any particular named author or authors. That said, there is some evidence to suggest that its first compiler might well have been a Franciscan. This is arguably implied by the colophon of its oldest manuscript, J, which speaks of the 'gesta imperatorum moralizata a quodam fratre de ordine minorum' (fol. 138r). This ambiguous designation of a 'certain brother of the order of the Minorites' might perhaps refer only to J's scribe, but it is far from impossible that the originator of the *Gesta* tradition is meant. The work's overriding concern with providing materials for preaching is, after all, firmly in line with established Franciscan interests, as indeed is the overall thrust of its theological message, which, as Weiske has demonstrated,[6] is compatible with Franciscan emphases, particularly of the early scholastic period before the advent of Duns Scotus. Moreover the *Gesta* texts themselves occasionally make positive references to the importance of preachers (see nos 85, 96, 131, 175), and no. 163 singles out the Franciscans and Dominicans in particular as being 'bound to be welcomed' by 'prelates of the Church'. One way and another, then, there is ample circumstantial evidence to suggest that the *Gesta*, along with several comparable collections such as the *Exempelwerk der englischen Bettelmönche*, were at least decisively influenced by the priorities and pedagogical techniques of mendicant friars.

Whatever their precise origin, the *Gesta* changed and developed enormously even in the course of their Latin manuscript tradition. In many ways, indeed, they could serve as an ideal example of the variability and 'openness' intrinsic to many medieval texts. Oesterley was perhaps using some poetic licence when he spoke of having to deal with 'almost as many texts as manuscripts',[7] but the frustration implicit in such a comment is understandable. Differences between *Gesta* texts abound, and go far beyond variations in individual words or phrasing; few manuscripts, indeed, preserve exactly the same corpus of exempla, and scribes and later printers clearly felt at liberty to add or subtract items at will. This means that no editor could responsibly seek to reconstruct an 'original' version of the *Gesta*, and could aspire to do no more than to produce a reliable version of a text or texts that were actually read in the Middle Ages. Oesterley's own text, on which Christopher Stace has based his translations in this volume, is based on two very early *Gesta* prints, those published by Nicolaus Ketelaer and Gerhardus de Leempt in Utrecht in 1472, and by Ulrich Zell in Cologne around 1473. The shorter Utrecht print contains the first 150 stories of Oesterley's volume, and he supplemented these by a further 31 from Zell's edition. Following Oesterley, scholars have tended to refer to this corpus of 181 items as the 'Vulgate' text – to which, in his edition, Oesterley proceeded to add some 82 others which stem from a rather arbitrary variety of manuscripts and prints. For reasons of space and coherence, only the first 181 stories are translated here. Oesterley's edition recommends itself as the basis for a new translation of the *Gesta* not least because the only more recent edition, that published by Wilhelm Dick in 1890, is fatally flawed.[8] It has the arguable advantage of being based principally on manuscript J, which contains some 220 stories, but, for reasons that now seem untenable, omits all of the work's allegorical interpretations – which, as much more recent scholarship has shown, are fundamentally important parts of the *Gesta* tradition, and of many other medieval exempla collections as well.[9]

Indeed, one could readily argue that the binary structure of story and spiritual interpretation, which is common to the vast majority of items in every version of the *Gesta*, represents the tradition's most powerful unifying force. The method used to convey the spiritual meanings behind the stories is in essence an allegorical one, and as such ultimately owes much to techniques used throughout the Middle Ages in the context of biblical interpretation. From the time of the Church Fathers onwards, scholars perceived in the Bible both a literal sense, a *sensus literalis*, and a spiritual sense, a *sensus spiritualis*; and the convention developed of dividing this spiritual sense into three levels, or layers. These consisted of the allegorical, concerned with the history of salvation, the tropological, which focuses on moral instruction for this life, and finally the anagogical, which relates to the end times and, as such, to heaven. Gradually these techniques designed to unearth the hidden, deep meanings of Scripture came to be applied, *mutatis mutandis*, to a wide range of non-biblical texts, and they underlie such exempla collections as the *Disciplina clericalis* of Petrus Alfonsi, the *De ludo scacchorum* of Jacobus de Cessolis, the *Moralitates* of Robert Holcot and, last but by no means least, the *Gesta* themselves[10] – at times to initially puzzling effect, as when we are told, for example, that figures such as Alexander the Great (no. 96), the tyrant Dionysius (no. 53) or a quarrelsome nobleman (no. 35) all, allegorically, represent God; or that a serpent can signify the devil (nos 37, 174, 176), yet also mankind (no. 99), a prelate or confessor (nos 105, 119), and indeed Christ (no. 141).

The compiler of the *Gesta* seeks, then, to disclose to his readers the 'true' meaning of the stories he tells, and lays particular, though not exclusive, emphasis on their allegorical significance: that is to say, he focuses on the devil and on human sinfulness, but also on the means available for their defeat, notably the salvific work of Christ and the sacraments of the Church (particularly penance). As one might expect from an author of his era, he often employs for this purpose the related method of point-by-point allegoresis: in our first story, for example, the king 'is' (or 'means' or 'represents') God the Father, his daughter the rational soul, the five soldiers the five senses, the burning lamp 'the will that is subject to God in all things', and so on. One of the *Gesta*'s most fascinating characteristics, however, is that this thorough if potentially tedious procedure is used frequently, but not altogether consistently. Some stories (such as no. 59, on Jovinian, or no. 110, on St Eustace) leave many parts of the story altogether uninterpreted and permit the narrative 'half' of the exemplum to take on an extensive life of its own; in others (e.g. nos 17, 97), this process is reversed, and a notably slight story is followed by a much more detailed moralization; and in at least a few others the basic structural division between narrative and interpretation is removed and the latter is either omitted entirely or subsumed within the story itself (see nos 36, 51).

For the modern reader at least, such obvious discrepancies of scale are not the only features that sometimes make the relationship between the two parts of a *Gesta* exemplum appear disconcertingly loose or, indeed, inappropriate. On occasion the tone of a narrative seems to jar somewhat with that of its accompanying interpretation, as when a jokily misogynistic anecdote such as no. 33, 'Of boastfulness',[11] gives rise to a decidedly serious moralization about Christ's Passion in which the three wives hanged on a tree are compared to the unholy trinity of sins from 1 Jn 2.15–16. Such jarring is perhaps an inevitable concomitant of the *Gesta* compiler's programmatic decision to impose Christian moral and theological lessons on Classical material – as we see, for example, when the story of Androcles and the lion (no. 104) or Seneca's cogitations about the lesser of two evils (no. 134) are used to teach lessons which bespeak a very different cultural and ideological awareness from that which will have informed their original authors and audiences. In instances such as these, one strongly suspects that, far from being in any way inessential or dispensable (as Dick, for one, plainly believed), the *Gesta*'s spiritual interpretations were regarded by contemporaries as ultimately more important than the stories that precede them – an impression that is reinforced by the numerous examples one could cite of motifs which appear to have been engrafted on to stories not for narrative reasons, but specifically in order to invite a particular moralization. In our no. 67, for example, the inclusion of the two paths (one hazardous and one light), each of which is guarded by a steward and three knights, is clearly called for primarily by the desired interpretation of the story as an allegory of God's judgement. Similarly, in no. 49, one is surely justified in surmising that Duchess Rosimila is specified as having two daughters and four sons simply because these have later to be interpreted as 'wicked pleasure and evil desire' and as the four cardinal virtues, respectively.

For all this, however, it is plain from comparably numerous instances of vivid, lively storytelling – apparent perhaps especially in longer tales such as those about Pope Gregory (no. 81) or Apollonius of Tyre (no. 153) – that the *Gesta*'s compiler(s) regarded the narratives as of interest for their own sake, rather than solely as vehicles for the conveying of sermonizing messages; and in general one can only admire the work's essentially pragmatic approach to its own allegorical content and method – one which facilitated a coherent presentation of its central didactic message, yet did not lose sight of the essentially literary nature of its basic material. This is no doubt one of the reasons for the *Gesta*'s remarkable popularity in the later Middle Ages: as Philippa Bright's recent survey of the circulation of Latin *Gesta* manuscripts written in England has implied, the collection, in its various forms, was used not only by preachers, but also by readers with more devotional, historical or literary interests.[12]

The sources of the *Gesta*'s stories are many and wide-ranging. Most versions of the *Gesta* ascribe roughly a quarter of their exempla to particular sources, though these attributions are by no means always reliable; and the matter is rendered still more complicated by the fact that much of the work's Classical material has certainly been transmitted indirectly, via more or less faithful medieval intermediaries. That said, Ella Bourne was able to establish that, of the 181 stories translated here from Oesterley's main corpus, some seventy-five are 'clearly classical in origin', while twenty others 'contain elements the classical nature of which in most cases is quite plain'.[13] Moreover, of these ninety-five items, roughly a third can be traced back to 'definite classical authors' and 'with a few exceptions deviate but slightly from the classical versions and contain few mediaeval additions'.[14] The Classical work used most frequently by the *Gesta* was the *Controversiae* of Seneca, material from which is found in our stories 2–7, 14, 73, 90, 100, 112, 116 and 134.[15] The next most frequently quarried Classical text is the *Facta et Dicta Memorabilia* of Valerius Maximus: stories 50, 52–3 and 149 are correctly attributed to Valerius, and 'several others are manifestly taken from him'.[16] Other important sources include Pliny the Elder (nos 37, 92, 139, 175–6 and 181 are based on his *Natural History*), Frontinus (nos 38, 88 and 152), Seneca the Philosopher (nos 32 and 140), Justinus (nos 21 and 169) and Macrobius (nos 87 and 126), while several stories 'have become so widely used in classical literature that they have, as it were, become standardized, with little or no variation to indicate individual authors'.[17] This is no doubt true also of the stories involving Alexander the Great (nos 36, 61, 96, 139 – though some of these contain seemingly inauthentic medieval elements). One way and another, it is clear that the subject matter of the *Gesta*'s narratives owes much to Classical literature and its medieval reception. Nevertheless by no means all of the *Gesta*'s narratives have Classical origins: there are Christian legends (such as nos 15, 18, 81, 110), anecdotes from medieval historiography (nos 38, 49, 162, 180), accounts of everyday life (nos 30, 82, 113, 133), humorous tales (nos 122–3, 125, 157) and not a few fables or accounts of natural historical *proprietates* whose genesis cannot always be dependably traced (nos 23, 68, 79, 83, 104, 175–6).[18] Certainly, to see our collection's use of Classical materials as in some way heralding or prefiguring the priorities of Humanism would be misguided – not least given that it evinces little or no interest in Classical culture in its own right, but rather shows a pervasive determination to use antiquity to promote an orthodox, medieval Christian world view. We should not be surprised to see Erasmus of Rotterdam, in his *Praise of Folly*, mock those preachers who 'bring in some popular story drawn, I judge, from the *Speculum historiale* or the *Gesta Romanorum* and interpret it'.[19]

What precisely, then, do these interpretations of the *Gesta*'s tales seek to teach their readers and hearers? In essence they present the human being, and his or her soul, in the context of a cosmic conflict between God and the devil. People are born with the potential to do good, and to become children of God; yet they have an equal propensity towards evil, and as such to be children of the devil. They therefore have free will; but they have been crucially assisted in any attempt to defeat sin and choose the path of salvation by the grace of God, by the redeeming death and resurrection of Christ, and by the sacraments of the Church. In particular, the *Gesta* tends to present the sacrament of penance, and especially its elements of contrition, confession and priestly absolution, as essential to human salvation. In ecclesiological terms, then, our collection is entirely orthodox, so much so that one can see it as constituting an 'attempt to assert the primacy of the Church's authority in moral and religious matters'.[20]

On the other hand, the individual reader or hearer of the *Gesta* is frequently urged to contribute to, or work out, his or her own salvation by approaching the sacramental process with willingness and determination, and by practising good works (see, for example, nos 7, 17, 20). The receipt of divine grace and forgiveness via the sacrament of penance, then, brings with it moral implications, responsibilities and challenges: those who have been made or re-made children of God should live in the light of this fact and seek to follow, to imitate Christ in their everyday lives. This emphasis on the *vita apostolica*, along with features such as criticism of avarice or worldly wealth (nos 31, 164) and the relatively frequent use of such biblical passages as Mt 25.34–41 (see nos 9, 14, 21) and 1 Jn 2.15–16 (see nos 107, 128, 132), are rightly seen by Weiske as 'at least not arguing against' the notion that the *Gesta* may have originated in Franciscan circles.[21]

All in all, this religious 'programme' of the *Gesta*'s moralizations undeniably sits, not least in the eyes of a modern reader, in an at times uneasy tension with the decidedly secular morality that underlies many of the stories to which it is applied. The latter tend to focus our attention less on matters concerning God and the soul, and more on a wide variety of social and relational concerns: problems to do with inheritance (e.g. nos 45, 87, 89–91), relationships between the sexes (nos 5–6, 120, 122), social barriers and the possibility of overcoming them (nos 17, 34), just or unjust judges (nos 105, 127, 140), and so on.[22] Indeed, despite being frequently set in the highest echelons of Classical, especially Roman society,[23] the stories typically thematize common and timeless human preoccupations with which readers and hearers of diverse social backgrounds were presumably able to identify.

If the dominant literary mode of the *Gesta*'s spiritual interpretations is allegoresis, then that of their narrative parts is dialogue – as befits subject matter that often foregrounds complex interpersonal relationships. While there exists in nearly all of the stories a clear narrative voice, the narrator in question often records a number of conversations, speeches, questions and answers. Rainer Nickel perceives in this the influence of Seneca's *Controversiae*, which either dramatize controversial legal debates or record advice given to people in difficult situations.[24] Be that as it may, the 'culture of conversation' that Nickel observes in the stories of the *Gesta* adds much to the work's liveliness and literary appeal.[25] Good examples of this include the judicious mixture of direct and indirect speech in no. 62, the quickfire exchanges of stories like no. 117 and, not least, the incongruous but often entertaining words uttered by a variety of animals (see nos 110, 141, 167, 174).

Furthermore, the concept of dialogue in its broadest and most inclusive sense is perhaps a fruitful one for attempts to comprehend and assess the *Gesta* tradition as a whole. Within the bipartite framework of individual exempla, the narrative and interpretative parts, responding to and shaping each other as they do, can be seen as engaging in a form of dialogue which is creative as well as problematic; and the same is true also of the distinct but related theological and moral (allegorical and tropological) sections into which several interpretations are in practice divided. Nor do individual exempla ever exist in a vacuum; rather, they are in an essentially dialogic relationship both with their sources and with the other exempla of the specific corpus in which they are transmitted. And the innumerable different versions of the *Gesta* as a whole inevitably exist in intertextual dialogue with those versions they have copied, translated, excerpted, extended, amended and indeed influenced. As we have seen, the *Gesta* seek in many ways to convey a basically monologic religious message – that is, the spiritual interpretations are intended to 'reduce the multiple voices and consciousnesses within a single text to a single version of truth imposed by the author'.[26] Nevertheless the modern reader will surely be disposed to hear this voice as only one of many that confront him or her when reading the translations that follow. It is a loud and insistent one, for certain; but it is in the end it is no more than one of the rich multiplicity of voices which, together, make reading the *Gesta Romanorum* a sometimes baffling but highly rewarding experience.

The *Gesta Romanorum* in English

As we have seen, the *Gesta* may well have originated in England, and hence it is not surprising that they seem to have been well known there in the Middle Ages and the early modern centuries. Within the Latin manuscript tradition, it is reasonable to designate, as English-speaking scholars have tended to, a particular group of *Gesta* manuscripts as constituting a discrete 'Anglo-Latin' tradition – which, while itself decidedly variable, differs from 'Germano-Latin' versions in the wording, ordering and, above all, quantity of its exempla (*Gesta* texts originating in England are almost invariably shorter, never exceeding 103 items).[27]

There can be no doubt that the fifteenth-century Middle English translation of the *Gesta* (assigned by its editor, Herrtage, to the reign of Henry VI, i.e. 1422–61) was based on one or other of these insular Latin manuscripts – though the three vernacular codices used by Herrtage in his edition include only seventy, forty-six and thirty-two stories, respectively.[28] These figures in themselves imply something about the extreme variability of the *Gesta*'s textual history, as does the statistic that only eight of these exempla (nos 8, 20, 27, 57, 60, 85–6 and 119) are shared by all three English vernacular manuscripts and by Oesterley's Latin corpus. Moreover, even those stories that are transmitted in both Latin and Middle English provide a revealing case study of the extent of the changes that *Gesta* exempla frequently underwent in the course of their transmission. Some differences are modest: in the English texts that correspond to our no. 74, for example, the king's golden apple is a golden ball, and an additional moralization is provided for the king's son, who becomes a peripatetic 'precheor and dyscrete confessoure'.[29] The English texts of Oesterley no. 99, however, record a significantly different account and interpretation of the enmity between the serpent and the toad. Instead of the knight being poisoned by the toad during the former's intervention on behalf of the serpent, he is followed home by the toad and poisoned by it while sleeping. The serpent appears and proceeds to fight and kill the toad while the latter is still in the knight's bedroom, and is given a bowl of milk for its pains. Whereas in our Latin version of no. 99 the knight is thereupon interpreted as Christ, the toad as the devil and the serpent as man, the allegoresis of the English version proceeds along quite different lines: the toad remains type-cast as the devil, but the serpent represents Christ and the knight 'every good christian man that lovith God with perfite herte', whose donation of milk to the serpent exemplifies the 'shewing of goode werkis'.[30] Finally, Herrtage's no. 47 is a highly idiosyncratic exemplum which clearly has its origins in a combination of, or contamination between, our corpus's nos 45 and 89. One day, in anger, a king's Spanish wife tells him that she has borne three sons, of whom only one is legitimate – which one, however, she declines to reveal. On his deathbed, the king bequeaths a ring to this (still unidentified) legitimate son, leaving them with an inheritance problem similar to that described in Oesterley no. 45. The sons seek advice from the King of Jerusalem, who has the father's body disinterred and asks all the sons to shoot an arrow at it. The youngest refuses to do so – an action which the following allegory interprets as a refusal to 'see God smitten by sin'.[31] The remainder of the interpretation shows an obvious affinity to Oesterley no. 89 and other versions of the 'ring parable' in presenting the three sons as the Jews and Saracens, 'fals Christen men'[32] and the children of God, respectively. All in all, an exemplum such as this is undeniably rather an extreme example of the essentially unstable nature of medieval textuality in general and of the *Gesta*'s transmission in particular; but it nevertheless powerfully underscores the truth that the work of medieval scribes and editors often went beyond a simple process of faithful copying and became instead a pro-active process of creative reception.

It remains only to survey the English versions of the *Gesta Romanorum* that have hitherto appeared in print. The first of these was made by Wynkyn de Worde in London at some point between 1510 and 1515, and consisted of some forty-three stories, taken in the main from the Middle English manuscripts, but considerably modernizing their language. This was followed by the far more influential version of Richard Robinson, which appeared in six editions between 1577 and 1601 and was patently known not least to Shakespeare.[33] Robinson's *Gesta* 'altered and modernized the language of Wynkyn de Worde, corrected [in a Protestant direction] the applications, and added an argument to each story, the number and order of which he has retained';[34] and so durable did his text prove that it received further reprints in Aberdeen in 1715 and Glasgow in 1753. By this time it was competing with a volume first printed by Richard Jakeway in London in 1703 (and reprinted in 1720 and 1722), which contained forty-five stories newly translated by one 'B. P.' from a Latin *Gesta* edition of 1514.

The most recent English translation of a corpus of Latin *Gesta* remains that of Charles Swan, published as long ago as 1824.[35] Swan used as his source an edition printed by Heinrich Gran in Hagenau in 1508, which was plainly very close to the 'Vulgate' text printed by Zell in 1473: his 181 items correspond to the first 181 subsequently published by Oesterley and newly translated here. Inevitably, Swan's translations are of their time. While by no means disastrous, they avoid or gloss over many difficulties, use much deliberately archaizing vocabulary and, more seriously, often make free with the actual contents of the text. The most notorious example of this comes at the end of story 28, which Swan changes fundamentally, in order presumably to accommodate his own and his nineteenth-century contemporaries' moral scruples. He shrinks from making specific mention of the climactic act of adultery between the lady and her youthful admirer which the ostensibly holy old woman has arranged, telling us instead that, on the night in question, 'the husband returned, and put the whole party to a shameful death. Thus did the wicked project of the old woman involve many in ruin.'[36] This of course necessitates an addition also to the accompanying moralization, which sees the returning husband as Christ, who 'will come during the night, and condemn the sinner to death'.[37] Whatever the merits of Swan's translation, so anachronistically moralistic and cavalier an approach to a medieval original cannot be viewed as appropriate for the twenty-first century; and this is one of the reasons why the translations that follow in this volume fill a significant gap in medieval studies which has been neglected for far too long.

Notes

1 The term 'exemplum' is used in this book to refer to a brief story which is used to make or reinforce a didactic point.
2 Of these, the German versions are the most thoroughly researched. See in particular Peter Hommers, *'Gesta Romanorum* deutsch. Untersuchungen zur Überlieferung und Redaktionengliederung', PhD thesis, University of Munich, 1968; Brigitte Weiske, *Gesta Romanorum*, 2 vols, Fortuna vitrea, 3–4, Tübingen: Niemeyer, 1992, Vol. 1, pp. 107–26. Also noteworthy is Geoffroy Hope's recent edition and study of the early sixteenth-century French version known as *Le Violier des Histoires Rommaines*, Textes Littéraires Français, 548, Geneva: Droz, 2008.
3 Details of such influence are given most conveniently by Udo Wawrzyniak, 'Gesta Romanorum', in Rolf Wilhelm Brednich et al. (eds), *Enzyklopädie des Märchens. Handwörterbuch zur historischen und vergleichenden Erzählforschung*, Berlin/New York: de Gruyter, 1987, Vol. 5, col. 1206. For a detailed analysis of Shakespeare's use of the *Gesta* in his *Merchant of Venice*, see Rebecca Krug, 'Shakespeare's Medieval Morality: *The Merchant of Venice* and the *Gesta Romanorum*', in Curtis Perry and John Watkins (eds), *Shakespeare and the Middle Ages*, Oxford: Oxford University Press, 2009, pp. 241–61. For a survey of the *Gesta*'s reception in vernacular English romance, see Diane Speed, 'Middle English Romance and the *Gesta Romanorum*', in Rosalind Field (ed.), *Tradition and Transformation in Medieval Romance*, Cambridge: Brewer, 1999, pp. 45–56.

Introduction

4 Nigel F. Palmer, 'Das *Exempelwerk der englischen Bettelmönche:* Ein Gegenstück zu den *Gesta Romanorum?*', in Walter Haug and Burghart Wachinger (eds), *Exempel und Exempelsammlungen*, Fortuna vitrea, 2, Tübingen: Niemeyer, 1991, pp. 137-72; Brigitte Weiske, 'Die *Gesta Romanorum* und das *Solsequium* Hugos von Trimberg', in ibid., pp. 173-207. See also Weiske, *Gesta*, Vol. 1, pp. 77-81.

5 See Hermann Oesterley (ed.), *Gesta Romanorum*, Berlin: Weidmann, 1872, p. 262; Sidney J. H. Herrtage (ed.), *The Early English Versions of the 'Gesta Romanorum'*, Early English Text Society, 33, London: Oxford University Press, 1879, pp. 175, 480; Weiske, *Gesta*, Vol. 1, pp. 30-41.

6 Weiske, *Gesta*, Vol. 1, pp. 172-94.

7 'fast so viele texte wie handschriften' (Oesterley, p. 255).

8 *Die 'Gesta Romanorum' nach der Innsbrucker Handschrift vom Jahre 1342 und vier Münchener Handschriften*, ed. Wilhelm Dick, Erlanger Beiträge zur englischen Philologie, 7, Erlangen: Junge, 1890.

9 This point is illuminated particularly tellingly by Christoph Gerhardt, *Die Metamorphosen des Pelikans. Exempel und Auslegung in mittelalterlicher Literatur. Mit Beispielen aus der bildenden Kunst und einem Bildanhang*, Trierer Studien zur Literatur, 1, Frankfurt: Lang, 1979.

10 For a classic account of this approach to interpretation, see Friedrich Ohly, 'The Spiritual Sense of Words in the Middle Ages', trans. David A. Wells, *Forum for Modern Language Studies*, 41 (2005), pp. 18-42.

11 As discussed in a note to the translation of this exemplum (pp. 94-5), Oesterley's baffling choice of title for it brings in another layer of apparent inconsistency.

12 Philippa Bright, 'Anglo-Latin Collections of the *Gesta Romanorum* and their Role in the Cure of Souls', in Juanita Feros Ruys (ed.), *What Nature Does Not Teach. Didactic Literature in the Medieval and Early Modern Periods*, Disputatio, 15, Turnhout: Brépols, 2008, pp. 401-24.

13 Ella Bourne, 'Classical Elements in the *Gesta Romanorum*', in Christabel Forsythe Fiske (ed.), *Vassar Mediaeval Studies*, New Haven, CT: Yale University Press, 1923, pp. 345-76, here p. 375.

14 Bourne, 'Classical Elements in the *Gesta Romanorum*', p. 376.

15 Bourne, 'Classical Elements in the *Gesta Romanorum*', pp. 349-51.

16 Bourne, 'Classical Elements in the *Gesta Romanorum*', p. 351. Into this category she places nos 8-9, 29, 41 and 48. Nos 33 and 42 are falsely attributed to Valerius.

17 For full details, see Bourne, 'Classical Elements in the *Gesta Romanorum*', pp. 349-67. The quotation is from p. 366.

18 For parallels to the *Gesta*'s fables in other collections, see the index to Gerd Dicke and Klaus Grubmüller, *Die Fabeln des Mittelalters und der frühen Neuzeit. Ein Katalog der deutschen Versionen und ihrer lateinischen Entsprechungen*, Münstersche Mittelalter-Schriften, 60, Munich: Fink, 1987, p. 849.

19 *Opera omnia Desiderii Erasmi Roterodami*, Leiden: Brill, 1969–present, Vol. 4, III, 9.
20 Bright, 'Anglo-Latin Collections of the *Gesta Romanorum*', p. 416.
21 Weiske, *Gesta*, Vol. 1, p. 193.
22 For a survey of much of the *Gesta*'s non-religious content, see Rolf Sprandel, 'Die *Gesta Romanorum* als Quelle der spätmittelalterlichen Mentalitätengeschichte', *Saeculum*, 33 (1982), pp. 312–22.
23 The *Gesta*'s presentation of its many Roman emperors is discussed by Johannes Schneider, 'Das Fortleben der römischen Kaiser in den *Gesta Romanorum*', *Klio*, 52 (1970), pp. 395–409.
24 See *'Gesta Romanorum'. Lateinisch/Deutsch*, trans. and ed. Rainer Nickel, Universal-Bibliothek 8717(3), Stuttgart: Reclam, 1991, p. 264. With regard to Seneca he mentions in particular nos 5–7 and 134.
25 Nickel, *'Gesta Romanorum'. Lateinisch/Deutsch*, p. 265.
26 Phyllis Margaret Paryas, in Irena R. Makaryk (ed.), *Encyclopedia of Contemporary Literary Theory. Approaches, Scholars, Terms*, Toronto: Toronto University Press, 1993, p. 596.
27 One is delighted to read (Bright, 'Anglo-Latin Collections of the *Gesta Romanorum*', p. 404) that Philippa Bright and Diane Speed are in the process of preparing an edition of this Anglo-Latin tradition, whose main characteristics are delineated by Bright in the article cited.
28 London, British Library, Harl. 7333 and Addit. 9066; also Cambridge, University Library, K. k. 1.
29 See Herrtage, *Early English Versions of the 'Gesta Romanorum'*, pp. 438–9 (quotation from p. 439).
30 Herrtage, *Early English Versions of the 'Gesta Romanorum'*, pp. 6–7.
31 Herrtage, *Early English Versions of the 'Gesta Romanorum'*, p. 170.
32 Herrtage, *Early English Versions of the 'Gesta Romanorum'*, p. 169.
33 Krug, 'Shakespeare's Medieval Morality', p. 243.
34 Herrtage, *Early English Versions of the 'Gesta Romanorum'*, p. xxiv.
35 *'Gesta Romanorum'. Entertaining Stories Invented by the Monks as a Fire-Side Recreation and Commonly Applied in Their Discourses from the Pulpit*, trans. Charles Swan, London: Routledge, 1824.
36 Swan, *'Gesta Romanorum'. Entertaining Stories*, p. 129.
37 Swan, *'Gesta Romanorum'. Entertaining Stories*, p. 129.

Translator's preface

This translation, the first in English since that of Revd Charles Swan (1824), is based on Hermann Oesterley's edition of 1872, though I have also consulted A. Keller's 1842 edition, occasionally a French translation of 1521, and a Latin text of 1555 printed at Lyon. The moralizations appended to 171 of the tales contain a large number of biblical references, many of them garbled or incorrect as to chapter and verse, and some even as to book. Correct references are given, wherever possible, in footnotes, along with references to lists of motif parallels in Oesterley's edition, in the *Index exemplorum* of F. C. Tubach, and in Geoffroy Hope's new edition of a French translation of the *Gesta*, *Le Violier des Histoires Rommaines*.

Translations (see also Bibliography)

English

Wynkyn de Worde, a translation of forty-three stories (unnumbered) from the *Gesta* (c.1510–15) together with moralizations. Eight of these are included in Herrtage, Text III, pp. 429–45.

Revd Charles Swan, *Gesta Romanorum* (Bohn Antiquarian Library, 1824) subsequently 'revised and corrected' by Wynnard Hooper (London: Bell, 1876), with introduction and notes. Swan's translation is unreliable; it regularly glosses over difficult passages and resorts to free invention. He gives very brief, often misleading or fanciful synopses of the moralizations.

Sidney J. H. Herrtage, *The Early English Versions of the 'Gesta Romanorum'* (1879), with full introduction, notes and glossary. This includes the moralizations, but they are generally quite different from those in Oesterley.

German

Johann Georg Theodor Graesse (1842; rev. edn, 1962): with two appendices containing additional stories and bibliography. Reliable and scholarly.

Winfried Trillitzsch (1973): includes the 102 further tales in Oesterley's appendix, and brief notes. Close to Graesse's version, and similarly reliable.

Rainer Nickel (1991): selections (forty-five tales) with some textual notes and an Afterword.

French

Le Violier des Histoires Rommaines: anonymous sixteenth-century translation of 149 of the 181 tales in Keller/Oesterley, including moralizations (sometimes very similar to, but often markedly different from those in Oesterley). Useful notes on sources and other versions. Now in a new edition (2008) by Geoffroy Hope.

Variant readings

Listed below are variant readings that differ from Oesterley's text (omitting minor points of orthography and punctuation, and misprints). References to Oesterley are to page and line numbers.

No. 4	Oest. 277.23	For *inicior*	*minor* (K., L.)
No. 17	Oest. 310.37f.	For *nec forcior fetet*	*Nec fortior efficitur* (K., L.)
No. 18	Oest. 311.23f.	For *cum Julianus, quinam essent inquisisset* etc.	*quos cum uxor Juliani videbat et Julianus non affuerat, quinam essent* etc. (K., L.)
	Oest. 313.7	For *consuetudines*	*consuetudines infigit* (K., L.)
No. 20	Oest. 317.38	For *cardinales et theorice*	*cardinales et theologicae*
No. 33	Oest. 332.17	For *sed non dividit*	*sed si non dividit* (L.)
	Oest. 333.14	For *venenoso*	*venenum* (L.)
No. 37	Oest. 337.20f.	For *quod si saepius venient*	*quae <si> saepius veniet* (K., L. *sibi*)
	Oest. 337.31	For *decepcionis*	*disceptationis* (L.)
No. 47	Oest. 345.12	For *cum coronis, quas portaverant in capitibus, preferentes*	*coronas in capitibus preferentes quas portaverat*
No. 54	Oest. 350.7	For *facias*	*facio* (K., L.)
No. 61	Oest. 369.29	For *impleverit*	*impleveris* (K.)
No. 63	Oest. 372.38	For *fuerit*	*fueris* (K.)
	Oest. 373.26	For *quia que*	*per quae* (K., L.)
No. 70	Oest. 384.31	For *verlebe*	*glebae* (K.)
No. 80:	Oest. 399.1	For *attrahas*	*detrahas* (K.)

No. 81	Oest. 405.39	For *video*	*videbis* (K., L.)
No. 109	Oest. 443.27	For *non tamen*	*non tantum*
No. 110	Oest. 445.31	For *medidianum*	*modo diabolum* (L.)
	Oest. 447.36	For *quod*	*quam* (G.L., L.)
No. 111	Oest. 452.17	For *more historico*	*more histrionico* (K.)
	Oest. 452.14	For *infidelis ero*	*filus mortis ero* (L.)
No. 119	Oest. 466.14	For *quantum Christus*	*quantum Christus exigit* (L.)
No. 121	Oest. 471.33	For *insequebantur*	*sequerentur* (L.)
No. 126	Oest. 477.10	For *ut parve rei*	*ut non parvae rei* (Macrobius, *Saturnalia* I.VI)
No. 127	Oest. 479.34f.	For *ut alter deus non esset*	*ut alter deus esset* (L.) (cf. Oest. 509.5)
No. 135	Oest. 490.24	For *in alia forma*	*in qua forma* (K., L.)
No. 142	Oest. 497.16	For *Sicut et cum enim*	*Cum enim* (K., L.)
	Oest. 498.2f.	For *quia si pars una eis vult dare aliquid, accipiunt de parte altera bursam plenam, dum illam trahant ad se*	*quia si pars vera eis nihil vult dare, accipiunt de parte falsa bursam plenam, ita quod illa trahat ad se decreta & decretalia* (K., L.)
No. 144	Oest. 501.7	For *perdicione*	*perditionem* (V.)
	Oest. 501.22	For *nuntii*	*meriti* (K., L.)
	Oest. 503.12	For *in justiciam*	*minus justam* (K., L.)
No. 153	Oest. 515.14	For *hic enim juvenis, ut suspicor, mihi comparandus, est Appollonius*	*hic enim juvenis, ut suspicor, mihi comparandus est*
	Oest. 524.13	For *Apoziatus*	*aporiatus*
	Oest. 527.7	For *Sic spinis rosa nescit violari et ullis*	*Sic rosa de spinis nescit violarier ullis* (1595 version)
	Oest. 527.8	For *Corruit et raptor gladium*	*Corripit et raptor gladii* (1595 version)
	Oest. 527.14	For *Fuge*	*Fige* (1595 version)
	Oest. 528.12	For *Per rotas et aedes*	*Per totas aedes* (H.A.T.)
No. 155	Oest. 534.23	For *per luta*	*per lora* (O.I. LIX)

Variant readings

No. 158	Oest. 538.30	For *curvi*	*Turni*
	Oest. 538.31	For *morte sua jacet*	*morte sua jacet hic*
No. 160	Oest. 540.19	For *dominus*	*domina (Le Violier)*
	Oest. 540.24f.	For *abducit*	*adducit* (K.)
	Oest. 540.30	For *vitam*	*viam* (L.)
No. 172	Oest. 566.10	For *mentis*	*mentio* (L.)
	Oest. 569.38	For *cum gladio potestatis diem latuit, quam sibi retinuit*	*cum gladio potestatis, quam sibi retinuit*
No. 177	Oest. 578.23	For *concors*	*consors* (L.)
No. 178	Oest. 582.5f.	For *veritas pertinet, scilicet vite contra omne peccatum contra affatum locutionis*	*veritas vitae pertinet, scilicet contra omne peccatum: primo contra affatum locutionis* (K.)
	Oest. 582.27	For *imitatione*	*invitatione* (L.)

Gesta Romanorum,
translation

1. Of love[1]

Pompey was a very rich and powerful king[2] who had a most beautiful only daughter. He loved her so dearly that he appointed five soldiers to guard her, ordering them on pain of severe punishment to protect her against every possible peril. The soldiers were armed and guarded her night and day, and set a lamp before her bedroom door so that no-one could get to her at night without them knowing, or while they slept. They also kept a little dog with a loud bark, so that its barking would wake them.

This girl had had a very sheltered upbringing, and she absolutely longed to see the sights of the world. One day when she was gazing out of her window, a duke came along, and as soon as he cast his unchaste eyes upon her he was smitten with love for her; for she was very lovely, and beloved by all, and the king's only daughter, and, after his death would by hereditary right succeed to the throne. This duke made her many promises to win her consent, and, trusting in his promises, she gave it. She promptly killed the dog, put out the lamp, got up in the night and went off with the duke.

The next morning an enquiry was made as to where she had gone. At that time there was in the palace a valiant champion who had always fought for justice in that kingdom, and when he heard

---

1 The titles are absent from the oldest versions of the text. Since some of those given in Oesterley's edition seem inappropriate, and at times inscrutable, translators have generally adapted them, or invented their own.
2 *Pompeius regnavit*: there is confusion between king (*rex*) and emperor (*imperator*) in this story, as often elsewhere in the *Gesta*. Needless to say, this is not Pompey the Great, who was neither king nor emperor: here 'Pompey' is used as a type of Roman potentate.

of the contempt the girl had shown towards her father, he hurried with all speed in pursuit of her. When the duke saw him coming, and that he was armed, he fought a duel with him. But the champion prevailed, chopped off his head and took the girl back to the palace. However, she did not see her father's face for a long time, but uttered sighs and groans without cease.

Now a wise man at the king's court heard of her plight. He had always acted as a mediator between the king and others, and was moved by compassion. Through him the girl was reconciled with her father and betrothed to a distinguished nobleman. After this she received a great variety of gifts from her father. First she had a multicoloured and richly embroidered tunic that reached down to her ankles and bore the inscription: '*I have forgiven you. Do not add to your offence.*' She also had from the king a golden coronet with the inscription: '*Your dignity comes from me.*' From the champion she had a ring with the inscription: '*I have loved you: learn to love [me].*' From the wise mediator she received another ring on which was engraved: '*What have I done? How much? Why?*' From the king's son she had another ring, on which was written: '*You are noble. Do not despise your nobility.*' From her own brother she also received another ring, on which was written: '*Come to me. Fear not. I am your brother.*' From her husband she received a golden signet by which she was confirmed as his heiress. On it was the inscription: '*Now you are married. Err no more.*' After receiving these gifts the girl kept them as long as she lived, and, beloved by all, ended her days in peace.[3]

[Moralization.][4] *Dear friends, the king is the Heavenly Father, who, through the Passion of his Son, has summoned us from the jaws of the*

---

3 This story is found in the *Moralities* (no. 24) of Robert Holcot, a Dominican friar who died in 1349. This was a collection of exempla for the use of preachers, and provided quite a substantial amount of source material for the *Gesta*. On this topic, see Nigel F. Palmer, 'Das Exempelwerk des englischen Bettelmönche: Ein Gegenstück zu den *Gesta Romanorum*?', in Walter Haug and Burghart Wachinger (eds), *Exempel und Exempelsammlungen*, Tübingen; Niemeyer, 1991, pp. 137–72 (especially pp. 142–6). For cognates of this story, see Oesterley, p, 718; Tubach, no. 1831; Hope, pp. 503–4.
4 A moral application (*moralisatio*) follows nearly all of the tales, some of them brief, some exceeding the length of the story itself.

1. Of love

devil. He is the King of Kings and Lord of Lords. Deuteronomy c. 32:[5] 'Is not he thy Father that hath possessed thee, and made thee, and created thee?' His only daughter is the rational soul, which is handed over to five soldiers, i.e., the five senses, for safe keeping, and they are armed by the virtues that man has received in baptism. These senses are sight, hearing etc., which have to guard the soul against the devil, the world and the flesh. The burning lamp is the will that is subject to God in all things, which must always shine brightly in good works so that it does not consent to sin. The little dog with the loud bark is the conscience, which has to fight back at sins, but – alas, alas! – the soul, wishing to see the sights of the world, often ventures abroad whenever it acts in defiance of God's commandment, and is at once, of its own volition, led astray by the duke, i.e., the ravisher from hell. And so the lamp of our good works is extinguished and the little dog of our conscience is slain, and accordingly the soul follows the devil in the night of sin. When our champion, i.e., God, hears[6] of this, 'because there is none other that fighteth for us, but only thou, our God,'[7] he at once fights against the duke, the devil, and takes the soul to the palace of the heavenly kingdom. The wise mediator is Christ, as the Apostle says in the First Epistle to Timothy, c.2:[8] 'There is one God, one mediator of God and men, the man Christ Jesus.' The king's son is Christ, for as the Psalmist says:[9] 'Thou art my Son etc.' Christ is also our brother, Gen 37:[10] 'He is our brother.' Christ is also our spouse, according to Hosea, c.2:[11] 'I will espouse thee to me in faith.' And again: 'A bloody spouse art thou to me.'[12] So through him we are reconciled to the Heavenly Father and called to peace. 'For he is our peace, who hath made both one', Eph 2.14. It is from him that we have received the aforesaid gifts: first the

---

5 Dt 32.6.
6 hears ... fights ... is: in the Latin these three verbs are in past tenses, but in the context it seems better to remain in the present tense.
7 One of the responses at Evensong: V: Give peace in our time, O Lord. R: Because there is none other etc.
8 1 Tm 2.5.
9 Ps 2.7.
10 Gn 37.27.
11 Hos 2.20.
12 Ex 4.25. The Vulgate has *Sponsus sanguinum tu mihi es*, an obscure expression. Zipporah has just circumcised her youngest son and touched Moses with the prepuce, and as a result the Lord allows Moses to escape his wrath.

tunic reaching down to the ankles, i.e., his most precious flesh, which is indeed of many colours, because it was embroidered with bloody stripes and bruises when he was scourged. And what does its texture signify but: 'I have forgiven you because I have redeemed you. Do not add to your sin?' 'Go,' he says, 'and sin no more.'[13] *This is Joseph's tunic that was dipped in the blood of a goat, Genesis 37.*[14] *That same Christ our King gave us a most glorious crown, i.e., when he was willing to be crowned for our sake; and indeed on it we find written: 'Your dignity comes from me.' Of this crown John writes, c. 19:*[15] *'Jesus came forth bearing the crown of thorns.' Christ is our champion, who gave us a ring, i.e., the opening in his right hand, and there we can indeed see it is written: 'I have loved you: learn to love [me].' Revelation 1:*[16] *'He hath loved us and washed us from our sins in his own blood.' Christ our mediator gave us a second ring, i.e., the opening in his left hand, where we can see written: 'What have I done? How much? Why?' What have I done? I emptied myself and took on the form of a servant. How much have I done? I made God man. Why? To save man that was lost. Of these three, Zechariah says, c. 14:*[17] *'What are these wounds in the midst of thy hands?' and he replies, saying: 'With these I was wounded in the house of them that loved me.' Christ is our brother, as Son of the eternal King. He gave us a third ring, i.e., the opening in his right foot. And what does that signify, but: 'You are noble. Do not despise your nobility'? Christ is likewise our own brother, and gave us a fourth ring, i.e., the opening in his left foot, on which is written: 'Come to me. Do not fear. I am your brother.' Christ is our spouse, who has given us the seal whereby the inheritance he bestowed on us is confirmed, i.e., the wound in his side which was pierced by the lance because of the immense love he had for us.*[18] *And what does that signify but: 'You are now joined to me through my compassion: sin no more'?*

Let us strive therefore, dear friends, to keep these gifts so undefiled that we may say, as we read in Matthew:[19] *'Lord, thou didst deliver*

13 Jn 8.11.
14 Gn 37.31.
15 Jn 19.5.
16 Rv 1.5.
17 = Zec 13.6.
18 *us*: the Latin (*te*) lapses into the second person singular. Such sudden changes of person are very common in the moralizations, and I have corrected the most awkward instances.
19 Mt 25.20.

1. Of love

to me five talents.' And so we shall without doubt reign in the bosom of heaven, which may [Father and Son] deign to vouchsafe us![20]

---

20 The moralizations usually end with a prayer for a safe passage to heaven or for delivery from hell. This formulaic coda is often abbreviated to just a few words (no. 71, e.g., has just one word: '*Ad* etc.'), but the meaning in the context is clear.

2. Of compassion, and the relief of one's kin

The emperor Titus enacted a law on pain of death that children should provide for their parents. Now it happened that there were two brothers, sons of the same father. One of them had a son, and seeing that his uncle was needy, in accordance with the law, but against his father's wishes, he at once made provision for him, and for this reason his father banished him from his house. Nonetheless, this did not prevent the son from continuing to provide for his needy uncle, and he gave him everything he required. Subsequently this uncle became rich and his father needy. In view of this, though his uncle forbade him to do so, he provided for his father, and because of it he was banished from his uncle's house. His uncle said: 'My dear nephew, as you know, I was once poor and against the wishes of your father you supplied me with everything I needed, for which I accepted you as my son and heir. An ungrateful son does not receive an inheritance, whereas an adopted son does. And you have been ungrateful in providing for your father against my wishes, so you shall not obtain my inheritance.' The son replied to his uncle: 'No-one should be punished for doing what the law commands and compels. The laws of nature and of Scripture compel a son to help his parents in time of need, and especially to honour them. So in justice I should not be denied the inheritance.'[1]

[Moralization.] Dear friends, the two brothers are the Son of God and the world, which have both proceeded from the Heavenly Father:

1 This story, like the following five, is drawn from the elder Seneca's *Controversiae*, five books of disputable questions of ethics or law designed to train young Romans in the oratory of the law courts. (For no. 2, see *Controversiae* I.1; for no. 3, I.3; for no. 4, I.5; for no. 5, I.6; for no. 6, II.2; for no. 7: cf. II.4.)

2. Of compassion, and the relief of one's kin

the Son of God by generation, the world by creation. From the beginning there was discord between them, and still is, such that he who is the friend of one is the enemy of the other. As James says, c.4:[2] *'Whosoever will be a friend of this world shall become an enemy of God.' But the son is any Christian, who is a son of Christ, and cleaves to him by faith. We should not therefore seek to please the world, with pride and avarice etc., if we wish to be sons of God; if we do other than this, we are undoubtedly banished from the fellowship of Christ in respect of our heavenly inheritance. If we wish to please Christ through works of piety, the world will hate us. But it is better that the world should hate us than that we should lose our heavenly inheritance.*

---

2 Jas 4.4. *constituetur*: Oest.; *constituitur*: V.

3. A just verdict

An emperor passed a law that if a woman committed adultery she should be thrown without mercy from the top of a mountain. Now it happened that a woman was found guilty of adultery, and in accordance with the law she was at once thrown from a mountain. But her fall from the mountain was so gentle that she received no injuries at all, and she was taken back to court. When the judge saw that she was not dead, he passed sentence that she should be thrown from the cliff again, and so executed. But the woman said: 'Lord, if you do this, you are acting against the law. The law says that no-one should be punished twice for the same crime. I have been thrown from the cliff once already for committing adultery, and God miraculously saved me. So I ought not to be punished a second time.' The judge replied: 'That is a very good defence. Go in peace.' And the woman was saved.

Moralization of the above tale: Dear friends, the emperor is our God, who lays down the law that if anyone subject to Christ, who is the spouse of the soul, is polluted in soul through the commission of a mortal sin, he must be cast from a lofty mountain, i.e., from the heavenly kingdom, as was the first man Adam. But God has saved us through the Passion of his Son. When man sins, because of His infinite mercy God does not instantly damn him, but saves him through His grace, so that he is not cast into hell.

4. Of the justice of those in judgement[1]

When Caesar was king, he passed a law that if a man took a woman by force and raped her, the woman should be permitted to choose whether he should die or marry her without a dowry. Now it happened that a man raped two women in the same night. One of them requested that he be put to death, the other that he should marry her. The rapist was captured and taken before the judge to answer to the two women according to the law.

The first woman insistently demanded his death in accordance with the law; the second claimed him as her husband. The first woman said: 'The fact is that the law ordains that I should obtain my wish.' The other replied: 'By the same token the law sides with me. But because my petition is less severe,[2] and more charitable, I believe that the judge will pass sentence in my favour.'

Both women appealed to the judge, and both demanded the benefit of the law. When the judge had heard both sides, he allowed the second woman to have the man as her husband. And that is what happened.

[Moralization.] Dear friends, the emperor is our Lord Jesus Christ, the ravisher any sinner, who ravishes, i.e., violates, two women, i.e., justice and mercy, which are both daughters of God. The ravisher is called before the judge when the soul is separated from the body. The first woman, i.e., justice, argues against the sinner that, according to the law of justice, he must suffer eternal death. But the second, i.e., divine mercy, argues that by contrition and confession he will be saved. Therefore let us strive so to please God [etc.].

1 Cf. Herrtage, Text III.XIX (Wynkyn de Worde).
2 *inicior*: Oest.; *minor*: K., L.; possibly *micior* (milder), as in Seneca *Controversiae* I.5?

5. Of aspiring to fidelity[1]

During the reign of a certain king, one of his subjects, a youth, was captured by pirates and wrote to his father for his ransom. But his father refused to redeem him, and so the youth wasted away a long time in prison. Now the man who was keeping him in chains had fathered a beautiful daughter who was much admired by men, and she had been brought up in his house until she was now in her twentieth year. She went to visit the prisoner frequently and tried to console him, but he was so downcast that he could not be comforted, and uttered sighs and groans without cease. It happened one day while the girl was visiting him that the youth said to her: 'Kind maid, if only you would try to set me free!' She replied: 'How could I ever do that? Your own father refuses to redeem you. Why should I, a mere stranger, consider such a thing? And if I were to set you free, I would incur the hatred of my father, because he would lose your ransom money. Nevertheless, grant me one wish and I will set you free.' 'Kind maid,' he said, 'ask me whatever you wish. If it is possible, I will do it.' She said: 'All I ask in return for your freedom is that, when an opportunity occurs, you take me as your wife.' He replied: 'I promise you this faithfully.'

At once, unknown to her father, the girl freed him from his chains and fled with him to his own country. When he got there his father said to him: 'My son, I am delighted at your return. But tell me, who is this girl you have brought with you?' 'She is a king's daughter,'[2] he said, 'and I am going to marry her.' His father replied: 'On pain of losing your inheritance I forbid you to marry her.' 'What are you saying, father?,' he said, 'I am more beholden to her than to you. When I was captured and in my enemy's

1 Cf. Herrtage, Text I.LXVII.
2 Evidently he was a pirate king.

5. Of aspiring to fidelity

hands and clapped in irons I wrote to you asking you to ransom me, and you refused to do so; whereas she delivered me not only from prison but from mortal peril. So I will marry her.' His father replied: 'My son, I can prove to you that you cannot trust her and consequently cannot possibly marry her. She deceived her father when she freed you from prison behind his back. And because she freed you her father has lost all the money he would have had for your ransom. It appears therefore that you cannot trust her and so cannot possibly marry her.[3] There is also another reason. I grant that she freed you, but that was only to gratify her desire to have you as her husband. So since it was desire that caused her to set you free, I do not think it right that she should be your wife.' When the girl heard these arguments she said: 'As to the first, your saying that I deceived my own father, my reply is that it is not true. He is deceived who is deprived of some good. But my father is so rich that he needs no help from any man. After weighing this carefully, I freed the young man from prison, and if my father had received his ransom, he would not have been much richer for it, while you said you would have been reduced to poverty if you had had to pay it. Therefore by doing what I did I saved you from having to pay the ransom, and did no injury to my father. As to the second argument, your saying that I did this to gratify my desire, my reply is that this cannot possibly be the case, because desire is kindled either by great beauty, or wealth, or physical prowess, and your son possessed none of these. His beauty had been impaired by imprisonment; nor was he wealthy, because he did not have the means to pay his own ransom; nor was he physically strong, because he had lost his bodily strength through wasting away in prison. It was compassion alone that moved me to set him free.'

When the father heard this, he could raise no further objections, so his son married the girl with great solemnity and ended his days in peace.

[Moralization.] Dear friends, the son captured by pirates signifies the whole human race held captive in the devil's prison, i.e., in his power, through the sin of its first parent. The father who would not redeem him is this world, which absolutely refuses to help him to escape from the

---

3 This argument is used in *Othello*, I.iii.293: 'She has deceived her father and may thee.'

devil's prison, but wants rather to keep him there. The daughter who visited him in prison is the divinity of Christ united to the soul, which took pity on mankind, and after his Passion went down to hell and freed man from the bonds of the devil. But the Heavenly Father has no need of our wealth, because he is pre-eminently rich and supremely good. So Christ, moved by compassion, came down to us from heaven and visited us when he took on flesh; and yet he sought no other reward for our redemption than that he be united with man, as Hosea says:[4] 'I will espouse her to me in faith.' However, our father, the world, whom many obey, always murmurs and argues against us: 'If you cleave to God, you will not have my inheritance', i.e., worldly wealth, because it is impossible to serve God and Mammon, Matthew c. 6:[5] But it is better to reject this world than to lose our fellowship with God, as we read in Matthew:[6] 'He who leaves his father and mother, his wife and lands for my sake, shall receive a hundredfold and possess life everlasting.' Which [may Christ grant] us etc.

---

4 Cf. Hos 2.20 (God takes back his unfaithful wife and showers her with gifts).
5 Mt 6.24.
6 Cf. Mt 19.29.

6. Of following reason

There was an emperor, a powerful tyrant, who married a very beautiful girl who was the daughter of a king. After the wedding each made a vow to the other that when one of them died, as a token of their great love the other should commit suicide.

It happened once that this emperor travelled to distant parts and remained there for a long time. Wishing to put his wife to the test, he sent a messenger to her to inform her that he had died. When his wife heard this news, in obedience to the oath she had made earlier to her husband, she cast herself from a lofty mountain, intending to kill herself. However, she did not die, and in a short while was restored to health. Then in her determination to die she decided to throw herself from the mountain a second time. When her father heard of her intention he forbade her to obey her husband's order and the oath she had sworn him, but she refused to listen to him. Her father said: 'Since you will not listen to me and obey me, you must leave my house at once.' She replied: 'I will not, and I can prove I am right for the following reason. When someone is under obligation to an oath, he is bound to fulfil it. I swore to my husband that I would kill myself as a token of my love for him. So I have done nothing wrong by wishing to fulfil my oath, and should therefore not be banished from your house on that account. Moreover, no-one should be punished for doing something commendable. And since a man and his wife are one flesh before God, it is a commendable thing for a wife to die for love of her husband. For this reason there was once a law in India requiring a wife, after her husband's death, to burn herself, or else to be buried alive with him in token of her grief and love.'

Her father replied: 'You said earlier that you were under obligation to an oath etc., but an oath is not binding when it results in an evil, such as death. An oath must always accord with reason, and thus your oath is null and void. As for your other argument, that it is commendable for a wife to die for her husband, that is not valid because, though they are one in the body through their carnal affections, yet they are two persons in their souls, which are essentially distinct from each other. And so your argument is not valid.'

When the girl heard his reasoning she could argue no further. She obeyed her father's command, and no longer desired to throw herself from a mountain, or to live any more with her husband.[1]

[Moralization.] Dear friends, the king is the devil. The girl is the soul, well-favoured and created in the likeness of God, but which through sin has become espoused to the devil. Now when a sin is committed there is a covenant that, if someone died in sin and was placed in distant parts, i.e., in hell, because of his pride, that the sinful soul should cast itself from a lofty mountain, i.e., from heaven, into hell. And so it was before the advent of Christ. But through Christ's Passion the soul was restored to health. However, it still frequently seeks to cast itself down, whenever it acts against God's commands. But God our Father does not wish us to be cast down into hell through sin, but rather that by contrition and confession we may wholly return to him and cleave firmly to him and possess everlasting life.

---

[1] Presumably she subsequently discovers that her husband is still alive and that she has been the victim of a ruse.

7. Of the envy of the wicked towards the good[1]

When Diocletian was emperor, among his subjects there was a well-born soldier who had two sons whom he loved dearly. Against the wishes of his father, the younger son married a harlot, and when his father heard he had done so, he was grief-stricken and banished him from his presence. This caused his son the greatest distress, and when his harlot wife presented him with a handsome son he was reduced to extreme poverty. He sent a messenger to his father asking him to have mercy on him, and when his father heard of his distress he was deeply moved, and took pity on him and was reconciled to him. After this reconciliation the son commended to his father the child which his wife, the harlot, had given him, and his father brought him up as his own son. When the elder brother heard about this he was angry and said to his father: 'You are mad, and here is my proof: anyone is mad who adopts as his heir, and supports, a son who has done him a great wrong. And my brother, who is the father of that son, did you a great wrong when he married that harlot against your wishes. You are therefore clearly mad to foster his son and to make peace with him.'

His father replied: 'My son, I have been reconciled to your brother because of the sincere contrition he has shown, and because of the entreaties of others. So it is fitting that I should love your brother more than you. And this is the reason: you have often offended me and never been reconciled to me because you would not humbly recognize your error. Now you are being hostile towards your brother, for you would have me banish him from my house, when you should rather be happy that he has been reconciled to me. And because you are being so hostile, you shall not receive the

[1] Cf. Herrtage, Text III.XXXVII (Wynkyn de Worde).

inheritance which you should have received by right. Your brother shall have it.' And that is what happened.

Moralization. Dear friends, by this father we are to understand the Heavenly Father, and by the two sons, the two natures, angelic and human. Human nature was joined to a harlot, i.e., iniquity, when it ate the forbidden fruit in defiance of God's command; so man was banished by his Heavenly Father. The son of the harlot is the whole of mankind which perished through its perverse sin. The son became ill because after his sin he was placed in this vale of tears, according to Genesis:[2] *'In the sweat of thy face.' But by Christ's Passion he was reconciled to God the Father, and is continually reconciled by the good works and prayers of the saints, who daily pour forth their prayers in heaven for humankind. Psalm [9]:*[3] *'The Lord hath heard the desire of the poor.' But the other brother, i.e., the devil, who is always hostile, assails us constantly and murmurs at our reconciliation, and argues that because of our sin we ought not to obtain our inheritance of the kingdom of heaven. But without doubt, if we lead holy and righteous and pure lives in this world, his arguments will not harm us at all; indeed, we shall obtain his own portion, i.e., the place which he himself lost in heaven.*

2 Gn 3.19.
3 Ps 9.17 (second part).

8. Of vainglory[1]

There was an emperor named Leo who derived an extraordinary pleasure from looking at beautiful women. He therefore had three statues made to stand in a temple and ordered all his subjects to worship them. The first statue had a hand outstretched towards the people, and on one finger was a golden ring on which was the following inscription: '*I am generous: behold the ring on this finger.*' The second statue had a golden beard, and on its forehead was written: '*I am bearded; let anyone who is bald come to me and take my hair.*' The third statue had a golden cloak and a purple tunic, and on its breast was written in letters of gold: '*I am one who fears nobody.*' The core of these three figures was of stone. When they were finished in accordance with his wishes, the emperor passed a law that anyone who stole the ring or the golden beard or the cloak would be condemned to a most ignominious death.

Now it happened that a baron[2] entered the temple, and when he saw the first statue and the ring on its outstretched finger, he drew the ring from its finger. He then went to the second statue and removed the golden beard from it. After that he went to the third statue, removed the cloak from it and left the temple. When they saw that the statues had been despoiled the people reported the matter to the emperor, and hearing what had happened, he was extremely

1 *De Vana Gloria*: It is not clear whether the vainglory is to be seen in the emperor's statues, and his command that his subjects should worship them, or in the thief's outrageous special pleading. Cf. Herrtage, Text I.LXVIII.
2 *quidam tyrannus*: this is likely to be some powerful landowner. The word *tyrannus* has a wide range of meanings and can be used of a feudal tenant or a baron. It may perhaps be used to indicate the character, as much as the status, of the thief.

displeased and summoned the baron who was the transgressor, and charged him with despoiling the statues in defiance of his edict.

'Lord,' he said, 'may I be permitted me to defend myself?' 'Very well,' the emperor replied. 'When I entered the temple,' the baron told him, 'the first statue, with the gold ring on its finger, stretched out its hand to me as if to say: "Take this ring." Even so I would not have taken it just because the hand was outstretched towards me; but then I saw what was written on the finger: "*I am generous: behold the ring,*" and at once I realized that it was the statue's wish that I should take the ring, and so I took it. Then I went up to the second statue and when I saw it had a golden beard, I thought to myself: "The man who created this never had a beard, because I often saw him, and it does not accord with reason that the statue should be nobler than its creator. It would be both a good and salutary thing to remove its golden beard." Nevertheless, I would not have taken it off until I read the inscription: "*I am bearded: let anyone who is bald come to me and take my hair.*" As you see, I am bald, and so I took the golden beard, and for two reasons: first, that then the statue should look like its creator and not be too proud of its golden beard; second, to relieve my own baldness with the aid of its hair. I then came to the third statue, which had a golden cloak. I removed the cloak because gold is cold in winter, and the statue is of stone, and stone is by nature cold, so if it kept the golden cloak, it would be adding cold to cold, which would trouble the statue. Moreover, if it had the cloak in summer time, it would be too heavy. And for all that I would not have taken it, until I read the inscription: "*I am one who fears nobody.*" And when I considered the great arrogance it displayed, I took the cloak from the statue to humble it.'

The emperor replied: 'My dear sir, when the law was passed expressly forbidding the despoiling of the statues, was it not laid down in that law that no-one should despoil the statues on any pretext? So, since you have interfered with things that did not belong to you, my sentence is that you be hanged from the gallows.'

And that is what happened.

Moralization. Dear friends, the emperor is our Lord Jesus Christ. The three statues are the three kinds of men of this world in whom God takes pleasure. As it is written:[3] *'My delights were to be with the children of men.' If we lead holy and righteous lives, God will remain with us.*

3 Prv 8.31.

8. Of vainglory

By the first statue, with the outstretched arm, we are to understand the poor and simple of this world, who, if they are to pass into the courts of princes and lords and accomplish anything, must stretch out their hands to offer gifts to the judge. For gifts blind the eyes of judges.[4] *And if a judge or one of his assistants is asked: 'Why have you accepted money from a poor man?', he will promptly reply: 'Can I not receive with a good conscience what is offered me willingly? He was kind to make me the offering, and if I had not accepted his gift, I would have been accused of boorishness, so to avoid having that said of me, I accepted the gift.'*

By the second statue we are to understand the rich of this world, who by the grace of God are raised to great wealth. Of these the Psalm says:[5] *'[The Lord dwelleth on high] lifting up the poor man out of the dunghill,' and he is at once judged by his rivals: 'Look, that wretch has a golden beard,' i.e., greater riches than his father had. 'Let us ruin him!' And, whether lawfully or unlawfully, they ruin this just man, saying: 'We are bald,' i.e., have no wealth; 'it is right that this rich oaf should share his riches with us.' Indeed, they often murder him in order to make off with his property. As we read in Timothy:*[6] *'The desire of money is the root of all evils.'*

By the third statue with its golden cloak we are to understand men in elevated positions, like prelates of the Church and earthly judges, who have to preserve the law, implant virtues and root out vices. So evildoers who refuse to submit to their discipline rise up against their prelates and superiors and conspire against them, saying: 'We do not want this man ruling over us.' Luke says:[7] *'The Jews, seeing Christ performing miracles and accusing them of sinning against the law, immediately conspired to kill him.' Such conspirators, who rob a man of his good name and virtuous reputation, shall die an evil death either here or elsewhere. Let us strive therefore so to amend our lives etc.*

---

4 Cf. Ex 23.8; Dt 16.19.
5 Ps 112.7.
6 1 Tm 6.10.
7 This is a conflation of Gospel texts: see e.g. Lk 19.47; Jn 5.18, 11.47ff.

9. Of overcoming natural malice through gentleness[1]

An extremely wise emperor called Alexander married the daughter of the King of Syria and she bore him a beautiful son. The boy grew, and when he attained his majority he continually plotted against his father and tried every way he could to kill him. The emperor was amazed at his behaviour and went to the empress, and said: 'My dearest, open your heart to me and tell me the truth; you may speak freely, have no fear. Have you ever been unfaithful to me with another man?' 'My lord,' she replied, 'why do you ask me such a question?' He answered: 'Your son is constantly seeking to kill me, and I find this astonishing, because if he were mine he would not be attempting such a thing.' 'God knows,' she said, ' that I have never been with another man, and I am prepared to go to any lengths[2] to prove my innocence. He is truly your son, but why he is persecuting you in this way I have no idea.'

When the king heard this, he spoke to his son and said, in the mildest tones: 'My dear son, I am your father. It was I who brought you into the world and you will be my heir. Why are you threatening to kill me? I have brought you up in the lap of luxury and all I have is yours. Put an end to this wickedness and stop trying to kill me!'

But the son took no notice of his father's words; day after day his spite towards his father increased and he continually strove to kill him, making attempts on his life both in public and private. In view of this Alexander took his son and went off to a secluded place, and holding a sword in his hand said to him: 'Take this sword and kill

1 Cf. Herrtage, Text I.L.
2 *per omnem viam*: if *viam* is right it could refer to some medieval trial by ordeal in order to establish the wife's innocence. Graesse and Trillitzsch translate *per omnem vitam* (for the rest of my life).

9. Of overcoming natural malice through gentleness 23

me here, because you will cause less scandal if you kill me in secret than in public.' At these words his son threw the sword away and knelt before his father, and weeping profusely begged for his mercy. 'My dear father,' he said. 'I have sinned against you, for I have wronged you, I have been wicked. I am no more worthy to be called your son.[3] Forgive me, I beg you, and love me, and from henceforth I shall be your beloved son and do your will in all things.'

Hearing this, his father fell upon his neck and kissed him, and said: 'My dearly beloved son, sin no more, be a faithful son to me, and I will be a kind father to you.' So saying he clothed him in costly garments and took him home with him, and held a great banquet for all the satraps[4] of his empire. He lived but a few days after this, and ended his life in peace. His son succeeded to the throne and ruled with great wisdom, and at the end of his life, when he was about to die, he had a banner carried through the whole of his empire and shown to everyone, on which was written: 'All things pass save the love of God.'[5]

[Moralization.] Dear friends, this emperor is our Lord Jesus Christ. The son who persecutes his father is a bad Christian, who is a legitimate son of God by virtue of his baptism. The boy's mother is the Holy Church, from which we receive our baptism and salvation, and through which the perverse sinner, who through sin is alienated from God, seeks the death of Christ. That Christ is himself the Father is clear from Deuteronomy c.32:[6] 'Is he not thy father etc.?' The Christian seeks the death of Christ whenever he acts in defiance of God's commands. Christ led us[7] into the desert of this world, and in that desert not only offered to die, but actually died for our sins. So for love of him and for the salvation of our soul we ought to resist sin and serve him faithfully. The father gave his son a sword with which to kill him. Even so God gives you a sword, i.e., the free will either to accept His love and grace,

---

3 The preacher's words are inspired by the story of the Prodigal Son, Lk 15.11ff., which is the theme of the moralization.
4 *satrapas*: the title of provincial governors in the ancient Persian empire.
5 *Omnia praetereunt praeter amare deum*: a medieval proverb, expressed in a dactylic pentameter.
6 Dt 32.6.
7 Here and in what follows, as in no. 1 and elsewhere, there is a switching of persons (*te, nostra*) in the Latin, which needs adjustment to avoid awkwardness in English.

or simply to thrust Him from you. Do therefore as the son did! Cast from you the sword of iniquity and malice, as he did of whom we read in the Gospel:[8] *'The son went abroad into a far country.' Like him, the sinner, when he loves carnal pleasures, abandons his lord, and the more he changes through sinning, the further he is estranged from his lord. He wastes his substance while devoting his life and thoughts to shameful acts, and so we read in the Gospel that the son 'began to be in want'. 'He went and cleaved to one of the citizens of that country. And he sent him into his farm to feed swine etc.' The son began to be in want when he abandoned his pursuit of virtue through sin. Thus the Psalm says:*[9] *'The rich have wanted, and have suffered hunger.'*

He 'cleaved to' one of the citizens, i.e., the devil, because demons are citizens and rulers of the darkness of this world, according to the Apostle:[10] *'For our wrestling is not against flesh and blood etc.' The swine is an unclean animal because it delights in filth, so demons are compared with pigs, because they will glut themselves on the filth of sins. The sinner feeds them with the filth of his crimes and he is their servant. Husks are the food of sinners, as fornication, drunkenness and gluttony are the food of devils. The sinner desires to fill his belly with husks, because no-one satisfies his appetite, since pleasure is always hungry, and very often the devil does not grant a man the means to satisfy his longing, knowing that he is dead through sin. However, the Lord through his grace often shakes the sword of iniquity from his grasp and the sinner says: 'Have pity on me!' as he recognizes his sins, and says: 'I have acknowledged my sin to thee.'*[11] *And God is moved to compassion and goes to meet him, and falls upon his neck and kisses him, and tells His servants: 'Bring forth quickly the first robe, and put it on him, and put a ring on his hand, and shoes on his feet, and bring hither the fatted calf and kill it, and let us eat, for this my son was dead and is come to life again: was lost and is found.'*[12] *So too the Heavenly Father sees His straying son when he is moved to repentance, and throws Himself upon his neck, when he imposes on himself the burden of penance, and kisses him, when the sinner delights in the words of His mouth, as we read:*[13] *'Let him kiss me with the kiss of his*

8 Lk 15.13ff.
9 Ps 33.11. The King James Bible (Ps 34.10) has 'the young lions'.
10 Eph 6.12.
11 Ps 31.5.
12 Lk 15.22ff.
13 Sg 1.1.

9. Of overcoming natural malice through gentleness

mouth.' He is clothed in the best robe when through penance he wins the love of Christ. The ring on his hand is the seal signifying his likeness to Christ in his good works. Therefore he wears the ring on his hand who never turns from Christ in any of his actions. The shoes on his feet are the examples of the saints who are dead, because, as shoes on the feet of animals protect their feet, so the examples of the saints protect our souls. The fatted calf is Christ, who was sacrificed for us on the altar of the cross, and fatted, because filled with the grace of the Holy Spirit. And then throughout the city of your heart you[14] will be able to display the banner of the valiant soldier of Christ, on which will be written: 'All things pass save the love of God,'[15] i.e., all my evil sins have been blotted out through penance and now I bear with me the fear of God and his grace, through which I shall obtain life everlasting; to which may [God] bring us etc.

---

14 Once again, there is a confusion of persons. The sinner has been spoken of as 'he': the speaker then applies his case to his audience: 'you', and finally, speaking of them individually, he refers to his sins as 'my'.
15 See note 5 above.

10. Of forgetfulness[1]

The emperor Vespasian[2] lived for a long time without children. Finally, on the advice of wise men he married a beautiful girl from distant parts and remained with her in her native land, where she bore him a child. After a time he wanted to return to his kingdom, but he could not get her to permit this. She always said: 'If you leave me, I will kill myself.'

The emperor therefore had two splendid rings made, and engraved upon gemstones images of special virtue, one an image of Memory, the other an image of Forgetfulness. These he inserted into the two quite similar rings, then gave the ring with the image of Forgetfulness to his wife, and himself took the other, so that, as they had been well matched in love, the rings they wore might also be well matched. And as soon as his wife took the ring she began to forget her love for her husband, whereupon the emperor happily departed for his kingdom and never returned to his wife, and there ended his days in peace.

[Moralization] Dear friends, by this emperor we are to understand the human soul, which must be taken up to its proper country, that is the kingdom of heaven, to the end that it may win its final salvation. Hence the Psalm says:[3] 'Save me, O God etc.' His wife is our flesh, which encumbers the soul with many pleasures which will prevent it from passing to eternal life, where the soul lives and reigns and has its every desire. And why does it not permit the soul to do so? Because the desire of the flesh opposes that of the spirit, and vice versa. Do

1 Cf. Herrtage, Text I.LI.
2 This is, of course, no more the historical Emperor Vespasian than the previous emperor was Alexander the Great.
3 Ps 53.3.

10. Of forgetfulness

therefore as the emperor did. Make two rings, one of Memory and one of Forgetfulness. These two rings are prayer and fasting, and both are permanent in their effect. In many countries if a woman wears a ring it is a sure sign that she is married. And indeed, when a man devotes himself to prayer and fasting, it is a sign that his soul is the bride of Christ. Now prayer is the ring of Memory, because the Apostle counsels us:[4] *'Pray without ceasing.' So man uses the Lord's Prayer that God may remember him, and indeed an angel will present his prayer to God, as in the case of Tobit.*[5] *Fasting can be called the ring of Forgetfulness, because it restrains the flesh and shuns it, lest it impede the use of reason and good works, which are the way to God. Let us strive therefore to keep these rings with us so that we may be found worthy to attain to life everlasting.*

---

4 1 Thes 5.17.
5 Tob 3.24f.

11. Of the poison of sin, on which we are nurtured daily[1]

Alexander was an extremely powerful emperor who had the philosopher Aristotle as his teacher, and Aristotle schooled him in every branch of knowledge. Hearing of his learning, the Queen of the North nurtured her daughter from the day of her birth upon poison, and when she attained to womanhood, she was so beautiful and men thought her so desirable that many of them were driven mad at the very sight of her. The queen sent her to Alexander to become his concubine. As soon as he set eyes on the girl Alexander fell in love with her and wanted to sleep with her, but seeing this Aristotle told him: 'Don't do any such thing. If you do, you will die at once, because she has been fed on poison all her life. And I shall prove the truth of this directly. There is a criminal who has been sentenced to death. Let him sleep with her, and then you will see if I am speaking the truth.'

And that is what happened. As they watched, the criminal kissed her and instantly fell dead. And when he witnessed this, Alexander heaped praises upon his teacher for saving him from death, and sent the girl back to her mother.

Moralization. Dear friends, this Alexander may be understood as any good Christian who is strong and powerful in the virtues he received in baptism, and remains powerful and strong as long as he preserves his charity and purity of life to arm him against the devil, the world and the flesh. The Queen of the North is abundance of worldly goods,

1 Swan notes that this based on the 28th chapter of the *Secretum Secretorum*, a medieval treatise which takes the form of a supposed letter from Aristotle to his pupil Alexander the Great. Cf. Herrtage, Text II.XXII. For parallels, see Oesterley, pp. 714–15; Tubach, no. 3830; Hope, pp. 475–6.

11. Of the poison of sin, on which we are nurtured daily

which seeks to kill a man, sometimes spiritually, and often physically. The poisoned girl is luxury and gluttony, which are nurtured upon delicious victuals that are poison to the soul. Aristotle is your conscience, or reason, which constantly murmurs at, and objects to those things that are harmful to the soul, and prevents a man from becoming involved with such things. The malefactor is the perverse man, who is disobedient to God and follows after the pleasures of the flesh rather than the commands of God. Such a person sleeps in sin all day long, by kissing, i.e., embracing, gluttony and luxury, through contact with which he is spiritually destroyed. Hence Ecclesiasticus says:[2] 'He that toucheth pitch shall be defiled with it.' Let us therefore strive to live sober lives, and thus we shall attain to life eternal.

---

2 Ecclus 13.1.

12. Of dissipation

In the reign of King Otto there lived in his kingdom a priest whose lustful behaviour often upset his parishioners and caused them great offence, and one of them would never attend any Mass when he was celebrating. Now it happened one feast day that at the time of Mass he was walking alone in a meadow and became so extraordinarily thirsty that it seemed to him that if he did not quench his thirst he would die. As he walked on it chanced that he came to a stream of the purest spring water, and seeing it he began to drink, and draw great draughts of it into his mouth. But having tasted it, the more he drank the more and more thirsty he became, and wondering at this he said to himself: 'I will look for the source of this stream, so that I can drink from the source itself.' And as he walked on he came upon an old man of distinguished appearance, who said to him: 'Where are you going, friend?' 'I am unbelievably thirsty,' he told him. 'I have found a stream and I drank the water, but the more I drank the more thirsty I became. So I am looking for the source of the stream so that I can drink from it and see if I can quench my thirst.' The old man said: 'Look, the source of the stream is over there. But tell me, why did you not go to church to hear Mass with the other Christians?' He replied: 'Truly, sir, our priest leads such a disgraceful life that I do not believe the Masses he celebrates are pure and pleasing to God.' The old man said: 'If you are thirsty, as you say, look, here is the source of the sweet water of the stream from which you have drunk.' So he looked, and saw a stinking dog with its jaws wide open, and through its mouth and teeth the water of the whole spring gushed in an amazing torrent. When he took a closer look, he was dumbstruck and terrified, and his whole body trembled, and because of the stench he did not dare to taste the water, though he was still unbelievably parched.

12. Of dissipation

Seeing him hesitate the old man told him: 'Don't be afraid, because you have drunk water from this stream. It will do you no harm.' So, reassured by this, he drank, and quenched his thirst, and said: 'Sir, no-one ever drank water so sweet!' The old man replied: 'Now consider how this sweet water, passing through the jaws of a foul-smelling dog, keeps its natural clarity and taste and is neither polluted nor changed. Dear friend, the same is true of a Mass that is said by an unworthy priest. And so, however displeasing the life of such priests, you ought nevertheless to hear their Masses.'[1] With these words the old man vanished from sight. And the parishioner revealed to others what he had seen, and thereafter heard Masses with devotion and ended his days in peace.

Moralization. Dear friends, this emperor is our Lord Jesus Christ, in whose kingdom, i.e., the world, there is an impure priest, i.e., the perverse Christian. As a priest has to keep watch over the souls of his parishioners, so too Christians have to keep watch over the virtues they received in baptism and carefully preserve them from defilement. This evil priest corrupts many people by his evil example. Hence Gregory says: 'For every bad example they give to their flock, they lose a soul.' So too the bad Christian drags many people down to hell both by word and example. If this happens to you, do as the parishioner did. Walk through the field, i.e., through town and country, until you come to the one your soul loves, in other words the old man, who is Christ, and you will find him through good works. But first you must drink of the stream, even if you do not slake your thirst. That stream from which you drink is baptism, which alone can slake the thirst caused by original sin; but if you fall once more into sin, your thirst cannot be slaked again until you go to the source of the spring itself. This fountain is our Lord Jesus Christ, as he says of himself: 'I am a fountain of water springing up into life everlasting', John c.4.[2] The rivulet or stream of this fountain, i.e., the words of Holy Scripture, can often come from the mouth of a foul-smelling dog, i.e., a preacher who is sinful. If it be asked why the waters of a fountain gush through the mouth of a foul-smelling dog, rather than from that of another animal, the answer is that in Holy

---

1 It is the ancient teaching of the Catholic Church that the personal sanctity of the priest does not affect the sacrament, which works *ex opere operato*, by its own power.
2 Cf. Jn 4.14.

Scripture priests are very often compared with dogs.[3] *And just as dogs have four good qualities, as the following verses tell us:*

*All dogs have four virtues; a tongue that brings healing,
Keen nostrils, steadfast love, and a bark that gives warning;*

so too, for the salvation of souls, in the business of the preaching of penance and confession, good priests should carefully preserve these four characteristics:

First, that their tongues should heal, licking and soothing the wounds of sinners, and not treating them too roughly. For dogs lick wounds and sores.

Second, as a dog tracks down a fox or a hare by the scent of its nostrils, so too a priest, by the scent of confession, skilfully and subtly tracks down the cunning of the fox, i.e., heretical perversity and falsehood, which results in the retention of sin; the timidity of the hare, due to detestation of evil or despair of pardon; and the ferocity of the wolf or lion, shown by a disdain for pardon; and other sins of this nature.

Third, just as the dog is known to be the most faithful of animals, because it exposes itself to danger for its master and its master's household and livestock, and fights off evil men; so too, for the Catholic faith and the salvation of souls, not only those of their own parishioners but those of all faithful Christians, priests must confidently risk body and soul, heeding the saying in John c.10:[4] 'The good shepherd lays down his life for his sheep.' Also 1 John:[5] 'He hath laid down his life for us. And we ought to lay down our lives for the brethren.'

Fourth, as a dog betrays the presence of thieves with his barking, and does not allow them to steal his master's treasures, so the faithful priest is the guard-dog of the Supreme King, and by his barking, i.e., preaching, and by his vigilant and continual prayer, he never ceases to drive thieves, i.e., the intrigues and machinations of the devil, from his Lord's treasure, i.e., the soul of his neighbour, which our Lord Jesus Christ has redeemed with the supreme treasure, i.e., that of his precious blood.

---

3 Comparisons between dogs and priests (and especially preachers and Dominicans, 'domini canes') were perhaps surprisingly common in the Middle Ages, the *tertium comparationis* often being the supposed healing properties of dogs' tongues. This tradition is surveyed in Meinolf Schumacher, *Ärzte mit der Zunge. Leckende Hunde in der europäischen Literatur. Von der patristischen Exegese des Lazarus-Gleichnisses (Lk 16) bis zum ‚Romanzero' Heinrich Heines*, Bielefeld: Aisthesis, 2003.
4 Cf. Jn 10.14f. These are the words of Jesus.
5 1 Jn 3.16.

13. Of unlawful love

An emperor had a beautiful wife whom he loved with a passion. In the first year of their marriage she conceived and gave birth to a son, and she loved the child so much that every night she slept with him in the same bed. When the child was three years old, the king died, and his death was deeply mourned. For many a day the queen bemoaned his death, and when he was placed in his sepulchre, she lived on her own, with her son, in a castle elsewhere, and she loved the boy so deeply that she could not bear to be without him. They continued to sleep together until the boy had reached the age of eighteen. And observing this passionate love between the mother and her son, the devil enticed them to commit an abominable sin, and the son had carnal knowledge of his mother. The queen immediately conceived, and when she became pregnant the son abandoned his kingdom in grief and went off to distant lands.

When the time came for her delivery, the queen gave birth to a beautiful son, but as soon as she set eyes on the child, she killed it by cutting its throat. But the blood that spurted from his throat fell on the palm of the queen's left hand, forming four round drops: O O O O. No matter what she tried the queen could not remove these drops from her hand, and she was so ashamed that she always wore a glove on that hand in case the drops of blood might be seen.

Now the queen was deeply devoted to the Blessed Virgin, but felt such shame at having conceived her own son's child and having killed her own son that she could not bring herself to confess this; yet every fortnight she confessed her other sins. She distributed generous alms for love of the Blessed Virgin Mary, and was beloved of everyone, because she was so kind to them.

It happened one night that her confessor was kneeling at his bed and saying five Ave Marias, when the Blessed Virgin appeared to him and said: 'I am the Virgin Mary. I have some secrets to tell you.' The confessor was overjoyed and replied: 'O most dear Lady, tell your servant whatever you please.' She said: "The queen of this kingdom confesses to you, but she has committed a crime which she dare not reveal to you because she is too ashamed. Tomorrow she will come to you to make her confession. Tell her from me that her alms and her prayers have been presented to my Son and have been accepted by him. I command her to confess the crime that she committed in the secrecy of her chamber; for she killed her only son. I have prayed for her and her sin has been forgiven if she will confess it. But if she will not agree to what you say, ask her to remove the glove from her left hand, and you will see in its palm evidence of the sin she has committed and not confessed. And if she refuses, remove the glove forcibly.' With these words the Blessed Virgin disappeared.

Next day the queen with great humility confessed all her sins with the exception of that one. When she had said all she wanted to say, her confessor replied: 'My dear lady, the people are forever wondering why you always wear a glove on your left hand. You need have no fear; just show me your hand so that I can see if anything is hidden there that might be displeasing to God.' 'Sir,' she replied, 'my hand is diseased, so I do not wish to show it to you.' When he heard this he took her by the arm and drew off the glove against her will. 'My lady,' he told her, 'do not be afraid. The Blessed Virgin, who loves you deeply, has commanded me to do this.' And when her hand was uncovered he saw the four circles of blood. In the first there were four Cs; in the second four Ds; in the third four Ms; and in the fourth four Rs. And round each of the circles, in the manner of a seal, was a blood-coloured inscription. They read as follows: *Casu Cecidisti Carne Cecata* [You have fallen to your ruin, blinded by the flesh]; *Demoni Dedisti Dona Donata* [You have given to the devil the gifts you were given]; *Monstrat Manifeste Manus Maculata* [The blemished hand reveals it clearly]; *Recidit Rubigo Regina Rogata* [The bloodstains vanish when the queen is questioned].[1]

At this revelation the queen fell at her confessor's feet and tearfully and humbly confessed the sin she had committed. And when she had received absolution and done penance, after a few days

1 *rogata*: 'questioned'. Here this clearly refers to the priest's interrogation of the queen. But the moralization (q.v.) interprets the queen as Mary, Queen of Heaven, and *rogata* as 'entreated', since she is our mediator.

13. Of unlawful love

she fell asleep in the Lord, and there was great lamentation for her death throughout the land.[2]

Application: Dear friends, this emperor is Jesus Christ, who espoused a beautiful daughter, i.e., human nature, when he took on our flesh. But he first became enamoured[3] *of her when the Father said to the Son and the Holy Spirit: 'Let us make man in our own image and likeness.' But alas, alas! After our Lord Jesus Christ begat in us a most lovely child, the soul, which was cleansed of all contamination through his Passion and the power of baptism, that soul was destroyed in us through sin and denied eternal life. Do you know how? Listen, I will tell you. Man has his own son with him, and lies with him in wantonness, when he indulges in carnal desire; and the consequence is that, knowingly and deliberately, you murder your own son, i.e., your soul or reason, with which you should control your feelings, but which is trampled by carnal desires. But the blood, i.e., sin, always remains on your hand, as the Psalm says:*[4] *'My soul is continually in my hands.' And this means: 'Whether we have done well or ill, it will be revealed to the Supreme Judge as if it were written on our hand.'*[5]

Or it can be interpreted another way: the queen is human nature, which was created in our first parent, Adam, and which conceived a child by its son, i.e., through carnal pleasure, when it ate of the apple. It then bore a son, i.e., the whole human race, which it slew through sin. As a result the blood on our hand, i.e., our sin, was so blatantly obvious that it could not be hidden by anything other than a glove, symbolizing our frailty in the face of the devil's deception, and so it could never be blotted out except by Christ's Passion. How? Here is the way. The confessor, i.e., the Holy Spirit, visited the Blessed Virgin, and by it she conceived a son, i.e., Christ Our Lord, by whom we have been saved.

But on the queen's hand there were four circles. The first circle is

---

2 A similar tale is found in the *Speculum Historiale* (VIII 93) of Vincent of Beauvais, a thirteenth-century Dominican friar who wrote, *inter alia*, a history of the world down to his own time. Cf. Herrtage, Text II.LXXIV. Other versions are listed by Oesterley, p. 715; Tubach, no. 2730; Hope, pp. 478–9.

3 *in amasiam accepit*: literally 'took as his concubine' or 'sweetheart'.

4 Ps 118.109, in which context it means: 'I would lay down my life at any moment.'

5 Note again the awkward change from third person (man) to second (you), then to first (we).

thought, which precedes sin; the second is pleasure; the third is assent; and the fourth is the act of sinning. Adam was marked with these circles when he sinned, as are we all when we commit sin.

In the first circle there were four Cs,[6] signifying: 'You have fallen to your ruin, blinded by the flesh.' That fall to ruin was the devil, because the whole of humankind was lost. 'You have fallen': Where? To hell, of course. 'By the flesh', i.e., with its impiety, its wickedness, its misery and its many afflictions. 'Blinded', i.e., you have become blind. In what way? Whereas before his sin man lived in Paradise, now because of sin he lacks that vision.

In the second circle there were four Ds,[7] signifying: 'You have given to the devil the gifts you were given.' What did you give him? Why, your soul, when you committed mortal sin. This was brought about by our first parent when he ate of the forbidden fruit. 'The gifts you were given' are the virtues with which God adorned you in baptism. These you have given to the devil by sinning.

In the third circle there were four Ms,[8] signifying: 'Reveals clearly', i.e., it is now perfectly clear in what wretched circumstances we are placed, because we were first created so that we should never die, but through sin we have become mortal. 'The blemished hand', i.e., except through Christ's Passion, no matter how many and good our works are, they will not be able to prevent us and the whole human race from going down to hell.

In the fourth circle there were four Rs,[9] signifying: 'Vanished', i.e., the burden of sin has vanished through Christ's Passion. 'Bloodstains', i.e., original sin is cleansed through baptism. 'The queen', i.e., the Virgin Mary [brought this about] through her holy conception of a child by the Holy Spirit. 'When entreated', because she is the mediator between God and man. Then, by the conception of her Son, through his birth, circumcision and Passion, as well as his holy resurrection and ascension, she brought us to eternal life.

---

6 *Casu Cecidisti Carne Cecata.*
7 *Demoni Dedisti Dona Donata.*
8 *Monstrat Manifeste Manus Maculata.*
9 *Recedit Rubigo Regina Rogata.*

14. Of one's duty to honour parents[1]

When Dorotheus was emperor he passed a law that children should provide for, and support their parents. Now at that time one of his subjects, a soldier, had married a beautiful and virtuous woman by whom he had a son. The soldier went off on his travels and on the way was taken captive and kept in close confinement. He at once wrote to his wife and son for his ransom. When his wife learned of his plight she was grief-stricken and wept so much that she became blind.

Her son said to her: 'I will go to my father and free him from prison.' 'Don't go,' his mother replied. 'You are my only son, my joy, and half of my soul. The same could happen to you as has happened to him. Would you rather ransom a father who has gone away than provide for a mother who is here? When you have to choose between two equally desirable things, it is best to cling to what you already have. You are my son as well as your father's, but I am here and he is not. So in my opinion you should certainly not leave me and go to your father.'

Her son replied with words of great wisdom: 'Although I am your son, my father is the principal cause of my being: he was the active partner, you the passive; my father went abroad while you sit at home; he has been captured and close bound in chains, while you are free; he is in the hands of his enemies, you are among friends; he is confined, you are free; true, you are blind, but he cannot see the light of day, only his chains, his wounds, his wretchedness. So I will go to him and ransom him.'

And so he did, and everyone commended him for the pains he took to secure his father's freedom.

1 Cf. Herrtage, Text I.LII; Seneca, *Controversiae* VII.4.

[Moralization.] Dear friends, this emperor is the Heavenly Father, who established the law that sons should support their parents in all things and obey them. But who are our father and mother? To be sure, our father is Christ. Deuteronomy 32:[2] 'Is not he thy father?' His affection for us is paternal, not maternal. You know that when a son does wrong his father corrects him severely; he beats him and scourges him, but his mother is soft and gentle and kind in the way she treats him. Christ, as our spiritual father, permits us to be scourged and to suffer greatly for our failings; but our mother is this world, which promises us pleasures and amusements. But our father goes off abroad; as the Psalmist says:[3] 'I am become a stranger to my brethren.' Christ is still bound and scourged, not personally, but in those who are his members. As the Apostle says to the Hebrews:[4] 'Whoever is guilty of mortal sin lies in the devil's prison.' But our father wants us to work for his redemption. Luke c.9:[5] 'Let the dead bury their dead,' said the Lord; 'but go and preach the kingdom of God,' and this is to redeem Christ. For whoever preaches the word of God fruitfully profits his brother and redeems Christ in him. Matthew 21:[6] 'What you did to one of these my humblest brethren, you did it to me.' But the mother, i.e., the world, does not permit a man to follow Christ in poverty, but makes him a variety of promises, and argues: 'I cannot live in abstinence, if you choose the way of penance in order to follow Christ.' And so it is with all the arguments she puts to a man. But do not yield to her! For truly she is blind. She will say to you: 'Come. Here I am. Let us relish the good things of life, and make haste to enjoy the world as we did in youth!' But, dear friend, if you are a good and grateful son, answer your mother, i.e., the world, as follows: 'My father is the principal cause of my being, i.e., my soul, and all I have he has given me willingly. Whereas my mother is the secondary cause, i.e., passive, that is, the wealth and the pomp of this world.'

I advise you not to hope for an old age that may bring suffering and blindness, because in your old age the world will abandon you, not you the world. If you could serve it longer, it would hold on to you. Let us therefore strive to amend our lives with all diligence, that we may be able to come to everlasting life. To which may God bring us, who lives and reigns, blessed for all ages to come. Amen.

2 Dt 32.6.
3 Ps 68.9.
4 I cannot trace this quotation. (The concept of mortal sin [*peccatum ad mortem*] is referred to first at 1 Jn 5.16f.)
5 Lk 9.60.
6 Cf. Mt 25.40.

15. Of the life of St Alexius,[1] son of the senator Euphemianus

In the reign of one of the emperors there lived in the city of Rome a youth named Alexius, the son of Euphemianus, a most noble Roman who was a leading figure in the imperial court. Euphemianus was attended by many boys and servants who wore golden girdles and were clothed in garments of silk. Now this Euphemianus was an extremely compassionate man, and every day three tables in his house were provided for the poor, for orphans, for pilgrims and widows, and he waited on them busily, and at the ninth hour together with other pious men he would take his supper in the fear of the Lord.

He had a wife named Agael[2] who was as devout as he was and of a like mind. Now since they had no child, in answer to their prayers the Lord gave them a son. After he was born, they resolved to live henceforth in chastity. The boy was given into the charge of teachers to be instructed in the liberal disciplines and he became proficient in all the philosophic arts. When he reached the age of puberty, a girl of the imperial house was chosen for him and she became his wife. On the night of the wedding, he and his bride entered the silence and secrecy of their chamber, and then the holy youth began to instruct his bride in the fear of God and to urge her to reserve the purity of her virginity. He then gave her his golden ring and the clasp of the sword belt he wore, and asked her to keep them for him, saying: 'Take these and keep them as long

---

1 Alexis of Rome was thought to have lived in the fifth century AD, but he probably never existed. His legend seems to be a conflation of the lives of two other holy men: St John Calibita and Mar Riscia of Edessa (D. H. Farmer, *The Oxford Dictionary of Saints*, Oxford: Oxford University Press, 1978).
2 *Agael*: *Aglaes*, G.L. XC.4.

as it pleases God, and may the Lord be always with us!' After this, he took some of his possessions and left for the coast, and there secretly boarded a ship and sailed to Laodicea. From there he went to Edessa, a city in Syria, where an image of our Lord Jesus Christ was preserved, an image on fine linen made by no human hand. On his arrival there he distributed all he had brought with him to the poor, and putting on ragged clothes he began to sit with other poor people in the porch of the church of Mary, Mother of God. When he received alms he kept what was sufficient for himself and gave the rest to the other poor people.

His father mourned the loss of his son and sent his servants to every corner of the world with instructions to search for him diligently. Some of them came to the city of Edessa and were recognized by the son, but they failed to recognize him, and gave him alms like the rest of the poor; and accepting them he gave thanks to God, saying: 'I thank you, Lord, for enabling me to receive alms from my servants.' And the servants returned and reported that he was nowhere to be found.

From the day of his departure his mother spread sackcloth on the floor of her bedroom and there she moaned aloud and gave voice to her misery, saying: 'Here I will stay for ever in mourning until I recover my son.' And Alexius's bride said to her father-in-law: 'Until I hear from my dearest husband, I will remain with you, like a turtle dove.'

When Alexius had remained in God's service in the porch of the aforementioned church for seventeen years, the image of the Blessed Virgin which was preserved there said to the sacristan of the church: 'Have the man of God come in, for he is worthy of the kingdom of heaven, and the spirit of God rests upon him, for his prayer rises like incense in the sight of God.' But the sacristan did not know whom she meant, so she spoke to him again: 'He is the man who is outside in the porch.' The sacristan then hurried out and brought him into the church, and when this occurrence became common knowledge, people began to regard him with reverence, and to avoid earthly acclaim Alexius left the place and boarding a ship there made for Tarsus in Cilicia. But under God's dispensation the ship was driven off course by winds and put in at the port of Rome. When he realized where he was, Alexius said to himself: 'I will stay unknown in my father's house and not be a burden to anyone.' Now he met his father returning from the

15. Of the life of St Alexius, son of the senator Euphemianus

palace surrounded by a crowd of servants, and began to call after him: 'Servant of God, have a pilgrim taken to your house and feed him on the crumbs of your table, that the Lord may deign to have pity on your own pilgrim.'[3] And hearing this, his father, out of love for his son, ordered him to be taken in. He gave him a room of his own in his house, and supplied him with food from his own table, and assigned him his own servant.

Alexius persevered in his prayers and mortified his body with fasts. The servants of the house laughed at him and would often pour water from the household utensils over his head, but he bore all this with great patience. Alexius remained unknown seventeen years in his father's house, and perceiving in spirit that the end of his life was approaching, he asked for paper and ink and wrote down the whole story of his life. On a Sunday after the solemnization of Mass, a voice from heaven thundered out in the sanctuary: 'Come to me, all you that labour, and are burdened, and I will refresh you.'[4] When they heard this everyone fell upon their faces. Then the voice came a second time saying: 'Seek out the man of God that he may pray for Rome.' So they sought him, but could not find him, and again the voice spoke: 'Search in the house of Euphemianus.' Euphemianus was duly questioned but said he knew nothing of this. At this point the emperors Arcadius and Honorius,[5] together with the Supreme Pontiff Innocent[6] went to Euphemianus's house, and the servant who attended Alexius came to his master and said: 'Consider, master: might the man they seek not be our pilgrim? For he is a man of exemplary life and patience.' Euphemianus went in haste to the pilgrim, and found him dead, and saw that his face was radiant, like the face of an angel; and he tried to remove the piece of paper he was holding in his hand, but was unable to do so. So he went and reported this to the emperors and the pontiff, and on entering Alexius's room they said: 'Sinners

---

3 *tui quoque peregrini*: generally taken as referring to his lost son, whose disappearance was presumably common knowledge. But the Latin might also mean 'on you who are also a pilgrim'.
4 Mt 11.28.
5 When Theodosius (the emperor referred to at the start of this tale?) died in AD 395, his two young sons, Arcadius and Honorius, divided the empire between themselves. But at the end of the tale we are told that Alexius died 'around AD 327'.
6 Innocent I (AD 402–17).

though we are, we govern the state and provide for the pastoral care of the whole world. Give us the paper so that we may learn what is written on it.' The pope then approached the body, and took hold of the paper, which was at once released, and he had it read out before Euphemianus and a great crowd of people.

When Euphemianus heard what was read out, he was horrified, and became faint; the strength drained from him and he fell to the ground. When he came to himself in a while, he tore his garments and began to pluck the grey hairs from his head, to tear at his beard and claw his face. He threw himself upon his son's body and cried aloud: 'Ah me, my son, why have you brought me such sorrow? Why have you caused me all this sadness, and brought upon yourself a life of pain and sorrow and lamentation for so many years? Ah, wretch that I am, to behold you, the guardian of my old age, lying dead upon a mattress and unable to speak to me! Ah me, what consolation shall I ever find?'

And when Alexius's mother heard the news, she appeared like a lioness breaking from a net; her garments were torn, her hair dishevelled, and she lifted her eyes to heaven, and being unable to get to the holy body because of the great crowds of people there, she cried: 'Make way for me, let me see my soul's consolation, who sucked at my breasts!' And reaching the body she lay upon it and wailed: 'Ah me, my dearest son, light of my eyes, why have you done this to me? Why have you treated us so cruelly? You saw your father and me weeping in my wretchedness and you did not reveal yourself to us! Your own servants ill treated you and you endured it!' Again and again she prostrated herself upon his body, now spreading her arms over it, now caressing his angelic face with her hands, and kissing it she cried: 'Weep with me, all of you here, because for seventeen years I had him in my own home and did not know him, and he was my only son! His own slaves insulted him and slapped him in the face! Alas, who will give my eyes a fountain of tears so that night and day I may vent my soul's anguish?'

Alexius's wife too came running; she was dressed in mourning,[7]

7 *veste adriatica*: generally interpreted as 'clothes of mournynge' (e.g. *Gilte Legende*, ed. Richard Hamer, Vol. I, EETS, 327, Oxford: Oxford University Press, 2006, p. 468), though I cannot parallel the usage. If the text is corrupt, *atrata* or *atrita* (black) would be an obvious emendation. E. Bensly suggested (*Notes & Queries*, April 1919, p. 92) that *adriatica* is a corruption of *Atrabatica,* originally meaning 'made by the

15. Of the life of St Alexius, son of the senator Euphemianus

and weeping, and saying: 'Ah me, for today I am all alone, I am a widow! I no longer have anyone to look to, no-one to follow with my gaze! Now my mirror is broken, my hope is gone! Now begins a grief that has no end!'[8] And when the people heard her, they wept bitterly.

The pope and the emperors then placed the body on a splendid bier and escorted it into the centre of the city, where it was announced to the people that the man of God whom the whole city was seeking had been found, and everyone ran to see the holy man. And if any sick person touched his holy body, he was instantly cured; the blind received their sight, the possessed were delivered from demons, and all the infirm, whatever illness they suffered, were cured when they touched the body. When they witnessed these miracles the emperors and the pope began to carry the bier themselves, that they too might be sanctified by the holy body. The emperors then had a large quantity of gold and silver scattered in the streets that, distracted by their love of money, the crowds might allow the body to reach the church; but the people forgot their love of money and more and more of them ran up to touch the holy body. And thus it was only with great difficulty that they at length got the bier through to the church of St Boniface the Martyr. There they laboured for seven days praising God, and erected a monument of gold and gems and precious stones in which, with great veneration, they placed the most holy body. And from the monument there burst forth a fragrance so sweet that everyone believed it was filled with all manner of perfumes. Alexius died around AD 327.

[Moralization.] Dear friends, Euphemianus can be seen as any man of this world who has a son he loves dearly, and whose best interests he strives day and night to serve. He gives him a wife, i.e., worldly vanity, in which he delights as a bridegroom delights in his bride; indeed, a man often takes more delight in worldly vanities than he does in his wife, because for worldly things a man often loses his life. The mother is this world, which loves its worldly children dearly. But the good son, like blessed Alexius, strives in all things to please God rather than to heed his parents and the vanities of this world, so that he can earn the

---

Atrebates' (a Gallic tribe), but subsequently associated with *atrum/ater* (black). See Du Cange s. *Atrabaticae*.

8 Here Swan comments: 'The reader will not perhaps comprehend much occasion for the lady's sorrow.'

reward spoken of in Matthew, c.11:[9] *'He that hath left land or house, father or mother or wife for my sake, shall receive a hundredfold and shall possess life everlasting.'*

Alexius boarded a ship etc. This ship is Holy Church, aboard which we must climb if we wish to obtain everlasting life; and we must lay aside our costly garments, i.e., the pomp of this world, and be numbered among the poor, that is, the lowly, in all we say and do. The sacristan who took Alexius into the church is the discerning confessor, who has to instruct the sinner and acquaint him with Holy Scripture to enable him to take better precaution against the things that harm his soul. But often a wind gets up and takes a man to his own country, as it did St Alexius. This wind is the devil's temptation, which strives day and night to keep a man from doing good. If therefore you feel that you are beset by some temptation, do as St Alexius did. Put on the garb of a pilgrim, that is, you must possess the virtues of the true pilgrim, so that you cannot be recognized by your carnal father or the world as anything but a man of God. But often when such a man chooses the life of penance, his parents grieve and are very downcast, seeing their children rejecting the world and embracing poverty for love of God. But it is safer to offend them than to abandon the way of perfection. Write on a piece of paper, therefore, as evidence of a clear conscience, proof that you have served God faithfully. Then the Supreme Pontiff arrives with the emperors, i.e., Christ with a multitude of angels, and will take your soul to the Church of St Boniface, i.e., to eternal life, where all goodness, i.e., all joy, abounds.

9 Cf. Mt 19.29.

16. Of an exemplary life

We read of a certain Roman emperor that he built himself a splendid palace, and while digging its foundations he discovered a golden sarcophagus fastened with three bands, and on the sarcophagus was the following inscription: 'I have spent; I have given; I have kept; I have had; I have; I have lost; I am punished. What I formerly spent, I possessed, and what I gave, I have.' When he saw this the emperor summoned all the governors of his empire and said: 'Go and consider among yourselves what this inscription means.'

They replied: 'My Lord, the meaning can only be this: there was an emperor before you who wished to set others an example, so that they should live life as he did. "I have spent" my life giving wise judgements, correcting others, and subjecting myself to the dictates of reason. "I have given" to my soldiers all they needed, given victuals to the poor, and to everyone, as to myself, according to their deserts. "I have kept" the rule of justice in all things, showing compassion to the needy, and paying workmen a fitting wage. "I have had" a generous and steadfast heart, giving riches to all who served me when I needed them, and showing kindness to everyone at all times. "I have" a hand ready to bestow gifts, a hand to protect and a hand to punish. "I have lost" my folly, I have lost the friendship of my adversaries and I have lost the lusts of the flesh. "I am punished" now in hell, because I did not believe in the one eternal God. "I am punished", alas, because for me there is no redemption.'[1]

1 The last two parts of the inscription are given no interpretation. The moralization says, in sum: what the Christian has expended was his time in works of mercy (for the seven spiritual works of mercy, see no. 83, note 3), for which he has received Christ's grace; he has given his whole obedience to prelates and so has eternal life.

When the emperor heard this, he governed himself and others more prudently all the rest of his life, and ended his days in peace.

[Moralization] Dear friends, this emperor symbolizes any Christian, whose bounden duty it is to create a basilica, i.e., a heart ready for God, that he may do His will in all things, and to excavate his heart by means of penance, and so he will be able to find a golden sarcophagus, i.e., a soul, gilded and full of virtues through God's good grace, which is fastened by three golden bands, which are faith, hope and charity. And what is written on it? First, 'I have spent.' Tell me, dear friend, what have you spent? The good Christian should answer: 'My body and soul in the service of God.' All of you who spend your life in this way will be sure of a rich reward in eternal life. The second thing inscribed is: 'I have kept.'² Tell me, dear friend, what have you kept? The good Christian should answer: 'A contrite and humble heart that is ready to heed God's will in all things, and do whatever pleases him.' The third thing inscribed is: 'I have given.' Tell me, dear friend, what have you given? The good Christian should answer: 'My love to God with all my heart and with all my soul and with all my mind, and love to my neighbour in accordance with God's commandment.' The fourth thing inscribed is: 'I have had.' Tell me, dear friend, what have you had? The good Christian should answer: 'Truly a wretched life, because I was conceived in sin, and born in original sin, and formed of base matter.' The fifth thing inscribed is: 'I have.' Tell me, dear friend, what do you have? The good Christian should answer: 'Truly, the grace of baptism, and through the virtues God gave me in baptism, I became a soldier of Christ, when I had been a slave of the devil.' The sixth thing inscribed is: 'I have lost.' Tell me, dear friend, what have you lost? The good Christian should answer: 'Truly, God's grace. But through penance I have made amends for all the sins that I committed to offend the Lord, because penance cleanses us from sin.' The seventh thing inscribed is: 'I am punished.' Tell me, dear friend, why do you say you are punished? The good Christian should answer: 'Because my soul is constantly troubled for my sins and wickednesses, and my flesh undergoes penance.' The eighth thing inscribed is: 'What I spent, I possessed.' Tell me, dear friend, what does that mean? The good Christian should answer: 'I have spent my time doing works of mercy

---

2 The second word of the inscription, according to the tale, was in fact *donavi* (I have given).

16. Of an exemplary life

through the grace I have received from my Lord Jesus Christ.' The ninth thing inscribed is: 'What I gave, I have.' Tell me, dear friend, what have you given that you now have?' The good Christian should answer: 'Truly, all my life I have given counsel, and I have given my assent, and subjected all my will to the will of my prelate for the love of God,[3] *and therefore I now have eternal life in heaven.'*

---

3 *consilium et assensum*: the Christian hardly gives his *consilium* (advice) to his prelate. Nor is it clear to whom the Christian has always given his *assensum* (assent, approval). Perhaps for *consilium* we should read *consensum*. He has consented to, and been compliant with, all his prelate has prescribed. (Cf. *Le Violier*: '*J'ay donné tout le temps de ma vie conseil, consentement, et bon propos de vivre; vers mes prelatz obédience de bon cueur et à Dieu service.*')

17. Of perfection of life[1]

An emperor enacted a law that whoever wished to serve him would obtain employment in his service if he knocked three times on the palace gate, and this would be the sign that he wanted to enter his service. It happened that there lived in the city of Rome a poor man named Guido, and when he heard of this law he began to think to himself: 'I am poor and of lowly birth. It would be better for me to serve and acquire wealth than to live like this in poverty for ever.' So he went to the palace, gave three knocks on the door as prescribed by the law, and the gatekeeper opened the gate and took him in. On bended knee Guido greeted the emperor, and the emperor said: 'Tell me, what do you want, my friend?' 'To serve you, my Lord.' 'What kind of service would you be able to give me?' the emperor asked. 'My Lord', Guido replied, 'I am skilled in six kinds of service. First, I can act as a prince's bodyguard night and day, make his bed, set his food before him, and wash his feet. Second, I can keep watch when others are asleep, and sleep when others watch. Third, I know the taste of good drink and can judge the quality of any drink by its taste. Fourth, I know how to invite people to a feast to do honour to their host. Fifth, I can make a fire without smoke that will warm all who are near it. Sixth, I can teach people a good way to get to the Holy Land so that they come back safe and sound.'

The emperor said: 'These are excellent services and extremely useful. You shall stay with me, and first I want you to be my bodyguard. You will be my bodyguard for a year.' 'My Lord,' Guido replied, 'I am ready to do as you wish.'

Every night Guido made the emperor's bed neatly, and washed

---

1 Cf. Herrtage, Text I.XXVIII.

17. Of perfection of life

and changed the sheets often. Every night he lay down at the door of the bedchamber ready armed, and kept a dog with him so that he would be woken by its barking if he fell asleep and someone came along. Once each week he washed the emperor's feet, and served him in every way so ably and well that no fault could be found with him and the emperor was full of praise for him. At the end of the year he made him his seneschal, and asked him to perform his second service, that of keeping watch. Once appointed seneschal, Guido worked hard keeping watch the whole summer and made all the necessary provisions for the winter. And when winter approached and others began to watch and toil, Guido rested and slept. And so he completed his second service, that of watching while others slept. When the emperor noted that he had faithfully performed these two services, he was delighted and called his butler and said to him: 'Friend, put some vinegar, some fine wine, and some new wine into my cup, and give it to Guido to drink, because that is his third service – to judge the quality of what he drinks. The butler did as he said, and when Guido had tasted the mixture. He said: 'It was good, it is good, it will be good. That is to say: the new wine *will be* good, the wine *is* good, and the vinegar *was* good.' Observing how prudently he had judged what he had drunk, the emperor said to him: 'Friend, go through the towns of my kingdom and invite all my friends to a feast, because it will soon be Christmas, and this will be the fourth service you perform.' 'Certainly, my Lord', Guido replied. So he went to all the towns of his kingdom, but he did not invite any of the emperor's friends; all those he invited were his enemies, and on Christmas Eve the emperor's court was filled with them. Seeing all his enemies there, the emperor was extremely annoyed. He called Guido and said: 'Friend, did you not tell me that you knew whom to invite to my banquet?' 'I did, my Lord,' he said. The emperor retorted: 'And I told you to invite all my friends, and you have invited my enemies!' 'My Lord,' Guido replied, 'allow me to answer you. Whenever your friends come to you, whatever the day or hour, they are welcomed with joy. The same is not true of these men, because they are your enemies. So I brought them here hoping that a smiling face and a fine banquet would convert them from enemies into friends.' And that is what happened, for before the feast was over they all became his friends, and the emperor was overjoyed, and said: 'My friend, blessed be the Lord! My enemies have become my friends! Now perform your fifth service: make me and my friends a fire that makes no smoke.'

'At once,' he said. And what did Guido do? In summertime he had placed a pile of logs in the heat of the sun and they were so dry that as soon as they caught fire the flames gave off great heat and did not smoke, and the emperor and all his friends were kept warm.

The emperor then said to Guido: 'There now remains your last service. If you perform this faithfully I will raise you to a position of wealth and honour.'

'My Lord,' Guido replied, 'all who wish to go to the Holy Land must follow me to the seashore.' When they heard this almost countless numbers of men and women and children followed him, and when they reached the sea, Guido said to them: 'Friends, can you see what I see?' 'What do you mean?' they asked him. He said: 'Look, there is a great rock out there. Lift up your eyes and look.' 'We can see it clearly enough, sir,' they said, 'but we don't know why you are saying this.' He said: 'On that rock is a bird that sits continually on her nest, and she always has seven eggs in her nest. And she loves these eggs dearly. The peculiarity of this bird is that, so long as she sits on her nest, the whole of the sea is tranquil and peaceful; but if she happens to fly from her nest, the whole sea is set in such commotion that anyone who tries to cross it will certainly be drowned. But as long as she sits on her nest, anyone making the crossing will go and come back without danger.' 'How shall we know when the bird is sitting on her nest and when not?', they asked. He replied: 'She never leaves her nest except for one reason: there is another bird that is her enemy, and it tries day and night to befoul her nest and break her eggs. And as soon as the nesting bird sees her eggs befouled or her nest defiled, she flies from her nest in grief and then the sea is disturbed and a really violent wind blows up. You should on no account try to put out to sea when that happens.'

'How can we stop this happening, sir?' they asked. 'Is there some way in which we can prevent this bird that is her enemy from approaching her nest, and so make the crossing in safety?'

'There is nothing under the sun,' he told them, 'that the hostile bird hates as much as the blood of a lamb. Sprinkle the outside and inside of the nest with lamb's blood and as long a single drop of that blood remains, the hostile bird does not dare go near the nest. So the bird will remain on her nest, the sea will be tranquil and calm, and you will be able to cross to the Holy Land and return in safety.'

17. Of perfection of life

When they heard this, they took the blood of a lamb and sprinkled it all over the nest, both inside and outside, and so they went to the Holy Land and all came back safe and sound. And because Guido had performed all these services so expertly, the emperor promoted him to high command in his army and rewarded him with great riches.

[Application.] Dear friends, this emperor is the Heavenly Father, who enacted a law that whoever gave three knocks on the gate, i.e., those of prayer, fasting and almsgiving, should at his entry become a soldier of the Church Militant and consequently obtain everlasting life. The poor Guido is any man who is poor and naked from his mother's womb, who knocks three times on the gate of the church when he seeks baptism. For every Christian promises to perform six services for God.

The first is to care for the body of his lord, i.e., Christ. How? Just as Guido did. First, he must be rich in virtues lest some temptation should enter the chamber of his heart and offend our Lord Jesus Christ. And he[2] *should have a little dog with a loud bark, i.e., a clean conscience that murmurs constantly at vices. Hence the Apostle says:*[3] *'Everything that is done contrary to your conscience, drags you to hell.' Second, he must prepare the bed of his heart well, change the linen, i.e., change his vices completely into virtues, and wash away the grime of sins by contrition, and keep the chamber of his heart always clean, so that it never offends the eyes of his lord, i.e., the body of our Lord Jesus Christ, whose body he has bound himself to keep pure. Then he must wash His feet twice each week, i.e., please Him by his confession and penance and loving disposition. That is the first service every Christian promises at his baptism, to keep the Lord within himself in purity.*

But concerning the body of this lord, i.e., the Lord, note that Christians must consume it fittingly in the form of bread, and be sure to respect it in its character as visible bread. The host therefore has an inscription, to make it known that all who are to be refreshed by the Eucharist must be inscribed. And they are inscribed in whose hearts the name of Christ is written through true faith, so that they can be called Christians by Christ. Hence the Lord says through Jeremiah:[4] *'I will write my law in their heart.' And the first law by which we are bound to*

---

2 The subject changes here from third to second person, as often in this moralization. Where necessary, I have made the person consistent.
3 This is Gratian: *Corpus Iuris Canonici* 1.1088.
4 Jer 31.33.

God is faith, the second is hope, and the third, charity. Likewise, next to the inscription, the host has a circle: by this is denoted eternity, which has neither a beginning nor an end, to which we come if we consume Christ's body fittingly. Likewise, the host has breadth, which symbolizes charity, which spreads itself everywhere. Likewise, the host is thin and dry, which signifies a twofold abstinence: its thinness denotes frugality in the taking of food; its dryness, sobriety, to avoid excess in the intake of fluids. For those who drink this are sober. Those therefore who wish to be refreshed by this bread are inscribed by faith, and possess a circle through their contemplation of things eternal, and are enlarged through charity. Likewise, the host is pure white, as we must be to combat wantonness. Likewise it is light,[5] as we must be to combat sloth.[6] Likewise it is little, i.e., humble, as we must be to combat pride. If we possess these qualities, then we can ask that our daily bread be given us for our use; otherwise it does not benefit us, but does us harm, as the Apostle says, 1 Cor 11:[7] 'He that eateth unworthily, eateth judgement to himself.' Likewise, the host is unleavened and yeastless, and this is contrary to the bitterness of hatred, which in spiritual terms is wickedness. Hence the Apostle says at 1 Cor 11:[8] 'Let us feast not with the leaven of malice and wickedness, but with the unleavened bread of sincerity and truth.' Likewise it is made of wheat, and this is contrary to anger. For a grain of corn is smooth and even and without harshness, but anger so irritates a man that because of his harshness hardly anyone dare touch him. Likewise, the host is unalloyed and simple, and this is contrary to covetousness and avarice. Likewise, it is round, contrary to sloth. For just as natural bread refreshes and sustains the body more than all other foods, and wine gladdens and inebriates man more than all other drinks, so the flesh of Christ refreshes and nourishes the inner man more than anything else, and His blood gladdens it more than any other drink, and inebriates him in a way that makes him sober. Hence the Psalm says:[9] 'My chalice which inebriateth me, how goodly is it!' Likewise, bread is the common food and wine the

---

5 *levis*: the adjective (with short '*e*') could mean 'nimble', but this can hardly be predicated of a host. (If the '*e*' is long, *levis* means 'smooth', but it is difficult to see how either lightness or smoothness would help the Christian fight *accidie*.)
6 *accidiam*: lethargy, apathy, indifference, especially in spiritual matters.
7 1 Cor 11.29.
8 = 1 Cor 5.8.
9 Ps 22.5.

17. Of perfection of life

ordinary drink for everyone on every occasion. Even so Christ offers himself as food to all the faithful on every occasion, to both poor and rich without distinction, and for this reason is also called our 'daily bread'. Likewise, as the philosophers say, the pre-eminent virtue of bread is nourishment, of which it is a symbol, because its consumption does not cause us to tire of eating it. So it is with the bread of Christ, of which Ecclesiasticus says, c.24:[10] *'They that eat me, shall yet hunger.' Likewise, just as wheaten bread is the food of adults, not of children, as the Apostle says,*[11] *so the body of Christ is the spiritual food of those who have matured in faith and the virtues. The question then arises: 'Who should eat this bread?' Clearly, those of whom it is said in the Gospel:*[12] *'Come to me, all you that labour, and are burdened, and I will refresh you.' The next question: 'How can the bread of Christ be converted into the body of Christ?' This is how: consider the nurse who feeds the child. If the nurse is starved and has no milk, the child becomes hungry and quickly fades away. But if, in her privation, the dregs of wine are given her to drink, these dregs, when taken through the mouth, are changed to blood to strengthen the woman, and into milk for the child's nourishment. And if this is the effect that nature has on a woman, how much greater is the supernatural power in the sacrament of the altar? Through the words that come from the mouth of a pure priest, i.e., Christ, the bread is changed into flesh and the wine into blood. And of those who consume it unworthily we can quote the words of Genesis:*[13] *'Some evil beast hath devoured my son.' Wine is wholesome to the healthy man or injurious to the sick man, indeed it could be the cause of his death. In the same way the body of Christ brings life to the healthy soul and death to the sinful soul. Even so the 70 famous men and 2,000 of the people were struck down, because they had seen the Ark uncovered.*[14] *(Yet we can say that they did not sin in seeing it, since they had not been forbidden to see it.) Let us see therefore that we keep the body of our Lord, i.e., Christ, in a state of decent cleanliness.*[15]

10 Ecclus 24.29.
11 Heb 5.14, 'Strong meat is for the perfect.'
12 Mt 11.28.
13 Gn 37.20, 33.
14 1 Kgs 6.19, where the figure is 50,000.
15 This lengthy excursus prompted the Anglican Swan to note: 'There is a curious defence of transubstantiation in this moral; and we may admire its ingenuity while we reprobate the absurd doctrine it is designed to promote.'

The second service we have promised is to be vigilant in our good works, when others sleep in sin; as has been written:[16] 'Watch, because ye know not at what hour the son of man will come.' And Paul said to the Ephesians:[17] 'Rise, thou that sleepest, and arise from the dead, and Christ shall enlighten thee.' So, dear friends, you must know that some travellers get up at the first cockcrow, others at the second, others at the third, and others at dawn, when the cocks cry out and say: 'There must be no more sleeping!' Listen, the cocks are calling: Let us arise! The first cocks were the prophets, who arose to see Christ in the flesh, and did not see him. The second cocks were the Apostles and Evangelists, who did see Christ. The third cocks are the Friars Minor who preach, and the Brothers of Blessed Mary the Mother of God of Mt Carmel, and others who preach the word of God, the Augustinians and parish priests. These are cocks who call out and say: 'Arise, be vigilant in your good works, as you promised the Lord! Sleep, when others are vigilant,' i.e., desist from sin when others are vigilant in the deeds of evil, as are robbers, thieves and wantons. Be vigilant in the summertime, i.e., when you are alive in the body, and make provision of all that is necessary for your souls, so that when the winter of death approaches, you will be able to rest happily with your Lord.

The third service is to know the taste of good drink. This drink is penance or martyrdom for love of God. Hence our Saviour says in Matthew:[18] 'Can you drink the chalice that I shall drink?' And they said: 'We can,' i.e., drink the cup of penance or martyrdom. Vinegar was good in its time, i.e., it was good for the saints in heaven, who lived in the world and who did penance and subdued the flesh, and thus they now reign in heaven. Wine is good: this means that it is good for us to do penance, through which we shall be able to attain to everlasting glory. It will be good, i.e., when the flesh rises again with the spirit on the Day of Judgement and enters into life everlasting. The Lord has a tavern with excellent wine, namely the joy of heaven, and has a lovely sign before his tavern, namely the cross. But when large numbers of customers flock to his tavern, the innkeeper sells his wine at a high price, and when the numbers of customers diminish, then he must sell it cheaply or keep it all for himself. After His resurrection the Lord distributed His wine by sending the Holy Spirit, and then people flocked to Him in multitudes, i.e., they were converted to the

16 Cf. Mt 24.42.
17 Eph 5.14, probably a quotation from an early Christian hymn.
18 Mt 20.22.

17. Of perfection of life

faith through the preaching of the Apostles and other saints, and then the innkeeper, i.e., our Lord Jesus Christ, sold his wine, i.e., the glory of paradise, at a high price. Did not Peter, who was crucified, buy that wine at an exceedingly high price, and Paul and Lawrence and the other martyrs who gave their bodies up to death to uphold and increase faith in Christ? But now the numbers of purchasers are diminishing, and thus Christ has to sell his glory at a low price or else keep it to himself. So let us taste the drink of penance in the present life and we shall win the prize of eternal life.

The fourth service is to invite people to a banquet. Guido invited his master's enemies etc. So too each one of us is bound to invite Christ's enemies to eternal life; as our Lord said:[19] *'I am not come to call the just, but sinners.' And so you must instruct the sinner by your good examples and works and reconcile him to God. But some sinners are millstones and will not be easily moved, indeed they are as it were in chains, as Peter was when Herod put him in prison; and that night Peter slept between two soldiers, bound with two chains, and there were guards before the door keeping watch over the prison, Acts 12.*[20] *Peter's sleep represents the sleep of the sinner in the habit of sin. The two soldiers symbolize death and the devil, because death lies in wait for life, as the devil does for the soul. The two chains are carnal pleasure and worldly vanity. The guards represent the expectation of an indulgent pardon and the presumption of a longer life, and when the devil holds the sinner fast with these bonds, he keeps him quiet. Therefore we must toil with the utmost care both by word and deed to invite such people to the everlasting banquet.*

The fifth service is to light a fire without smoke etc. This fire is charity, which everyone is obliged to possess if he desires to obtain eternal life; and this he must do without the smoke of wrath. So you must not express in your words anything other than what is in your heart, as many people do who say they love others, when in their hearts they hate them. That is not real charity, rather it is a fire full of smoke; so we must banish hatred from our hearts. To illustrate this allegorically: Pliny says there is a certain fish which, when it swallows the hook, vomits up its insides, i.e., its intestines, until the hook comes out, and then it draws its intestines back into their proper place again. This is what the sinner must do if ever he swallows the hook of hatred or

---

19 e.g. Mt 9.13.
20 Acts 12.6.

some other sin. Ecclesiastes 9:[21] 'As a fish is taken with the hook, and as a bird is caught with the snare, so are men taken in the evil time.' They must therefore spew all their inner parts through their mouth until the hook, i.e., all the hatred and sin, comes out, because all their inward thoughts must be revealed through confession until they are perfectly free from sin, and then the sinner will be able to prepare a fire without smoke, by which God will be warmed, i.e., satisfied.

The sixth service is to teach men the way to the Holy Land, i.e., heaven; but to get to heaven one must cross the sea. The sea stands for this world, and for many reasons. First, because as winds conflict at sea, so too in this world there is conflict and warfare of many kinds. Likewise, just as at sea the waves are storm-tossed, so too in the world there is wave after wave of adversity. Likewise, as in the sea the waters are bitter, so too in the world there is the bitterness of sin. And as the waters of the sea are boundless, so too in the world there are boundless miseries. And as at sea the there are cruel monsters, so in the world there is the cruelty of rulers. Further, because of these and many other dangers one must make the crossing in a ship. Now men have to embark on a ship for four reasons. First, because of a flood, Gen. 9;[22] and we too must do this because of the flood of sins; as Hosea says, c.4:[23] 'Lying, cursing, killing and theft and adultery' have flooded the earth, 'blood hath touched blood, therefore shall hell be manifest to you and all things that dwell therein';[24] and thus we must of necessity embark upon the ship of a good life. Second, ships are boarded to pass over waters. Mt 9:[25] 'Jesus entered the boat and passed over the water and came into his own city.' So too must we, if we would reach the heavenly city. For we have no abiding home here, therefore we must board a ship. He is a fool who must cross the sea and will not climb aboard a ship. He is a fool who has the appropriate time, but delays, because from dawn to dusk the sea will change. They are fools moreover who delay boarding ship when the sailors call to them. Third, men board ships for the purpose of trade. Prov 31:[26] 'She[27] is like the

21 Cf. Eccles 9.12.
22 = Gn 7.
23 Cf. Hos 4.2f.
24 *lucebit*: the Vulgate has *propter hoc lugebit terra et infirmabitur omnis qui habitat in ea* (therefore shall the land mourn and every one that dwells in it shall languish).
25 Cf. Mt 9.1.
26 Prv 31.14.
27 i.e., the valiant woman who 'brings bread from afar' to provide for her husband.

17. Of perfection of life

merchant's ship.' The holy soul is like a good ship which has an abundance of earthly goods, i.e., groans, sighs, poverty, humility and charity, and our Lord Jesus Christ comes seeking these goods in our land. And when our soul comes to port with such a cargo, it receives the warmest welcome from the lord of the land, and he takes these goods and lades the ship with the goods of his land, i.e., with honour and riches. Fifth, men board ship to fish, as Peter did. So too we must board ship to fish for sinners, drawing them from the water of their sins by our good works and examples. But we must take care not to pay too much attention to saving others, lest neglecting ourselves we sink, as happens sometimes to fishermen. But there are many who are not fishermen, but thieves, who go in search of drowning people not to rescue them, but to take their clothing, and, what is even worse, they drown people sailing the sea for their plunder. And these are sometimes those who have the duty of steering God's ship. And note that, in order to save a ship in a great storm, one man throws the cargo overboard, another bales out water, another casts the anchor, another strikes the sails, another holds the tiller, another tries to steer the ship through the waves; so no-one is idle, rather everyone is anxious for his safety, and in this way the ship is saved and does not perish. These are the things that must be done spiritually in such a situation in order to avoid temptation, and so a man will be saved from the peril of eternal death. But anyone who is negligent in doing any of these things will perish. So Paul says to Timothy:[28] *'They that will become rich fall into the snare of the devil, and into temptation, into destruction and perdition.' If therefore you wish to be saved, jettison the riches from your heart, which are an exceedingly heavy burden. Second, humility drains the water from the ship of the soul, clearing the water of sin from the tongue*[29] *and casting it away. As Jeremiah says:*[30] *'Pour out thy heart like water.' Third, fear closes up the breaches. For he who knows fear closes up the opening of the senses through which death enters into the soul. Now this fear arises from a consideration of God's power, and the Judge's sentence, and the lack of an advocate or favourable evidence, and the multitude of his accusers. As Job says:*[31] *'If strength be demanded, he is strong; if equity of judgement, no man dare bear witness for me. If I would justify myself, my own mouth condemns me,' because of my consciousness of guilt which speaks continually to me.*

28 Cf. 1 Tim 6.9.
29 *lingua*: possibly: 'with its tongue'.
30 Lam 2.19.
31 Cf. Jb 9.19f.

Fourth, hope casts anchor. Fifth, wisdom strikes the sail. Sixth, wisdom controls the helm to steer a straight course. Seventh, justice cleaves the waves. The ship is the holy soul, whose wares are works of charity; its sheets, God's commandments; its mast, patience; its sail, perseverance; its anchor, faith; its helm, charity; its helmsman, the Holy Spirit; and the crew who sail the ship are the examples of the saints. Of this ship Proverbs 31 says:[32] *'She is like the merchant's ship,' which contains all these things. This ship carries fruits, i.e., works of holiness that give off a sweet fragrance before God and men, of which you must make a gift to God himself. And just as fruits are distributed after a meal to bring pleasure and refreshment, so after this life we shall be granted the benefit and enjoyment of our good works in heaven. At sea, i.e., in the world, there is a great rock, namely the human body, that is composed of four elements,*[33] *and in this body there is a nest, namely the human heart, in which a bird, i.e., the Holy Spirit, dwells by virtue of our baptism, which always has seven eggs, namely the seven gifts of the Holy Spirit. As long as this bird, i.e., the Holy Spirit, dwells in your heart, you will certainly be able to cross to the Holy Land, i.e., to eternal life. But if it happens that through sin the bird flies away from its nest, the sea, i.e., the world, the devil and your own flesh will oppose you and terrible storms will arise that you cannot escape. And so you must get your heart ready in proper cleanliness after the manner of a worldly house. Soot is removed from a house, and soot signifies the bitterness of sin, which must be removed. Likewise, dust must be removed, which is love of earthly things, and dust is the special breeding place of fleas, i.e., the proud, who leap too high. Likewise, the woman who is tidying the house first cleans it and sweeps up the dust, and then casts it out of the door; and when the floor is clean she puts water on it and finally straw. So too the man who would clean his house, i.e., his heart, gathers up the dust by considering all the evil things he has done and all the good things he has left undone. Then he must cast them out by a full confession, apply water by the shedding of tears, and deck*[34] *his house with straw by doing a fitting penance; and thus his Lord will be a willing guest in a house so well prepared. For at the approach of a noble guest, we see that the*

---

32 Prv 31.14.
33 In medieval times it was believed that the body reflected the macrocosm of nature, and like it was composed of four elements: fire (digestive enzymes and secretions, heart, liver, stomach); air (lungs, chest, thorax); water (vital fluids); and earth (all the solid parts: bones, nails etc.).
34 *ornat*: Oest.; *ornet*: K., L.

17. Of perfection of life

whole house is cleaned, but when he goes, nothing of his remains but the dung of his horses. So too, at the coming of God, the body and soul are sustained through his grace, but when his grace departs, nothing remains except dung, i.e., earthly things, because the more man clasps dung in his embrace, the less he has of it, and becomes no more powerful.[35] *The same is true of the man who loves wealth. Ecclesiastes:*[36] *'He that loveth riches shall reap no fruit from them.' Nothing is more wicked than to love money. The bird that is hostile is the devil, who goes about seeking whom he may devour, who strives day and night to banish the Holy Spirit from our hearts. Because if you would have the Holy Spirit within you, do as Guido did. Sprinkle the nest with the blood of a lamb, i.e., you must always keep fresh in your heart the memory of Christ's Passion, which he endured for you, and thus the hostile bird, the devil, does not dare to come hear you, and consequently the Holy Spirit will remain in you, and so you will be sure to attain to the Holy Land, i.e., to life everlasting.*

---

35 *nec fortior fetet*: Oest.; *nec fortior efficitur*: K., L. In the context *fetet* (stinks) is attractive, but it is hard to make sense of the *nec*. Possibly *fiet*?
36 Eccles 5.9.

18. All sin, however grave in predestination, is pardonable, unless subject to the hell of despair

There was a soldier named Julian[1] who unwittingly killed both of his parents. This Julian was a nobleman and, being a young man, devoted to hunting, and one day he was pursuing a stag he had tracked down, when suddenly the stag turned round and said: 'You, who are pursuing me, will cause the death of your own father and mother.'[2]

When he heard this, Julian was terrified that the stag's prediction might come true. He left all his possessions and secretly went away and came to a distant country where he attached himself to a certain prince. He displayed such energy in all he did, both in war and at court, that this prince made him a knight, gave him the widow of a castellan[3] in marriage, and he received a castle as dowry.

Now Julian's parents were heartbroken at the loss of their son, and went around everywhere looking anxiously for him. At length they came to the castle of which he was lord. Julian's wife[4] asked them who they were, for Julian was absent. And when they told her all that had happened to their son, she realized that they were actually the parents of her husband, for she had often heard the story from him. So she welcomed them kindly, and out of love for her husband gave them her marriage bed and got another bed ready for herself elsewhere. Next morning she went off to church. And Julian, coming into his bedchamber early to wake his wife was startled to find two persons there, both asleep. And suspecting that it was his wife with a lover, he silently drew his sword and killed them both.

1 This is Julian the Hospitaller, *G.L.* XXX.
2 Cf. the story of St Eustace, see no. 110; *G.L.* CLVII.
3 The officer in charge of a castle, a châtelain.
4 *Cum Julianus quinam essent inquisisset*: Oest.; *Quos cum uxor Juliani videbat, et Julianus non affuerat*: K., L.

18. All sin, however grave in predestination, is pardonable

He then left the castle and to his amazement saw his wife coming back from church. He asked her who were the couple sleeping in her bed, and she replied: 'They are your parents. They have been looking for you for a long time and I put them in our bedroom.'

At these words he almost fainted. He began to weep bitterly, and cried: 'Woe is me! What am I to do? I have slain my own beloved parents! And the stag's prediction has come true! While attempting to avert it, I have fulfilled it, accursed wretch that I am! Farewell now, dearest sister, for henceforth I shall never rest until I know that God has accepted my repentance.'

'No, dearest brother!' she answered. 'God forbid that you should abandon me and go without me! No, I have shared your joy and shall share your grief also.'

So they left together, and they came to a broad and dangerous river on which many people's lives were endangered, and there they established a great hospice where they could do penance, and promptly carry all who wanted to cross the river to the other side, and give hospitality to all the poor who came there.

After many years, at midnight one cold and frosty night while Julian was asleep, worn out by his exertions, he heard a woeful voice calling his name: it was someone asking him in the most pathetic tones to take him across the river. He got up at once and found a man almost dead with the cold, and he carried him into the house, and lighting a fire tried to warm him. But he could not get him warm, and fearing that he would die, he carried him to his own bed and carefully covered him up. And after a little while this man, who had seemed so ill and seemed almost leprous, rose heavenwards in splendour and said to his host: 'Julian, the Lord has sent me to you to tell you that he has accepted your penance, and you will soon both go to your rest in the Lord.'

So saying, he vanished. And not long afterwards, full of good works and almsgiving, Julian and his wife went to their rest in the Lord.

Moralization. Dear friends, this knight Julian signifies any good Christian and prelate, who must manfully war against the devil, the world and the flesh, and devote himself to the hunt, that is, win souls for God and pursue the stag, i.e., Christ. Hence the Psalmist says:[5] *'As the hart panteth after the fountains of water etc.' And if the prelate faithfully*

---

5 Ps 41.1.

pursues Christ, he will understand and learn from Holy Scripture that he must kill his parents, i.e., completely abandon them for the love of God, as Jesus says:[6] *'He that hath left father and mother for me, shall receive a hundredfold and shall possess life everlasting.' This soldier journeyed to a far-off place etc. So too the prelate must travel to a far-off place, that is, travel far from the world and those who are in the world, by living in holiness and purity, and serve a prince, i.e., Christ, and with him fight many battles against the devil, the world and the flesh. When Christ sees that his soldier is winning these battles, he will give him a châtelaine to wife, that is, his grace, to watch over the castle of his heart, so that he will be able to please God in all things. But often we see it happen that his carnal parents and the vanities of the world pursue such a man, inciting him to evil, and are placed in the bed of his heart to try him, as Job was tried. But resist boldly, and destroy them with the sword of repentance, as is prefigured in the story of Absalom, who, while pursuing his father, was hanged by his hair in an oak tree, and Joab thrust three lances into his heart.*[7] *This oak tree is lust; his hair is carnal desires; the wound that transfixed him is mortal flesh; and Joab is the devil, who while man lives pierces him*[8] *with three lances, namely his thoughts, deeds and habits; and at his death with three torments, namely the wrath of God, whom he has offended, the deprivation of heaven, which he has lost, and the pains of hell, which he has merited. These parents you must kill with the sword of repentance, and after this you must hasten to the waters of Holy Scripture and there erect a place of healing, i.e., engage in prayer, fasting and almsgiving, and in consequence you will be able to look for God in the bed of your heart and attain to everlasting life, to which etc.*

---

6 Cf. Mt 19.29.
7 2 Kgs 18.14. In the Vulgate there are four books of Kings (= 1 and 2 Sm, 1 and 2 Kgs).
8 *consuetudines*: Oest.; *consuetudines infigit*: K., L.

19. Of the sin of pride

We read in the Roman histories that there was a Roman prince[1] named Pompey. He had married the daughter of a noble called Caesar. These two conspired together to force the whole world into subjection. Now it happened that Pompey sent Caesar out to subdue certain distant lands, because he was young[2] and suited to undergoing such hardships, while Pompey, as head of state, was to guard the city of Rome against those countries. He fixed the time for Caesar's return as within five years; and if he failed to return by then he would forfeit his citizenship for ever.

Caesar duly assembled an army and went off to the countries he was to subdue, but he came up against a warlike people and was unable to conquer them in the predetermined time. Choosing to offend Pompey rather than abandon the war, he decided to stay away for a further five years. Pompey took a serious view of this and banished him from Roman territory so that he would not dare come near him again. But after concluding the war Caesar headed for Rome, and he and his army came to a river called the Rubicon. There, in midstream, a gigantic spectre appeared to him and said to him: 'Caesar, if you come with peace for Rome, you may continue; but if not, you may not presume to enter it.'

Caesar replied: 'I have always fought for, and am prepared to undergo any hardship for, the honour and advantage of the people of Rome; and that is all I ever desire. Let the gods I worship be my witnesses.'

At these words the phantom disappeared. Caesar then spurred

1 *princeps*: the historical Pompey was no such thing. The tale is a confused medieval version of the rivalry between these two men.
2 In fact Pompey (b. 106 BC) was only a few years older than Caesar (b. 102 or 100 BC).

on his war-horse and crossed the river, but when he had got across and was standing on the other side, he said presently: 'Here[3] I have violated the peace and resign my citizenship.' And from that day on he never ceased pursuing Pompey and doing all he could to destroy him.

[Moralization.] Dear friends, by this Pompey I understand God the Creator of all things, who always was from the beginning and shall be without end. By Caesar I understand Adam, who was the first of all men, and whose daughter, i.e., soul, God betrothed in faith, Hosea c.2:[4] 'I will espouse thee to me in faith.' So God, wishing to prove Adam, placed him in paradise to cultivate and safeguard it. But Adam at once became haughty at his privileged status, and wishing to please his wife and follow the devil, disobeyed the only command that God had given him, and for this God banished him not only from paradise but from His kingdom. But Adam, hoping that he could recover what he had lost, laboured with all his might subsequently to that end, but in truth he was unable to achieve this until the coming of our Lord Jesus Christ, our likeness, who revealed himself when he was baptized in the waters of the River Jordan. And our Lord and Saviour said to all of us who wish to get to heaven, in John c.3:[5] 'Unless a man be born again of water and the Holy Ghost etc.' But many, when they come to this water, promise before witnesses to serve God and avoid sins, and to fight manfully against the devil. But alas and alack! I fear, and one must fear in the case of many such, that when they have made their vows, they forget them and scorn the commandments. Even as Absalom did, Kings c.3,[6] after he had been reconciled with his father David, for he had killed his brother. Seeing that the people were inclined to make him king, he said to his father:[7] 'Let me go, and pay my vows which I vowed to the Lord in Hebron.' And his father said to him: 'Go in peace.' And he went to Hebron and the people made him king. And from that day until the day of his death he did not cease to persecute

---

3 By crossing the Rubicon, Caesar was entering Roman territory, defying Pompey's decree of banishment and so declaring war.
4 Hos 2.20.
5 Jn 3.5.
6 The reference is to 2 Kgs 13.29. Absalom had Amnon, his half-brother, killed for raping his sister Tamar, and was only reconciled with his father some years later.
7 2 Kgs 15.7ff.

19. Of the sin of pride

his father. But Caesar and Absalom were killed by their servants. In the same way bad Christians never cease to persecute God their Father through their evil deeds, and for this they will be handed over to the ministers of hell, whom they feared and worshipped. But mark, after Absalom had killed his brother, he was exalted, as was Caesar after he had broken the command of Pompey. But Joab, making peace between him and his father, brought him back, and Absalom, seeing how he was honoured, opposed his father, and gathering an army around him made himself king. But in the war he was hanged by the hair. And Joab, who had made peace between him and his father, thrust three lances into his heart. This Absalom symbolizes the man who commits mortal sin, who destroys his brother, i.e., his soul. Christ made peace, but many who had been reconciled made war against God. And then Christ came, who made peace and thrusts three lances into the sinner's heart. The first is separation from God, the second his curse, the third eternal fire.

20. Of misfortune and tribulation[1]

In the reign of the emperor Conrad there was a count named Leopold, who in fear of the emperor's wrath fled with his wife into a forest and took hiding in a little cottage there. Now the emperor Conrad was hunting in this forest when night fell and had to lodge in this same cottage. His hostess, who was pregnant and close to her confinement, made up a bed for him as best she could and provided him with all he needed. The same night she gave birth to a son, and the emperor heard a voice saying: 'Receive, receive, receive!' He woke from his sleep and shaking all over with fear said to himself: 'What does that voice mean? "Receive, receive, receive!" What am I to receive?' he thought, and went straight back to sleep. Then he heard the voice speaking to him a second time. 'Give back, give back, give back!' He woke from his sleep in great consternation and said to himself: 'What does this mean? First I heard: "Receive, receive, receive!" Now it says "Give back, give back, give back!" What am I to give back when I have received nothing?' He went back to sleep again. Then he heard the voice speaking to him a third time. 'Flee, flee, flee,[2] Conrad! This newborn child will become your son-in-law.' Now when he heard this the emperor was deeply disturbed. Next morning he got up early, called his two attendants and told them: 'Go and snatch that baby from its mother's arms, cut its body in two and bring me its heart.' They were terrified at this, but went off and seized the child as it lay in its mother's lap. However, when they saw what a beautiful child it was, they were

1 Cf. Herrtage, Text I.XLVIII. The tale is told at *G.L.* CLXXVII.302ff. (St Pelagius). For other versions, see Oesterley, pp. 715–16; Tubach, no. 647; Hope, pp. 487–9.
2 Riddles are a common motif in the *Gesta*. In *G.L.*, the voice speaks just once, when it makes the prediction about the newborn child.

20. Of misfortune and tribulation

moved to compassion, so they placed it at the top of a tree to keep it from being eaten by wild beasts, then cut up a hare and took its heart to the emperor.

That same day a duke was riding through the forest and heard the child crying, and there being no-one about, he placed it in his lap, and since he had no child of his own, he took it to his wife and had her nurse it. He pretended that it was a child of their own, and gave it the name of Henry.

As the boy grew up he was extremely handsome, well spoken and popular with everyone, and when the emperor noted his good looks and intelligence, he asked his father to let him live at his court. But then, seeing how popular the youth was with everyone and how highly they all thought of him, he began to worry that he might succeed to the throne after him, and that he might even be the child he had ordered his men to kill. So wishing to ensure his own safety, he wrote a letter to his wife in his own hand to the following effect: 'If you value your own life, as soon as you receive this letter you will kill this young man.' But on his travels he went into a church and fell asleep on a pew, and the priest, seeing the purse with the letter in it hanging from his waist, was overcome with curiosity, and opened the purse, and was horrified when he read of the intended crime. So he cunningly erased the words 'You will kill this youth' and wrote instead 'You will give him our daughter in marriage.'

The queen duly read the letter, and since she saw that it was stamped with the imperial seal and recognized the emperor's own handwriting, she called all the princes in the empire together, gave the youth her daughter's hand and celebrated the marriage, which took place in Aachen. When the emperor Conrad was informed of the solemnization of his daughter's marriage, he was dumbstruck, but on learning the truth from his two attendants, the duke, and the priest, he realized that there can be no opposition to the ordinances of God. So he sent for the youth, confirmed him as his son-in-law, and appointed him as successor to the throne.

[Moralization.] Dear friends, the emperor is God the Father, who was angered by the sin of our first parent and banished him from paradise, and he fled and lived in the forest of this world. But God, wishing to hunt for souls, sent his son into the forest of this world when he was born of the glorious Virgin and took flesh, and was born in the night. The king who heard the voice saying to him: 'Receive, receive,

receive!' can be taken as any man, who should be ruler of himself through self-government with respect to the health of his body and soul. So the command 'Receive etc.' is addressed to each one of us. By the first 'Receive!' we should understand first and foremost that we have received a soul created in the likeness of God. By the second 'Receive!' we must understand the body with its five senses and all the four elements that are ready to serve us. By the third 'Receive!' we must understand that, if we serve God faithfully, we will receive everlasting life. Dear friends, consider these three commands carefully. For heaven will speak first, and say to you: 'I provide you with light during the day so that you may be active; with darkness during the night that you may rest; and I change the seasons for you so that their variety may alleviate monotony.' Earth will say to you: 'I support you, I feed you, I comfort you with bread and gladden you with wine, I fill your table with meats of many kinds.' Water will say to you: 'I provide you with drink, I wash the dirt from you, and provide many kinds of fish for your use.' Air will say to you: 'I provide you with the breath of life, and send you all kinds of birds to serve you.' It is a word of admonition when the world says: 'See, man, how He loved you who made me for your sake! I serve you because I was made for you. Receive my benefits, and return your love!' It is a word of menace when fire says: 'You will be burnt by me'; water says: 'You will be drowned by me'; earth says: 'You will be devoured by me'; and hell says: 'You will be swallowed up by me.'

The second thing the voice said: 'Give back! etc.' What must you give back? First, of course, you must give back to God a pure soul, the soul that God created in his own likeness and redeemed through his Passion. What are you to do in answer to the second: 'Give back!'? By serving God you must give him tithes and oblations, that by willingly offering your whole body in service to him you may be able to say with the Psalm:[3] 'I will pay thee my vows'. By the third 'Give back!', understand that first you must give your whole body to God, that you may love him with all your heart, with all your soul and with all your mind, that you may be ready to endure all things patiently for love of him; and second, that you should love your neighbour as yourself.

The third thing the voice said: 'Flee! etc.' By the first 'Flee!' you are to understand that you must flee the devil through works of mercy and humility, the world through poverty, and the flesh through fasting and

---

3 Ps 65.13.

20. Of misfortune and tribulation

chastity. By the second 'Flee!' understand that you must with all your might avoid sin, your own will, worldly vanity and evil company. By the third 'Flee!' understand that you must flee hell and its punishment through contrition, confession and penance, because a boy is born to us, and the government is upon his shoulder.[4] *Many persecute this child Jesus Christ and seek with all their might to destroy him with their vices and evil desires. But his two squires, i.e., his divine power and grace, take the child Jesus away from the hearts of such men, because he can only repose happily in a place that is pure. The child Jesus is placed in a tree, that is, in a church, where the duke, a good prelate, will find him through his works of merit, and nourishes him on wholesome food; but wretched man, not fearing God, receives him on the altar, and then we can say of him what is said concerning Joseph, Genesis c.16:*[5] *'An evil wild beast hath devoured my son,' i.e., Christ. If you would therefore proceed in safety, kill the hare, that is, your flesh, your carnal affections through prayer, fasting and almsgiving, and remove your heart so that the child Jesus may be saved and remain with you, and espouse your daughter, i.e., your soul. But it often happens that man falls back into sin and writes a letter in his own hand etc. This letter is the wicked and perverse thoughts that lead him to do evil, by which the child would be utterly destroyed. And he writes this letter to his wife, i.e., his flesh, by pursuing gluttony and wantonness, but the wise priest, that is, the confessor and preacher, must open the Holy Scriptures to him and change the writing of the letter, i.e., of his evil deeds, by penance, and then the child Jesus will undoubtedly espouse his soul. And to this betrothal the princes, i.e., the cardinal and theological*[6] *virtues, will be invited, and so he will be able to reign with Christ.*

---

4 *cuius imperium*: cf. Is 9.6: *et factus est principatus super humerum eius* (and the government has been placed on his shoulder).
5 Cf. Gn 37.33.
6 *cardinales et theorice*: Oest.; *cardinales*: K., L., *Le Violier*. If *theorice* is right, it must mean 'speculative' or 'contemplative'. But the Church has always defined the virtues as cardinal or theological. The theological virtues, faith, hope and charity, are distinguished from the four natural, or cardinal, virtues: prudence, temperance, fortitude and justice.

21. Of guile and conspiracy and the caution required to oppose them

Justin relates[1] that the citizens of Lacedaemon conspired together against their king, and prevailing against him banished him from the city and the whole kingdom. Now it happened at that very time that the King of Persia was plotting to destroy that same city and assailed[2] it with a vast army. But the banished king,[3] ungrateful though his fellow citizens had been to him, could not overcome his love for his city, and so took pity on it. Having investigated and learned of the machinations of the King of Persia against Lacedaemon, he considered how he might cunningly inform his people in secret of all their plans. So he took some tablets and on them wrote down all these plans, and he also gave specific information as to how they might resist Xerxes and defend the city against him. Having written all he wished, he smeared wax over the writing, and selecting a trustworthy messenger sent him to the heads of state[4] in Lacedaemon. They duly received the tablets, but after inspecting them carefully they could see no writing, only the smooth surface of the wax. The councillors met together to discuss the tablets, and though each gave his opinion as to what should be done with

1 II 10.13ff. Marcus Junian(i)us Justinus (probably third century AD) made an epitome of Pompeius Trogus's *Historiae Philippicae* which was widely read in the Middle Ages.
2 *obsedit*: the verb must have other than its normal meaning ('besiege') here. The siege of Sparta never took place, because Xerxes was defeated at Salamis and Plataea and withdrew from Greece.
3 Demaratus, who was in exile in Persia.
4 *magnates*: later they are referred to as *satrapae*. These would be the ephors, five supreme magistrates, or perhaps members of the Gerousia, the Council of Elders (twenty-eight men over 60 years of age, plus the two kings).

21. Of guile and conspiracy and the caution required to oppose them 71

them, no-one was found who could disclose their meaning. Now it chanced that the sister of the aforementioned[5] king heard of the perplexity these tablets were causing and asked the authorities for permission to see them. After closely inspecting them, with a woman's cunning she lifted a little of the wax from the tablets, and at once the hidden writing became visible. And when she removed more of the wax, more of the writing could be seen. So when all the wax was removed from the writing in this way, the whole message could be read. Overjoyed at this discovery, the councillors put into action the advice contained in the tablets, defended the state bravely and delivered it from any threat of siege.[6]

[Moralization.] Dear friends, by this king I understand God Almighty, who was banished from his own city, i.e., from human society, when our first parents conspired together in paradise and transgressed his commandments, as if to say: 'We do not want him to reign over us.' Notwithstanding this, the king, our Lord Jesus Christ, could not fail to love his city, i.e., the whole of humankind. For he loved us when we were his enemies, because, as the Apostle says at Romans c.2:[7] *'When we were enemies, we were reconciled to God by the death of his Son.' The king, our Lord Jesus Christ, considering that the devil, who is king over all the sons of insolence, was striving to destroy them all with machinations almost beyond number, took some tablets, to which there is explicit reference at Exodus c.3,*[8] *i.e., the tablets he gave to Moses, and wrote upon them information enabling them to combat the devil and his machinations. And so he delivered them by sending a faithful messenger, i.e., Moses, to the city of humankind. But the writing was hidden under a layer of wax, i.e., certain religious rites, so that the principles of the law could not be read plainly and clearly by everyone at the time this law was given, and there were many issues that were not properly understood by the ancients in the interpretation of these tablets. And indeed no-one was ever found who could reveal the meaning of these tablets until the sister of the king, a very wise girl of noble family, stepped forward. This noble young lady was the Blessed Virgin Mary, the blessed and sanctified Mother of God and man, and*

5 This was Gorgo, the wife of King Leonidas, not the sister of Demaratus.
6 For this story, see Herodotus VII.239; also Oesterley, p. 716; Tubach, no. 5219; Hope, p. 489.
7 = Rom 5.10.
8 = Ex 31.18.

also the sister of Christ the King. For since she was the daughter of King David according to the flesh, she is also, spiritually speaking, the daughter of God, in accordance with the saying of Luke:[9] *'He had a sister called Mary.' So it was she, i.e., the Virgin Mary, who revealed the meaning of the tablets of the Old Law. How? Why, by removing the wax. You know that when the light comes, shadows vanish, and wax melts when warmed by fire. Now these rituals were like shadows. And Christ, our God, was the fire, and his Mother Mary the bringer of light on the day of her purification. Freely and willingly she submitted to the rites of the law, though she did not need to, that she might present her son, the divine fire, in the temple. The inevitable consequence is, and was, therefore, that the shadows vanished and the wax itself melted and was erased. As the Psalmist says:*[10] *'As wax melteth before the fire, so let the wicked perish at the presence of God.' And on the day of her purification she did away with the rituals and thus fulfilled the law and freed us from servitude to the devil through the birth of her son, and obtained life everlasting for us, to which etc.*

9 Lk 10.39. *Et huic erat soror nomine Maria.* The Latin can bear the meaning I have given it, and which the moralization requires, but in the context the pronoun *huic* refers to Martha. 'And she had a sister called Mary, who sitting even at the Lord's feet, heard his word.'
10 Ps 67.3.

22. Of worldly fear

Augustine relates[1] that when in days of yore the Egyptians deified Isis and Serapis, they proceeded in the following way: they set up two images and first enacted a law that anyone who said they were mortal, or said anything about their birth, should be put to death. Second, in order that this law should be known to everyone, they also placed near them, in every temple where they were worshipped, a small idol with a finger pressed to its lips, as a sign that those who entered these temples should keep silence, and that thus the truth should be suppressed by everyone.

[Application.] Dear friends, this is in fact what men of the world and of darkness do, who suppress the truth and undermine the dignity of the Church when they seek to deify and glorify themselves or others like them. Before the very eyes of prelates they promptly set up an idol signifying that silence is required; and they do this plainly so that no-one may dare to reprove them, or utter the truth about their doings, but rather that they should keep their heresies secret or better still commend them, so that in the absence of any contradiction they may seem righteous to the people. This idol is clearly fear of the world, because of which no-one dares to speak the truth, or to die for the truth, or to endure excessive persecution; indeed, because of this idol, those whose principal concern it is to die for their flock become as timid as hares; or rather, what is worse, they themselves become an idol enjoining silence on others, because they assume that, if they themselves did not exist, there would be others to defend the truth. Therefore let us keep God, who is truth, before our eyes in all our works, and he will deliver us and lead us to eternal life. To which etc.

[1] *De Civitate Dei* XVIII.5.

23. Of spiritual medicine

St Augustine relates that in ancient times it was customary that, after their deaths, the bodies of emperors were cremated and their ashes placed in a prominent place. Now it happened that an emperor died whose heart could not be burnt. This caused widespread astonishment, and all the rhetoricians and wise men of the state were summoned. When they were asked the reason for this they at length replied that the emperor had been poisoned, and his heart would not burn because of the poison within it. They then removed the heart from the fire, applied theriac[1] to it, and so rid it of the poison; and when the heart was put back in the fire, it was quickly reduced to ashes.

[Moralization.] Dear friends, even so, spiritually speaking, it is impossible for the hearts of men infected with the poison of mortal sin to be kindled with the fire of the Holy Spirit, unless first the stain of sin is destroyed by theriac, i.e., by confession and contrition.

---

1 *teriacam*: theriac, an antidote, originally used to nullify the effects of the poisonous bites of animals, especially snakes. It is the word from which 'treacle' ultimately derives.

24. Of the devil's enticement by means of worldly goods

The story is told of a magician who had a most beautiful garden full of so many fragrant flowers, delicious fruits, and such rich and sumptuous delights, that it was a great joy to be in it. But he would never show the place to anyone except fools or those who were his enemies. And when they were let in they saw so many wonderful things that they were amazed, and immediately asked if they could stay there. But he would not let anyone do so unless he made over his inheritance to him. The fools believed it was paradise, and that they would always remain there, and gave up their inheritances to him. But the magician got up in the night, and finding them asleep slew them; and so, by means of this garden, he perpetrated immeasurable evils.

Dear friends, the magician with his garden is this world with its riches and glory. It is symbolized by a magician because it seduces many people with its enchantments, as jesters[1] do. Such a person puts down a bowl and places nothing inside it, and in the meantime he talks and tricks and deceives the spectators. Then he asks: 'What is inside?' and coppers or gold coins appear. He shares them out and gives them to his audience, and they take them gratefully, but after closing their hands, thinking that they are holding a coin, when they open them again they find nothing. Even so this world deceives and tricks many people. It is the case with many that, so long as there is nothing actually under the bowl or dish, that is, as long as a man has nothing except those things that are necessary for his subsistence, he cares little about the world. Seeing this, the world, wishing to deceive such people, lifts the bowl

---

1 *joculatores*: jugglers, entertainers, jesters. Jesters performed tricks to delight their audience.

and shows them what is hidden underneath; i.e., it elevates a person somewhat and raises him above a need for the necessities of life, for example to a church living or a benefice, and then begins to show him life's riches and delights. At once the wretched man desires and covets things which work against the salvation of his soul; and many things are given to him, and he believes that he is being greatly enriched and is in an excellent position, but at length, if he opens his hands, he will find nothing there. As the Psalm attests:[2] *'All the men of riches have found nothing in their hands.' Let us therefore strive to reject this world if we desire to come to everlasting life, to which etc.*

---

2 Ps 75.5.

25. Of ingratitude and the forgetting of benefits[1]

A noble lady was suffering many injuries at the hands of a tyrant who was laying waste her land. As she received reports of his doings she wept day in and day out and her heart was filled with anguish. It so happened that a pilgrim arrived in her neighbourhood, and seeing her anguish he was moved to compassion and promised to make war on her behalf, on condition that, if he died fighting, she would keep his staff and bag in her bedchamber in order to preserve his memory and to show her gratitude. She promised him faithfully to do so, and the pilgrim made war on the tyrant and defeated him, but was himself fatally wounded in battle. When the lady heard of his death, she did as she had promised, and hung his staff and bag by her bed in her bedchamber. The report quickly spread through town and country that this noblewoman had recovered all the land she had lost, and when they heard the news, three kings came to her in great pomp to ask for her hand in marriage. She at once put on her finery and walked out to meet them, and received them with great honour, thinking to herself: 'If these three kings mean to enter my bedchamber, I shall be in disgrace if they find the pilgrim's bag and staff by my bed.' So she gave orders for them to be removed and put permanently out of sight. And so she forgot her promise, and proved ungrateful.

[Application.] Dear friends, the lady is the human soul, and the tyrant is the devil, who for long ages had robbed her of her inheritance of the heavenly kingdom, which caused her much pain. And no wonder, for she had been consigned to hell for a long time, until the pilgrim arrived, i.e., Christ, who came down from heaven to sojourn in this

[1] Cf. no. 66 below and Herrtage, Text I.IX; also Oesterley, p. 716; Tubach, nos 338 and 4585; Hope, pp. 492–3.

world. His bag is his most pure flesh beneath which his divinity lay hidden, and upon which he received the wounds. His staff is the wood of the cross on which he hung for us sinners. For he won a victory for the soul on the sixth day,[2] that he might deliver you from punishment, and that there all that had been lost might be restored. He therefore begs you insistently to keep his bag and staff for love of him, that is, to keep the remembrance of his Passion ever fresh within the chamber of your heart. The three kings are the devil, the world and the flesh, which come to man tempting him, seducing him and abetting him in sin. Wretched man, without a thought for the future, adorns himself with vices and desires and goes to meet them, and very soon yields to them, and so turns from the remembrance of Christ, and in consequence forgets God. Let us therefore strive to remember his benefits if we wish to win our prize in heaven.

---

2 i.e., Good Friday.

26. Of humility

A noble queen conceived a son by a lowborn servant. This son subsequently lived a disgraceful life and behaved badly towards his putative father, the king. In his concern, the king asked the queen if he was really his son; and hearing, when she confessed, that he was not his son, yet reluctant to deprive him of the kingdom on this account, he gave him his kingdom, but ordered him to wear clothes made of material of two different kinds and colours – one half of them of poor cloth, the other of precious material, so that when he looked at the poor material, he would be deterred from pride and all other vices, and when he looked at the fine material he would not be altogether disheartened, nor appear too humble.

[Application.] Dear friends, even so, speaking spiritually, our flesh, like a wife, in its love of things of the flesh seeks to prevent us from journeying to the promised land whenever we commit mortal sin. What then are we to do? Clearly, we must give the flesh a ring of forgetfulness,[1] that it may be drawn from the pleasures of the senses, that so it may forget carnal pleasures. But the soul must keep the ring of memory for itself, so that it may constantly keep in remembrance the torments of hell and the end of its life, and that the flesh may thus forget sin. Hence it has been written: 'Remember your last end, and thou shalt never sin,' Ecclus 7.[2] We must wear a tunic of poor cloth, because we are uncouth sons, i.e., sons of the earth. Job 7:[3] 'I have said to rottenness: "Thou art my father etc."' For if we were asked: What is man?, we would certainly answer that man is poor or weak, foolish or ignoble. If he is poor, he lacks wealth; if weak, he lacks power; if uncouth, he

1 See no. 10.
2 Ecclus 7.40.
3 = Jb 17.14.

lacks nobility; if foolish, wisdom. I can prove that you are poor. You have nothing of your own except sin. If you give the sheep back his wool, the ox your leather shoes, the earth its corn, you have nothing left with you but sin. Second, you are weak, because of yourself you can do nothing good. Hence man is compared to a flower, which in the morning is lovely and bright, but in the evening languishes. Likewise to smoke. The Psalmist says:[4] 'As smoke vanisheth, so let the wicked perish at the presence of God.' Likewise to vanity. The Psalmist says:[5] 'Man is like to vanity.' Third, you are not wise, because you do not know yourself. How then can you know anything else? Fourth, you are not of noble parents, but of the stock of which Job speaks, c.7:[6] 'I have said to rottenness: "You are my father etc."' Fifth, you are not lovely, because you swiftly pass away, and your beauty is vain.[7] So one side of the cloth is worthless, the flesh; the other side most noble, i.e., the soul; and if we regard these two sides in the light of their true nature, we shall be able to reach the eternal kingdom.

---

4 Ps 67.3.
5 Ps 143.4.
6 = Jb 17.14.
7 See Prv 31.30.

27. Of just repayment[1]

There was a very rich and powerful emperor who had an only daughter, who was very beautiful, and he loved her so much that he appointed five soldiers to ensure her safety. These soldiers were armed at all times and every day they received a fixed wage from the king's treasury for guarding his daughter.

The emperor[2] had a seneschal and a dog, to both of whom he was deeply attached; and this dog was held by a triple leash of chains because he was very fierce and killed anyone he could get hold of. Now it happened one day that as the king lay in bed he determined to visit the Holy Land, and when he got up he called the seneschal and told him: 'I wish to visit the Holy Land. I am leaving my only daughter in your safekeeping, together with the soldiers and the dog I love. On pain of death I charge you: my daughter is to want for nothing. You are to provide the soldiers with everything they need, as appropriate; you are to keep my dog chained up, and not give him too much to eat. Let him go hungry so that his bloodthirstiness and viciousness are curbed.'

The seneschal promised faithfully to carry out these instructions. But when the emperor went off to the Holy Land, he did the very opposite of all he had promised to do. He always gave the dog the best foods and did not guard him as he ought to have done; he denied the young girl the necessities of life, and robbed the soldiers of their wages, so they disbanded and wandered all over the country. The girl, left unguarded as she was, walked about the palace alone weeping and wailing. And when the dog saw her on her own, he broke the triple chains that tethered him and killed her,

1 Cf. Herrtage, Text I.XXXVI.
2 *rex* (king): there is confusion here, as commonly, between *imperator* and *rex*.

and her death plunged the whole kingdom into deepest mourning.

When the emperor heard of the death of his daughter he was distraught. He summoned the seneschal and asked him why on earth he had let his daughter go unguarded, the soldiers unpaid, and fed the dog contrary to his orders. The seneschal was silent and could say nothing to excuse his behaviour.

So the emperor commanded the torturers to bind him hand and foot and throw him into a blazing furnace. And everyone applauded the emperor for passing such a sentence.

[Moralization.] Dear friends, this emperor is our Lord Jesus Christ, and the beautiful daughter is the soul created in the likeness of God, for whose safekeeping he appointed five soldiers, i.e., the five senses, to be armed continually with good works and to receive the wages of God's grace. The dog is our wretched flesh that strives day and night to disturb the spirit and destroy the soul. So it is absolutely necessary that it is permanently bound by three chains: that is, by the fear of God, the love of God, and our shame at committing sin. It is bound by the fear of God, because God is just and justly condemns the sinner to everlasting punishment. This is the first chain by which the wretched flesh is bound lest it offend God and destroy our chance of salvation. The second chain is the love of God, because man is bound to love him above all things, even more than himself. For love of him you must refrain from sin and beware of inordinate desires. Why must you love him so much? To be sure, because he created you, formed you, made you in his likeness, redeemed you and will give you eternal life. The third chain is man's shame at sinning in God's sight, for He sees everything, even the most trivial thought in your heart. These are the three chains by which man must tether himself, and so never offend God by sin. The seneschal is man, to whom God has given a soul together with the five senses, and his flesh to control in such a way that he can answer for them when our Lord Jesus Christ comes to his judgement. But wretched man, who does not love God, breaks his chains, because he neglects the fear of God, and does not trouble to think that God's judgement is just when he damns man eternally. He neglects the love of God, and does not trouble to consider all the tokens of love He has manifested, in that He formed him from nothing, made him in His own likeness, adorned him with His divine image, humbled Himself for him, assumed his nature and redeemed him with His own blood; and he feels no shame at sinning in the sight of his Lord God. He does the very opposite of

all he should do, and destroys his soul. So when the Day of Judgement arrives, the sinner will stand before him and not be able to answer his charges, and then God will hand him over to the tormenters of hell, as Matthew himself attests, c.25:[3] *'Go, you cursed, into everlasting fire.' Let us therefore strive before all else to keep our soul from sin if we desire to attain to everlasting life.*

---

3 Cf. Mt 25.41. This is quoted in seven other moralizations, and always at their very end, as if the preacher wanted to send his flock on its way with a terrifying reminder of hell fire.

28. Of the abominable cunning of old women[1]

There was an empress in whose kingdom there lived a knight who had a noble, chaste and lovely wife. It happened that this knight had to travel abroad, and before his departure he said to his wife: 'I am not leaving you a guard, because I am sure you do not need one.' He then got together his retinue and left, and his wife remained at home living a chaste life. Now it chanced one day that she was prevailed upon by the entreaties of a neighbour to attend a feast, and after it was over, she went back home, and a youth saw her and fell passionately in love with her. He sent her countless messages hoping that she might return his passion, but she scorned them and utterly rebuffed him. The youth was so deeply wounded by her rejection of him that he fell ill. He would often go to her house, but it did him no good because she treated him with contempt.

One day he happened to be going towards the church, all downcast and miserable, when he met an old woman who had a reputation for holiness of life. Seeing how sad he looked, she asked him the reason for his unhappiness. 'What point is there in telling you?' he replied. 'My dear young man,' she said, 'as long as the sick man hides his illness from the doctor he cannot be cured. So tell me the reason for all this unhappiness. With God's help I will cure you.'

At these words the youth told her of his love for the lady, and the old woman said: 'Quick now, go home, and I will cure you in no time.' So the youth went home, and the old woman returned

---

1 This story can be found in Peter Alfonsi's *Disciplina Clericalis*, XII. Alfonsi was a converted Spanish Jew, who compiled this collection of moralizing tales at the beginning of the twelfth century. Cf. the conclusion of *Decameron*, Day 5, nov. 8, which has a similar theme; and Day 5, nov. 10, in which the bawd is very like the old woman here. See also Oesterley, pp. 716–17; Tubach, no. 661; Hope, pp. 494–6.

28. Of the abominable cunning of old women

to her own house. Now this old woman had a little dog, and she made it go without food for two days, then on the third day she made a loaf of mustard powder and gave it to the starving animal. As soon as it tasted the loaf, its eyes watered all day because of its pungent bitterness. The old woman then went with her little dog to the house of the lady whom the youth loved so much, and because of her reputation for holiness she was at once given a respectful welcome by the lady. As they sat there together, the lady noticed the little dog weeping, and finding this very strange asked what was the reason. 'Ah,' said the old woman, 'dear friend, don't ask me the reason! Her misery is so great I can hardly find words to tell you.' But the lady kept pressing her to speak, and the old woman told her: 'This little dog was my daughter, a most chaste and lovely girl. A young man fell madly in love with her, but she was so chaste that she utterly rejected his love, and he was so grief stricken that he died, and to punish her for this God changed her into the little dog you see here.' So saying, the old woman began to weep: 'Whenever my daughter remembers what a lovely girl she was, and that now she is a little dog, she weeps, and is inconsolable; indeed her bitter grief makes everyone weep.'

When she heard this story the lady thought to herself: 'Ah me! It is the same with me: a youth loves me, and is ill with love for me.' So she told the old woman the whole story.

The old woman said: 'My dear lady, don't reject the love of this young man or you may be changed into a little dog like my daughter, and that would be a punishment too cruel to bear.'

'Good woman,' the lady replied. 'What would you advise me to do to avoid becoming a little dog?'

'Send for the youth at once,' she told her, 'and do as he wishes. Don't put it off a moment longer. Give him what he wants.'

'Then, please, your holiness,' the lady said, 'go to him and bring him back with you. It would cause a scandal if anyone else went.'

The old woman replied: 'I pity you, and I will bring him to you with pleasure.'

So she hurried off and brought the youth back with her, and he lay with the lady. And so, by means of the old woman, the lady committed adultery.

[*Moralization.*] Dear friends, the knight is Christ; the chaste and lovely wife is the soul, washed clean by baptism, to which God gave free will and which he left to its own will when he ascended from this world to his Father. The woman, i.e., the soul, is invited to a banquet whenever she is inclined to the desires of the flesh, for the banquet of carnal man is to live constantly for pleasure. At once a youth, i.e., worldly vanity, does everything he can to entice her to yield to him. And if she will not agree, a little old woman, i.e., the devil, is at hand, who 'goeth about seeking whom he may devour,'[2] i.e., he tempts her soul with all his powers to give way to sin. How? Why, he shows her the little dog weeping. The little dog is the hope of a long life, and an excessive assurance of God's mercy, which many people have to such a degree that they are soon led astray to sin. For just as the little dog wept because of the mustard, so hope often overwhelms the soul and prevents it from arriving at the truth, so that man yields to sin. If therefore we wish to preserve purity of soul and be on our guard against the deceits of the world, let us flee the world with all our might, because 'all that is in the world is either pride of life, or the concupiscence of the eyes or the concupiscence of the flesh',[3] and so the supreme remedy is to abandon it, if we wish to obtain the eternal prize.

2 1 Pt 5.8.
3 Cf. 1 Jn 2.16.

29. A noteworthy tale concerning wicked judges

There was an emperor who enacted a law that all judges should administer justice fairly or face the severest penalty: any who did otherwise could expect to find no mercy at all. Now it happened that a judge was bribed and gave a dishonest judgement, and when the emperor heard of this he commanded his servants to flay him alive. His command was duly carried out, and he placed the dead man's skin on the seat on which the next judge would sit, so that he might think of this and be deterred from ever giving false judgements. Then the emperor appointed the dead judge's son as judge, and told him: 'You will sit on your father's skin to deliver justice. If anyone offers you a gift to divert you from the path of justice, look upon your father's skin, lest the same fate befall you.'[1]

[Moralization.] Dear friends, the emperor is our Lord Jesus Christ, who established this law, of which Deuteronomy speaks:[2] 'Thou shalt appoint judges and magistrates etc .' He indeed judges us justly at all times, for our Heavenly Father granted him all power to give judgement. The judge whose judgement was unjust is any man, who must judge himself according to the righteousness of his life, and consider what sins he has committed against God, and their gravity. And if any one of you is corrupted by bribes, i.e., by evil desires, he must be flayed, i.e., stripped of all his sins by penance, so that he can say with Job:[3] 'Skin for skin, and all that a man hath he will give for his life.' The skin that was placed on the judgement-seat as a reminder is the memory of Christ's Passion, which man must preserve upon the judgement-

---

1 Cf. the tale of Sisamnes and Cambyses, Herodotus V.25. For cognate versions, see Oesterley, p. 717; Tubach, no. 2859; Hope, pp. 496–7.
2 Dt 16.18.
3 Jb 2.4.

seat of his heart, lest he sin against God and his soul's salvation; as has been written:[4] 'Remember thy last end, and thou shalt never sin.' Christ gave not only his skin on the judgement-seat of the cross for us, but also his life. Therefore if we are true sons we should not offend him by sinning. And if it happens that we stumble, let us consider how much he endured for us upon the cross, that we may make amends with works of mercy, and accordingly we shall obtain everlasting life.

4 Ecclus 7.40.

30. Of crime and judgement[1]

A certain king ordered that when a victor returned from war he should receive three honours and suffer three vexations. The first honour was that the people should go to meet the victor with shouts of joy. The second was that the captives should follow behind his chariot with hands and feet bound. The third honour was that, clad in the tunic of Jupiter, he should sit in a chariot drawn by four white horses and be conducted in this to the Capitol.

But in case he should forget himself because of these honours, he had to endure three vexations. The first was that alongside him in the chariot a slave of the lowliest degree was seated, to show that anyone who had sufficient integrity might attain to such honour, however lowly his status. The second vexation was that the slave was to buffet him to prevent him from being too proud, and say to him: 'Know yourself, and do not be too proud because of this great honour! Look behind you and remember that you are a man!' The third vexation was that on the day of the triumph anyone could say anything he wanted, i.e., utter any kind of personal insult, against the victor.

Dear friends, this emperor is the Heavenly Father, and the general victorious in war is our Lord Jesus Christ, who won a victory against the devil, and so was accorded triple honours on the Day of Palms. First, the people went to meet him, when everyone came out of Jerusalem with the branches of palms and garments and the children shouted:[2] *'Hosanna to the Son of David!' The second honour, that all the captives [should follow him]. These captives were the Jews and sinners bound*

---

1 Cf. Herrtage, Text I.XLV (which also contains the three cockerel motif of no. 68, below).
2 Mt 21.8f.

fast by their sins, who followed the chariot of his humanity, seeing the signs and prodigies he performed. The third honour, that the victor was clad in the tunic of Jupiter. This tunic was Christ's divinity, inwardly united with his humanity, which was drawn by four white horses, i.e., the four Evangelists, who discoursed of his humanity and divinity. To balance these three honours he endured three vexations, namely that someone of servile status was placed beside him,[3] i.e., a most evil robber. The second vexation was that slaves struck him. This is what the Jews did to Christ, saying:[4] 'Prophesy unto us, who is he that struck thee?' The third vexation was that people hurled all kinds of insults at him: this the Jews did when they spat on his face and mocked him so cruelly.

---

3 i.e., on the cross.
4 e.g. Mt 26.68.

31. Of the harshness of death

We read that, when at Alexander's death a golden sepulchre was built,[1] a great company of philosophers gathered beside it. One said: 'Alexander made a treasure of gold; and now, on the contrary, gold has made a treasure of him.'[2]

Another said: 'Yesterday the whole world was not enough for him: today three or four yards of cloth are sufficient for him.'

Another said: 'Yesterday Alexander could save a thousand people from death: today he could not avoid the shafts of death himself.'

Another said: 'Yesterday he burdened the earth: today he is burdened by it.'

Another said: 'Yesterday everyone feared Alexander: today everyone thinks of him as nothing.'

Another said: 'Yesterday Alexander had many friends: today he has none.'

Another said: 'Yesterday Alexander led an army: today he is led by the same men to his grave.'

Dear friends, Alexander is any rich man of this world who cares only about worldly things. When they die, the worldly care more about the great pomp of their funerals than about their soul, which undergoes punishment. The philosophers who were drawn to the sepulchre are the Doctors and interpreters of Holy Scripture, who are the rich of this world; they make a treasure of worldly gold, which is to say that man must abound in worldly goods, i.e., in virtues, such as almsgiving, clothing the naked etc., and in this way he makes a treasure in heaven for his soul. Likewise they say: 'The world is not sufficient for the

1 *quod antea*: Oest.; *cum sepultura eius fieret aurea*: K., L.
2 *et nunc e converso aurum ex eo fecit thesaurum*: I take this to refer to the golden sepulchre.

greedy man, because the more he has, the more he wants to have, and this is folly, because at his death the world will fail him. And if for all his toil he obtains two or three yards of cloth, that is plenty.' They also say: 'The rich, while they live, give the orders, but after they die, any poor man can command them; and as long as the rich man lives, he can save many from death, yet no rich man, however powerful, can escape the darts of death in his hour of need.' Likewise, man is master of the earth, but in death the earth is his master, because man's whole body is consumed by the earth, and as long as man lives, he is feared, as it is written: 'The face of a man is the face of a lion';[3] but in death everyone considers him contemptible. Likewise, as long as he lives he has friends, but in death they all depart and leave him on his own. As long as he lives, man can win many friends and be their leader, but in death he will be led by them; as Christ said to Peter:[4] 'Another shall gird thee and lead thee whither thou wouldst not.'

3 Cf. Ez 1.10.
4 Jn 21.18.

32. Of good inspiration

Seneca relates[1] that when bodies are poisoned, because of the evil properties of the poison and its coldness, no worm is begotten in them. But if they are struck by lightning, in a few days they produce worms.

Dear friends, by poisoned bodies I understand the man who is poisoned by mortal sin. Such men cannot produce a worm[2] because of the coldness of sin, and so God strikes them with lightning when he imbues them with his grace, and if the sinner wishes to receive this, he can quickly be converted. It is therefore a sound counsel that we should quickly turn to Christ through contrition. And so let us win eternal life. To which etc.

1 L. Annaeus Seneca, the younger (d. AD 65), *Quaestiones Naturales* II.31.2.
2 Swan suggests that the worms symbolize virtues.

33. Of boastfulness[1]

Valerius tells the story of a man named Peratinus who tearfully exclaimed to his son and all his neighbours: 'Alas, wretch that I am! I have a tree in my garden that is cursed. My first wife hanged herself on it, then my second, and then my third. It has caused me endless grief.' But one of his neighbours, a man called Arrius, replied: 'I am amazed that you are weeping after such singular good fortune. Give me three cuttings from that tree, I beg you, because I shall divide them up among my neighbours so that each of them can have a tree for his wife to hang herself on.' And that is what he did.

Dear friends, the tree is the holy cross on which Christ hung. This tree must be planted in a man's garden, while his mind keeps a continual remembrance of Christ's Passion. On this tree the three wives of men are hanged, namely pride of life, concupiscence of the flesh and concupiscence of the eyes. For when man is placed upon the earth he marries three wives: one is the daughter of the flesh, and her name is pleasure; the second is the daughter of the world, and her name is avarice; the third is the daughter of the devil, and her name is pride. But when a sinner through God's grace devotes himself to repentance, these wives, not able to have their own way, hang themselves. Avarice hangs herself with the rope of alms, pride with the rope of humility, pleasure hangs herself with the rope of fasting and chastity. The man who asked for the cuttings is the good Christian, who must make every effort to look for and seek this cutting, not only for himself, for but for others who

1 *De Jactantia*: neither the tale itself nor the application explains the choice of this title. The story is not in Valerius Maximus but is told by Cicero, *De Oratore* II.LXIX.278. Cf. Chaucer, Wife of Bath's prologue, ll. 757–65.

33. Of boastfulness

are his neighbours. The man who wept is the wretched man who loves the flesh and the things of the flesh more than the things that are of the Holy Spirit. But often such a person can be brought to the way of righteousness by the instruction of a good man, and so will obtain eternal life.

34. Of the consideration of life

We read that Alexander had Aristotle as his tutor, and profited greatly from his teaching and learned many virtues from him. Among other things he asked his tutor to tell him what would be the most profitable advice for himself as well as for others.

His tutor replied: 'Listen carefully, my son, and if you observe my teaching you will attain to great honours. I will give you seven counsels. The first is, do not overleap the balance.[1] The second: do not feed a fire with the sword.[2] The third: do not rail at the crown.[3] The fourth: do not eat the heart of a little bird.[4] The fifth: once you have started, do not turn back. The sixth: do not walk along the public highway.[5] The seventh: do not let a twittering swallow live in your house.'[6]

The king paid the closest attention to these seven counsels and profited from them as long as he lived.

Dear friends, the balance is human life. There are two things to be weighed: our entry into the world and our leaving it. So let man be placed in one scale, i.e., in the poverty in which he entered the world, and in the other scale with the poverty in which he will leave the world, and he will find that he weighs the same. Just as he comes into the world

---

1 *ne transilias stateram*: the Latin version of a Pythagorean maxim: do not exceed what is just. The balance was a symbol of justice/equity.
2 Another Pythagorean maxim (more usually *ignem gladio non fodias [=poke]* or *scalpas [rake]*): do not provoke anger with harsh words. A. Otto, *Sprichwörter der Römer* [1890], Hildesheim: Olms, 1971, 171.4.
3 i.e., respect the authorities.
4 i.e., respect weak and timid creatures.
5 i.e., the road leading to death.
6 i.e., do not let sin enter your heart.

34. Of the consideration of life

poor, so he leaves it poor. *Ecclesiasticus c.2:*[7] *'As he came forth naked from his mother's womb, so he returns*[8] *and takes nothing away with him of his labour.'* Likewise place on one side of the balance the time in which you have sinned, and then I ask the question Christ asked of the father of the sick child:[9] *'When did this happen to him?'* And the father replied to Christ: *'From his infancy etc.,'* as is made clear. And I ask of you: *'When did you begin to sin?'* Alas, you will reply: *'Not yesterday, nor the day before, but from my infancy.'* So put the time of your sinning on one side of the balance and it will weigh the scale down.[10] So you must not *'overleap the balance'*; but consider well how [you are to avoid this]: put the time for your repentance on the other side. But you do not know how long you have to repent. Then multiply your works of penance that they may weigh the same as your ill deeds. As Zacchaeus says:[11] *'If I have wronged any man of anything, I restore him fourfold.'* Further, do not *'overleap the balance'* in this respect: do not desire more than is necessary for your nourishment. As is said of the vulture: when a vulture captures its prey it sees if it can carry it all and fly away with it, or not; if not, it divides it up,[12] and carries away with it as much as it can fly away with, and so has as much as is sufficient for it. Man should behave in the same way. There are many who regard riches as their prey; they labour night and day to become rich, they rob other people of their goods, and when they have them they put them in a secret place, and this prevents them from being able to fly up to God. And this is a great folly, that they should have any use for those things that they cannot take with them. Therefore let the prey, i.e., wealth, be divided up, and let a man keep only what is necessary. The rest he should give to the poor, and thus he will be able to fly up to God.

The second counsel: Do not feed a fire with the sword, i.e., do not provoke a wrathful man with harsh words. Wrath is compared with

---

7 = Eccles 5.14.
8 *revertitur ... aufert*: Oest.; *revertetur ... auferet*: V.
9 Cf. Mk 9.20ff. Jesus asks how long the child has been suffering in this way.
10 *minus ponderabit*: this would normally mean 'it will weigh less', but surely the weight of his sins will weigh the scale down, an imbalance which he redresses by putting his acts of repentance in the other scale. (*Le Violier*: 'Mectz le temps de penitence lors avesques le temps de peché et garde bien que pesché ne transcende.')
11 Lk 19.8.
12 *sed non dividit*: Oest., K.; *si non, dividit*: L.

fire because, when a wrathful man lacks something, his wrath is at once kindled. This fire is not to be fed with the sword. The sword is truly man's tongue, which is broad and sharp on both sides after the fashion of a sword. The Psalmist says:[13] *'Their tongue is a sharp sword.' It is the same with the wrathful man as with lime: in lime there is dormant heat; if water is poured on it, it is at once heated and gives off smoke. So too with the angry man, whose wrath is dormant; as soon as he hears harsh words, his anger is kindled and he lets the smoke of wrath and conflict issue from him. And so we should not feed a fire with the sword.*

The third counsel: Do not rail at the crown, i.e., do not find fault with civic laws. The city in which we live is the Church. The laws of this city are the doctrines of the Church, which no wise man should criticize, but humbly obey and follow. But this teaching has many critics, as is obvious from the fact that it has few followers, and so we must obey the words of God and his precepts and hold fast to them if we wish to come to the eternal kingdom.

The fourth counsel: Do not eat the heart of a little bird, i.e., do not suffer sorrow, hatred or envy in your heart because of any temporal adversity, because Proverbs c.15 says:[14] *'As worms damage wood and moths clothing, so sorrow damages the heart of man.' Let man therefore unite himself with God by leading a good life, and keep his remembrance of Him always fresh in his heart, and thus he will feel no grief, indeed he will rejoice the more in adversity. 'The Apostles went forth rejoicing etc.'*[15]

The fifth counsel: Once you have started, do not turn back; i.e., when you have withdrawn from a state of error, do not return to the vomit of sin. This wise counsel is given in Ecclesiasticus c.21:[16] *'My son, hast thou sinned? Do so no more.' But I fear that many behave like the dog, and of them Peter says:*[17] *'The sinner who returns to his evil ways is just like the dog that returned to its own vomit.' Many people also behave like the viper. For when it wants to couple with a lamprey, the lamprey flees from its poison; the viper then vomits up its poison somewhere,*[18] *and so couples with the lamprey, and then returns to its poison. Similarly many who wish to be united with Christ upon*

13 Ps 56.5.
14 Cf. Prv 15.13.
15 Acts 5.41.
16 Ecclus 21.1.
17 Cf. 2 Pt 2.21f.
18 *venenoso*: Oest., K.; *venenum*: L.

34. Of the consideration of life

the altar vomit up their poison when they confess their sins, but afterwards return to sin. And of such people Proverbs c.16 says:[19] *'As the dog returneth to his vomit etc.'*

The sixth counsel: Do not walk along a public highway. The public highway is the way of the sinner, along which the greater part of the world passes, because it is broad. Matthew c.7:[20] *'Broad is the way that leadeth to destruction, and many there are who walk it.' Note that there are many wild beasts that never pursue a straight path, lest they be hunted down by dogs. So too man, while he is in the world and in danger, should flee because of the hounds of hell that are pursuing him. As the Psalmist says:*[21] *'Many dogs have encompassed me.' We must flee from such a path, because on it are the devil's huntsmen who employ three kinds of hunting. There are three varieties of hunting and all of them are full of guile. The first is when men hunt beasts that flee them, and to catch them dig pits. These pits are usury, and temporal possessions, and lies, false oaths and acts of duplicity, in which the covetous are ensnared. The second kind of hunting is when men hunt wild fowl. To catch them they set snares, which are false advocates and judges, who are corrupted by bribes and who make laws to ensnare the poor. The third kind of hunting is that of fishermen, who put out their nets to catch all humankind. They are the lecherous. Women are the devil's nets, in which people of almost every walk of life are caught.*

The seventh counsel is: Do not allow a twittering swallow to live in your house; i.e., do not let sin into your heart, for your conscience will always murmur against it. As we read of Jonah, as long as he was in the hold of the ship, there could be no calm at sea. In the same way, as long as sin lodges in the heart of man, because of it a raging storm arises, while the conscience murmurs against God, and there can be no tranquillity; not until Jonah is expelled from the ship and sin is expelled from the heart, and the storm, i.e., the remorse of conscience, will cease, when sin is plunged into the depths of hell. So let us not allow a swallow, i.e., sin, into our heart, but let us desire to obtain eternal life, to which etc.

---

19 = Prv 26.11.
20 Cf. Mt 7.13.
21 Ps 21.17.

35. Of the restoration of peace and the punishment of those who disrupt it

We read in the chronicles of Rome that when peace was to be made between nobles who had quarrelled, it was customary for them to climb a great and lofty mountain taking with them a lamb. This was then sacrificed, and its blood poured out before them to symbolize the restoration of peace, and as a sign that if anyone were to disrupt the peace, he would suffer the severest penalty for it, and his blood would be shed.

Dear friends, the noble lords were God the Father and man. Of God the Psalmist says:[1] *'Of his greatness there is no end.' Of man, who was made in the likeness of God, the Psalmist says:*[2] *'Thou hast subjected all things under his feet etc.' There was such discord between these nobles that when men died they went down to hell. Then peace was made between God and man, and at the restoration of this peace the lamb, i.e., Christ, was led to the top of Mount Calvary and slain, and his blood was poured out as a sign that if were anyone were to disrupt the peace he would suffer the severest penalty and his blood would be shed. So if you break the compact with God, severe punishment will follow. And how severe do you think your punishment will be if you have broken the promises you made at your baptism?*

1 Ps 144.3.
2 Ps 8.8.

36. Of the course of human life

We read of a certain king who wished above all things to understand the nature of man. In his kingdom there lived a philosopher of exceptional wisdom upon whose advice many people acted. When the king heard of his reputation, he sent a message to him commanding him to appear before him without delay, and as soon as he learned of the king's wish, the philosopher went to him.

The king said to him: 'Master, I wish to learn from your wisdom and hear your teaching. Tell me, in the first place, what is man?' The philosopher replied: 'Man is wretched all the days of his life. Consider your beginning, middle and end and you will find that life is full of miseries. Hence Job said:[1] "Man born of a woman, [living for a short time, is filled with many miseries]." If you consider your beginning, you will find that you are poor and helpless; if the middle of your life, you will find the world oppressing you and perhaps bringing your soul to damnation. If you consider your end, you will find the earth receiving you. So, my lord king, there will be nothing then to recall all your worldly pomp.'

The king replied: 'I have four questions for you, and if you answer them well, I will raise you to a position of wealth and honour. The first is: What is man?[2] The second: What is he like? The third: Where is he? The fourth: What companions has he?'

The philosopher said: 'My lord, I will answer your first question. If you ask What is man?, I say that he is the slave of death, a guest wherever he is, a passing traveller. He is a slave because he cannot escape the hand of death, for death robs him of all his

---

1 Jb 14.1.
2 The question has been asked, and answered, before. The style of the philosopher's speech suggests that the tale has become conflated with the *moralisatio*.

works and days, and he will be rewarded or punished according to his deserts. Also, man is a guest wherever he is, because he is consigned to oblivion. Also, he is a passing traveller: whether sleeping or waking, eating or drinking, whatever he is doing, he is always hurrying on towards death. So we should provide victuals for our journey, that is, virtues. My answer to your second question, What is man like?, is that he is like ice, which dissolves rapidly in the heat. So too man, who is composed of earth and the elements, rapidly dissolves in the heat of his infirmity and is destroyed. He is also like a young apple as it hangs on the bough, which instead of swelling as it should, rots because a little worm has grown inside it, and suddenly drops to the ground and is good for nothing. The same is true of man; as he grows in his adolescence, suddenly a sickness develops within him, his soul is driven from him and his body destroyed. How then can man be proud? My answer to your third question, Where is man?, is that he is at war on all fronts against the world, the devil and the flesh. My answer to your fourth question, Who are his companions?, is that he has seven, and they are hunger, thirst, heat, cold, fatigue, sickness and death. Prepare your soul therefore to fight the devil, the world and the flesh, for their assaults, that is, temptations, are of various different kinds. So the soul must be armed in different ways in order to resist them. The flesh tempts us with lust and sensual pleasures; the world with the vanity of riches; the devil with the base sin of pride. So if the flesh tempts you, apply the following remedy: always remember that the flesh that prompts you to sin, though the day and time is unknown, will turn to dust, and the soul will undergo eternal punishment for its sin. Wisdom 2:[3] 'Lifeless, our body shall be ashes.' And it continues: 'Then we shall be forgotten and no man shall have any remembrance of our works.' And if we keep that dust in mind it will prevent us from succumbing to temptation. If the world tempts us to vanity, apply the following remedy: consider carefully its ingratitude, and you will never have any desire to be its slave; for the world is so ungrateful that, though you may be its devoted slave all your life, it permits you to take with you nothing but your sins. For the world is like the partridge. When a partridge has chicks and knows the hunter is approaching her nest, she runs towards him to divert him from her young, pretending she cannot fly, and

3 Cf. Wis 2.3f.

36. Of the course of human life

the hunter, believing this to be the case, gradually follows her. She then takes flight, and he goes after her hoping to catch her, and she keeps doing this until he has been drawn far from the chicks; and so the hunter is deceived because he gets neither the partridge nor her chicks. And so it is with the world. The hunter who approaches the nest with its chicks is the good Christian, who gets food and clothing and all other necessities by hard work. But the world is unwilling to stand by man: she applauds him and pretends that she will attend him and he will always be honoured. Under this illusion man often abandons his good works and follows after the world's vanities, and then the world draws him away from the love of God and good works. And then death removes him from the world and he is a deceived and wretched thing, because he has neither the world, which he followed after, nor the fruit of his good works, which he has been kept from pursuing. See how the world repays its servitors! This is what St James says, c.2:[4] 'The whole world is seated in wickedness; everything that is in the world is the pride of life etc.' Third, if the devil tempts you, apply the following remedy: keep in mind Christ's Passion, before which the proud yield and which they have no power to resist. Hence the Apostle says:[5] 'Put on the armour of God that you may be able to stand [against the deceits of the devil].' Solinus relates[6] in *De Mirabilibus Mundi* *[Of the Wonders of the World]* that Alexander had a horse called Bucephalus, who, when armed ready for battle, would let no-one except Alexander sit upon him, and if anyone else mounted him, he immediately threw him. But when he was not armed for battle, even the servants were permitted to do so. So too the man who is armed with the Passion of Christ can receive no-one in his heart except God the Omnipotent Commander, and if some temptation of the devil tries to take control of his heart, through the virtue of Christ's Passion he has the power to cast it out. But if he is without the armour of God, he will at once be vulnerable to every kind of temptation. Let us therefore strive to arm ourselves with virtues, that at length we may attain to the glory of God.

4 = 1 Jn 5.19; cf. 1 Jn 2.16.
5 Eph 6.11.
6 Gaius Julius Solinus, *Collectanea Rerum Mirabiliorum* c. XLVI. This work, which is almost wholly cribbed from Pliny's *Natural History* and Pomponius Mela's *De Chorographia*, was written soon after AD 200.

37. Of lifting the mind to heaven

Pliny relates that an eagle flew to a high peak and there built her nest, and a kind of serpent called pervas[1] lay in wait to kill her young. This serpent, finding that he could not reach the nest because of its great height, went upwind of it and spat out poison so that the air infected with her venom might pass over the young birds and kill them. But the eagle, relying on her native instinct, guarded against this with remarkable cunning. She fetched a stone known as agate[2] and placed it in that part of her nest which faced the wind, and the special virtue of the stone prevented the poison from reaching her young, and so their lives were saved.

Dear friends, the eagle, who flies high and has acute vision, signifies man, whose life and desires must be raised above earthly things, so that he can say with the Apostle, Philippians c.2:[3] 'Our community is in heaven.' It is in that lofty community that we must place our chicks, i.e., our good works. Then the old serpent, i.e., the devil, tries to kill man by tempting him to some mortal sin, but, perhaps because of his loftiness of life he cannot achieve his purpose. The devil then goes and tries to kill them[4] by means of the wind, by commending to man the praise of mankind, and if this comes to him often, so that man repeatedly performs good works because of his thirst for such praise, his chicks will die, and his merit be lost.[5] Let us therefore occupy the rock,

1 *pervas*: Oest.; *parnas*: K., Graesse, Trillitzsch; *parnes*: L. There is no such story in Pliny. See Oesterley, p. 718; Tubach, no. 1831; Hope, pp. 503–4.
2 *Achates*: on the supposed virtues of this stone, see Pliny, *N.H.* XXXVI. 34; *N.H.* XXXVII.54.
3 = Phil 3.20.
4 i.e. his chicks, or good works.
5 *quod si saepius venient ut*: Oest.; *quae sibi saepius veniet, ut*: K.; *quae sibi*

37. Of lifting the mind to heaven

i.e., Christ, and place it between our works and the wind of vainglory, that thereby we may direct our works towards God and so win a great reward. For, as you must be aware, the Lord will shoot three exceedingly sharp arrows at men: the first, that of summons, the second, that of disputation,[6] the third, that of conviction. The arrow of summons comes when he says: 'Rise up, you dead, and come to judgement!' It is of this summons that we read at John c.12:[7] 'All that are in the graves shall hear the voice of the Son of God.' Jerome too says:[8] 'Whether I eat or drink, it always seems to me that I hear the cry: "Arise, you dead,"' etc. The arrow of disputation comes when at the judgement sinners are told:[9] 'I was hungry and you gave me not to eat.' The arrow of conviction comes when the judge says: 'Go, you cursed, into everlasting fire.'[10]

---

saepius veniet; et si: L. The text is uncertain. The general sense seems to be that the chicks are a man's good works: if he neglects them to win worldly praise, they die and his merit is cancelled.

6 *decepcionis*: Oest.; *deceptio* (trickery, deceit) sometimes occurs in the form *disceptio*. Perhaps the author was thinking of *disceptatio* (examination, trial, dispute), which is the reading of L.
7 = Jn 5.28.
8 A saying attributed to Jerome, quoted e.g. in *G.L.* XIII.146.
9 Mt 25.42.
10 Cf. Mt 25.41.

38. Of the forethought required to extinguish sin

In the time of the emperor Henry II we read that when a certain city was besieged by its enemies, a dove flew down into the city which was found to have a letter hanging round its neck. It read as follows: 'A generation of dogs is coming and it will be a contentious nation, against which you and your allies must defend your laws.'

Dear friends, what are we to understand by this dove but the Holy Spirit, who descended upon Christ in the form of a dove, and who brings us a letter when he reveals our sins, and announces to us that an insolent nation is coming to besiege us, i.e., to bring men to perdition? So while we have the light of the Holy Spirit, let us read the letter, i.e., reveal our sins through confession, that we may be able to keep God's law and escape death, lest at the last judgement causes for our death be discovered that have not been cleansed by confession. You are wealthy, therefore, for you have the sign of the Son, who with his wisdom is able to apportion wealth and to take it away; you are powerful and mighty, for you have the sign of the Father, who with his power can make you strong and overcome weakness. If you have sins, they are opposed by the sign of the Holy Spirit, who in his mercy wishes us to call our sins to remembrance. If God did not first show him these signs, man would not believe in His judgement as he should. As John himself says, c.4:[1] *'Unless you see signs and wonders, you believe not.'*

---

[1] Jn 4.48.

39. Of the reconciliation between God and man

We read in the annals of Rome that once there was such a violent quarrel between two brothers that one of them laid waste all the lands of the other. Hearing of this, Emperor Julius was exceedingly angry with the offending brother. This brother, realizing that he had offended the emperor, went to the brother whom he had injured so often and begged his forgiveness. He also asked him to make peace between himself and the emperor. All who were present at the meeting said that he deserved not pardon but punishment. But the brother who was being sued for peace replied to them: 'No-one loves the prince who in war is as gentle as a lamb and in peace as fierce as a lion. So although as a man my brother does not deserve peace with me, I will be reconciled with him, if I can, because the injury he has done me is sufficiently atoned for by the fact that he is begging for my mercy.' And thus he restored peace between the emperor and his brother.

Dear friends, the two brothers are the Son of God and man, between whom there is great discord when man yields to mortal sin. Yet man then persecutes the Son of God, his own brother, because he strives with all his might to crucify him a second time. So we read in Hebrews:[1] *'Crucifying the Son of God etc.' And because of this the supreme emperor, the Heavenly Father, is offended. Let us therefore go to our brother, i.e., Christ, and ask him for mercy with heartfelt contrition, and in his mercy he will account that as payment, so that he pardons our guilt and re-establishes peace between the Heavenly Emperor and us. If therefore you fear his justice, have recourse to his mercy, because*

---

1 Heb 6.6. Paul is warning the Christians of Palestine against falling into apostasy, 'crucifying again to themselves the Son of God'.

his mercy is greater than our wretchedness. Hence the Psalmist says:[2] 'His mercy is over all his works; the mercies of the Lord I will sing for ever.'

2 Cf. Ps 144.9 and 88.2.

40. Of skill in the manner of examination[1]

We read in Macrobius[2] that there was a knight who, because of things he had heard and seen, suspected his wife of loving someone else. He often asked his wife if this was true, but she flatly denied that she loved anyone as much as him. However, this did not put the knight's mind to rest, so he went off to a clerk and engaged him to establish the truth of the matter. But the clerk told him: 'I shall not be able to do this, unless I see the lady and talk with her.' The knight replied: 'Then I cordially invite you to dine with me today, and I shall seat you next to my wife.'

So at dinner time the clerk went to the knight's house and was seated next to the lady, and when the meal was over, he began to converse with her on a variety of subjects. Finally he took the lady's hand and felt her pulse, then spoke of the man whose name was linked with hers and whom she was strongly suspected of loving. At once her pulse began to quicken, betraying her joy, and remained feverish as long as he spoke of him. Noting this, the clerk then began to speak of her husband, and her pulse immediately stopped its feverish beating. The clerk knew from this that she loved the man with whom she was accused of committing adultery, and so, through the clerk, the knight got to the truth of the matter.[3]

Dear friends, the knight is Christ, the Son of God, who fought for us against the devil and won the victory. His wife is the soul, united

1 *de modo temptationis et peritia:* here it is probably best to translate *temptatio* as 'trial' or 'examination', referring to the clerk's ruse.
2 There is no such story in Macrobius.
3 The idea of using the pulse as a guide to the emotions recurs in *Decameron*, Day 2, nov. 8, and was taken up by Charles Reade in *The Cloister and the Hearth*.

with him through baptism. Hosea c.2:[4] 'I will espouse thee to me in faith.' But the wife very often loves another more than her husband, i.e., than God, and this can be fully tried and tested nowadays. For if someone speaks as men of the church do, preaching the word of God, and proclaiming the salvation of the soul, he will at once be hated by many, and they will regard whatever he says as wearisome and comfortless. And why? Because the heart's impulse puts love of carnal delights and the world before the love of God, in defiance of Holy Scripture, which says: 'You must love God before all else.' But if anyone begins to say anything of worldly vanities and the things people love, they are at once jolly and merry, and though they sit there all day, the time they spend like this seems to them short.

---

4 Hos 2.20.

41. Of the triumph of Christ and his measureless charity

When Cosdras,[1] King of Athens, had gathered together an army to fight the Dorians, he consulted Apollo on the outcome of the war. Apollo answered that he would not win unless he himself perished by the sword. Now the Dorians heard of this oracle and gave the order that no-one should do violence to Cosdras's person. But Cosdras got to know of this, and took off his regal clothing, armed himself and fought his way into the midst of the enemy. Seeing this, one of the enemy pierced him to the heart with his spear, and so by his death Cosdras delivered his people from the hands of their enemies. In the end his death was deeply mourned by the people of both countries.

Dear friends, even so our beloved Lord Jesus Christ consulted God the Father, and because humankind could not be redeemed unless he himself died, he came to fight in the war against the devil. And knowing that he would be recognized, he changed his appearance when he assumed human nature. 1 Corinthian, c.1:[2] 'If they had known it, they would never have crucified the Lord of Glory.' Now when the day for war was imminent, one of the soldiers standing near the cross pierced him to the heart with his spear, and thus by his death he delivered the whole of humankind from the death to which it had justly been sentenced. And there was grief on both sides for his death: the demons grieved greatly because by his death humankind had been saved; and for their part the Apostles were downcast at the death of their Lord.

1 Codrus, last King of Athens.
2 = 1 Cor 2.8.

42. Of the lack of charity

Valerius relates[1] that on a column in Rome he saw four letters, each of them written three times: three Ps, three Ss, three Rs and three Fs. After considering them he said: 'Alas, alas! I see this means ruin for the city.' When the nobles of Rome heard him they said: 'Master, tell us how you understand this.' He replied: 'The meaning of the letters is as follows: *Pater Patriae Perditur* (The father of the fatherland is lost); *Sapientia Secum Sustollitur* (Wisdom is extinguished with him); *Ruunt Regna Romae* (The Roman Empire is brought low); *Ferro, flamma, fame* (By the sword, by fire, by famine).

And the prediction came true.

Dear friends, spiritually speaking, the father of the fatherland is charity, which is love of God and one's neighbour, a principle to which every man should be subject, because, as you know, it behoves a father to provide what is necessary for his sons. Consequently true charity will provide us with infinite riches in everlasting life, because without charity it is impossible for us to obtain everlasting life. But alas, alas! The father of the fatherland, i.e., charity, is lost upon the earth; for hardly anyone loves anyone else, and without doubt wisdom is extinguished along with him, because there are few who know how they should behave towards God and their neighbour, and if they do know, there are few who put it into practice through lack of wisdom. What then is the consequence? The kingdoms of Rome and those in many different parts of the earth are brought low by the sword, by fire and by famine, because there is no charity on earth, and no wisdom. If we speak of human wisdom, it is folly before God.[2] How many nobles and princes have within a short period of time perished by the sword in war,

1 This story is not in Valerius Maximus.
2 Cf. 1 Cor 1.25.

or died, and died a most ignominious death! How many poor people have perished of hunger! And all this is because there is no love or wisdom on earth, whereas railing and murder are common.

43. Christ closed hell by his Passion and willing death

In a place in the centre of Rome the earth once opened up and revealed a gaping chasm beneath. The gods were questioned about this and they answered: 'This abyss will not close unless someone plunges into it of his own free will.' But no-one could be persuaded to do this until Marcus Anilius declared: 'If you allow me to live in Rome as I please for a year, at the end of it I will happily and willingly throw myself into the chasm.' When they heard this the Romans were delighted; they agreed wholeheartedly and denied him nothing. Anilius then made free with men's wives and possessions, and at the end of the year he mounted a noble horse and with one swift leap plunged into the abyss, and the earth at once closed up.[1]

Dear friends, Rome signifies this world, in the middle of which, at its centre, is hell, which was open before Christ's birth, and countless men fell into it. Then we received a response from the gods, i.e., the prophets, that it would never be closed until a virgin brought forth a son who would fight against the devil for humankind, and whose soul with its divinity went down into hell. So you must know that in future it will never be open unless someone wishes to open it of his own volition through mortal sin.

---

1 *F.D.M.* V.6.2 (of Marcus Curtius, who sacrificed himself in 362 BC).

44. Of envy

Before Tiberius became emperor he was known for his wisdom, famed for his eloquence, and prosperous in war. But afterwards he made no use of his military skills and undertook no more campaigns, and was the scourge of the Roman people. He put to death his own sons, and many patricians and consuls. Then an inventor came to him claiming that he could produce a glass that was flexible, and when Tiberius threw this glass against a wall it did not crack; however, it bent, so the craftsman took a hammer to it and, beating at the glass as if it were copper, soon corrected the curve. When Tiberius asked him how this was possible, he replied that he was the only person on earth who knew the secret. So Tiberius immediately ordered him to be beheaded, saying: 'If this secret becomes common knowledge, gold and silver will be considered worthless.'[1]

Dear friends, Tiberius symbolizes those monks and others who, before they are elevated to high office or wealth, are most humble and patient, but after their preferment behave in a wholly differently manner; hence it will commonly be said of them: 'Honours change manners.'[2] And the Psalmist says:[3] 'Man when he was in honour did not understand etc.' The craftsman who presented the vessel can be taken as the poor man who offers gifts to the rich man; who, if they are not to his liking, casts them to the ground and refuses to accept them. Indeed this only makes him more angry with him, and he strips him, and indeed often chastises him so severely that he dies.

1 The story is related in Pliny, *N.H.* XXXVI.66. See also Oesterley, p. 719; Tubach, no. 4861; Hope, pp. 508–9.
2 *Honores mutant mores*: a Latin adage, which is often completed by *sed raro in meliores*: 'but rarely for the better'.
3 Ps 48.21.

45. How only the good will enter the kingdom of heaven[1]

There was a very noble, wise and wealthy king who had a wife whom he loved, but she, forgetful of the love she owed him, gave birth to three illegitimate sons who were constantly rebellious towards the king and quite unlike him. Subsequently she conceived and bore the king a fourth, legitimate son and brought him up. But it happened that the king completed the course of his days and died, and his body was buried in a royal sarcophagus. After his death the four sons began to dispute the succession to the kingship. Finally they came to an agreement that they should consult one of the dead king's veterans, a knight who had been his special confidant, and defer completely to his judgement. So that is what they did. When this knight had patiently heard them out, he said: 'Heed my advice. If you do so it will be to your good. You must remove the dead king's body from the sarcophagus, and each of you have a bow and arrow ready, and whoever shoots an arrow deepest into his body shall win his kingdom.' This plan met with their approval, so they took their father's body from its resting-place and tied it to a tree.

When the first of them let fly his arrow it pierced the king's right hand, and at this they began to hail him as sole heir to the throne and successor to the kingdom. The second son's arrow, to his delight, went closer to the mark and struck the king's face, so that he was even more certain of victory. But the third son's arrow pierced the king's heart, so he considered that he had beaten his brothers and was absolutely certain to possess the kingdom. However, the fourth son approached the body, gave a most pitiful cry and groaned: 'Oh, my poor father! That I should see your body wounded like this by your own sons! Far be it from me ever to strike my father's body,

[1] Cf. Herrtage, Text I.XLII.

45. How only the good will enter the kingdom of heaven 117

living or dead!' When he spoke these words all the nobles of the realm and all the people lifted the young man on their shoulders and set him on his father's throne as the true heir and successor to the kingdom. The other three sons were stripped of all rank and wealth and banished for ever from the kingdom.

Dear friends, the wise, noble and wealthy king is the King of Kings and Lord of Lords. And he is an apt symbol for one who, as a special privilege, united all human creation with him like a beloved bride; but forgetful of the love she owed him she went whoring after other gods, and in her adultery bore three sons, namely the pagans, the Jews and the heretics. The first of these wounded the king's hand, by rejecting the teaching of Christ, who sits at the right hand of the Father, and by putting to death his servants, sent by God, in a variety of ways. The second putative son literally wounded the [mouth of the] King of Kings when the Jews said:[2] *'Come, let us strike him with the tongue,'*[3] *by giving him gall and vinegar to quench his thirst. The third most treacherous son repeatedly pierces his heart with a poisoned dart, when the heretics strive to wound the faithful, who have one heart and one soul in their Lord, with the arrows of evil doctrine. Hence the Psalmist says:*[4] *'They have sharpened their tongues like serpents etc.' And again:*[5] *'They have prepared their arrows in the quiver.' The fourth son, who is in anguish and refuses to shoot, is the good Christian, who fears God greatly and grieves for the sins of others, and would not on any account offend God by sinning; and if he does offend him, is prepared to atone for his sin. Such a one on the Day of Judgement will be lifted in glory to the eternal kingdom.*

---

2 Jer 18.18.
3 *percutiamus eum lingua*: in its biblical context the saying is variously interpreted, but means something like 'let us trump up some charges against him [Jeremiah]'. Here the author seems to understand it as 'let us strike him by means of the tongue', i.e. in the mouth, as the second son did.
4 Cf. Ps 139.4.
5 Ps 10.3.

46. Of the seven mortal sins

Julius relates that in the month of May a man went into a forest in which stood seven trees in full leaf, and he picked so many branches that he could not carry them. Then three strong men came along and escorted him to the edge of the forest. But as he came out of it he fell into a deep pit and plunged to the bottom because of the weight of his load.

The philosopher also relates, in his book *On Animals*, that if you wish to stop a crow hatching her chicks from their eggs when she has built a nest in a tree, you should place powdered glass[1] between the tree and its bark, and as long as the glass remains there, she will never hatch her chicks.

Dear friends, the forest is this world, in which a variety of lovely trees, i.e., mortal sins, grows. In this forest, i.e., the world, are seven trees which signify the seven mortal sins, of which man collects such a heavy load that he that he cannot carry it or even lift it, i.e., he cannot move on from his sin or attain to God's grace as long as he remains in sin. But along come three men, the wardens of this forest, who help him; and they are the world, the flesh and the demons (and these are visible),[2] which abet man in his various sins and lead him on until he leaves the forest, i.e., leaves his body. But then he sinks into the abyss of hell because of the magnitude of his sins. Likewise the crow is the devil; its nest is the dwelling it makes in man's heart at the commencement of sin. The glass, which can be of many colours, symbolizes human flesh, and powdered glass is the remembrance of death, because glass is made

1 *cineres vitri*: literally 'the ashes of glass'.
2 *et ista visibilia*: this might also mean 'and those visible/earthly things'. But this would make four categories, unless the *demonia* and *visibilia* are taken together.

from ashes and returns to ashes. Let the remembrance of death therefore be placed between the tree and its bark, i.e., between the soul and the body; the body is like bark, protecting the soul, and so the devil will never bring forth his offspring of evil works. Which may God vouchsafe us etc.

47. Of the three kings

A king of Denmark was devoted to the three kings who, guided by a star, came from the East to Jerusalem and offered gifts to the newborn Christ, and he would invoke them to come to his aid. So he set out with a large retinue to Cologne, where their holy bodies are preserved with due honour, and offered up to them three golden crowns of wonderful, regal magnificence; and besides this, with great devotion, he distributed more than 6,000 marks to the churches and poor people, thus leaving in the city an example of his faith for all believers.

Now one day, as he was returning to his kingdom, he dreamed in his sleep that he saw the three kings wearing upon their heads the crowns he had brought them; they were coming towards him in a great halo of light, and he heard each of them address him. The first, who was eldest, said: 'My brother, your coming here was blessed with good fortune, but your return home will be blessed with greater good fortune.' The second said: 'You have given much, but you will take much more back with you.' The third said: 'My brother, you have shown faith, but in twenty-three years time you will reign with us for ever in heaven.'

Offering him a pyx filled with gold, the first king said: 'Receive the treasure of wisdom, by which you will justly rule over your subject people, for it is the glory of kings to love justice.'

The second offered him a pyx filled with myrrh, and said: 'Receive the myrrh of repentance with which you will also curb the seductive promptings of the flesh, for the best ruler is he who firmly masters himself.'

The third then gave him a pyx full of incense and said to him: 'Receive the frankincense of devotion and pious clemency, with which you will relieve the downcast, for as the dew moistens the grass, enabling it to grow, so too the sweet clemency of a king uplifts him and exalts him to the stars.'

Marvelling at the strangeness of this vision, the king suddenly woke up and found the pyxes placed beside him, which he accepted joyfully as God's gifts. Returning to his own kingdom he most devoutly fulfilled all the things he had heard in his dream, and at the end of the time predicted, he was found worthy to possess the kingdom of heaven.

Dear friends, the king signifies any good Christian, who must offer three crowns to three kings, namely the Father, Son and Holy Ghost. You are bound to render to the Father a crown of honour and faith, because he is powerful. It is not good to offend one who is powerful, because he can crush you and destroy you. You promised to render to him the crown of faith at your baptism, when you renounced the devil and his vanities. You must render to the Son a second crown of wisdom and hope, because he is wise and suffered for us; thus we must have hope in him, and there are many reasons for this: first and foremost, because he loved us so much that he came down from heaven, assumed our nature, and won a victory for us against the devil. Third, we must offer a crown of love to the Holy Ghost, for he is the love of Father and Son, and through him we can win the love of man and God. If we offer these three things with pure heart and perfect charity, we shall without doubt obtain from the Father and Son and Holy Ghost the following things. From the Father, a treasure of virtues, with which we shall be able to direct our soul and body in its fight against the devil, the world and the flesh, and in consequence gain the heavenly kingdom. From the Son, a pyx containing myrrh. The pyx signifies a pure heart cleansed of sin, and the myrrh penitence, because Christ first revealed the life of penitence upon the cross, and daily gives his grace to those who seek it from him. From the Holy Ghost, the frankincense of devotion, i.e., he pours upon us his virtue, which makes us devout and full of charity, because God is charity, and consequently we shall be able to atone for the habitual offences which we commit through sinning against God, and so obtain life eternal. To which etc.

48. Of the just consequence of evil

Dionysius[1] relates that when the cruel tyrant Phalaris[2] was wreaking havoc upon the Agrigentines and causing them the most excruciating suffering, Perillus,[3] a worker in bronze, offered him a brazen bull he had just constructed, something well suited to his cruel nature. In one of its sides it had a secret door which people sentenced to death had to enter so that they could be burnt to death by a fire lit beneath it. And when in the agony of death they screamed inside the bull, their cries would not sound human, but like those of a beast, and so the king would not feel the slightest compassion. Phalaris was impressed by the invention but warned Perillus: 'You yourself shall be the first to enter and test it; because though I am cruel, you were crueller still in offering it to me.' For, as Ovid says, 'there is no juster law than that the contriver of death should perish by his own contrivance.'[4]

Dear friends, the craftsman is a bad seneschal serving a tyrant king, who robs the Agrigentines, i.e., simple, righteous folk, and afflicts them with all manner of torments. A simple man brings gifts to escape the persecution, but this does him no good. A brazen bull is offered him. A new statute is enacted and an evil law is established, by which the simple believe they will be able to escape persecution, but by which they are then often punished, and lose their goods, and though they are

1. Perhaps Diodorus Siculus (IX.19.1). But many classical authors tell this story.
2. Phalaris, tyrant of Acragas c.570–554 BC. The story is alluded to in Pliny, *N.H.* XXXIV.89. Cf. Gower, *Confessio Amantis* 3295ff. See also Oesterley, pp. 719–20; Tubach, no. 811; Hope, pp. 511–12.
3. = Perilaüs, an Athenian artisan.
4. Ovid, *Ars Amatoria* I.655f.

burnt alive in bitterness of heart and cry aloud, theirs is not thought to be a human voice, because the powerful do not like to hear the cry of the poor; they say: 'It is a slave or a peasant: all his goods are mine.' But often such people, who oppress others, suffer the same or a greater punishment and end their days badly. Hence the Psalmist says:[5]*'I have seen the wicked highly exalted, and lifted up like the cedars of Libanus. And I passed by, and lo, he was not.'*

5 Ps 36.35f.

49. Of the cunning delusions of the devil

Paul, who wrote the history of the Lombards, relates[1] that Conan,[2] King of the Hungarians, was besieging a castle in Forum Julii[3] called Sondat. Now the duchess Rosimila,[4] who had four sons and two daughters, saw how exceedingly handsome he was, and wrote to him in secret. 'If you marry me,' she said,' I will give up this castle to you.' He promised to marry her, she surrendered the castle to him, and her sons all fled. King Conan kept his promise and married Rosimila the very next day. But the day after that he handed her over to twelve Hungarians to be publicly abused;[5] and the next day he had her whole body impaled as far as the throat, and remarked: 'A wife such as this, who brought ruin on her own country to satisfy her personal lusts, deserves such a husband.'

Dear friends, Conan is the devil, who lays siege to a castle, i.e., the human heart, with vices and desires. The duchess Rosimila, i.e., the soul, having been seduced by the devil, looks beyond the wall, i.e., hankers after forbidden things, like a man looking at a woman to lust after her;[6] and the same applies to his other senses. And wretched man is so delighted that he surrenders his castle, i.e., his heart, when he consents to sin. Consequently his four sons, i.e., the four cardinal virtues, flee from him, and so the devil occupies the soul with his two daughters, i.e., wicked pleasure and evil desire. Then he hands it over to twelve Hungarians, i.e., all the vices, to be abused. After this he destroys it when he takes it to hell.

1 Paul the Deacon (c.720-c.799), *History of the Longobards* IV.37.
2 Paul says the Avars called their king the Cagan.
3 This is probably Cividale del Friuli, near the Slovenian border.
4 Romilda, wife of Gisulph, Duke of Friuli.
5 According to Paul, Romilda's daughters escaped a similar fate by making their bodies stink of raw meat.
6 Mt 5.28.

50. Of the praise of those who judge justly[1]

Valerius relates[2] that the emperor Zelongus[3] enacted a law whereby anyone who deflowered a virgin should lose both of his eyes. It chanced that his own son deflowered the only daughter of a certain widow. When the mother learned of this she went to the emperor and said: 'My lord, you must implement the law you have passed. Your only son has assaulted my daughter and taken her by force.' When he heard this the emperor was horrified, and commanded that his son should lose both his eyes. But his nobles said to him: 'Lord, he is your only son, he is your heir. It would be calamitous for the whole realm if your only son were to lose his eyes.' He replied: 'But don't you understand? I myself passed this law. It would be a disgrace if I were to break a law once I have laid it firmly in place. Since my son is the first to have broken the law, he shall be the first to undergo the punishment.' 'Lord,' his councillors said, 'in God's name we beg you to spare your son.' Finally he was won over by their entreaties, and replied: 'Dear friends, in such a situation, here is what I propose. My eyes are my son's eyes, and his mine. Pluck out my right eye and my son's left eye. Then the law is fulfilled.' And that is what happened, and everyone praised the emperor's wisdom and justice.

Dear friends, the emperor is our Lord Jesus Christ, who enacted a law that if anyone deflowered a virgin, i.e., the soul washed clean by baptism, he should lose his two eyes, i.e., forfeit the divine vision[4] *and*

1 Cf. Herrtage, Text I.XLI.
2 *F.D.M.* VI.5 ext. 3.
3 This is Zaleucus, a seventh century BC ruler of Locri in southern Italy.
4 The beatific vision, or the vision of God in heaven, the final destiny of those who are redeemed.

eternal glory. The emperor's son, who broke the law, is man, who has deflowered the soul through sin. Thus it is necessary for him to undergo punishment, because Mother Church cries to God daily, praying that man should atone for his sins in this his mortal body. Isaiah:[5] 'Cry, cease not! Lift up thy voice like a trumpet!' The emperor, i.e., the Lord Jesus Christ, lost one eye, so that he had only one eye left, when he laid down his life for us, and therefore we must pluck out our left eye, that is, all inordinate desires, that is, we must destroy the pleasures of the flesh through penance, and accordingly we shall obtain eternal life.

5 Is 58.1.

51. Of unjust administrators

Josephus relates[1] that when Tiberius Caesar was asked why he kept provincial governors so long in office, he replied with a fable. 'I once saw a sick man covered in ulcers and plagued by flies,' he said, 'and when I tried to drive them away with a whisk, he said to me: "You think to relieve me, but you cause me twice the pain if you drive flies away that are gorged on my blood, and send others to replace them that are empty and starving. For who can doubt that, unless a man is made of stone and not flesh, the bite of a starving fly is twice as painful as that of one that is full?"[2] I therefore keep my governors in office long, for once they are enriched by their booty they are more likely to leave their subjects alone, whereas new and empty-handed governors are more likely to abandon justice and oppress their subjects with unfair taxes and burdens.'

1 *Antiquitates Judaicae* XVIII.6.5. Cf. Aesop's fable as related at Aristotle, *Rhetoric* II.20
2 As it stands, this is one of only two tales in Oesterley's collection without a moralization (eight others have moralizations integrated into the narrative of the tale). K. and L. end the tale here and begin the moralization with the usual *Carissimi* ('Dear friends'). *Praesules* (which I translate as 'governors') might mean 'bishops' or 'prelates', but then the first-person singular *teneo* ('I keep') is problematic. For *teneo*, however, L. has *tenti*: 'So too prelates kept long in office etc.' *Le Violier* also has a moralization, but of rather different content.

52. Of fidelity

Valerius relates[1] that Fabius promised money to redeem some Roman captives, and when the Senate refused to pay this money, he sold the only farm he possessed and paid the money he had promised, preferring to be deprived of his patrimony rather than show a lack of personal integrity.

Dear friends, Fabius is the Lord Jesus Christ, who, to ransom the captives, i.e., the whole human race ensnared by the devil, gave not money but his own blood, preferring to be deprived of his patrimony, i.e., his own life, than to abandon the human race.

---

1 *F.D.M.* IV.8.1. The story concerns Fabius the Delayer (*Cunctator*), dictator in 217 BC. See Livy, *Ab Urbe Condita* XXII.23. Other versions are listed by Oesterley, p. 721; Tubach. no. 4034; Hope, p. 515.

53. Good rulers should not be changed

Valerius Maximus[1] relates that when all the Syracusans desired the death of Dionysius,[2] King of Sicily, just one person, a woman of extreme old age, besought the gods each morning that he might outlive her. Wondering why she made this prayer, Dionysius asked her the reason. She answered: 'When I was a girl and lived under a cruel tyrant, I wanted to be rid of him, and then I got another I wanted to be rid of, and then I had a third. So fearing one even worse might follow you, I pray every day that you may live on.' When he heard this Dionysius troubled her no further.

Moralization. Dear friends, in the Old Testament God was very stern and spared no-one, because the law was 'eye for eye, tooth for tooth.'[3] But now, because he assumed our mortal flesh, he has become merciful and forgiving, and so we ought to pray to him continually that we may have no other lord but our Lord Jesus Christ. May he deign to grant us this etc.

1 *F.D.M.* VI.2 ext. 2.
2 Dionysius I, tyrant of Sicily 405–367 BC.
3 Ex 21.24.

54. Of the celestial kingdom

The emperor Frederick II constructed a remarkable marble gate over a fountain of running water near Capua. On it was a statue of the emperor in majesty together with two other judges. In a semicircle above the head of the judge on the right the following verse[1] was inscribed:

Enter here in safety all those who would lead pure lives.

In a semicircle above the head of the left-hand judge was inscribed this verse:

Let him who is envious fear banishment or imprisonment.

In a semicircle above the emperor's head was inscribed:

How wretched I make[2] those who stray from the path of justice!

In a semicircle above the gate was inscribed:

In the reign of Caesar I became guardian of the kingdom.

Dear friends, the emperor is our Lord Jesus Christ; the marble gate is Holy Church, the gate through which we must enter the heavenly kingdom, and it is situated above a fountain of flowing water, i.e., above the world, which runs by like water. On the gate is sculpted an image of our Lord Jesus Christ with figures on either side of him: Mary, the Mother of Jesus, and John the Evangelist, who signify his mercy and justice towards us. Then there is the verse: 'Enter here in safety,' i.e., let pagans, Jews and Saracens enter here through baptism, and they will be able to live pure lives cleansed of all sin, like innocent children. Another verse says: 'Let him who is envious', i.e., the sinner who lives in sin, fear banishment from the Church Triumphant, and thus imprisonment for

---

1 Verses 1, 2 and 4 are dactylic hexameters; line 3 is a pentameter.
2 *facias*: Oest.; *facio*: K., L., *Le Violier*.

54. Of the celestial kingdom

ever in the prison of hell. Above the emperor's head was an inscription speaking of the wretchedness of those who stray from the path of truth; and another says: 'In the reign of Caesar', i.e., the reign of our Lord Jesus Christ shall be our safeguard and our everlasting home.

55. Of the recall of a sinful soul sent into exile to make atonement[1]

A noble king had a son who was handsome, clever, valiant, affable and loving, and four daughters whose names were Justice, Virtue, Mercy and Peace. This king wanted to present his only son with a bride, so he despatched a messenger to find a beautiful virgin. At length he found one, the daughter of the King of Jerusalem, who was exceedingly beautiful, and she was married to his son, who loved her with a passion. Now this son had a servant, and because he had complete trust in him, he entrusted one of his duchies to him for his safekeeping. But this servant turned traitor, seduced his master's wife, dishonoured her and ravaged the duchy he had been given. When the prince heard of his wife's adultery he was heartbroken, and he repudiated her, giving her a bill of divorce and depriving her of her every honour. As a result she was reduced to a state of such poverty that in despair she went from place to place begging her bread, and when her husband heard of her plight he took pity on her and sent a messenger to her to recall her. 'Come back to your lord,' he said. 'You are quite safe, so don't be afraid.' But she refused, and said to the messenger: 'Tell my lord that I would willingly come to him, but I cannot. If he wants to know why I refuse, tell him it is because the law says that if a man has a wife who commits adultery he must give her a bill of divorce and after that she cannot go back to him.' The messenger replied: 'My master is above the law, since he is the one who made it. So since he has taken pity on you, you can go back to him without any misgivings.' 'But what sign will he give me that I can safely go back to him?' she asked. 'I should feel safe if he does this: if my love would come to me and kiss me with the kiss of his mouth,[2]

1 Cf. Herrtage, Text I.XXXIV.
2 Sg 1.2.

55. Of the recall of a sinful soul sent into exile to make atonement 133

then I can be sure that he will look on me with favour again.'

When this was reported to the prince he summoned all the nobles of his court and kingdom to a council, and it was finally decided that he should send someone of proven judgement to get her to return; but not a single person in the whole kingdom could be found who was willing to undertake this mission. In view of this the prince sent another messenger to say to her: 'What am I to do with you? I have not found a single man willing to bring you back to me.' When she heard that no-one was willing to take her back to him, she wept bitterly, and hearing how wretched she was, the prince went to his father and said to him: 'Sir, if you agree, I will go to my wife and put an end to her sorrow and grief, and, with your permission, bring her back.' 'Go in your strength,' his father told him, 'and bring her back.' So he sent a messenger ahead of him to tell her: 'Be of good cheer now. I am on my way and will bring you back in person.'

When his older sister, Justice, heard what was happening, she went straight to the king and said: 'Sir, you are just and your judgement is just. I am your daughter, Justice, and your judgement of that harlot was right; it was just that she should no longer be my brother's wife, and that you authorized the bill of divorce. So hold fast to justice; and if you act in defiance of what is just, I tell you, Justice shall no longer be a daughter of yours.'

Then the second sister, Truth, came and said: 'Father, your judgement of that harlot was true, because she dishonoured my brother's marriage bed by committing adultery. If you wish her to return, you are acting in defiance of truth, and if that is the case, Truth, shall certainly no longer be a daughter of yours.'

Then the third sister, Mercy, came to her father and said: 'Sir, I am your daughter, Mercy. So have mercy on this poor sinner for her offences, as she is suffering greatly for what she has done. And if you do not show mercy, Mercy shall be no longer a daughter of yours.'

Then the fourth sister, Peace, hearing her sisters squabbling among themselves, decided to leave the country, and fled. When she had gone, Justice and Truth produced a sword and offered it to the king, saying: 'Sir, this is the sword of justice with which to kill that harlot who has put us and our brother to shame.' But seeing this, Mercy snatched the sword from their hands and said: 'You have ruled and had your way long enough. It is now time for my father to listen to me. I am his daughter as much as you are.'

Justice replied: 'It is true. We have reigned a long time, and we wish to go on doing so. But since there is such disagreement between us, let us call our brother, who is wise in all matters, and let him judge between us.'

So that is what they did. And when their brother arrived and heard their opposing arguments, how Justice and Truth on the one hand desired revenge, and Mercy pardon, he said: 'Dearest sisters, because of your quarrelling our sister Peace, so beloved of our father, has left the kingdom. This I cannot possibly allow, for I am ready to be punished myself for my adulterous wife.'

'If you do this,' said Justice, 'we cannot oppose you.'

The prince said to Mercy: 'Strive to secure my wife's return. But if I do have her back, and she commits adultery again, do you intend to intercede for her again?'

'No,' replied Mercy, 'not unless she is really penitent.'

When the prince heard this, he got Peace to return and made the sisters exchange kisses. And harmony having been restored, the prince left the kingdom, made war[3] for his wife, and brought her back to his father's kingdom. And so they both ended their days in peace.

Dear friends, the king is our Heavenly Father, his wise son is our Lord Jesus Christ, his beautiful wife is the soul created in the likeness of God, and his four sisters are Justice, Truth, Mercy and Peace. The soul committed adultery with her lord's servant, i.e., with the devil, when she yielded to him, and her lord banished her. After this her dutiful husband gave her a bill of divorce and put her away, and deprived her of every honour she had had when set over the works of her lord's hands; as the Psalmist says:[4] 'Thou hast subjected all things under his feet.' He also gave her a province, i.e., paradise, and took that also from her and set her amid the misery of this world, and said:[5] 'In the sweat of thy face shalt thou eat bread.' Bernard bemoans this and

---

3 *bellum pro sponsa dedit*: the prince has declared himself ready to accept punishment in his wife's place. The moralization explains that the king is the Father, the son is Christ (*filius de regno descendit* – the Son came down from his kingdom) and his bride is the soul. The son makes war in atonement for his bride's sin.
4 Ps 8.6.
5 Gn 3.19.

55. Of the recall of a sinful soul sent into exile to make atonement

says:[6] 'Remember your nobility, feel shame at your banishment.' Now the lord took pity on his wife and sent a messenger to her to recall her and say:[7] 'Arise, arise, stand up, stand up, O Jerusalem! Loose the bonds from off thy neck, O captive daughter of Sion!' But she refused to come and said: 'Lord, I would willingly come back, but I cannot. Why? Because you said through Jeremiah:[8] "If a man has a wife and she fornicates with another, her husband shall give her a bill of divorce, and shall not go back to her again." So I dare not return to you. What then shall I do? Those are your own words, and you are just and judge all things with justice. How then can I return to you?' The Lord replied through the prophet Isaiah:[9] '"Is my hand shortened that it cannot redeem?" Far from it! As I said through Ezekiel:[10] "In whatsoever hour the sinner shall grieve, I will not remember all his iniquities." And although you have committed adultery, you will return to me, and I will receive you, with the words of the Song:[11] "Return, return, O Sulamitess etc.". Return and be reconciled to God the Father, return and be reconciled to God the Son, return and be reconciled to the Holy Ghost, return and be reconciled to the angels, whose society you have lost.' She replied: 'What sign will you give me that you will take me back?' The Lord said: 'Ask me for a sign in the depths of hell, or in the heights above.' But she said: 'I will not ask, but let my beloved come to me and kiss me with the kiss of his mouth, that I may be sure that he will look on me with favour again.' The Lord replied: 'Even though a mother should forget her little child, I shall never forget you: I think the thoughts of peace and not of conflict; and therefore I shall hold a council.' The Lord then held a secret council with the whole court of heaven to decide whom he should send to deliver his wife, but he could find no-one among either angels or men who was worthy to redeem her. The angels each said: 'I am of free status, she of servile, why should I debase my status?' Man said: 'I am not worthy to suffer for your wife, because I am a sinner.' In view of this the Lord sent to his wife to say: 'What am I to do? For I can find no saviour for you, no-one who will or can save you.' When she heard this she wept, because no-one had been found in heaven or on earth to save her. The Father of Mercies

---

6 *Serm.* XII.1109.2.
7 Is 51.17, 52.2.
8 Cf. Jer 3.8; Dt 24.1ff.
9 Is 50.2.
10 Cf. Ez 18.21f.
11 Sg 6.12.

and God of all Consolation then consoled her, saying: 'Jerusalem, my spouse, my city, do not weep so, because your salvation will come speedily. Why do you waste away in sadness? You are never without a counsellor, because your grief has renewed you. I will save you and deliver you, do not fear!'[12] *Therefore the Son rose up before his Father and said: 'Here, I am ready to suffer for my spouse; I have done so, and I will do so;'*[13] *I will support you and I will deliver you.' The Father replied to him: 'Go in your strength and deliver my daughter, your spouse, from the prison of Midian,' i.e., the devil. Hearing this, Justice opposed her brother; then Truth intervened and sided with Justice; but Mercy sided with her brother, and Peace, the fourth sister, fled, because there was no peace between God and man. Justice said to Mercy: 'I wish to reign, because the Lord Solomon is immortal and just and will never die. Hence my judgement has no limitation and length of time does not diminish it, but rather confirms it.' Mercy replied: 'It is true that you are immortal and everlasting, but that applies to the future, not now. I wish to intercede for her, because she is now doing penance, and just as you, Justice, are my father's daughter, so I, Mercy, am also his daughter. Therefore reason dictates that he should hear me as he hears you.' At this disagreement between his sisters, the wise son said to Justice: 'I am prepared to make atonement to you, that Mercy's plea may prevail.' Justice said: 'Very well, but I would like to know how.' 'I will take flesh,' the Son said, 'and assume human nature. Is this enough?' And Justice replied: 'No.' The son said: 'I will be circumcised, suffer hunger and thirst, be tempted, endure misery, suffer weariness, sweat drops of blood. Is this enough for you?' She replied that it was not. The Son said to Justice: 'I will be scourged with stripes, be beaten about the head, I will be spat on, mocked and abandoned and despised etc. Is this enough for you?' Justice replied that it was not. 'I will carry a cross and have my hands and feet pierced and be bound. Is this enough for you?' She said it was not. 'I will drink vinegar, be drained of all my blood and die upon a cross, and when dead be pierced in the side by a lance, then rise again from the dead, ascend to heaven, and prepare a place for my spouse. Is this enough for you?' 'My good brother,' she said, 'as I can see, and from what I hear, you love your spouse more than yourself. What you have now said is suffi-*

---

12 Based on the last stanza of *Rorate caeli desuper*, a text frequently used in Mass and the Divine Office during Advent.
13 Oest.: *ego feci, ego faciam*. Is 46.4. The Vulgate has *ego feci, et feram*: 'I have made you and I will bear (you).'

55. Of the recall of a sinful soul sent into exile to make atonement

cient.' The Son then said to Mercy: 'If I do all the things I have said and purposed in my heart, and my spouse disdains them, will you intercede for her a second time?' She replied: 'Not unless she does penance.' 'Very well,' he said. 'When a man has sinned, if he does penance afterwards, I will have mercy on him.' With these words he had the sisters summoned, i.e., Justice, Truth, Mercy and Peace, and they kissed each other. Then the Son fulfilled all his promises and gave his spouse the heavenly kingdom. Bernard, rousing the spouse to consider the grace conferred on her by the Lord, speaks words of great solemnity. He says this: 'See, O spouse, your Spouse upon the cross, his head inclined to kiss, his hands outstretched to embrace, the opening of his side inviting love, the exposure of his whole body inviting disdain.' He therefore shed his own blood, and offered it as a gift to his Father for his beloved spouse. So the Heavenly Father accepted the noble gift from the hand of his Son, and thereby we were saved for life eternal. To which etc.

56. Of the remembrance of death

There was a prince who loved to hunt, and it once happened that when he went out hunting a merchant chanced to be taking the same path, and seeing how handsome and elegant the prince was, and the costly clothing he wore, he said to himself: 'Lord God, that fellow is greatly beholden to you! Look how handsome he is, how dashing and debonair, and all of his company so finely clothed!' With these thoughts in his head he said to one of the prince's servants: 'Tell me, my good man, who is your master?'

He replied: 'He is lord of many estates and possesses gold and silver and servants in plenty.'

'He is greatly beholden to God,' said the merchant. 'I have never seen anyone more handsome or elegant.'[1]

On hearing this the servant reported all the merchant had said to his master, and around the hour of Vespers, as the prince made his way home, he asked the merchant to stay the night with him. The merchant dared not refuse him, so went with the prince to his city. When he entered the castle, he saw so much wealth and so many rooms decorated with gold that he was lost in wonder. Then when it was time for supper the prince sat the merchant next to his lady at table, and seeing how beautiful and elegant she was, he was quite carried away and said to himself: 'My God, this prince has everything his heart desires, a beautiful wife, sons and daughters and hundreds of servants!'

But as he was thinking these things, the dishes were set before the lady and him, and to his horror, the finest food was contained

---

1 *sapiens*: normally 'wise', 'prudent'. But the merchant is in no position to appraise the prince's wisdom. Perhaps here the adjective bears the sense of 'having (good) taste' (*sapire*).

in a dead man's skull;[2] and this was set before the lady, whereas everyone else in the hall was served by waiters from dishes of silver. When the merchant saw the skull on the table before him he was horrified and said to himself: 'Alas, I fear I shall lose my head in this place!' But the lady did her best to comfort him, and when it was night he was taken to a fine bedroom, where he found his bed made with the curtains drawn round it; and in one corner large lamps were burning. As soon as he got into bed, servants fastened the door and he was left alone in the room. Then he looked at the corner from which the light came, and saw two dead men hanging by their arms. The sight so terrified him that he was unable to sleep. In the morning he got up and thought: 'Alas, I fear I shall hang beside these two fellows!'

When the prince himself got up, he had the merchant summoned and asked him: 'My friend, what do you see of mine that pleases you?'

'Everything,' he replied, 'except for the fact that my food was served in a dead man's skull and I was so appalled that I could not eat it. And when I got into bed, I saw two young men hanging in the corner of my room, and was so terrified that I could not sleep! So, please, for the love of God, let me go my way.'

The prince replied: 'Friend, you saw my beautiful wife and the dead man's skull set before her. The reason is this: the skull is that of a nobleman who seduced my wife and slept with her. I actually caught them in the act of adultery and I drew my sword and cut off his head. So I set his skull before her every day as a token of her shame to remind her of the crime she committed. The son of the dead man killed the two young kinsmen of mine that are hanging in your bedroom, so every day I go to look upon their corpses to whet my appetite to avenge their murder. And as long as I recall my wife's adultery and remember the death of those young men, I shall never be able to feel joy again. So, my friend, go your way in peace, and henceforth never judge any man's life until you know the truth of it more fully.'

2 A similar story, apparently historical fact, is told of Alboin, King of the Lombards, who made his wife Rosamund drink his health from a goblet made out of her father's skull; see *G.L.*, St Pelagius, CLXXVII.23ff.; Edward Gibbon, *The History of the Decline and Fall of the Roman Empire*, Vol. V: *Justinian and the Roman Law*, London: The Folio Society, 1987, pp. 308–9. See also Oesterley, pp. 721–2; Tubach, no. 2475; Hope, p. 518.

So the merchant bade him farewell and went back to his trading business.[3]

Dear friends, the prince is any good Christian, enriched by virtues through baptism, who must have a splendid retinue, i.e., interior and exterior senses[4] *without the stain of sin, which must serve him, and often go hunting, i.e., perform works of merit. The merchant is a good prelate or discerning confessor, who is obliged to consort with such a man, to visit the house of his heart and to plant virtues there, as Christ did to the two travellers on their way to Emmaus, when 'he went into their lodging etc.'*[5] *The beautiful wife is the soul created in the likeness of God, who must be placed at table next to the authority on Holy Scripture in order to learn what is necessary for her salvation. But often the soul is polluted by the devil when it commits a mortal sin. What then is to be done? Draw the sword of your tongue and pray to God in secret. For the Psalmist says:*[6] *'Their tongue is a sharp sword.' With the sword of your tongue you will be able to defeat the devil, i.e., with contrition of heart and the confession of your mouth you will be able to cut off his head and place it always before the eyes of your heart, for God will give you grace to defeat him, to do perfect penance, i.e., works of mercy. The two youths hanging in the bedchamber, slain by your adversary, are love of God and one's neighbour, which were extinguished by the sin of our first parent, and so you ought always to keep them in the chamber of your heart, that you may love God with all your mind and all your soul, and always remain in fear of him, because we do not know if we are worthy of love or hatred, and to recall to the memory how much God endured for us on the cross.*

---

3 See Paul the Deacon, *History of the Longobards* II.28, and cf. the story told in *Heptameron*, no. 32.
4 Aquinas speaks of interior and exterior senses in discussing the specific powers of the soul.
5 Cf. Lk 24.29.
6 Ps 56.5.

57. Of perfection of life[1]

When Titus was emperor of Rome he enacted a law that his first-born son's birthday should be held sacred by everyone, and anyone who profaned that day by performing any servile work should be put to death. Having promulgated this law he called Master[2] Virgil and said: 'My friend, I have made this law, but violations of it will often be committed in secret, and I shall not be informed of them. So we wish you to use all your power to invent some device that will enable me to discover those who violate the law.'

'Lord,' he replied, 'it shall be as you wish.'

With the aid of his magic powers Virgil at once set up in the centre of the city a statue which informed the emperor of all the offences committed that day, and an almost countless number of people were condemned to death on the evidence provided by the statue.

Now at that time there lived in Rome an artisan called Focus who worked on that day as on all the rest. And one day as he lay on his bed he got to thinking of the many people who were losing their lives because of the accusations of the statue. So in the morning he got up and went to the statue and said: 'O statue, statue! Many people have been executed because of your accusations. I vow to God that, if you accuse me, I will break your head in pieces!' Having uttered this threat, he went back home.

At the first hour, as he was wont, the emperor sent his messengers to the statue to enquire if anyone had violated the law. When they got there and told it what the emperor wished to know, the statue replied: 'Friends, lift up your eyes and read what is written on my forehead.' They did so, and saw quite clearly three sentences

---

1 Cf. Herrtage, Text I.X.
2 A title indicating someone skilled in the occult, a necromancer, a magician.

written there: *The times are changing. Men are becoming worse. He who wishes to speak the truth will have his head broken.* 'Go and tell your master what you have seen and read.'

The messengers went back and told all this to the emperor, and when he heard what they had to say he commanded his bodyguard to arm and go to the statue, and if anyone did it any violence they were to bind him hand and foot and bring him to him. The soldiers went to the statue and told it: 'It is the emperor's will that you tell him of those who have violated the law and who they are who have threatened you.'

The statue replied: 'Arrest Focus the artisan. He breaks the law every day and has threatened me.' So they seized him and brought him into the emperor's presence.

'My good man,'[3] said the emperor, 'what is this I hear of you? Why are you breaking the law I passed?' 'Sire,' he replied, 'I cannot keep that law because every day I have to make eight denarii, and I can't make them if I don't work.' 'Why eight denarii?' asked the emperor. Focus replied: 'Every day I have to pay back two denarii which I borrowed in my youth; two I lend; two I lose and two I spend.' 'You must explain this to me more clearly,' said the emperor.

'Listen to me, my lord,' the artisan replied. 'I have to pay two denarii every day to my father, because when I was a young boy, my father spent two denarii on me every day. And now my father is poor, so reason dictates that I must help him in his poverty, so each day I hand him two denarii. I lend two more to my son, who is now a student, so that if I should ever chance to be poor, he can pay me back the two denarii, as I am doing to my father. And I lose two further denarii every day on my wife, who is always arguing with me, and of a wilful, sly temperament, so because of her nature whatever I give her I lose. And I spend another two denarii on myself for food and drink. I can't easily get by on less, and I can't make the eight denarii without working every day. Now you have heard my defence. So let your sentence be a just one.'

'My friend,' replied the emperor, 'your defence is just. Go now and in future work as hard as you wish.'

Soon after this the emperor died, and because of his wisdom Focus the artisan was unanimously elected as his successor, and he

---

3 *carissime*: literally 'most dear', a form of address used repeatedly in these tales without any special connotation of friendship.

57. Of perfection of life

ruled the empire with great prudence. When he died, his portrait, with the eight denarii above his head, was painted and placed beside those of the other emperors.

Dear friends, the emperor is the Heavenly Father, who established a law that anyone who violated the sanctity of his first-born son's day should die the death. That day is the Lord's Day, or a day ordained as a feast by the Church; hence in both the Old Law and the New we are told:[4] *'Remember that thou keep holy the Sabbath day.' But alas, alas!, many commit greater sins on those days than on other day! Such people can be likened to a fish in the sea, which is healthy so long as it is in the sea, but if it should happen to leap out at a time of rain and the rain touches it, it begins to die, and will not return to its former state for many days, until it has had its fill of sea water. In the same way, some people believe that all is well with them as long as they labour the whole week in the sea of this world; but if they happen to go to church on feast days and hear a good sermon or Mass, they believe that they are in great trouble, until they are revived once again by their worldly activities. Virgil, who made the statue, is without doubt the Holy Spirit, who ordered the preacher to proclaim virtues and vices, punishment and glory. But alas, alas!, the preacher can now say, as the statue said: 'The times are changing.' We can see the truth of this quite clearly in the primitive church; for every class of person in those times was better than now, intercessions and prayers more fervent than today. The earth gave forth its fruit more abundantly and all the elements gave what was theirs to give, but all has been changed because of man's sins. This was apparent at Noah's flood. Second: 'Men are becoming worse,' as we can clearly see. In old times men were more devout, more generous with alms, more charitable than they are now. And why? Because 'the whole world is seated in wickedness.'*[5] *Third: 'He who wishes to speak the truth etc.' Today, if a preacher denounces the sins of the powerful, he will immediately receive threats and complaints. Hence Isaiah says:*[6] *'Speak pleasant things!' And the Apostle says:*[7] *'There shall be a time when they will not endure sound doctrine.' Focus is any good Christian who labours faithfully as a soldier of Christ. For every good Christian*

---

4 Ex 20.8; Mt 19.17 ('If thou wilt enter into life, keep the commandments').
5 1 Jn 5.19.
6 Is 30.10.
7 2 Tim 4.3.

is bound every day to pay his Heavenly Father two denarii, i.e., love and honour; love, because he loved us so much that for love of us he allowed his only son to come down from heaven and be condemned to an ignominious death; honour, because all things come from him and without him we can do no good. Likewise we lend two denarii to his son. What kind of son is he? He is the son of whom Isaiah says:[8] *'For a child is born to us etc.,' i.e., the Son of God. And what are these denarii we must lend him? We must lend him two every day, i.e., good will and good works, as long as we inhabit this earthly body; and when we are in need on the Day of Judgement, when we shall appear naked, then he will repay us these denarii with eternal life, as it is written:*[9] *'You shall receive a hundredfold and shall possess life everlasting.' Likewise we lose two denarii on our wife. This wife is our wretched flesh, which is always at variance with the spirit. The denarii we lay out on it are evil desire and evil action, which work continually with hostile will. We lose these two denarii because we shall be severely punished for this, either here or elsewhere. Likewise, every day, if we are good Christians, we spend two denarii on ourselves, and these are loving God with our whole heart, and loving our neighbour as ourself. Dear friends, if you spend these eight denarii you will attain to joy everlasting.*

8 Is 9.6.
9 Cf. Mt 19.29.

58. Of confession[1]

A king named Asmodeus passed a law that when any criminal was taken and brought before the judge, if he could state three unquestionable truths which no-one could contradict, however great his crime he should retain his life and all his property. It happened that a certain soldier had broken the law and subsequently fled and hid in a forest where he perpetrated many wicked crimes, robbing or killing all who entered it. When the judge got to hear of this he had the forest surrounded, caught the man, and had him bound hand and foot and brought before him for judgement. 'My good man,' said the judge, 'do you know the law?' 'I do,' the soldier replied. 'If my life is to be spared, I must declare three truths, otherwise I cannot escape death.'

'Then take advantage of the law,' the judge told him, 'or today you shall not taste food before you hang.'

He replied: 'Then call for silence, sir.' When this was done, he continued: 'Sir, this is the first truth: I declare to you all that all my life I have been a wicked man.' Hearing this the judge asked those present: 'Is what he says true?' 'If he were not a criminal,' they replied, 'he would not be standing here now.' So the judge said to him: 'Tell me a second truth.' He replied: 'The second truth is this: I am extremely unhappy at being in the present situation.' 'We can well believe you,' the judge said. 'So tell me a third truth, and you have saved your life.' He replied: 'This is the third truth: if I ever get out of here, I will never end up like this again.' 'Amen to that,' said the judge. 'You have been clever enough to win your freedom. Go in peace.'

And so, by telling three truths, the soldier was saved.

1 Cf. Herrtage, Text I.XXVII.

Dear friends, the emperor is our Lord Jesus Christ, who established a law that if any malefactor, i.e., sinner, is captured by the grace of God and taken before a discerning judge, i.e., a confessor, and tells three truths so incontrovertible that the demons are not able to object, he will obtain the inheritance of the heavenly kingdom. The first truth is: 'I am an evil man', i.e., because of such and such a sin, and likewise every other sin I have committed. Confession! The second truth is: 'I am unhappy etc.,' i.e., I am extremely unhappy because I have offended my God so deeply. Contrition! The third truth is: 'If I can ever escape by way of penance, I will never willingly return to sin.' And in consequence he will win life everlasting.

59. Of excessive pride, and how the proud are often brought to extreme humility: a notable tale[1]

Jovinian was an emperor who possessed immense power, and one night as he lay on his bed he became extraordinarily elated at the thought, and said to himself: 'Is there any other god than I?' And thinking these thoughts he went to sleep. Next morning he rose and called his troops. 'Comrades,' he said, 'it would be a good idea to eat something, because I want to go hunting today.' They promptly did as he commanded, and after breakfast they set off to the hunt. Now as the emperor rode along he became unbearably hot, so hot in fact that he thought he would die if he could not plunge into some cold water. He gazed into the distance, and seeing a stretch of water there told his men: 'Stay here until I have cooled myself down.' He spurred his horse and rode in haste to the water's edge. Dismounting he stripped off all his clothes, got into the water, and remained there a considerable time until he was quite refreshed. But while he lingered there, up came a man like him in every respect, in looks as well as bearing, and he put on his clothes, climbed on his horse and rode off towards the emperor's men, where he was received by everyone as the emperor himself. And when the sport was over, he went back with them to the palace.

Soon after this Jovinian got out of the water and could not find his clothes or his horse. He was puzzled and annoyed, because he was naked and could see no-one about, and he thought: 'What am I to do? I have been wretchedly used.' At length he recovered his composure and said to himself: 'A soldier lives hereabouts whom I promoted to knighthood. I'll go to him, get some clothes and a horse, and ride to the palace and find out how this happened and who has treated me so shamefully.'

1 Cf. Herrtage, Text I.XXIII.

So, completely naked, Jovinian went to the knight's castle and knocked at the gate. The porter asked him why he was knocking and Jovinian told him: 'Open the gate and see who I am.' The porter opened the gate and was dumbfounded at what he saw, and said: 'Who are you?' 'I am the emperor Jovinian,' he replied. 'Go to your master and tell him to provide me with some clothing, because I have lost my clothes and my horse.' 'You are lying, you evil rascal,' the porter said. 'Just before you came, the emperor Jovininan passed here on his way to the palace with his guard, and my master went with him, then came back, and he is now sitting at table. But you have called yourself emperor, and that I will report to my master.' The porter went into the castle and told his master what the man had said, and he commanded him to bring him in. This he did. But when the knight saw Jovinian he did not remember him at all, though the emperor knew him at once.

'Tell me,' the knight said, 'who are you and what is your name?' Jovinian replied: 'I am the emperor Jovinian. It was I who promoted you to knighthood on such-and-such a day.' 'You evil rascal!', said the knight. 'How dare you call yourself emperor! My lord the emperor rode off to the palace before you arrived. I kept him company along the way and have just come back. Well, you shan't get away with calling yourself emperor!' And he ordered him to be soundly flogged and then thrown outside.

So Jovinian was flogged and thrown out, and weeping bitterly, exclaimed: 'My God, how it is possible that a man whom I promoted to knighthood should not remember me, and not only that but he has had me soundly beaten!' Then he thought to himself: 'A duke lives near here, one of my councillors. I will go to him and let him see the plight I am in and he will provide me with clothes so I can go back to the palace.' So he made his way to the duke's residence and knocked on the gate. The porter heard him knocking and opened the gate, but when he saw a naked man there, he was taken aback and said: 'Friend, who are you, and why have you come here all naked like this?'

'I am the emperor,' he told him. 'Unfortunately I have lost my horse and my clothes, so I have come to ask the duke to help me out of my predicament. So I beg you, make my request known to your master.'

The porter was astonished to hear this and went into the hall and told his master everything. 'Have him come in,' said the duke. But

59. Of excessive pride

when Jovinian was brought in he had no recollection of him at all. 'Who are you?' the duke asked. 'I am the emperor,' he replied, 'and I promoted you to riches and honours when I made you a duke and appointed you my councillor.'

'You mad wretch!', said the duke. 'A little while ago I accompanied the lord emperor to the palace and have just returned. And since you have laid claim to such rank, you shall not go unpunished.' He had him clapped in prison and put on a diet of bread and water. Then he removed him from prison, had him soundly beaten then thrown from his estate altogether. After being ejected in this manner Jovinian uttered groans and sighs beyond measure and said to himself: 'Alas, what am I to do? I am an outcast, the laughing-stock of my people. I had better go to the palace; the palace servants will recognize me. And even if they do not, my wife will know me from certain things I can tell her.'[2] So he went on his lonely way to the palace and knocked on the gate, and hearing the knocking, the porter opened the gate. When he saw him he said: 'Tell me, who are you?' Jovinian replied: 'I am surprised you do not recognize me when you have been with me so many years.' 'You lie!', the porter said. 'I have always been here with my lord the emperor.' 'I am he,' replied Jovinian,' and if you do not believe me, I beg you, for the love of God, go to the empress and when she hears the secrets I shall tell you, she will send you to me with my imperial robes, for unfortunately I have lost everything. These secrets that I want you to convey to her are known to no-one else on earth but us two.'

'You are obviously mad,' the porter said. 'My master the emperor is at this moment sitting at table with the empress next to him. but since you claim to be the emperor, I will inform the empress, and I have no doubt that you will be severely punished.' The porter went to the empress and told her all he had heard. She was deeply disturbed at this, and turning to her husband said: 'My lord, what a strange story! There is some rascal at the gate, and through this porter he is repeating details of our private lives, things we have often done together, and he says he is the emperor and my lord!' When the false emperor heard this he ordered the porter to bring the stranger in before everyone assembled. And

2 *per certa signa*: through certain signs, i.e., secrets known only to Jovinian and his wife. Signs and tokens are the formulaic means of recognition in such tales.

when he was brought in, totally naked as he was, a dog, which had formerly loved him, leapt at his throat and would have killed him if the servants had not prevented it, and enabled him to escape unhurt. And a falcon that he kept tied to its perch broke its jesses and flew out of the hall as soon as it saw him.

The emperor then said to all who were seated in the hall: 'Friends, listen to what I say to this rascal. Tell me, who are you and why have you come here?'

'My lord,' Jovinian said, 'that is a strange question. I am the emperor and lord of this place.'

The emperor then said to all who were at table or standing nearby: 'Tell me, on the oath of allegiance you have sworn to me, which of us is your emperor and lord?'

They replied: 'Lord, on the oaths we have given you we can answer that without difficulty. We have never seen this rascal before. You are our lord and emperor, we have known you from our youth. So we beg you with one voice to punish him so that he may serve as an example to others, and warn them never to aspire to such audacity themselves.'

Then turning to the empress the emperor said: 'My lady, tell me on your honour, as you are bound, do you know this man who says he is the emperor and your lord?'

'My good lord,' she said, 'how can you ask me such a thing? Have I not been your companion for more than twenty-six years and borne your children? Yet there is one thing I wonder at: how did this rascal come to know of things that we have done together in secret?'

The emperor said to the man who had been brought in: 'My friend, why have you dared to call yourself emperor? We sentence you to be drawn at the tail of a horse this very day, and if you dare make this claim again, I shall condemn you to the most shameful death.' He then called his servants and told them: 'Go and have him drawn at the tail of a horse. But do not kill him.' His command was duly carried out. After his ordeal Jovinian was in such a terrible state that he almost despaired of living. He said to himself: 'I wish I had never been born! My friends have abandoned me, my wife and my children do not know me!' But then he fell to thinking: 'My confessor lives near here. I shall go to him. Perhaps he will remember me; he has often heard my confessions.' So he went to the hermit and beat at the door of his cell.

'Who is there?' asked the hermit.

59. Of excessive pride

'It is the emperor Jovinian,' came the reply. 'Open the window so that I can speak to you.'

At his request the hermit opened the window, but as soon as he saw him he hastily shut it again and told him: 'Get away from me, you wretch! You are not the emperor: you are the devil in human form!'

Grief-stricken, Jovinian fell to the ground; he tore at his hair and beard and said: 'Alas, what am I to do?' And then he recalled the vainglory he had felt in his heart as he said to himself as he lay in bed: 'Is there any god other than I?' Instantly he began beating at the hermit's cell and cried: 'For the love of him who hung upon the cross, hear my confession with the window closed.' 'Very well,' the hermit replied.

Then Jovinian tearfully confessed every sin of his whole life, and in particular that he had exalted himself above God, saying that he believed there was no other god than himself. After he had completed his confession and received absolution, the hermit opened the window and recognized him. 'Blessed be the Lord Most High!' he said. 'Now I know you. I have a few pieces of clothing here. Put them on and go to the palace, and they will recognize you, I'm sure.'

The emperor clothed himself, went to his palace and knocked on the gate. The porter opened the door and received him with great deference. 'Do you recognize me?,' Jovinian asked him. 'Of course, my good lord. But it is strange that I have been standing here all day and didn't see you go out.'

Jovinian entered the hall and everyone bowed heir heads on seeing him. The other emperor was with the empress in a private chamber, and a guard coming out of the chamber took a close look at Jovinian, then went back into the chamber and said: 'Lord, there is someone in the hall to whom everyone is bowing and doing reverence, and he looks so exactly like you in every detail that I do not know which of you is emperor.'

Hearing this the false emperor said to the empress: 'Go and see if you know him.' So she left the chamber and when she saw Jovinian she was amazed. She went straight back into the chamber and said: 'My lord, all I can say is that I have no idea which of you is my lord.' 'In that case,' he replied, ' I will go and find out the truth of the matter.' He then went into the hall, took Jovinian by the hand, and placing him at his side, called all the nobles in the hall, as well as the empress, and said: 'On the oath of allegiance you have sworn me, which of us is the emperor?'

The empress was first to speak. 'Lord, it is I who should speak first. As God in heaven is my witness, I have no idea which one of you is my lord.' And they all gave the same response.

'My friends,' he said, 'this man is your emperor and lord. But at one time he exalted himself above God, so God scourged him in punishment and made him unrecognizable to everyone until he had atoned to him for his sin. I am the guardian angel of his soul, and I have watched over his kingdom while he was doing penance. His penance is now complete, and he has atoned for his sins. From now on give him your obedience, and I commend you to God.' And instantly he vanished from their sight.

Jovinian gave thanks to God, and lived all the rest of his life happily and in peace until he rendered up his soul to God.

Dear friends, the emperor signifies any man who is entirely devoted to the world, and because of his wealth and position is lofty and vain, like a second Nebuchadnezzar, who did not obey God's commandments. He summons his soldiers, i.e., his senses, and goes off to hunt worldly vanities, and at times he is overcome by such an intolerable heat, i.e., the devil's temptation, that he cannot find peace until he is wholly refreshed in the waters of the world. This refreshment is damaging to the soul, and so the soldiers, i.e., his senses, release him from their custody whenever he proposes to bathe in the water of the world. First he gets down from his horse, i.e., strays from the faith, because at baptism he has firmly promised God to cleave to it and renounce the vanities of the devil. But how quickly he immerses himself totally in the waters of the world, and breaks his promise! This is what 'getting down from the horse' signifies. Then he takes off his clothes, i.e., the virtues he received at baptism, and naked as he is the wretch wallows in worldly vanities. What is to be done? Clearly some other person, i.e., a prelate, who possesses faith and virtues, must protect him, i.e., recover his clothing, because a prelate is given power to absolve the sinner when he turns to God with a pure heart. 'When Jovinian got out of the water etc.' Even so, when through God's grace a wretched man purposes to get out of the waters of the world, he will find no virtue to assist him, because he has lost all he had through sin, so this causes him great anguish. How then can these virtues be recovered? Why, he must first go to the house of the knight. The knight is reason, which must chastise you, because reason dictates that you must atone in your heart for all that you have done against God, and so you will not be able to

59. Of excessive pride

call yourself emperor, i.e., a Christian, because through sin you have destroyed the good works of a Christian. Reason therefore drives you away from every vice. What then are you to do? Have recourse to the duke's castle, i.e., to your own conscience, which is murmuring bitterly against you, until you are reconciled to God; and indeed he casts you into prison, i.e., great perplexity as to how and by what means you can please God and receive wounds from Him, i.e., the heartfelt compunction through which the blood, i.e., sin, may come out. Then beat at the palace of your heart, i.e., consider deeply how and why you have sinned against God. The porter, i.e., the will, which is free, has to open the door of your heart, and return you to the original status you received at baptism. The dog that leaps up to kill you etc., is your own flesh, which is so often the cause of man's death, were God not to prevent it. And the falcon on her perch flies out of the window etc.; i.e., God's power will not remain with you as long as you continue in a life of evil; and your wife, i.e., your soul, will not know of your salvation. What then can be done? Why, you are dragged at the tail of a horse. To be dragged at the tail of a horse is nothing other than to grieve deeply for all the sins you have committed from the beginning of your life to the present day, and to make atonement. Then, after you have done so, go to the hermit, i.e., a discerning confessor, in the forest of Holy Church, and make a sincere confession of all the sins you have committed against God, and do so when you have closed the window, i.e., in private, not for the applause of mankind, but for your own comfort, and at once God and all the angels will know you. After making your confession you will be able to clothe yourself, i.e., in virtues, and go in secret to the palace of your heart, and all your senses,[3] together with your wife, i.e. your soul, will know you, because you have become the true emperor, i.e., a good Christian, and consequently will obtain life everlasting. To which may He bring [us all] etc.

---

3 i.e., soldiers.

60. Of avarice and its subtle temptations[1]

There was once a king who had an only daughter, a beautiful, loving and charming girl, named Rosamond. When she was ten years old she was such a good runner that she always reached the finishing line before anyone could catch her. The king had it proclaimed throughout the whole of his kingdom that anyone who ran a race with his daughter and beat her to the finish should have her as his wife and inherit the whole kingdom after his death. But anyone who attempted this and failed should lose his head. At this proclamation large numbers of suitors came forward to race with her, but all those who did so failed and lost their heads.

Now at that time there lived in the city a poor man named Abibas, who thought to himself: 'I am poor and low born. If I can somehow beat this girl, I should not only advance my own status but that of all my kin.' So he provided himself with three things by way of precaution: first, a garland of roses, because girls love them; second, a silk girdle which girls delight in wearing; and third, a silk purse containing a golden ball on which was inscribed: 'Whoever plays with me will never tire of play.' With these three objects in his bosom he went to the palace and knocked at the gate. The porter asked him what he wanted, and he told him: 'I am prepared to race with the princess.'

Now the princess happened to hear this and opened a window to look, and when she saw Abibas she was utterly repelled by him, and said to herself: 'Just look at that good-for-nothing I have to run against!' But she could not object, so she got ready for the race.

1 Cf. Herrtage, Text III.I (Wynkyn de Worde) and Text I.XXII. This is a version of the story of Atalanta and the three golden apples. See e.g. Ovid, *Metamorphoses* X.560–680. For other versions, see Oesterley, p. 722; Tubach, no. 405; Hope, pp. 523–4.

60. Of avarice and its subtle temptations

They both set off, and the girl quickly ran a considerable distance ahead of him, but Abibas threw the garland of roses in her path, and when she saw it the girl bent down, picked it up and put it on her head, and she was so delighted with the garland and paused so long that Abibas got ahead of her. When she saw him pass her, the girl thought: 'Never shall a daughter of my father be married to a ne'er-do-well like him!' She threw the garland into a deep ditch, ran after him, and caught him, and when she drew level she gave him a slap, and said: 'Stop, you wretch! It would not do for any son of your father to have me as his wife!' And she ran swiftly past him. As she did so, Abibas threw the silk girdle in her path. Seeing it, she stopped and picked it up, put it round her waist, and was so delighted with it that she gave Abibas time to run a long way past her a second time. The girl wept bitterly when she saw what he had done. She snatched at the girdle, tearing it in three pieces, and ran after him and caught him; and as she drew level she raised her hand and slapped him, saying: 'You wretch, you shan't have me as your wife!' And in an instant she ran far ahead of him. Abibas waited until she was near the finish, then threw the silk purse in her path. When she saw it she stooped and picked it up, and opened it, and inside found the golden ball, and read the inscription: 'Whoever plays with me shall never tire of play'. And she began to play, and played so long with the ball that Abibas reached the finish first and won her as his wife.

Dear friends, the king is our Lord Jesus Christ, and his beautiful daughter is the soul created in God's likeness, which runs swiftly doing good works as long as it remains in purity of life, so that mortal sin cannot vanquish it. A proclamation was made etc. This is nothing other than a proclamation that man should defend and protect himself against the devil, the world and the flesh, and if he goes to war against these three things and wins the victory, then mortal sins are defeated, and 'lose their heads'. Abibas is the devil, who, when he sees that a man has overcome him through his works of mercy, provides himself with three safeguards, i.e., with a garland [etc.]. The garland is pride, because just as a garland is always put upon the head so that it can be seen, so the proud man wants always to be seen; hence Augustine says: 'When you see a proud man, do not doubt that it is the son of the devil.' Therefore when man uses the garland of pride, the devil at once runs past him. What then is to be done? Clearly, the garland of pride must be cast into the ditch of humility, and so you will deal the devil a blow and banish him. After this the girl 'bent down and picked up the girdle etc.' The girdle is lechery, which the devil casts in front of man. However Gregory warns us against this: 'Gird your loins in chastity.' If therefore you gird yourself with the girdle of lechery, the devil at once runs past you and prevents you from leading a good life. What then is to be done? Clearly, the girdle of lechery must be torn in three parts, i.e., prayer, fasting and almsgiving, and consequently you will vanquish the devil. Next the devil throws a purse in front of man. Now you know that a purse has two strings to open it, and the purse is the heart, which must be closed below to earthly things, and open above to heavenly things in the hope of grace. The two strings that shut it are fear of God and eternal punishment, and by these two things the heart is closed against the entry of sin. A ball is often found in the purse in our hearts, that is, avarice, greed; for just as a ball travels in every possible direction, so too the avaricious man travels the earth and travels the sea, and his feet never stop running, and his heart never stops wondering how and by what means he can acquire worldly goods. The inscription reads: 'Whoever plays with me [etc.],' i.e., he who begins to lead a life of avarice, will scarcely or never be able to sustain it.[2] As Seneca says:[3] 'When all other sins wax old, avarice alone waxes young.' We must therefore beware of those who play much with the ball of avarice, because the devil will possess them; as the Apostle says:[4] 'The desire of money is the root of all evils.' Let us therefore strive to direct our lives in the performance of good works, that [we may win] eternal life etc.

2 *sustinere*: we might have expected *satiari:* 'be satisfied', as in the preceding tale.
3 A proverbial saying quoted e.g. by Augustine (*Sermon* 48). I have not been able to find it in Seneca.
4 1 Tm 6.10: the Latin word is *cupiditas*, commonly translated as 'love of money'.

61. Of the necessity of foresight[1]

King Claudius had an only daughter who was both charming and very beautiful. One day as he lay in bed he fell to thinking seriously about how he might best provide for her. 'If I marry my daughter to a rich fool,' he said to himself, 'I shall ruin her, but if I marry her to a wise man, even if he is poor, he will amply provide her with all she needs through his wits.'

There lived in the city at that time a philosopher named Socrates whom the king loved. Claudius sent for him and asked him: 'My friend, would you consent to marry my daughter?' 'Indeed, my good lord,' he replied. 'In that case,' said the king, 'I will marry you to her on one condition: if my daughter dies while wedded to you, you too shall lose your life. Do you choose to take her or not?' Socrates replied: 'I agree to take her on that condition.'

The king celebrated the marriage with great solemnity. For some time the couple lived a peaceful life and enjoyed perfect health. Then Socrates's wife fell ill, and was close to death. Socrates was heart-broken and retired into a forest where he wept bitterly. And as he gave vent to his grief, King Alexander came hunting in the same forest and one of his guards saw Socrates, and rode up to him and asked: 'My good man, whose service are you in?' Socrates replied: 'I am the servant of a master so great that his servant is master of your master.' 'There is no greater lord than mine in the whole world,' retorted the guard. 'But since you say there is, I shall take you to my master and we shall hear who this master of yours is about whom you make such arrogant claims.' Socrates was then taken before King Alexander, who said to him: 'My friend, who is your master?' Socrates replied: 'My master is reason, and his servant is the will. Now thus far you have governed your kingdom in obedience to

[1] Cf. Herrtage, Text III.IV (Wynkyn de Worde).

your will, and not reason, therefore the will, which is servant of my master, is your master.' Alexander replied: 'My friend, you have spoken wisely. Go in peace.' And from that day the king began to govern his kingdom in obedience to reason and not his will.

But Socrates went back into the forest and wept bitterly for his wife. Then an old man came up to him and asked: 'Good sir, why are you so downcast?' 'I married the king's daughter,' Socrates told him, 'on the condition that if she ever died while wedded to me, I should die too. And now she is at death's door. That is why I am so wretched.'

'Take my advice,' the old man replied, 'and you won't regret it. Your wife is of royal blood. When the king is bled, let your wife smear her chest and breasts with her father's blood. Then there are three herbs you must find in the forest: make a potion of one, and grind the other two, make a poultice and place it where she feels the pain. If you do exactly as I have told you, she will be perfectly well again.'

Socrates carried out all these instructions, and his wife was restored to perfect health; and when the king heard of the pains Socrates had taken to cure his daughter's illness, he raised him to a position of great wealth and honour.

Moralization of the preceding tale: Dear friends, the king is our Lord Jesus Christ, and his lovely daughter is the soul, created in the likeness of God, and he gave this girl not to a rich man but to the poor Socrates, i.e., to man. Job c.1:[2] *'Naked came I out of my mother's womb etc.' But, dear friends, you must know that our Lord Jesus Christ gave man a soul on condition that, if through mortal sin it should die while wedded to him, he would lose his life, i.e., everlasting life. If therefore your soul has become diseased through sin, do as Socrates did: go into the forest, i.e., Holy Church, in which you will find an old man, i.e., a discerning confessor, and following his counsel you will be restored to health. Alexander, who went hunting, is the worldly man who is governed rather by his will than by reason, but is corrected by holy teaching. If you are stained with sin, first anoint your breast with blood, i.e., keep fresh in your heart the memory of Christ's Passion; then gather three herbs, namely confession, contrition and penance. Make a potion of the first, i.e., grieve always for your sins, and a poultice of the others, i.e., penance, and you will receive such health that you can then be raised to a position of great wealth, i.e., to the riches of everlasting life, to which may He bring us etc.*

2 Jb 1.21.

62. Of the beauty of a faithful soul[1]

There was a very wise emperor called Caius among whose subjects was a woman called Florentina, who was extraordinarily lovely and charming; indeed her beauty was so great that three kings laid siege to her and one of them took her by force. Subsequently these kings waged war against each other and almost countless numbers on each side were slain. When they learned of this the nobles of the realm came in a body to the emperor and said: 'Lord, this citizen of yours Florentina is so beautiful that untold numbers of men are being slain every day because of the love she inspires, and unless some measure is taken to stop this, everyone in the kingdom will be dead.'

In response to this, the king had a letter written and sealed with his signet, telling Florentina to come to him without any delay. A herald went to her with the letter but before he reached her she died, so the herald returned and reported her death to the king. He was deeply disappointed at not being able to see her in all her beauty and had all the artists in the kingdom summoned to him. When they had assembled he said to them: 'Friends, the reason why I have sent for you is this: there was a woman called Florentina whose beauty was such that for love of her almost countless men have lost their lives. She has died, and I never set eyes on her. So go and take great pains to paint her likeness, in all her beauty, so that I can see why so many men have lost their lives for her.'

'Sire,' they replied, 'what you ask is difficult. She was so ravishingly beautiful that there is only one painter in the world who could do her beauty complete justice, and he lives hidden away in the mountains. He alone could do what you ask, and no other.'

1 Cf. Herrtage, Text II.XXXIX.

So the king sent for this painter, and when he came he said to him: 'My friend, we have been told of your skill. Go and paint an accurate likeness of Florentina, in all her beauty, and I will give you a fitting reward.'

'What you ask is difficult,' he said. 'But let me have before me all the beautiful women in your kingdom for an hour at least, and I will do as you wish.'

The king summoned them, and had these women stand before him. The painter picked the four most beautiful of them and gave the others leave to return home. Then he began to paint the portrait with a red pigment, and choosing from the features of the four women the loveliest face, nose and so on, he used that in his painting; and so, by using some part of each of them, he completed the portrait. And when it was finished the king came to view it, and seeing it he exclaimed: 'Oh Florentina, Florentina, had you lived you must have loved this painter more than anyone in the world for portraying you in such great beauty!'[2]

Dear friends, the king is our Heavenly Father, and the beautiful Florentina is the soul created in God's image. The three kings are the devil, the world and the flesh. Through the sin of our first parent the soul was besieged by these three kings and violated by each of them, and so many died through sin, because before Christ's coming everyone went down to hell. In view of this the nobles, i.e., the patriarchs and prophets cried for help, saying: 'Lord, send us the one you are to send.'[3] Others said 'O Lord, send forth the lamb, the ruler of the earth.'[4] And God sent a herald, namely St John the Baptist, as it is written in Malachi 1:[5] 'Behold I send my angel who will prepare [the way before my face].' But alas, alas!, the soul died long before his coming. Painters were summoned, but they made their excuses etc.; i.e., not one could be found in heaven among the angels, or on earth among men, i.e., the patriarchs and prophets, who had the knowledge or skill to paint its likeness, i.e.,

---

2 A similar story is told (e.g. Cicero, *De Inv.* II.1) of the Greek artist Zeuxis (fl. late fifth century BC), who chose five beautiful women of Croton and united their best features to achieve a perfection of beauty in his famous *Helen*.
3 From the *Rorate caeli* section of *The Advent Prose*, attributed to Prudentius (fourth century).
4 Is 16.1.
5 = Mal 3.1.

62. Of the beauty of a faithful soul

portray the soul in its proper beauty. The painter who came from the mountains is our Lord Jesus Christ, who came down from heaven to recreate that likeness. How? Why, with a red pigment, i.e., with his own blood. 'He chose four most beautiful women etc.': from the first he gave us the being of stones, from the second the growth of plants, from the third the feeling of animals, and from the fourth the understanding of angels.[6] *When the king saw the result he said: 'O Florentina,' i.e., soul, 'you ought to love this painter, our Lord Jesus Christ, above all else, for he has portrayed you in such great beauty with his own blood!'*

---

6 It was the doctrine of Gregory the Great (c. 540–604) that man possesses qualities in common with all created things 'Man shares his being with the stones, his life with the plants, his feeling with the animals, and his understanding with the angels' (Homily XXIX, Migne, vol. 76: 1570, p. 1214).

63. Of the pleasures of worldly things[1]

The emperor Vespasian had a most beautiful daughter named Aglae, and she was so lovely and found such favour with men that no other woman could rival her. It happened one day that, as his daughter stood before him, the emperor considered her closely and told her: 'My darling, I am going to change your name. Because of your natural beauty in future you must be called the Lady of Solace, to make it known that all who come to you in sadness may leave you in joy.'

Now the emperor had near his palace a most lovely garden in which he would often walk for the purpose of recreation. He had a proclamation made throughout the whole of the kingdom that anyone who wished to marry his daughter should come to the palace and spend three or four days walking about this garden; then he could come out and claim his daughter in marriage. In answer to the proclamation many men came to the palace, went into the garden and were never seen again. Not a single one of them ever came out.

Then a knight who lived in far-off parts heard the rumour that if a suitor went to the palace he might marry the emperor's daughter, so he went up to the palace gate and knocked. The porter opened it and took him in, and he went up to the emperor and said: 'My lord, I have heard it noised abroad that the man who enters your garden shall marry your daughter, and that is why I have come.'

'Enter my garden,' said the king, 'and if you come out again you shall have her.'

'Allow me one thing,' said the knight. 'Before I go into the garden, I beg you to let me have a few words with the young lady.'

'Very well,' he replied.

[1] Cf. Herrtage, Text I.XXXI, and the story of Ariadne, Theseus and the Minotaur.

63. Of the pleasures of worldly things

So the knight went to the girl and said: 'My dear, your name is Lady of Solace, and it was given to you so that all who come to you in sadness should leave you in joy. I come to you in great sadness and loneliness; so give me your advice and aid that I may leave you in joy. Many have come before me and gone into the garden, but they have never been seen again. If the same thing happens to me – ah, how I shall rue the day I ever desired to have you as my wife!'

'I will tell you the truth,' she said, 'and turn your sorrow to joy. In that garden there is a savage lion who kills all who venture inside, and all those who have done so in order to marry me have perished. Arm yourself from head to toe and smear all your armour with gum. When you go into the garden the lion will rush at you. Fight him manfully, and when you[2] tire move away from him. He will sink his teeth into your arm or foot, but then he will get the gum on your armour in his teeth and will not be able to do you much harm. When you see this working, unsheathe your sword and cut off his head. But there is yet another danger in the garden. There is only one way in, and so many different pathways that, once in, it is almost impossible to find the way out. So I shall give you something to help you overcome this difficulty: a ball of thread. Take it and when you get to the garden entrance, tie one of the ends to the gateway, and go into the garden holding the ball. And, as you love your life, do not let go of the thread!'

The knight did all that she had told him and went fully armed into the garden. As soon as he saw him, the lion attacked him with all his might; the knight defended himself manfully, and when he became weary he sprang back from him. The lion then seized hold of his arm and held on so tightly that his jaws were locked by the gum; so the knight drew his sword and cut off the lion's head. But he was so delighted at his victory that he lost hold of the thread he had been holding when he came into the garden. In deep dismay he combed the garden for three days looking for the thread, and on the third night he found it, and in great joy retraced his steps with the aid of the thread until he reached the gateway. Then, untying the thread, he went to the emperor and claimed his daughter, the Lady of Solace, as his wife, which brought him much joy.

---

2 *fuerit*: Oest., K.; but *fueris*, which is the reading of L. (and Herrtage, Text I.XXXI) makes better sense.

Dear friends, the emperor is our Lord Jesus Christ, and his beautiful daughter, the Lady of Solace, is the everlasting kingdom. He who wishes to possess the everlasting kingdom must first enter the garden of this world and wait there for some time, however long God wishes. The Psalmist says:[3] *'You have appointed his [man's] bounds which cannot be passed.' Job:*[4] *'There is one entrance for men and beasts.' But in the world there are so many different pathways, i.e., dangers, and because of them*[5] *man does not know his goal, nor where, nor how he is to die. The lion is the devil, who 'goeth about seeking whom he may devour', and so almost countless numbers are slain by him. What then are we to do? Without doubt, if we wish to gain the heavenly kingdom we must be armed with virtues, so that our arms are covered with gum. By gum we are to understand alms, because just as gum joins two things together, so alms joins us with God; hence the prophet says:*[6] *'As water quencheth fire, so alms resisteth sins.' You must then take a ball of thread etc. This ball is baptism; for you must go into this world at the beginning of your life with baptism, then with confirmation, and so on through the other sacraments. But the lion, i.e., the devil, is ready to fight against you. You must fight against him manfully, and remove his head, i.e., his power, through good works. But it often happens that after a man has triumphed over the devil, as many do in Lent, after Easter they return to their sins and so lose the ball of thread, i.e., the power of the sacrament. So do as the knight did. If you have lost your virtues through sin you should be sorely troubled. Go searching for three days, i.e. by contrition, confession and penance, and you will find what you have lost, and thus when you come to the haven of death, when the soul is separated from the body, you will win the Lady of Solace, i.e., joy everlasting. To which etc.*

3 Jb 14.5.
4 *introitus*: Oest.: this is a conflation of Eccles 3.19 (the death [*interitus*] of men and beasts is one) and Wis 7.6 (all men have one entrance into life).
5 *quia que*: Oest.; *per quae*: K., L.
6 Cf. Ecclus 3.33.

64. Of our Lord's incarnation[1]

There was a king who was blessed with three gifts: first, he was physically stronger than all other men; second, he was wiser; third, he was more handsome. After he had been a bachelor for many years his friends came to him and said: 'Sire, it would be good for you to marry and have children. It is not good to remain unmarried.'

'My friends, ' he replied, 'you know that I am extremely rich and powerful and therefore have no need of wealth. So go through every town in the realm and seek me out a girl who is beautiful and wise, and if you can find these two qualities in a girl, even if she is poor, I will marry her.'

So they went through every town in the country, and finally found a girl who was exceedingly beautiful and wise, and of royal blood, and they told the king of her virtues. But the king desired to test her wisdom, and called a herald and told him: 'Friend, here is a piece of linen cloth three inches square. Go to the girl, greet her in my name, and give her this piece of cloth. Ask her to use her wits to make me a shirt with it, one that is big enough to fit me. If she can do this, she shall be my wife.'

The messenger went to the girl, greeted her in the king's name, and said to her: 'Here is a piece of linen cloth three inches square: if you can make a shirt big enough to fit the king's person from this cloth, he will marry you.'

She replied: 'But how can I do that, when the cloth is only three inches in length and breadth? It is impossible to make a shirt out of it. But if he gives me a vessel[2] in which I can work, I promise I

---

1 Cf. Herrtage, Text I.XLIII.
2 *vas*: the nature of this vessel is not made clear. For an interpretation of this tale, see D. S. Maccoll, 'Grania in Church: of the Clever Daughter', *The Burlington Magazine*, 8 (November 1905), pp. 80–5. The typical

can make a shirt big enough for him.'

The messenger returned to the king and told him what the girl had said, and the king at once sent her a costly vessel of the appropriate size, and using this vessel she made out of the tiny piece of cloth a shirt big enough to fit the king's person. And in view of this the king married her.

Dear friends, this king is God himself, who is powerful and wealthy, and the girl of noble, kingly stock is the Blessed Virgin Mary, Mother of God and man, who was beautiful and noble because full of grace. The messenger sent to her was the Archangel Gabriel, who greeted her on the part of God saying:[3] *'Hail, full of grace.' The piece of cloth that was sent her is the working of the Holy Spirit in her, because she was sanctified before she was born. It was three 'inches' long, because in the conception of her son there was the power of the Father, the wisdom of the Son and the clemency of the Holy Spirit. From them she asked for a vessel, that is, her womb that had been sanctified in her mother's womb, and in it she made the shirt, i.e., Christ's humanity, the humanity which was worked in her. Seeing this the Heavenly Father crowned her Queen in heaven, where she intercedes for us with her Son, and the Son with the Father, according to the saying of Saint Bernard:*[4] *'O man, you have a sure means of approaching God etc.'*

---

version of the 'clever wench' tale involves an exchange of impossible demands and counter-demands until an impasse is reached. Here the narrator has omitted important links in the tale. In one version the king sends the girl a pot without a bottom, and tells her to sew a bottom on so that no stitch or seam can be seen. She replies by telling the king first to turn the pot inside out, for cobblers sew from the inside, not the outside. This is presumably the 'vessel' referred to here. In the *moralisatio*, the girl is interpreted as the Virgin Mary, who was the chosen vessel. The vessel is her womb in which she made Christ's humanity.

3 Lk 1.28.
4 A saying commonly attributed to Saint Bernard (*Manipulus Florum, confidentia* d.), but the source is Arnaud de Bonneval (d. 1156), *De Laudibus Beatae Mariae Virginis* (Migne 189:1725).

65. Of the care of the soul

Once a king passed from one city to another and came upon a cross completely covered with inscriptions. On one side was written: 'O king, if you ride this way, you will be well entertained personally, but your horse will be ill cared for.' On another side was written: 'If you ride this way, you will stay somewhere where your horse will be excellently looked after, but you will be poorly served.' On the third side was written: 'If you go this way, you and your horse will be adequately provided for, but before you leave you will be soundly beaten.' On the fourth side was written: 'If you go this way, you will both be splendidly looked after, but you will have to leave your horse behind you and then go on foot.'

When he had read all these inscriptions the king wondered at them, then began to think which way he should go. He said to himself: 'I will choose the first, because I shall be looked after if my horse will not. One night will swiftly pass.' He spurred his horse on and came to a castle where a knight lived, who gave him a kindly reception and provided for him splendidly, while his horse had little or nothing. Next morning he got up and rode on to his palace, where he related all that he had seen.

Moralization. Dear friends, this king represents any good Christian, who has to ride in search of his soul's salvation. The horse that carries him is his body, composed of the four elements; the cross that stands in the middle of the way is your conscience, extended in the manner of a cross: one way spurring you to good, the other to fight bravely against evil; and if you go the way where you will be well served, but your horse ill served, you are acting in your best interests. Dear friends, this way is the way of penance; the inn is Holy Mother Church, where your soul will be well looked after, but your horse, i.e., flesh, must undergo penance. He who goes this way is acting wisely. There is another way, where you will find an inn where your horse will be excellently looked after, but you will be poorly served. This way is the way of the gluttonous and wanton, who lodge in an inn of fleshly pleasures; of them the Apostle says:[1] *'Whose god is their belly and whose glory is in their shame.' In this inn the soul will be very poorly served. There is another way, where your horse will be excellently looked after, and you will be beaten. This is the way of the covetous and greedy, who want to live in luxury here, and to do few works of merit, but when death drives them from the inn of this world, then after death their soul will be soundly beaten in hell. There is a fourth way, and if you go this way, all will be well with you, but you will lose your horse. This way is the way of the good religious, who is content with anything in the way of food and clothing. He loses his horse, i.e., all his carnal desires and worldly vanities, for God's sake, and thus the Saviour says:*[2] *'He that shall lose his life for me etc.' 'He that hath left his father and mother etc. shall receive a hundredfold and after this life shall possess life everlasting.'*

---

1 Phil 3.19.
2 Mt 10.39; cf. Mt 19.29.

66. Of steadfastness[1]

There was once a king who had a beautiful daughter, who after his death succeeded to the throne, being his only child. When he heard of this, a villainous duke came to her and made her extravagant promises if she would only yield to him. She was seduced by him and he took her virginity, at the loss of which she wept bitterly. The villain then drove her from the kingdom she had inherited.

Banished as she was, she spent her days groaning and sighing and would sit beside the public highway to beg alms of passers-by. One day as she sat there weeping, a well-born knight came by her on his horse and seeing how beautiful she was, was captivated as he gazed at her. 'Who are you, my dear?' he asked.

'I am the only daughter of a king,' she told him, 'and after my father's death I inherited the throne by rightful inheritance, but I was seduced and deflowered by a villain, who then robbed me of my inheritance.'

'Are you willing to become my wife?' the knight asked.

'I am, my lord,' she said. 'I would like that more than anything.'

He said: 'Give me your word that you will have no-one else but me, and I will make war on that villain and win back your land. But if I die in battle winning back your inheritance, there is one thing I beg of you: keep my bloodstained armour by you as a token of your love, so that if anyone comes along who wants to marry you, you may enter the chamber in which my arms hang, and consider them carefully, and remember how I lost my life for love of you.'

'Lord,' she replied, 'I promise faithfully to do this. But God forbid you should lose you life in battle!'

So the knight armed himself and went to meet the villain, who, learning of the threat, opposed him with all his might. They fought

1 Cf. Herrtage, Text I.IX.

a duel in which the knight was victorious and cut off the villain's head, so he won back the kingdom. But in the fight he sustained a mortal wound and two days later died. The princess mourned his death for many a day, and hung up his bloody armour in her chamber, and often went to look at it, and wept bitterly each time she saw it.

Many nobles came to her to ask her hand in marriage, and they made her lavish promises, but before she gave them her answer, she entered her chamber to look at the armour, and cried: 'Oh my lord, you died for love of me and restored my kingdom to me. God forbid that I should agree to marry another!' Then she came out again and said: 'I have made a vow to God never to marry.' And when they heard this they went away, and so she lived all the rest of her life in chastity.[2]

Moralization. Dear friends, this king is the Heavenly Father, and his beautiful daughter is the soul created in God's image. She was given the kingdom of paradise, but at the prompting of the duke, i.e., the devil, she lost it, and was deflowered, when she ate of the apple. Then she sat at the roadside, i.e., in the world: 'In the sweat of thy face' etc.[3] She begged alms from passers-by, i.e., she waited to receive God's grace from the four elements.[4] The knight who came riding by her was the Son of God, who entered this world on the horse of his humanity and had compassion for humankind. And you, O man, promised faithfully at baptism to accept no other husband but him. So he armed himself with the arms of humanity and made war against the devil on your behalf; he won the victory, but sustained a fatal wound for your sake, and won us our inheritance. Do then as the girl did, and keep his bloody armour in the chamber of your heart, i.e., keep fresh your remembrance of Christ's Passion, the Passion he endured for you upon the cross. And if any temptations come to you through the devil, the world or the flesh, have recourse to Christ's Passion, and recollect how for love of you he endured death upon the cross, and thus you will overcome temptations and win life everlasting.

2 Cf. no. 25, a very similar tale, in which, however, the lady forgets her gratitude.
3 Gn 3.19.
4 *a quatuor elementis*: the princess/fallen soul has to beg alms 'in the sweat of its brow' from passers-by; she begs bodily bread from transient things, i.e. the world, but has to wait until the knight, i.e. Christ, comes along and gives her spiritual bread, i.e., the grace she needs for her restoration.

67. Of defences which are inadmissible in extreme cases[1]

In the realm of the wise king Maximian there lived two knights who were close friends, one of them wise, the other foolish. The wise knight said to his friend: 'Do you want to strike a bargain with me? It will be to our mutual advantage.' 'Certainly,' said his friend. 'Then let us draw blood from our right hands,' the wise knight said, 'and I shall drink your blood, and you mine, as a token that neither of us shall ever abandon the other in prosperity or adversity, and whatever profit one makes, the other shall have half of it.' 'Gladly,' said the foolish knight. So they drew blood at once and drank each other's blood, and afterwards always lived in the same house together.

Now the king had had two cities built. One of them was at the top of a mountain, and everyone who went there could receive an abundance of riches and remain there all their lives. The road to this city was narrow and stony, and three knights with a large army barred the way, and everyone who travelled that road had to fight them or lose their lives and all their possessions. The king also appointed a seneschal in this city with orders to receive all those who entered it without exception, and to provide for them liberally as their status and rank warranted.

He had the other city built in the valley below this mountain and the way there was level and pleasant to travel. Three knights were stationed along the road who gladly received all who passed by and gave them all they desired. In this city the king had appointed a seneschal with orders to throw all who entered the city, or even came near it, into prison, and to present them before the judge when he arrived, and he was to spare none of them.

The wise knight said to his companion: 'My friend, let us go

---

1 Cf. Herrtage, Text I.VIII. This is an awkward title: the defences referred to are presumably inadmissible in any circumstances.

about the world like other knights, and we will make our fortunes and live lives of plenty.' 'Gladly,' said the other.

So they set out together until they came to a fork in the road. 'My friend,' the wise knight said, 'there are two roads here, as you can see. One leads to a most noble city, and if we go that way, we shall come to the city in which we can have whatever our hearts desire. The other is the road that leads to the other city which is built in a valley, and if we go that way we shall be seized and imprisoned, and brought before a judge, and then hanged. So I think we should forget that road and take the other.'

'My friend,' said the foolish knight, 'I heard of these two cities a long time ago, but the way to the city on the mountain is very narrow and dangerous, because three knights are stationed there with a large army, and they attack all who seek to enter it, and kill them or rob them; whereas the other way is absolutely level and there are three knights there who receive all who enter kindly, and give them all they need. This I can see quite plainly, and I trust my own eyes rather than you.'

The wise knight replied: 'Admittedly one way is level and easy to travel, but it leads us to everlasting ignominy, because we will end up on the gibbet. If you are afraid of taking the narrow path because of the fighting, and robbers, then that is to your eternal shame, because you are a knight and it is the knight's duty to fight against the foe. And another thing: if you agree to take that road with me, I promise faithfully to go before you into battle and to cut a way through the enemy, however many they are, if only you agree to help me.'

'I tell you truly,' the other said, 'I will not take that road. I will go this way.'

The wise knight replied: 'Since I gave you my word, and as a sign of my good faith drank your blood, I will not let you go alone. I will go with you.'

So they both took the same road and had a very comfortable journey along the way, just as they would have wished, until they reached the lodging-place of the three knights, where they were given an honourable reception and magnificently provided for. As they ate, the foolish knight said to the wise one: 'My friend, didn't I tell you? Look at all the comforts we are enjoying because we came this way. We would have had none of this had we gone the other way.'

67. Of defences which are inadmissible in extreme cases

'If this ends well,' he replied, 'then all will be well. But I am not sanguine.'

They spent some time with the three knights, during which the seneschal of the city heard that two knights were near the city in contravention of the king's prohibition and sent his men there to arrest them and bring them to the city. As soon as he saw the foolish knight he had him bound hand and foot and thrown into a ditch; the other he put in prison. When the judge arrived in the city, all the lawbreakers were brought before him, and among them the two knights.

The wise knight said to him: 'My lord, I wish to lodge a complaint concerning my companion, since he is responsible for my death. I told him of the law of this city and the dangers we would face, but he simply would not believe what I told him, or listen to me or follow my advice. His response was: "I trust my own eyes rather than your words." Now since we were mutually bound on a sworn oath not to abandon each other whether in prosperity or adversity, when I saw him setting off here alone, I went with him, because of that oath. And so he is responsible for my death. Let your sentence therefore be just.'

The foolish knight told the judge: 'He is responsible for my death. The whole world knows that he is wise and I am naturally foolish, so in his wisdom he should not so readily have become party to my folly. And if he had not followed me when I went off alone, I would have turned back to take the road he wanted to take and accompanied him because of the oath I swore him. So since he is wise and I am foolish, he is responsible for my death.'

The judge then addressed both of them, and first the wise knight. 'Since you, who are wise, so readily associated yourself with his folly and followed him; and since you, who are foolish, did not believe the words of a wise man, but did as your folly dictated, I sentence you both to hang today.'

And so it befell.

Dear friends, this king is our Lord Jesus Christ; the two soldiers are the soul and the body; the soul is wise, the body is foolish. These two were joined together at baptism, so that each drank the other's blood. A person drinks another's blood when he puts himself in danger on his behalf, and so, if the flesh wishes to have its pleasures, the soul must mortify itself in penance rather than allow the flesh to expose itself to such danger. But if the soul should waver, which God forbid!, the flesh must suffer fasting and vigils on its behalf, and this is to drink another's blood, and never to abandon another in time of need. The 'two roads' they come to etc. One is the way of penance, the other of worldly glory. Of the 'two cities', the one on the mountain is highest heaven; the other, in the valley, is hell. The road to heaven is narrow, like the way of penance, and few walk it. On this road there are three soldiers, i.e., the devil, the world and the flesh, and anyone who wants to get to heaven must fight these three and walk the way of penance. In this city there is a seneschal, i.e., God, who gives to all in abundance according to their merits; as the prophet says:[2] 'It hath not entered into the heart of man [what things God hath prepared for them that love him].' On the road to hell are three soldiers, namely pride of life, the concupiscence of the eyes and the concupiscence of the flesh,[3] and for a time the sinner finds these three things most delightful for his body. The road to hell is level and easy to walk, but before a man knows it, the seneschal, i.e., death, sends out his spies, i.e., infirmities, to seize him, when the soul is separated from the body. The soul will be imprisoned in hell, while the body is bound and placed in the grave, but on the Day of Judgement, when the Lord appears to judge the living and the dead, then the soul will give evidence against the body, and the body against the soul, and the judge, i.e., God, will pronounce sentence. If we are found to be in sin, we shall without doubt go to hell – from which may Father, Son and Holy Spirit protect us!

2 1 Cor 2.9; cf. Is 64.4.
3 Cf. 1 Jn 2.16.

68. Of proclaiming the truth until death[1]

In the reign of Gordian there was a certain well-born knight whose beautiful wife committed adultery on many occasions. It happened one day that her husband went on his travels and she immediately sent for her lover. Now this lady had a maid who could understand the singing of birds, and when the lover came, there were at the time three cocks in the courtyard. In the middle of the night, as the lover lay with the lady, the first cock began to crow. The lady heard it and called to her maid: 'Tell me, dear, what is the cock saying?' She replied: 'It says that you are wronging your husband.' 'Then kill it,' said the lady. So the cock was killed. In due course the second cock crowed, and the lady said to her maid: 'What is the cock saying?' She replied: 'My companion has died for speaking the truth, and I am ready to die for it too.' 'Kill it,' said the lady. So the cock was killed. Then the third cock crew, and when the lady heard it, she said to her maid: 'What is the cock saying?' She replied: 'Hear and see, but silent be, if you desire tranquillity.'[2]

'Let that one live,' the lady said. And her command was obeyed.

Moralization. Dear friends, the emperor is our Heavenly Father; the knight is Christ; and his wife is the soul, wedded to him at baptism. The one who seduced her is the devil, who ensnares us with worldly deceits, so that, whenever we consent to sin, we are unfaithful to Christ. The maid is your conscience, which murmurs at sin, and urges man constantly to do good. The first cock that crew is of course Christ, who rebuked sin from the first, because of which the Jews killed him; and we likewise do all we can to kill him as long as we remain in sin. By the

1 Cf. Herrtage, Text I.XLV; also Oesterley, p. 723; Tubach, no. 1134; Hope, pp. 530–1.
2 *Audi, vide, tace: si vis vivere in pace.*

second cock we should understand the martyrs. So too there were many others who proclaimed his way of life and teaching, and because of this they were murdered for Christ's name and the truth. By the third cock, which said: 'Hear, see etc.,' we may understand the preacher, who must be diligent in proclaiming the truth, but these days does not dare to speak the truth. Let us strive therefore to fear God more, to proclaim the truth, and thus we shall come to Christ, who is Truth.

69. Of chastity

There was an exceedingly wise emperor called Gallus who once decided to build a palace, and since among his subjects there was a very accomplished builder,[1] Gallus engaged him to build his palace. Now at that time there lived a knight who had a lovely daughter, and seeing how skilled this builder was he got to thinking: 'If I marry my daughter to him, with his skill and craftsmanship he will enable her to lead a splendid life.' So he called the builder and said to him: 'Friend, ask what you wish of me and if it is possible I will give it to you, but on condition that you marry my daughter.' 'Gladly,' replied the builder. So they agreed on the matter, and the builder married the girl. After the marriage the girl's mother called her son-in-law and said to him: 'Son, you have married my daughter, so look, I am going to give you this shirt', and she showed him the shirt, which was a very fine one, and told him: 'This shirt has a curious power: it will never need washing for the rest of your life; it cannot be torn, worn out, or change its colour as long as you and my daughter love each other faithfully. But if you do not, if one of you breaks your marriage vows, the shirt will at once lose all its power.'

Delighted at hearing this, the builder took the shirt and said: 'What a precious thing you have given me, mother! Now neither of us can break our marriage vows without the shirt revealing the fact.'

A few days later the builder was summoned to the palace to begin the new building. He took the shirt with him, left his wife at home, and stayed with the emperor until the new palace was finished. While he was working away, many people marvelled at how his

[1] *carpentarius:* normally 'carpenter' or 'wagon maker', but such a specialized meaning is clearly not intended here.

shirt always stayed so white and clean. The emperor said to him: 'Master, I beg you, tell me, how can it be that, although you never stop working, your shirt never needs washing and always remains so spotless and clean?'

'I will tell you, my dear lord,' he replied. 'So long as my wife and I are faithful to each other, my shirt never needs washing. But if either of us breaks our marriage vows, my shirt would need washing just like other shirts.'

Now a knight overheard this, and thought to himself: 'I'll make you wash your shirt, if I can.' And off he went to the builder's house, behind his back, to seduce his wife. She received him with pleasure, and the soldier pleaded with her, urging his ungovernable passion. 'Such affairs need to be conducted in privacy,' she told him. 'Come with me.' And she took him into a private room and having done so, locked the door and left him, telling him: 'Wait there for me there until I have the time to come and let you out.'

After that she visited him each day, giving him only bread and water to live on. He begged and begged her to let him out, but she would not agree to.

Subsequently two other knights came from the king's court, one after the other, to seduce her, but it was no use. She shut them up in the same room and fed them on bread and water. They remained there for many a day, and there was great concern in the emperor's household about these three knights, and an inquiry was held into what had become of them.

When the palace was completed the builder received his wages and went home, and his wife, overjoyed, received him with all honour and asked him anxiously how he was. 'Well,' he replied, 'well in every respect.' And looking at his shirt and seeing that it was spotless, she cried: 'Blessed be God! It is clear from your shirt that we have been faithful to each other.'

'Dearest,' he said, 'while I was working on the palace three knights came along, one after the other, and asked how my shirt remained white without washing, and I told them the truth. After that I have no idea what became of them. There has been a big inquiry at court into their disappearance.'

'My lord,' she said, 'the three knights that people are talking about came to me and made me lavish promises if I would yield to them. But I would not hear of it. I shut them up in a closet and until today have fed them on bread and water.'

69. Of chastity

The builder was delighted to learn of his wife's fidelity. He let the knights go free, and the two of them loved each other truly for the rest of their lives.[2]

Moralization. Dear friends, the emperor is the Heavenly Father, who has to build a palace, i.e., the human heart replete with virtues, and in this palace he delights to stay; as we read:[3] *'My delights are to be with the children of men.' The knight with the beautiful daughter is Christ, who has the soul as his daughter. His wife is Holy Mother Church; the builder is the good Christian who takes the daughter to wife with the shirt. This shirt is our faith, because, as the Apostle says,*[4] *'without faith it is impossible to please God'. As long as man remains in holiness in this life, his faith is inviolate. What follows then? Why, you*[5] *must erect a palace, that is, a heart purified through works of mercy. The three knights are pride of life, concupiscence of the eyes and concupiscence of the flesh. You must shut these three knights up in the closet of penance until you receive your everlasting reward from the everlasting King. Which may the Lord Jesus Christ grant us etc.*

---

2 Cf. *The Lady Prioress and her Three Suitors*, a metrical tale, one of the minor works of the prolific John Lydgate (?1370–1449). Other cognates are listed by Oesterley, p. 723; Tubach, no. 4336; Hope, pp. 531–2.
3 Prv 8.31.
4 Heb 11.6.
5 i.e., the good Christian/builder.

70. Of the compunction of a faithful soul[1]

A king had a beautiful and wise daughter for whom he wished to find a husband, but she had made a vow to God that she would never take a husband unless he could perform three tasks. First, he must state precisely how many feet there were in the length and breadth and depth of the four elements. Second, he must change the direction of the North wind. Third, he must carry fire in his bosom, next to his flesh, without suffering injury.

When the king learned of her vow, he had it proclaimed throughout the whole kingdom that anyone who could faithfully perform these tasks should marry his daughter. Many suitors arrived, but they all failed. However, there was a certain knight from distant parts who heard of the princess's vow and came to the royal palace with a single servant and a wild horse. He presented himself before the king and said: 'My lord king, I wish to marry your daughter and am prepared to perform the three tasks.' 'Very well,' the king replied.

The knight then called his servant and told him to lie upon the ground. When he had done so, the knight measured him from head to toe. Having done so, he said to the king: 'There, Lord. I can find scarcely more than seven feet in the four elements.' 'What has this to do with the four elements?' asked the king. 'Lord,' he replied, 'every man and every animal is composed of the four elements.'[2] 'That is true,' the king said. 'You have proved the point quite clearly. Let us proceed to the second task: change the direction of the wind!'

The knight at once had the wild horse brought to him and gave it a draught to drink, after which it became quite normal. He then turned the horse's head to the east and said: 'There, Lord, the wind has changed from north to east.' 'What has this to do with the

1 Cf. Herrtage, Text II.XXXV.
2 See note 33 on the moralization of no. 17.

70. Of the compunction of a faithful soul

wind?' asked the king. The knight replied: 'Is it not clear to you with your wisdom that the life of every animal is in its wind? While my horse was ill he was in the north; but now the draught has made him well again, and I have turned him to the east, so that he is now ready to carry a burden.' 'You have proved the point quite clearly,' said the king. 'Let us proceed to the third task.' 'Lord, said the knight, 'I am ready to perform this task before everyone present.' He scooped up some burning coals in his hands and put them in his bosom, and his flesh was not burnt in the slightest.

'You managed the other two tasks very well,' said the king, ' but tell me, how is it that the coals[3] do not burn you?'

'It is not from any power of my own,' replied the knight. 'It is by virtue of a stone I always carry with me. No-one who carries this stone in a place of purity will ever be burnt by fire. Look!, here it is.' And he showed everyone the stone.

The king said to him: 'You have performed all three tasks satisfactorily.' He gave orders for the wedding to take place, married his daughter to the knight and heaped riches upon him, and they both ended their days in goodness of life.

Moralization. Dear friends, the king is our Lord Jesus Christ; his beautiful daughter is the soul, created in God's image, who made a vow to God at baptism that she would never marry a man unless he could accomplish three tasks: the first, to measure [the elements] etc., means you must calculate how much your servant, i.e., your flesh, has sinned, and do penance for every sin; to 'measure the elements' is to subdue your flesh. The second task, to change [the direction of the wind] etc.; this means to amend your life. The wild horse is the sinner who remains in sin, and he must be given a draught so that he has contrition in his heart, confession upon his lips and repentance in his actions; and this is to 'change the wind'. As Job says:[4] 'My life is as the wind.' The third task was to carry fire without being harmed. This fire is the fire of wantonness, avarice and pride, which often destroy the soul and body. But if you want the fire not to harm you, you must keep the stone in your pocket, i.e., our Lord Jesus Christ in your heart through works of merit. And if you carry it in purity, the fire of sin will never harm you and in consequence you will win life everlasting.

3 *verlebe*: Oest.; *glebas*: K.; *glebae*: L. *Gleba* can mean 'piece' or 'lump'. It is attested as meaning 'spark' only in a glossary of 1483.
4 Cf. Jb 7.7.

71. Of the reward of the heavenly home[1]

A king held a great feast and sent out heralds to proclaim that everyone of any rank whatsoever should come to this feast, and not only would they enjoy a good feast, but also receive untold wealth. Now when the heralds went through the kingdom from town to town carrying out their king's command, there happened to be living in the same city two men, one of whom was strong and sturdily built, but blind, and the other was lame and weak but had excellent sight. The blind man said to the lame: 'My friend, we are a poor couple. It has been proclaimed throughout the land that the king is to hold a feast at such-and-such a time, and not only will everyone have all the food he wants but great riches into the bargain! But you are lame, and I am blind, so we shall not be able to go to the feast.'

The lame man said: 'If you do as I suggest, we shall both go together, and have the money and food like everyone else.' 'I am ready to do anything you suggest that will help us,' replied the blind man. 'You are strong and sturdily built,' the lame man said, 'while I am weak because lame. You can carry me on your back and I will guide you along the way, because I can see very well. This way we shall both go to the feast and get our reward like the rest.' 'So be it,' said the blind man. 'That is an excellent plan. Climb on my back at once.'

This he did. The lame man showed him the way while the blind man carried him, and in this way both arrived at the feast and received their money like the rest.

[1] Cf. Herrtage, Text I.VI.

71. Of the reward of the heavenly home

Dear friends, the king is our Lord Jesus Christ, who has prepared an everlasting banquet for us all; like the man in Luke:[2] *'There was a certain man who made a great supper etc.' Many have been invited to this feast and anyone who goes will have eternal riches. The blind man is any rich and powerful man of this world who is strong in body, i.e., in wealth and worldly power. For they are blind with regard to eternal life; they do not know the way to salvation, as a mole sees clearly under ground and knows many winding paths, but above ground becomes blind and helpless. So too the rich see quite clearly in temporal matters, and are blind in those that are spiritual. The lame man is the good religious, who is lame in both feet, that is, he possesses nothing either in common or of his own, but such a man sees quite clearly the way to the eternal banquet. So if you who are the rich and mighty of the world mean to go to the eternal banquet and there receive your rewards, it will be necessary for you to carry the religious and other poor folk on your backs. And this should be noted carefully: the rich must 'carry' the poor by giving them alms and aiding them in their distress – this is to 'carry' the poor – and faithfully pay men of the church their tithes. If you do so, we religious are bound to show you the way of salvation, and enable you to attain to life everlasting.*[3] *The heralds who proclaimed this feast are the doctors of Holy Writ, i.e., preachers and confessors, who have to teach us in public and in private how to get to the eternal banquet.*

---

2 Cf. Lk 14.16.
3 This was a recurrent theme of the monks: 'Pay us your tithes, or find your own way to heaven.'

72. Of the destruction of the ungrateful[1]

We read that a certain king had an only son whom he loved deeply and brought up with every care. As soon as he had attained his majority, he began, day in and day out, to urge the king to resign to the kingdom to him, on the grounds that his father was weak and he was strong.

'My dear son,' said the king, 'if I were sure that you would treat me with kindness and respect for the rest of your life, I would grant your wish and treat you with all the civility that a father owes his son.'

'Sire,' the son replied, 'I will swear an oath before all the ministers and nobles of the kingdom that you will never want; indeed I will hold you in greater honour than myself.'

The king believed him, gave him his throne, and retained no power of his own. But when the son was crowned king and set upon the throne, his heart grew incredibly swollen with pride. For some years he showed respect to his father, but then he neither respected him nor made provision for him. So his father began to complain to the wise men of the kingdom that his son was not keeping his word, and the wise men, who had always loved the old king, accused the son of ill treating his father. This sent him into a great rage, and he shut his father up in a castle where no-one could gain access to him, and where he had to endure hunger and many other miseries.

Now it happened that on one occasion the king spent the night in that same castle, and his father went to him and said: 'My son, have pity on your old father who brought you into the world and gave you everything. I endure hunger and thirst in this place, and now I have become seriously ill and a draught of wine would be a comfort to me.'

[1] Cf. Herrtage, Text II.XXI.

72. Of the destruction of the ungrateful

The king replied: 'I don't know if there is any wine in this castle.'

'There is, my son,' said his father. 'There are five casks of wine that the seneschal of the castle has, but he dare not open them and give me some to drink without your knowledge. So I beg you, my son, give me some wine from the first of these casks.'

'I will not,' replied the son. 'It is new, and not good for elderly people.'

'Then give me some from the second cask,' his father said.

His son replied: 'I will not do that either. I am keeping that for my personal use and for the young men I have with me.'

'Then give me some wine from the third,' he said.

'No. That wine is too strong, and you are weak and infirm. It could be the death of you.'

'Then give me some from the fourth cask.'

'No,' he said. 'It is old and vinegary and not much good, especially for someone of your constitution.'

'Then give me some from the fifth cask, my son.'

'God forbid!,' he replied. 'It is just dregs. The nobles would accuse me of having killed you if I gave you dregs to drink.'

In sorrow at his son's words the father left him, and at once wrote a letter secretly to the nobles of the kingdom, telling them how his son was treating him and asking them, for the love of God, to deliver him from the miseries he was enduring. The nobles were united in their compassion for him and immediately regained control of the kingdom, restored the father to his former throne, and put his son in prison, where he died in misery.

Dear friends, the king is our Lord Jesus Christ, and his son is any Christian, whom he loves very dearly as long as he remains in purity of life. He gave everything to man that man possesses, and he himself became poor, according to the testimony of Scripture:[2] 'The foxes have a hole etc.' But Christ suffers hunger and thirst every day, i.e., in his members, the poor and weak; as it is written:[3] 'What you did to one of my least brethren, you did it to me.' And when God asks us for a draught of the first cask, this cask is our childhood, and God requires of us that we serve him in our childhood. But the wicked child replies: 'It is new wine,' i.e., 'I am a child, I cannot fast, pray and be forever

---

2 Cf. Mt 8.20; Lk 9.58.
3 Cf. Mt 25.40.

serving God.' Then God asks us for wine from the second cask. The wicked son replies: 'I cannot give up my youth to serving God, because the world will laugh at me and say: "Look, that stupid youth doesn't want to keep company with other men!" So I will keep my youth for myself, banqueting, and drinking and serving the world.' Then God asks us for wine from the third cask: the wicked child replies: 'This is wine of iron,'[4] i.e., 'I am now physically in my prime; if I do penance I shall diminish my strength. I want to fight battles and compete in tournaments and follow other worldly pursuits, and then do penance when my strength is gone.' And seeing that he could have nothing from these three casks, God asks for a draught from the fourth cask. The wicked son replies: 'This wine is too old and vinegary,' i.e., 'I am now an old man; I can no longer fast or keep vigils, because my constitution is weak.' Then God asks for a draught from the fifth cask. The wicked son replies: 'These are dregs.' That is to say, 'Alas, I am enfeebled, my hope of salvation is gone. When I could do good, I did not do so, and now I am unable to,' and such a person sinks into despair, and so dies a wretched death. A grave charge will be laid against such as these, and on the Day of Judgement God with the whole heavenly court will pass sentence, saying:[5] 'Go, you cursed, etc.' From which may he deign to deliver us.

---

4 *vinum ferratum*: chalybeate wine. This is a medicated, ironated wine, one of the six medicated wines in the British pharmacopoeia, supposed to cure a variety of ailments. In the tale itself the son says only that the wine is strong: *forte*.

5 Mt 25.41.

73. Avarice makes many blind[1]

There was a certain king of Rome who ordained that all blind men should get 100 shillings every year from their ruler. It chanced that a company of twenty-four men came to the city and went into a tavern for a drink. They stayed there seven days eating and drinking, and when they wanted to settle with the innkeeper, they gave him whatever money they had. 'My friends,' he told them, 'this is a good 100 shillings short. I assure you, you'll not leave here until you have paid me the last farthing and settled up.'

'What are we going to do?' they asked each other. 'We haven't the money to pay.'

Then one of them said: 'I have a good idea. Listen: the king has passed a law that anyone who is blind will received 100 shillings from his treasury. Let's cast lots among ourselves, and blind whoever is chosen, and then he can go to the palace and get the 100 shillings and settle up for all of us.'

'That is an excellent idea,' they all exclaimed. So they cast lots, and the one chosen was the one who had suggested the scheme. They at once put out his eyes, took him to the palace and knocked at the gates. When the gatekeeper asked them why they were knocking, they told him: 'Look, here is a blind man who wishes to take advantage of the law.'

'I will inform the seneschal,' he replied. He then went to the seneschal and told him: 'There is a blind man at the gate who wishes to take advantage of the law.'

'I will go and see him,' said the seneschal.

When he saw the blind man he looked at him very closely, and after considering him he asked: 'What do you want, friend?'

1 Cf. Herrtage, Text I.XI.

'The 100 shillings ordained by the law,' he said.

'Listen to me,' replied the seneschal, 'I saw you yesterday in the tavern, and you had both eyes then and could see perfectly. You have misunderstood the law. The law that was passed specified that a man must have been blind through some infirmity or unavoidable accident in order to benefit from its generosity. You lost your eyes voluntarily. After drinking in the tavern you formed a plan to have your eyes put out. So look for consolation there, because you won't get a penny piece here.'

So, put to shame, the blind man went away.

Moralization. Dear friends, the law of God is such that anyone who sins in ignorance, or through infirmity, or the devil's temptation, if he is contrite and confesses, God will forgive him; as the prophet says:[2] *'In whatsoever hour the sinner [is converted] etc.,' God will forgive him. Every sinner, inasmuch as he is a sinner, is blind. If someone sins through pure malice and without cause, and then falls into despair, he will scarcely, if ever be forgiven. The innkeeper is the devil, who receives all such in the inn of hell. Let us therefore strive etc.*

2 Cf. Ez 18.21.

74. Of foresight and forethought[1]

There was a king who had an only son whom he loved dearly. This king had a golden apple made at great expense, but no sooner was it finished than he became mortally ill. He called for his son and said: 'My dear son, I shall not recover from this illness, so after my death go with my blessing through all the towns of the kingdom. Take with you the golden apple I have had made, and give it as a gift from me to the biggest fool you can find.'

His son promised faithfully to do so, and the king turned his face to the wall and breathed his last. His son gave him a magnificent funeral, and as soon as it was over he took the apple and went through all the towns of the kingdom. He found and saw many fools, but did not give the apple to any of them. Then he travelled to another kingdom and entered its principal city. There he saw the king riding through the city centre with a large retinue, and asked some of the citizens about the customs of that region.

'It is the custom here,' they told him, 'that no king shall reign over us longer than a year. When the year is over, he is driven into exile and dies an evil death.'

When he heard this he thought to himself: 'Finally I have found the one I was looking for.' He went to the king, did him obeisance on bended knee, and said: 'Hail, king! My late father bequeathed you this golden apple in his will.'

The king took the apple and replied: 'How can this be, dear boy? The king never set eyes on me and I never did him any favours. Why has he given me such a precious object?'

'My lord king,' he replied, 'my father commanded me to give it to the greatest fool I could find, and though I have travelled

---

[1] Cf. Herrtage, Text III.V (Wynkyn de Worde).

through many kingdoms and towns I have certainly never come across such a fool and idiot as you. So in obedience to my father's command I have given the apple to you.'

'Pray tell me,' said the king, 'why you consider me such a fool.'

'Very well,' he said, 'I will explain to you. It is the custom in this realm for a king to reign for one year only, then at the end of the year for him to stripped of all his honours and wealth and driven into exile, where he dies an evil death. In all truth, therefore, I conclude that there cannot in all the world be anyone as foolish as you, who must reign for such a short time and then end your days in wretchedness.'

The king replied: 'What you have said is quite right, so this year, while I am still king, I shall send an abundance of supplies ahead of me to my place of exile, so that when I go there, I shall have ample provisions to live on for the rest of my days.'

And that was what he did. At the end of that year he was removed from the throne and driven into exile, and there he live for many years on the provisions he had made.

Moralization. Dear friends, this king is God, who bequeathed a golden apple to fools. The round apple stands for this world, which God gives to the stupid who desire the world and the things that are in the world more than God. The king, who reigned for one year, can be taken as any man living in this world, who, though he live a hundred years, lives but a single hour in comparison with the future life, yet the wretched man never stops toiling day and night, and after death is sent into exile, i.e., hell, if he dies in mortal sin, where he will find endless torments. And there are few who think of this exile. Let us therefore do what the king did: while we are in the fullness of our powers in this life, let us send before us works of mercy, generous alms, and engage in prayer and fasting, that after this life we may enter paradise, and be sure of finding there the works of merit that we have performed in this life, and so reign there in glory! May God bring us to that glory.

75. Of the avoidance of worldly cares[1]

There was a king who had three beautiful daughters whom he married to three dukes, but all three of these dukes died in one and the same year. So the king decided that his daughters should marry again, and he summoned the first and said to her: 'My dear, your husband is dead. I propose to marry you to another.'

But she replied: 'I will never seek to marry again, and my reason is this: if I had to have another husband I would have to love him as much as my first husband, or love him more, or perhaps less. But to love him as much would be impossible, as my first husband took my maidenhead, so I could not love a second husband as much. If I loved him more, that would be an even greater injustice; if less, then there would be no true love between us. So I have decided never to have another husband.'

When the king heard this he called for his second daughter, and said: 'My dear, your husband is dead. I propose to wed you to another.'

'Sire,' she said, 'I will never seek to marry again, because if I did have another husband, I would marry him for his wealth or prowess or looks; and I would not do so for wealth, because I have plenty; nor for his prowess, because I have friends to defend me; nor for his looks, because I thought my husband the most handsome man in all the world. My decision is therefore never to marry another man.'

So the king called for his third daughter. 'My dear,' he said, 'your husband is dead, I want you to remarry.'

'I will never seek to do so,' she replied, 'because if I had another husband, he would agree to marry me either for my beauty or my

1 Cf. no. 78 below, and Herrtage, Text I.XLIV.

wealth; and it would not be for my beauty, because I am not beautiful; and if he did so for my wealth, it could never be true love, because his love would change if my wealth were gone. So I will not on any account have another husband. Moreover the Doctors of Holy Scripture say that a man and woman joined in matrimony are one body, but two souls. My husband's body is therefore my body, and vice versa. I can visit my husband's tomb every day and see his bones there, and it is as if he were there before me. And so I will not marry again.'

After hearing their arguments, the king no longer urged his daughters to remarry.

Dear friends, this king is God, and his three daughters represent the soul, which reflects the working and image of the Trinity, as we read in Genesis 2:[2] 'Let us make man to our image and likeness.' Now through the sin of our first parent the image of the Trinity was defiled and delivered up to three husbands, namely, the devil, the world and the flesh. If the devil is slain by Christ's Passion, never take another such husband again, but always remain under Christ's protection. If the world is slain by voluntary poverty, never take another husband, but remain under Christ's protection. And if the flesh is slain by fasting and mortification of the flesh, never take another husband, but remain under Christ's protection.

Or the tale can be interpreted in another way. The king is God, and his three daughters are the three types of men, i.e., the powerful and rich of this world, such as kings and worldly potentates; the wise of this world, such as secular judges and pious ecclesiastics; and perfect Christians, as are those who obey God's laws in everything. These three were united with three dukes at baptism, i.e., to the Father in power, the Son in wisdom, and to the Holy Spirit in clemency. If these die, i.e., are extinguished and taken from you because of your sin, never strive to be joined to another, but make every effort to perform works of mercy through which you may be reconciled with Him, because you will never find another who loves you so much. Note that a woman takes a husband for four reasons: either for his riches, his beauty, his might or his wisdom. If you wish to take a husband for his riches, you will certainly never find one as rich as our Lord Jesus Christ, who is Lord of heaven and earth; so hold fast to him and no other. If you

2 = Gn 1.26.

75. Of the avoidance of worldly cares

wish to take a husband for his might, fly to our Lord Jesus Christ, who is mightier than any man, mighty in heaven and on earth; and in hell there is no-one who can oppose him. If you wish to take a husband for his beauty, fly to our Lord Jesus Christ, who is fairer than any man; he is, as the Psalmist says,[3] *'beautiful above the sons of men'; so you must have him and no other. And if you wish to take a husband for his wisdom, fly to our Lord Jesus Christ, because he is wiser than any man; as we read in Romans:*[4] *'O the depth of the riches of the wisdom and of the knowledge of God! etc.' You must therefore have him and no other.*

3 Ps 44.3.
4 Rom 11.33.

76. Of concord

It happened that in a certain city there were two doctors who were highly skilled in every branch of medicine. They cured all who came to them no matter what their infirmity, so that people could not possibly tell which of them was better. And in due course the two men fell to disputing which of them was greater and more skilled.

One said to the other: 'My friend, let there be no strife or envy or quarrelling between us as to which of us is more skilled. Let us put our skills to the test, and let whichever of us is found wanting be the servant of the other.'

'What do you mean?' said the other. 'Tell me.'

'I will take out your eyes without harming you, place them on the table, and whenever you please, I will replace them in your head without doing you any harm. And if you can do the same thing, exactly as I did, let us regard ourselves as equals and look after each other as brothers. But if either of us fails, he will be the other's servant.'

'An excellent test,' the other said. 'I wholly approve of the idea.'

So the one whose suggestion it was took up his instruments and first smeared his colleague's eyelids both on the inside and outside with a precious ointment; then he removed his eyes and placed them on the table. 'My friend,' he said, 'how do you feel?' 'All I know is that I can see nothing,' he replied, 'because I have no eyes. But I felt no pain at all. Now please put them back as you promised.' 'Willingly,' he said, and took the ointment and smeared it over his eyelids, inside and outside as before, and replaced his eyes. 'My friend, how do you feel now?'

'Fine,' he replied,' because I felt no pain at all when you took them out.'

'Then it remains for you to do the same to me,' said the other.

76. Of concord

'I am ready,' he said. He took up his instruments and ointments, as his colleague had done, smeared his eyelids inside and out, then removed his eyes and placed them on the table. 'My friend,' he said, 'how do you feel?' 'It seems that I have lost my eyes,' the other replied, 'but I felt no pain at all. But now I would very much like to have my eyes back again.'

So his colleague got ready his instruments to replace the eyes. But the window of the room happened to be open, and a crow flew in, and seeing the eyes on the table, it swiftly seized one of them and few off. The doctor was horrified at this and said to himself: 'If I do not restore both my friend's eyes, I shall become his servant!' Then as he gazed out of the window he noticed a goat in the distance, so he removed one of its eyes and put it back in his friend's eye socket in place of the one that had been stolen.

When he had finished, he asked his colleague: 'My friend, how do you feel?' He replied: 'I felt no pain at all when you removed them or replaced them, but one of my eyes keeps looking up at the trees.'

'I have performed this operation perfectly,' said the other, 'as you yourself did, so from now on let us both be equals, and put an end to our rivalry.'

And so from that day on they lived in mutual harmony.

Moralization. Dear friends, these two doctors represent the New Law and the Old, both of which were concerned with the salvation of the soul. There was a dispute, which still continues, between the Jews and Christians as to which Law is better and a more perfect expression of the truth. Each of them 'extracted the other's eyes'; this means that there were many things from the Old Law that God extracted,[1] as for example the Ten Commandments of the Old Law. As the Saviour says:[2] 'I am not come to destroy the law but to fulfil.' So if anyone purposes to see God, he must have recourse to the New Law and clothe himself with the tunic of baptism. The crow came and seized the one eye of the Jews so that they were unable to see the truth, and in its place put a goat's eye, i.e., certain rites which they observe, by means of which they think to see God;[3] but they will go to the outer darkness, where there will be wailing and gnashing of teeth.

1 *extraxit*: extracted, i.e. for the New Law. *Extrahere* can mean 'to copy'.
2 Cf. Mt 5.17.
3 The Revd Swan notes: 'The Catholic ceremonies are open to the same censure, and are equally prejudicial in their consequences.'

77. One must not covet riches[1]

A king had two daughters, one of whom was most beautiful and loved by all, while the other was dark-skinned and universally loathed. This difference in their appearance influenced the king in the names he gave them. He called his beautiful daughter Rosamund, and the swarthy one Graziaplena. He then sent a herald throughout his kingdom to proclaim that any suitors should present themselves, and he would marry his daughters to those who were found worthy of them. But whoever married his beautiful daughter would have nothing but her beauty, whereas the one who married his swarthy daughter should succeed to the throne after his death.

On hearing this proclamation, many came to the royal palace and, when they saw the two daughters, they all paid court to the beautiful one and asked for her hand in marriage. This caused Graziaplena, the swarthy one, great unhappiness.

'Daughter, why are you so heartbroken?' the king asked her.

'Sire,' she said 'no-one comes to me and speaks to me. They all pay their attentions to my sister and scorn me.'

'My daughter,' he replied, 'you are forgetting that all that is mine is yours, and the man who marries you will possess my kingdom.'

This thought comforted her, and she dried her eyes.

Then along came a king to the royal palace and as soon as he saw Rosamund's beauty, he asked for her hand in marriage for her beauty alone. Her father the king agreed, gave him his daughter, and celebrated their marriage with great joy. The other daughter remained unmarried for many a year, until at length a certain duke, well born but poor, thought to himself: 'The girl may be ugly, but whoever weds her will also possess the kingdom.'

---

1 Cf. Herrtage, Text II.XXXIV.

77. One must not covet riches

So he went to the king and asked for Graziaplena's hand, and the king was delighted, and married her to the duke with great joy. And after the king's death the duke possessed his kingdom as well as his daughter.

Moralization. Dear friends, this king is our Lord Jesus Christ, and his beautiful daughter Rosamund is this world, and many are found who desire this world above all things, but will gain nothing with it but its beauty, i.e., vanity and riches. And just as beauty is destroyed by infirmity, hunger and old age, so the riches of this world pass away at death, and often before, and thus they are fools who espouse the world. The second daughter, Graziaplena, who is ugly and loathed by all, is of course poverty, which God loves exceedingly; and so she is called Graziaplena,[2] because through her one attains to riches. However, there are few who want to espouse her; indeed she is hated by everyone. Yet he who does espouse her will have life everlasting.

---

2 *Graziaplena*: literally 'full of grace'.

78. Of the constancy of mutual love

A king had a beautiful daughter who was married to a most noble duke, and they had bonny children and loved each other deeply. But the duke died. His death was greatly lamented throughout the country and his lady gave him burial with all honours. After his death her friends came to urge her to take another husband, arguing that she still had her youth and beauty.

But she replied: 'I will not have another husband, because the husband I had, who died, was so good and kind and rich in every virtue, and his love for me was so deep, and because of our great love for each other his death has so overwhelmed me that I am not sure I can go on living. And even suppose I could find such another man, and possibly he died before me, what grief would then be mine! So I am resolved never to take another husband. And if I married a bad man, what a torment it would be to me to have one so evil after one so good!'[1]

Dear friends, the king is God, and his daughter is the soul, created in the likeness of God, and espoused to a most noble husband, namely our Lord Jesus Christ, by virtue of baptism. And he loved us with supreme love, because he died for us upon the cross. Therefore do not accept another husband in his place, i.e., do not love anyone else as much, and so you will reign with him.

---

1 Cf. no. 75 above, and Herrtage, Text I.XLIV.

79. One should not make ignorant presumptions

There was once a king who loved little dogs with a loud bark so much that he allowed them to lie and be fed on his lap; and they were so accustomed to sleep and feed on his lap that they hardly ever wanted to leave it, and sometimes put their paws around his neck. So the king had much pleasure and amusement with them.

Now there was an ass who observed all this and thought to himself: 'If I could sing and dance before the king and put my feet around his neck he would give me all kinds of food to eat and let me lie on his lap.' So he left his stable, went into the hall of the palace and began to sing before the king. Then he danced this way and that, and finally ran to the king and put his feet around his neck. When the servants saw this they thought the ass had gone mad, so they caught him, gave him a sound thrashing and led him back to his stable.[1]

Dear friends, the king is our Lord Jesus Christ, and the little dogs with loud barks are preachers who zealously proclaim God's word and so are worthy to rest in the bosom of heaven. The ass represents the man who presumes to take upon himself the office of preacher and to proclaim the word of God, but has neither the learning nor the grace to do this; and such a person is in danger of being thrashed, i.e., chastised by the Lord and rejected by the people.

---

1 Cf. Aesop's fable, *The Ass and the Lapdog*.

80. Of the devil's cunning and the hidden judgements of God

There was once a hermit who lived in a cave and served God devoutly both day and night. Near his cell a shepherd tended his sheep and it happened one day that the shepherd fell fast asleep, and as he slept a robber came along and went off with all his sheep. When the owner of the flock arrived, and asked the shepherd where his sheep were, he swore he had lost them and had no idea where they were. Hearing this, the owner was so furious that he killed the man. The hermit witnessed this and said to himself: 'Lord above, look! That fellow has put the blame on an innocent man and killed him! If you allow such things to happen, I shall return to the world and live my life as others do.'

With these thoughts in his head he left the hermitage and returned to the world. But God did not wish him to leave, and sent him an angel in human form to keep him company. This angel met him as he was setting off on his journey, and said to him: 'Where are you going, my friend?' 'To the city that lies ahead,' he told him. The angel replied: 'I will keep you company, for I am a messenger from God and have come to you to be your companion along the way.'

So they travelled together towards the city, and when they entered it, they begged a knight to give them shelter for the love of God. The knight was very happy to receive them, and gave them the most lavish and splendid entertainment, zealously providing them with all they could need. Now this knight had an only son who was lying in his cradle, and he loved him greatly. After dinner, a room was opened for the angel and the hermit, and richly ornamented beds were prepared for them. But around midnight the angel got up and strangled the child in his cradle. Witnessing this, the hermit thought to himself: 'Can this possibly be one of God's

80. Of the devil's cunning and the hidden judgements of God

angels? The knight gave him all he needed for the love of God, and he had only the one son, an innocent child, and he has killed him!' But he did not dare say anything to him.

In the morning they both got up and went on to another city where they were received with every honour and splendidly provided for at the house of one of the citizens. This man possessed a golden goblet which he prized greatly. But in the middle of the night the angel got up and stole the goblet. The hermit saw him do this and thought to himself: 'This is a wicked angel, surely. Our host has treated us excellently, but he has stolen his goblet!' But he said nothing to him because he was afraid of him.

Next morning they got up and travelled on until they reached a river spanned by a bridge, which they began to cross. On it a poor man met them. 'My friend,' said the angel, 'show me the way to such-and-such a city.'

So the poor man turned and pointed with his finger at the road to the city. As he turned, the angel caught him by the shoulders and threw him off the bridge, and he sank beneath the waters below. When he saw this, the hermit thought to himself: 'Now I know this is the devil and not one of God's angels. What harm did that poor man do? Yet he has killed him!' From that moment on he planned to leave his companion, but he was afraid, and said nothing to him.

Around the hour of Vespers they reached the city and went to the house of a rich citizen and begged shelter for the love of God. But he flatly refused them. 'For the love of God,' the angel said, 'at least give us a roof over our heads, or we may be eaten by wolves or other wild beasts here.' The man replied: 'There is the sty where my pigs sleep. If you want, you can lie there with them. If not, be off with you, because I am not giving you anywhere else.' 'If that is all there is,' said the angel, 'we will lie down with the pigs.' So that is what they did.

In the morning they got up and the angel called their host and said to him: 'My friend, this goblet is a gift.' And he gave him the goblet he had stolen from their previous host. At this, the hermit said to himself: 'Now I know for certain that this is the devil! That good man took us in and attended to our every need, and he stole his goblet and gave it to this evil fellow who refused to give us lodging.' He said to the angel: 'I will stay with you no longer. I commend you to God.'

The angel replied:[1] 'Hear me before you go. First, when you were in your hermitage, the owner of the sheep unjustly killed his shepherd. That shepherd did not deserve to die for what he did then, but you should know that there were other things he had done, and for them he deserved to die. He was guiltless on that occasion, but God let him be killed so as to avoid punishment for his sins after his death. For he had committed sins on former occasions for which he would have to do penance. The robber who made off with his sheep will endure everlasting punishment, and the owner of the sheep who killed the shepherd will amend his life by abundant almsgiving and works of mercy, and so atone for the crime that he ignorantly committed. Now as for the child whom I strangled in the night, the son of the knight who gave us such good hospitality, you should know that, before the child was born, the knight was the most generous almsgiver and performed many works of mercy, but after he was born he became mean and grasping, and saved everything to make his child rich; and so this was the cause of his ruin. That was why I killed the child; and now the knight has become a good Christian again, as he was before. Then I stole the goblet belonging to that citizen who had been so hospitable to us. But you should know that before that goblet was made there was not a more sober man in all the world, but after it was made he was so pleased with it that he drank from it all day long and was drunk two or three times every day. So I took the goblet away and he has become sober again. Then I threw the poor man into the river. That poor man was a good Christian, but you should know that if he had gone half a mile further he would have killed someone and committed a mortal sin. But now he has been saved and reigns in heavenly glory. Then I gave the hospitable citizen's goblet to the man who refused us hospitality. But nothing on earth is done without cause. He let us sleep in the pig sty, and so I gave him the goblet, and after this life he will reign in hell. So in future watch your tongue and do not slander[2] God; for he knows all things.'

At these words the hermit fell at the angel's feet and begged for pardon. He then returned to his hermitage and became a good Christian.[3]

1 At this point *Le Violier* (*Exposition sus le Propos*) and L. (*Sensus moralis*) begin a moralization.
2 *attrahas*: Oest.; *detrahas*: K.
3 This story was adapted by Thomas Parnell (1674–1718) for his poem *The Hermit*.

81. Of the wonders of God's providence and the rise of Pope Gregory[1]

There was a king named Marcus, an exceedingly wise man, who had an only son and daughter whom he loved very much. When he reached old age he was stricken with a grave illness, and seeing that he had not long to live, he summoned all the nobles of his kingdom. 'Dear friends,' he said, 'you should know that today I must render up my soul to God. But I am not so much worried for my soul as for my daughter, because I have not given her in marriage. So I charge you, my son and heir, on my blessing, to see that she is married with all honours, as is fitting, and until then to respect her always as you do yourself.' So saying he turned his face to the wall and gave up the ghost. His death was deeply mourned throughout the land, and he was buried with all due solemnity.

His son began his reign with great wisdom, and treated his sister with all possible respect, for he loved her so deeply that everyday he sat facing her on the same chair at table, though he had nobles with him, and they ate all their meals together and slept on separate beds in the same bedchamber. But one night he was seized by a terrible temptation, and felt he would die if he could not satisfy his desire to possess his sister. He got out of bed and went over to his sister, who was asleep, and woke her.

'My lord,' she cried as she was woken, 'what do you want at this hour?' 'If I cannot sleep with you,' he told her, 'I shall die!' 'God

[1] Cf. Herrtage, Text I.LXI. This is in outline the same story of Pope Gregory as that told in Hartmann von Aue's *Gregorius* and Thomas Mann's *Der Erwählte* (both translated into English, the latter as *The Holy Sinner*). For a survey of the whole tradition, see Brian Murdoch, *Gregorius, An Incestuous Saint in Medieval Europe and Beyond*, Oxford: Oxford University Press, 2012 (the Gesta version is discussed on pp. 139–52).

forbid I should commit such a sin!,' she said. 'Think how before his death your father charged you, on his blessing, to treat me with all possible respect. If you commit such a crime, you will inevitably anger God and outrage mankind.' 'Come what may,' he replied, 'I will have my way.' And he slept with her. He then returned to his own bed, and the girl wept bitterly and refused to be comforted. The king did his best to console her, and his extraordinary love for her constantly increased.

Some six months later she was sitting at table when her brother looked closely at her and asked: 'Dearest, what is the matter? Your skin has changed colour and your eyes have lost their sparkle!' 'No wonder,' she said. 'I am pregnant and so I am covered in shame.'

At this her brother was grief-stricken. He wept bitterly and cried: 'Perish the day on which I was born! I have no idea what I am to do!'

'My lord,' she replied, 'do as I say and you will not regret it. We are not the first who have offended God so deeply. Near here lives an old knight, one of our father's counsellors. Our father always acted on his advice. Call him, and we will tell him the whole story under the seal of confession. He will give us sound advice so that we can both make atonement to God and avoid the condemnation of the world.' 'Very well,' said the king, 'but let us first strive to be reconciled to God.' They both made their confessions with pure hearts and profound contrition. Then they sent for the knight and in private tearfully told him everything.

'My lord,' he replied, 'since you are reconciled to God, this is my advice, so that you may avoid public scandal. To propitiate your sins and those of your father you must visit the Holy Land, so on such-and-such a day call all the nobles of your realm into your presence, then make the following statement: "Friends, I wish to visit the Holy Land. As you know, I have no heir but my sister, so in my absence you must obey her as you do myself." Then before them all say to me: "And I charge you, my friend, on pain of your life, to take my sister into your safekeeping." And I will keep her in such privacy and seclusion that no-one will know of your plight either before or after she gives birth, not even my wife.'

'Your advice is sound,' said the king. 'I will do everything you suggest.' He at once called all his nobles and made the abovementioned announcement, exactly as the knight had advised him. Having done so he bade them farewell and went to the Holy Land.

The knight took the king's sister to his castle, and when his wife

81. Of the wonders of God's providence and the rise of Pope Gregory

saw her, she went up to him and asked: 'My reverend lord, who is this lady?'

'She is the king's sister,' he told her. 'Swear to me by Almighty God, on pain of your life, that you will always keep secret what I am going to tell you.' 'Readily, my lord,' she replied. And after she had sworn, the knight told her: 'Our mistress has been made pregnant by our lord king. I therefore charge you that no living creature attend her but yourself, so that the whole business may be kept secret from start to finish.' 'My lord,' she replied, 'I will do exactly as you wish.' The lady was then taken to a private chamber where she was provided with every possible comfort. When the time came for her to give birth, she was delivered of a handsome son. As soon as the knight heard the news he said to her: 'My lady, the right and proper thing would be to call a priest to baptize the child.' But she replied: 'I vow to my God that I will never allow this child born of a brother and sister to receive baptism.' The knight said: 'As you are well aware, the sin you and my lord have committed is grave, but do not for this condemn the child's soul to death.' 'I have made a vow,' she replied, 'and I shall steadfastly keep it. Now I command you to bring me an empty cask.' 'At once,' he said, and he brought a cask to her bedchamber, and she lay the child comfortably in his cradle, and on some writing tables wrote the following words: 'Dear friends, you should know that that this child has not been baptized because he is the offspring of a brother and sister. So for the love of God have him baptized. Under his head you will find a quantity of gold which will enable you to feed him, and at his feet there is a quantity of silver to provide for his studies.' When she had finished writing, she placed the tablets underneath the child in the cradle, and put the gold beneath his head and the silver at his feet. Then she covered the cradle with cloths of silk and gold brocade. When she had done so, she instructed the knight to place the cradle in the cask and cast it into the sea, so it could float wherever God ordained.

The knight carried out all her wishes. When he had cast the cask out into the sea, he stood on the shore until it was no longer visible, then returned to his mistress. As he was approaching his castle a royal messenger from the Holy Land met him. 'Where are you from, friend?', he asked the man. 'From the Holy Land,' he replied. 'What news have you?' the knight asked. 'My lord the king is dead and his body has been taken to one of his castles.' At this news the knight wept bitterly. His wife now appeared, and learning of the king's death she was distraught with grief. When the knight had collected himself, he said to his wife: 'Do not weep in case our mistress should notice. We will say nothing to her until she has recovered from giving birth.' So saying he went in to his mistress and his wife followed him. As soon as she saw them she observed how downcast they were, and asked: 'Dear friends, why are you so sad?' 'We are not sad,' said the knight's wife. 'On the contrary, we are happy that you have been delivered from the grave peril you have been in.' 'No,' she replied, 'that is not so. Tell me. Do not hide anything from, me, whether good or ill.'

The knight said: 'A messenger has come from the Holy Land with news of our master, your brother the king.'

'Call him,' she said. And when he came she asked him: 'How is it with my lord?'

He replied: 'Your lord is dead and his body has been brought from the Holy Land to one of his castles, and he is to be buried alongside your father.'

When she heard this the lady fell to the ground, and seeing his mistress's grief, the knight threw himself to the ground with her, as did his wife and the messenger. For a long while they all remained there, rendered speechless and insensible by the great grief they felt. Finally, after some considerable time, the lady got up; she tore her hair and clawed her face until it bled, and cried in a piercing voice: 'Ah me, perish the day on which I was conceived! Let the night in which I was born never be spoken of! How many are my iniquities![2] My woes are now complete: my hope, my strength, my only brother, the half of my soul – all gone! What I shall do now I have no idea.'

The knight got to his feet and said: 'My dearest lady, listen to me. If you kill yourself for grief, the whole kingdom will perish. You are all that is left and the kingdom is yours by right of heredity. So if you kill yourself the kingdom will pass to foreigners. Come now, let us go to his resting-place and give his body honourable burial. Then let us consider how best to rule the kingdom.'

Comforted by the knight's words the lady bestirred herself and went with a noble escort to her brother's castle. On entering she found the king on a bier and fell upon his body, kissing it from the soles of his feet to his head. When they observed the intensity

---

2 Jb 13.23. 'How many are my iniquities etc.!' The 'etc.' implies that the queen completed the quotation: '... and sins! Make me know my crimes and offences.'

81. Of the wonders of God's providence and the rise of Pope Gregory

of her grief, the knights pulled her from the body and led her to a private chamber, then gave the body burial with due solemnity.

After the burial the Duke of Burgundy sent a formal embassy to her to ask her hand in marriage, but she replied at once: 'As long as I live I shall never marry.' The messengers duly reported her decision to their master, and when he heard it the duke was angry with her and said to himself: 'If she had agreed, I would have been ruler of that kingdom. But since she has scorned me, she shall have little joy of her kingdom.' He mustered an army, entered her kingdom and laid waste to it with fire and the sword, committed numberless atrocities, and won every battle he fought. The queen sought refuge in a well-fortified city where there was a redoubtable castle, and there she remained for many a year.

Now let us return to the boy who was cast into the sea. The cask containing him swept past many countries until on the sixth day[3] it arrived in the vicinity of a monastery. That day the abbot of the monastery went to the seashore and said to his fishermen: 'Friends, get ready to fish.' So they got their nets ready, and while they were doing so the cask was washed by the waves to land. The abbot said to his servants: 'Look, a cask! Open it up and see what is in it.' So they opened the cask and to everyone's surprise a little child wrapped in costly clothing looked up at the abbot and smiled. But the abbot was deeply distressed at the sight. 'My God!' he said. 'How can it be that we find a child here in his cradle?' He lifted him out with his own hands and discovered underneath him the tablets his mother had put there. He opened them and read that the boy had been born of a brother and sister, and had not been baptized, and that he was requested, for the love of God, to give him the sacrament of baptism; and that the gold at his head should provide for his nourishment, and the silver at his feet for his studies. Now when the abbot read all this and saw the cradle adorned with rich fabrics, he realized that the boy was of noble blood. He at once baptized him and gave him his own name, which was Gregory. Then he handed him over to a fisherman to be cared for, giving him the money he had found.

As the boy grew he was loved by everyone. Then when he was seven years of age the abbot arranged for him to begin his studies,

3 *sexta feria*: Swan takes this to mean 'six monkish holy days from the time of its departure'. But niceties of time are regularly disregarded in legend. *Feria sexta* can also mean 'Friday'.

and in them he made remarkable progress. All the monks loved him as if he were one of their own number, and in a short time he had surpassed them all in his learning. Now it happened one day that he was playing ball with the son of the fisherman whom he thought to be his father, and by chance he hit him with the ball, and this made him weep bitterly, and he ran home and complained to his mother: 'My brother Gregory has hit me!' Thereupon his mother came out of the house and gave him a severe scolding. 'Gregory,' she said, 'how dare you hit my boy – why, we don't even know who you are or where you came from!'

'My dearest mother,' he replied, 'am I not your son? Why do you speak to me so unkindly?'

'You are not my son,' she told him, 'and I don't know where you came from. All I know is that you were found in a cask. The abbot gave you to me to care for.'

When he heard this Gregory wept bitterly; he ran to the abbot and said: 'My lord, I have lived with you a long time and thought I was the fisherman's son, but I am not, and so I do not know who my parents are. Please, let me become a knight, because I cannot stay here any longer.' 'My son,' the abbot replied, 'do not think of such a thing. All the monks here have such a deep affection for you that after my death they will make you abbot.' 'Lord,' Gregory said, 'I can certainly not remain here. I must find my parents.'

At this the abbot went to his treasury and fetched the tablets he had found in his cradle, and showed them to him. 'Now read this, my son,' he said, 'and it will be clear to you who you are.'

When Gregory read that he was the offspring of a brother and sister, he fell to the ground and cried: 'Ah me! Then these are my parents? I will go at once to the Holy Land and fight there to atone for my parents' sins, and there I will end my life. So, my lord, I beg you to make me a knight.' The abbot did so, and when he received permission to leave there was great lamentation in the monastery, and all the people in the neighbourhood mourned his departure.

He made straight for the coast and there agreed terms with some sailors for his passage to the Holy Land. But no sooner had they set sail than the winds were contrary and they were immediately driven back to the very country where his mother's castle was. The sailors had no idea where the place was, or what kingdom they were in. But when the knight Gregory entered the city, a citizen met him and asked him: 'My lord, where are you going?' 'I am looking for lodging,' he replied. At this the citizen took him and all the ship's

81. Of the wonders of God's providence and the rise of Pope Gregory 209

company to his own house and entertained them royally. While they were sitting at table, the lord Gregory asked his host: 'What city is this, and who is lord of this land?' 'My friend,' he replied, 'we had a king, a very powerful man, who died in the Holy Land and left no heir but his sister. A duke wanted to marry her, but she had no intention of being wedded, and he was so indignant at this that he forcibly annexed the whole kingdom except this one city.'

The knight then said: 'Can I safely tell you of a secret desire I have?'

'Yes, my lord,' he replied, 'quite safely.'

'I am a knight,' he told him. 'Please go to the palace tomorrow and tell the seneschal that if he pays me I will fight this year on the queen's behalf.'

The citizen replied: 'I have no doubt that he will be delighted that you have come here. Tomorrow I will go the palace and settle the matter.'

As soon as he got up next day he went to the seneschal and told him of the knight's arrival. The seneschal was overjoyed and sent a messenger to fetch the lord Gregory, and on his arrival he was presented to the queen and recommended to her in glowing terms. When she saw him, she looked at him closely, but was quite unaware that he was her son, who she thought had been abandoned at sea many years ago. So the seneschal, in the presence of the queen, engaged him to serve her for the whole year. Next day the lord Gregory prepared for battle; he commanded a large army in the field, and when he entered battle he forced his way through all the foe until he came face-to-face with the duke, and slew him there and then, cut off his head, and so won the victory.

Thereafter Gregory continued to prosper and his fame spread everywhere throughout the kingdom, and before the year was up he had wrested the whole kingdom from the hands of the enemy. So he went to the seneschal and said: 'Friend, you know how things stood when I found you, and how they stand now. So, please, pay me my wages, because I plan to go on to another kingdom.' 'Lord,' the seneschal replied, 'you have earned more than our agreement obliges us to pay you. I shall therefore go to the queen and settle the matter of your employment[4] and your payment.'

4 *de statu*: in the context *status* could refer to the state of the kingdom (the sense in which it has been used twice just before) rather than Gregory's position/employment.

So he went to the queen. 'My dear lady,' he said, 'I would like to say a few words that will be to your advantage. Because we were without a leader, we suffered all manner of troubles. So it would be good if you were to take a husband who could ensure our security in the future. Your kingdom has more than enough wealth, so I would not advise you to marry a man for his riches. In which case I do not know where you could find a husband more appropriate to your station or more acceptable to your people than the lord Gregory.'

Now the queen had formerly always replied: 'I vow to God that I will never marry again.' But she requested a day in which to deliberate before she replied to the seneschal's proposal. The day for her answer came, and before all her court she said: 'Since the lord Gregory has valiantly delivered us and our kingdom from the hands of the enemy, I will marry him.' At this announcement everyone was overjoyed. The queen appointed a day for the wedding, and with great jubilation and with the approval of the whole kingdom the two were joined in matrimony, the son to his own mother, though neither of them knew of their true relationship. They grew to love each other dearly.

But one day, when the lord Gregory went off hunting, the queen's maid told her: 'My dear lady, have you offended our lord in some way?'

'Not at all,' the queen replied. 'I don't believe that any two married people could be found in the whole world who love each other as my lord and I do. But tell me, my dear, why did you ask such a question?'

She said: 'Every day when the table is laid, our lord king goes off happily into his private chamber. But when he comes out, he is sighing and weeping; then he washes his face. But why he behaves like this, I have no idea.'

When she heard this, the queen entered the private chamber on her own, and there closely inspected every nook and cranny until she came to the hiding place of the tablets which Gregory read every day, and which told of how he was the child of a brother and sister. Then she wept bitterly, for these were the tablets that had been found in his cradle. When she discovered the tablets, she knew them at once, and opened them, and read her own handwriting. She thought: 'No-one could have come by the tablets but my son!' Then she cried aloud and said: 'Alas that I was ever born and came into the world! Would that my mother had died the day I was conceived!'

81. Of the wonders of God's providence and the rise of Pope Gregory

Hearing this sudden outcry in the palace the queen's guard and everyone else ran to her aid, and found her lying on the ground. They stood around her for a considerable time before they could get a word out of her, but finally she moved her lips and said: 'If you value my life, go at once and seek my lord!' The guard mounted their horses immediately and rode off to the king. 'Sire,' they told him, 'the queen is at death's door!' As soon as he heard this he abandoned his sport and hastened back to the castle and entered the room where the queen lay. When she saw him, she said: 'My lord, send everyone away. I want no-one else to hear what I have to say to you.' And when they had been dismissed, she said: 'Dearest, tell me, who were your parents?' 'That is a strange question,' he replied, 'but I can tell you this for certain, I am from a far-off country.' 'I vow to God,' she said, 'that if you do not tell me the truth, you[5] will shortly see me die!' 'I can only tell you that I was poor,' he replied. 'I had nothing but the arms with which I delivered you and the whole kingdom from slavery.'

'Just tell me what country you came from, and who your parents were, and if you do not tell me the truth, I shall never touch food again.' 'I will tell you the truth,' he said. 'I was brought up from my infancy by an abbot, and he often told me that he found me in my cradle in some cask, and from that time on he brought me up, until I came here to these parts.'

The queen then showed him the tablets. 'Do you recognize these tablets?' she asked him. As soon as he saw them, he fell to the ground, and she cried: 'My dearest child! You are my only son, my husband and my lord! You are my brother's son and mine! Ah, my sweetest son, it was I who placed you in the cask with these tablets after I bore you. Ah me, why did you draw me forth from my mother's womb, my Lord God, to commit so many deeds of wickedness? I knew my own brother, and gave you birth! Would I had died before anyone ever set eyes on me! Would I had never been born!' And she dashed her head against the wall, and cried out: 'O my Lord God, do you see? This is my son, my husband, the son of my brother!'

'I thought I had escaped this danger,' the lord Gregory said, 'but now I have fallen into the toils of the devil. My lady, give me leave to bemoan my misery. Ah woe is me, woe! My mother is my darling, my wife! So the devil has ensnared me!'

5 *video*: Oest.; *videbis*: K., L.

Seeing her son's great anguish, his mother told him: 'My dearest son, I will wander for the rest of my life to atone for our sins, while you shall rule the kingdom.'

'No, no!' he retorted. 'You shall remain here to rule, mother, and I will go wandering until our sins are forgiven by God.'

He got up that night, took his lance, put on the garb of a pilgrim and bade farewell to his mother. He walked barefoot until he reached the borders of the kingdom and then, in the darkness of night, came to a city where he found the house of a fisherman whom he asked for lodging for the love of God. The fisherman looked at him closely, and observing his handsome appearance and elegant figure, said: 'Friend, you are not a real pilgrim, that is quite clear from your physique.' 'I may not be a true pilgrim,' Gregory replied, 'but I beg you for lodging tonight for the love of God.'

When the fisherman's wife saw him she was moved to pity him, and begged her husband insistently to let him into the house. So he let him in, and had his bed made up behind the door. He gave him some fish with bread and water, and, among other things, told him: 'Pilgrim, if you would find holiness, you should go somewhere solitary.' 'Sir,' he replied, 'I would gladly do so, but I do not know such a place.' 'Tomorrow,' said the fisherman, 'come with me and I will take you to a place that is remote.' 'May God reward you!', said Gregory.

Next morning the fisherman woke the pilgrim, but was in a such a hurry that he caused him to leave his tablets behind the door. The fisherman and pilgrim together put out to sea and they sailed some sixteen miles before reaching a rock which was encircled at its foot with chains which could not be undone without a key. The fisherman undid the chains, threw the keys into the sea, and then returned home. The pilgrim remained there doing penance for seventeen years.

Then it chanced that the pope died. At the time of his death a voice came down from heaven saying: 'Search out the man of God named Gregory and appoint him as my successor.'

When the electors heard this they were overjoyed, and sent messengers out into different parts of the world to find him. At length certain of them spent the night in the fisherman's house, and while they were at supper they told the fisherman: 'Friend, we have been to great trouble searching through town and country for a holy man named Gregory whom we are to appoint as pontiff,

81. Of the wonders of God's providence and the rise of Pope Gregory

but we cannot find him.' Remembering the pilgrim, the fisherman replied: 'It is seventeen years now since a pilgrim stayed in this house, and I took him to a rock out at sea and left him there. But I am sure he died long ago.' It happened that on the same day he caught a great haul of fishes, and as he was gutting one of them, he found inside the key he had thrown into the sea seventeen years earlier. At once he shouted at the top of his voice: 'Friends, look, the key I threw into the sea! This gives me hope that your labours will not have been in vain.' At this the envoys were overjoyed, and when they got up next morning they asked the fisherman to take them to the rock, and he did so. When they got there and found Gregory, they said: 'Gregory, O man of God, in the name of Almighty God, come away with us, for it is his will that you be appointed his Vicar on earth.' Gregory replied: 'If it please him, God's will be done.'

So they took him off the rock, and as he approached Rome all the bells of the city rang of their own accord. When the citizens heard them they said: 'Blessed be the Most High, for the one who will be Christ's Vicar is coming!' They all went to meet him and received him with every honour, and appointed him Christ's Vicar. Once appointed pope, blessed Gregory conducted himself admirably in every respect, and the news that such a holy man had been appointed Christ's Vicar soon spread through the world. Many people came to him from all over the world to ask for his counsel and aid. And when his mother heard that such a holy man had been appointed Christ's Vicar, she thought to herself: 'Could I do anything better than to go to such a holy man and tell him of my life?' Completely unaware that he was her son and husband, she hastened to Rome and made her confession to Christ's Vicar. Before her confession neither knew the other, but when the pope had heard her confession, he remembered every detail about her, and said: 'My dearest mother, wife and friend, the devil thought to take us to hell, but by God's grace we have escaped him.'

At these words she fell at his feet and wept copious tears of joy, until the pope lifted her to her feet. He subsequently founded a monastery in her name, and made her its abbess, and a short while afterwards they both yielded up their souls to God.

Moralization. Dear friends, the emperor is our Lord Jesus Christ, who united his sister, i.e., the soul, with her brother, i.e., man, because we who are Christians are Christ's brothers, and the soul is his sister and

God's daughter; but inasmuch as the soul is united with man, the flesh is properly termed his sister.[6] In the beginning the flesh accords the soul every honour, while it does nothing against it that would displease God; in accordance with God's command it is obliged to be wedded to a noble husband, i.e., God, through works of mercy. These two, the body and soul, love each other so much that they lie in one chamber, that is, in one heart, in one mind, as long as they carry out God's commandments; and they eat from one dish, that is, they act with one will, after they have received baptism and renounced the devil's vanities. But alas, alas! At the instigation of the devil man often violates his sister, i.e., corrupts the soul with vices and evil desires so that she becomes pregnant and bears a son. This son represents the whole human race that issued from the first parent. Adam was the first-born son, whose inheritance was to be the kingdom of this world, as the Psalmist says:[7] 'Thou hast subjected all things under his feet etc.' Now among his commandments he had to treat God's daughter, his sister, i.e., soul, with all honour, but deceived by the devil he corrupted her when he ate of the apple, and then a son, i.e., the whole human race, sprang from him, and this son, with the complicity of the knight, i.e., the Holy Spirit, was put in a cask, i.e., thrown into the misery of the sea of this world, where he floated for a long time. The first father died and went down to hell, and the soul was left naked, so the duke, i.e., the devil, assailed her, until the Son of God, i.e., God and man, came and delivered not only his mother, but also the whole kingdom and humankind through his Passion, because he fought against the duke, i.e., the devil, and won the victory and regained for us the land we had lost, i.e., paradise. After this he espoused his mother, i.e., Holy Church, who had written on the tablets, i.e., the Ten Commandments which Moses received from God. We must consider them every day and imprint them on our hearts, and consider, read and understand Holy Scripture, where we shall find that the holy Job spoke to the earth and said:[8] 'Thou art my father' and to the worms, 'thou art my sister.' If we ponder that

---

6 *eius soror*: if the text is sound, the argument seems to be: the soul is Christ's sister, and is wedded to her brother, man, and since she is one with him, the flesh can be called Christ's sister. (*Le Violier*, as often, is much simpler: 'Cest empereur est Nostre Seigneur Jesuchrist, qui a sa seur l'âme fort aimée quant à ce qu'elle est en la chair conjoincte; la chair proprement est dicte sa seur.')
7 Ps 8.8.
8 Cf. Jb 17.14.

81. Of the wonders of God's providence and the rise of Pope Gregory 215

deeply, we have reason enough to weep. But we must ask: who drew us from the cask etc.? It was of course the abbot, i.e., God himself, who through his only-begotten son daily draws us by his grace from the misery of sin and gives us to a fisherman to be fed. The fisherman is any prelate, who has to feed the sinner with good works and help him to join the army of Christ; then he will be able to live among monks, i.e., holy men, and be holy, as the Psalmist says:[9] *'With the holy, thou wilt be holy etc.'; and then to depart upon the ship of the church, i.e., obeying its commandments, and fight manfully against the devil and in consequence attain to great riches. These riches are the virtues by which man's soul is enriched, and he is received in the house of the citizen, i.e., prelate, and the prelate takes him to the seneschal, i.e., to a discerning confessor, by whom he is guided to the way of salvation. By what means? He fights for the lady, i.e., the soul. But it often happens that man falls back into sin and goes out hunting, i.e., for worldly vanities; the lady, i.e., the soul, grieves when it recalls the writing on the tablets, i.e., the sins it has committed, and so the knights, i.e., all the senses, are obliged to call him away from worldly sport; indeed God calls him, saying:*[10] *'Return, return etc.' But when man sees the soul laid low by sin, he must throw himself to the ground, that is, prepare to embrace all humility, strip off his garments, i.e., vices, and break the lance of his evil life by confession, and as he journeys he must continue in all the virtues until he comes to the house of the fisherman, i.e., the prelate. On his advice you*[11] *must be imprisoned on the rock of penance, until, when you have completed your penance, messengers, i.e., men of the church, take you to the city of Rome. This city is holy Mother Church, in which you must remain, i.e., fulfil its commands, and then the bells will be rung, i.e., give glorious testimony to you for your works of mercy restored through penance, and the citizens will rejoice, i.e., God's angels will rejoice over the sinner, as is written in Luke:*[12] *'There is joy before the angels of God upon one sinner that doth penance.' And then you will be able to conduct the lady, i.e., soul, to the monastery of the kingdom of heaven, to which etc.*

9 Ps 17.26.
10 Sg 6.12.
11 The subject changes here from the third to the second person, with one lapse, which I have ventured to correct.
12 Cf. Lk 15.7, 10.

82. Of the judgement of adulterers[1]

There was a knight who had a very fine castle on whose roof a pair of storks built their nest. Below the castle was a clear spring in which the storks used to bathe. It chanced that the female produced chicks, and the male would fly about the country to gather food for the chicks. In his absence the female was unfaithful to him, but before her mate returned she went down to the spring in case he smelled the stench of adultery on her. Now the knight saw this happen on many occasions, and was puzzled, and he closed up the spring so the female could not wash or bathe in it; and when, after another act of infidelity she saw that the spring was closed off, and she was unable to wash herself, she returned to her nest. On his return her mate smelt the stench of adultery on her and flew off; then, within the space of a day he brought back with him a great flock of storks, and together they killed the female in the presence of the knight.

Moralization. Dear friends, the two storks are Christ and the soul; the soul is Christ's spouse, and whenever through sin she commits adultery, she should have recourse to the spring of confession so that she can be cleansed, lest Christ her spouse should smell the stench of adultery. The knight who closes off the spring is the devil, who hardens man's heart, and is always striving to stop man hurrying to the spring of confession and making his confession. So if on the Day of Judgement Christ finds you have not washed, i.e., made confession, he will without doubt come against you with a multitude of angels and put you to death for all eternity.

[1] Cf. Herrtage, Text II.XXVIII.

83. Of the meticulous safeguarding of the soul[1]

The emperor Trajan had a special love of gardens, and after laying one out and planting all kinds of trees in it, he appointed a keeper and instructed him to watch over it carefully. But a wild boar got into the garden and rooted up the trees and overturned them. Seeing what it had done, the keeper, whose name was Jonathan, cut off its left ear, at which the boar gave a cry and went off. But the boar got into the garden a second time and caused untold damage, so Jonathan cut off its right ear, and with a great yell the boar went away. Nonetheless it got in a third time, whereupon Jonathan cut off its tail, and with a shriek it made off in ignominy. But despite this it got in a fourth time and did a great deal of damage. So Jonathan ran it through with a lance and when it was dead he delivered it to the cook to be prepared for the emperor's table. Now the emperor loved the heart of an animal more than any other part. But when the cook was preparing the boar and saw its heart was a plump one, he ate it himself. When the boar was served up to the emperor he inquired after the heart, and his servants went back to the cook and asked for the boar's heart. 'Tell my lord,' he replied, 'that the boar had no heart, and if he doesn't believe me, I undertake to prove it with a variety of arguments.'

The emperor's servants reported this to the emperor, word for word, and he said: 'What is this I hear? There is no animal without a heart. But since he offers to prove what he claims, we shall hear him.' So the cook was summoned to give the emperor proof that the boar had no heart.

'My lord,' he said,' listen to me. All thought proceeds from the heart, so it clearly follows that where there is no thought, there is no

[1] Cf. Herrtage, Text I.XXXVII.

heart. The boar, firstly, entered the garden and did a lot of damage, and when I[2] saw this I cut off his left ear. If he had had a heart, he would have thought about the loss of his ear, but he did not do so, because he entered the garden a second time; therefore he had no heart. Also, if he had had a heart, when I cut off his right ear he would have reflected on this, but he did not think about losing his right ear, because he came in again and lost his tail. So if he had had the tiniest bit of heart he would have thought about losing his ears and tail, but he did not, because after all this he came in yet again. So I killed him. And these three arguments are proof that he had no heart.'

When the emperor heard this, he accepted his reasoning, and so the cook escaped punishment.

Dear friends, the king is our Lord Jesus Christ, who has an especial love of gardens and vineyards, i.e., men of goodly estate, such as devout clerics and good Christians, in whose hearts our Lord daily plants different kinds of trees, i.e., virtues, for example the Ten Commandments, the seven works of mercy,[3] the four cardinal virtues[4] and the three theological virtues;[5] and their keeper is the prelate, who has to keep watch over them. The boar is the rich and powerful worldly man who trusts in his own feelings rather than another man's. He ruins the estate he received at baptism, and does untold damage, when he commits mortal sin, because he mars the virtues that he received at baptism. Seeing this, God, by means of Jonathan, i.e., death, cuts off your left ear, i.e., kills some relative of yours, that thereby you may amend your wicked life. But wretched man grieves for a time and soon returns to his vomit and disobeys God's commandments again. Seeing this, God cuts off man's right ear, i.e., kills your son or daughter, that thereby you may amend your ways. But wretched man mourns their death for a short time and returns to his evil works. And then God cuts off his tail, i.e., his wife, that chastened by this he may mend his ways. And when such punishments do not cause him to mend his ways, God then kills him and hands him to the cook, i.e., the devil, on the Day

---

2 There is confusion here between the cook and the keeper.
3 Converting the sinner, instructing the ignorant, counselling the doubtful, comforting the sorrowful, bearing wrongs patiently, forgiving injuries, and praying for the living and the dead.
4 Prudence, temperance, fortitude and justice.
5 Faith, hope and charity.

of Judgement. There is nothing in man that God loves more than his heart, i.e., soul. Then the devil will charge the man with having a soul that was not obedient to God, and he will say to Christ: 'This man was obedient to me and disobedient to you. If he had had a righteous soul he would never have broken your commandment.' And so God will be deprived of his soul, which would be lamentable. Let us strive etc.

84. Of the need for continual remembrance of God's goodness

When Pompey was king there lived in his kingdom a lady who was extraordinarily beautiful and loved by all. In her neighbourhood there lived a well-favoured and noble knight who often visited this lady and was dearly loved by her. One day when he visited her he saw a falcon on her wrist, which he passionately desired to possess.

'Good lady,' he said, 'if I have ever served you well, and if you love me, give me that falcon.'

'I will,' said the lady, 'but on one condition: that you do not give it so much of your affection that you deprive me of your company.'

The knight replied: 'Heaven forbid that I should let anything part me from you! And now I must love you even more than before.'

So the lady gave him the falcon, and he bade her farewell, but took such delight in the bird that he did not visit her and thought little about her as day after day he hunted with the falcon. She sent him messages repeatedly, but he did not come to her. Finally she wrote telling him to come to her with the falcon without delay, and this he did. When he arrived the lady said to him: 'Show me the falcon.' And as soon as she had hold of it, she tore its head from its body as the knight looked on.

The knight was horrified. 'My lady,' he cried, 'what have you done?'

'Don't upset yourself,' she told him. 'Be glad, be happy. The falcon was the reason for your not visiting me as you did formerly. So I killed it so that you might come and see me again as often as you used.'

And realizing that her motive had been just, the knight was content and visited her as he had done before.

Moralization. Dear friends, the king is our Heavenly Father, and the beautiful lady is our human nature joined to the deity in Christ. The knight is any Christian, who is bound to love his Lord God above all things, and to visit him often through works of merit. The falcon represents the temporal goods that God gives to man to make trial of him; but when wretched man becomes wealthy, he becomes like the beasts of the field, because he does not remember God's goodness to him, and does not visit Him as he used to do. In view of this God removes these temporal blessings from man, his health and prosperity, so that he may love Him as before; not that God hates the one he chastises in this way, but because He loves him. As Scripture says:[1] 'God chastiseth every man whom he loves.'

[1] Cf. Heb 12.6.

85. Our prayer is like sweet music before God[1]

The emperor Tiberius was extraordinarily fond of music, and it once happened when he went hunting that he heard the sound of a harp to his right, and he was so enchanted by its sweetness that he fell into a rapture, and turning his horse about rode towards the place from which the sound was coming. When he got there, he saw in the distance a broad stretch of water, and on the bank a poor man was sitting with a harp in his hands.

'Tell me, my friend,' the emperor said, 'how you make your harp sound so sweet.'

'Sire,' he replied, 'for thirty years and more I have sat at the waterside here, and God has given me such a gift for playing the harp that as soon as I touch the strings, a melody comes from them so sweet that the fishes come up to my hand; and this is how I support myself and my wife and family. But alas, woe is me!, some whistler has come here in the last few days from somewhere, and he whistles so sweetly that the fish are abandoning me and going to him. So, sire, as you are powerful because you are lord of the whole empire, give me your help to combat this whistler.'

'Friend,' the emperor said, 'I can help you in only one way, and that must suffice you. In my saddlebag I have a golden hook. I will give it to you. Tie it to the top of a rod and then touch the strings of your harp. As soon as you play, the fishes will be enchanted and you can quickly draw them to land by means of the hook. If you do this, the whistler will leave the place in confusion.'

The poor man did all he had been told, and before the fish could get to the whistler, he pulled them to the land with the hook. And when the whistler observed this, he left the place in confusion.

1 Cf. Herrtage, Text I.XXXV

85. Our prayer is like sweet music before God

Dear friends, the emperor is our Lord Jesus Christ, who loves sweet music, i.e., holy prayer, when he hears it, and he goes hunting for certain animals of his, i.e., souls, which the devil was attempting to carry off. The water in which the fishes are is this world, which is full of sinners. The poor man at the water's edge is the preacher, who has a lyre, i.e., Holy Scripture, with which he has to lure the fish, i.e., sinners, to dry land, i.e., to the heavenly kingdom. The Psalmist says:[2] '[Praise him] with timbrel and choir etc.' But alas, alas!, these days, when the preacher begins to touch the lyre of Holy Scripture and to preach, a whistler promptly comes along, i.e., the devil, who whistles so sweetly as the preacher is preaching that men are reluctant to listen to the preaching. And note that the devil has different kinds of whistling: with the first, he makes some people sleep to prevent them from hearing the word of God; with the second, if he cannot entice them to sleep he makes them talkative; and those he cannot make talkative, he causes to leave the place, or to understand nothing the preacher is saying. It is therefore necessary for the preacher to seek the hook of divine grace, with which he will be able to draw sinners to God, and that this may be so, at the beginning of a sermon preachers always ask for God's grace.

---

2 Ps 150.4.

86. God has compassion on sinners who beg for divine mercy[1]

There was an emperor who passed a law that if a woman were guilty of adultery she should be imprisoned for life. Now it happened that a knight married a noble woman whom he loved dearly, and when he went off on his travels to distant lands she committed adultery and as a result conceived a child. She was charged with adultery and lawfully convicted, and in accordance with the emperor's law she was sent to prison. While in prison she gave birth to a beautiful boy. As the boy grew up he was beloved by all who set eyes on him, while his mother groaned and sighed continually and was inconsolable. It chanced one day that, seeing his mother weeping, the boy said to her: 'Dearest mother, why are you so unhappy?' 'My darling son,' she replied, 'I have much to weep about. Above our heads people can move about freely, and the sun shines brightly; but here we are in the darkness and have no light.' 'Dearest mother,' her son said, 'I have never seen that light which you say shines above our heads, because I was born in this prison. As long as I have enough food and drink I am content to stay here all my life.'

Now while they were having this conversation the emperor was standing with his guards by the door of the prison, and one of the guards said to him: 'Sire, do you hear the pitiful things that mother and her son are saying?' 'I do,' he replied. 'I can hear them quite clearly and I pity them.' 'Sire,' the soldier said, 'we beg you, have mercy on them and show your compassion.' 'Your prayers are granted,' the emperor told them. And they released them from prison and absolved them from further punishment.

1 Cf. Herrtage, Text I.V.

86. God has compassion on sinners who beg for divine mercy

Dear friends, the emperor is our Heavenly Father, who passed a law that if a woman, i.e., a soul, under a husband's, i.e., Christ's, authority, through mortal sin commits adultery, she shall be condemned for ever to the prison of hell. The lady wept bitterly in prison. Why? Because of course she had defiled her soul, lost the everlasting kingdom, degraded Holy Church and stripped herself of the virtues she had received at baptism. The boy who said: 'As long as I have food, I am happy to stay here', represents the powerful and rich of this world, who say that if God gave them the world and all the delights of the flesh they desired, they would never long for the light of heaven. We must really grieve for such people. The soldier who stood near the door represents the good prelate, who must pray to God from the bottom of his heart on behalf of sinners that He may give them grace to rise from the prison of sin, so that they can enter into life everlasting. Which etc.

87. Christ gave himself up to death for us[1]

In the course of a murderous battle an emperor became exposed to danger and was on the point of death when a knight, seeing him, placed himself between the emperor and his foe, so that the emperor escaped without being wounded. But the knight received multiple wounds in defending him and needed lengthy treatment before he recovered. The scars, however, remained with him for ever and he was commended by all for fighting with such distinction for his master.

It happened subsequently that this knight was in danger of being cheated out of his inheritance, so he went to the emperor and asked him to help him and pass sentence in his favour.

'My friend,' said the emperor, 'I cannot attend to you at present, but I will appoint a judge who will investigate your case and do what is just.'

'Sire,' the knight said, 'how can you speak like this?' And at once, before the whole court, he tore away his clothes until his naked flesh was revealed, and showed him the scars of his wounds. 'Look!' he said, 'This is what I suffered for your sake, and you will not help me and pass sentence in my favour? Is it just, after all I suffered for you, that anyone other than yourself should be my judge and advocate?'

When the emperor heard this he replied: 'Dear friend, you are right. When I was in danger of death it was you and no-one else who saved me.' And the emperor at once presided at the tribunal and passed judgement in the knight's favour.

1 Cf. Herrtage, Text I.XIII.

87. Christ gave himself up to death for us

Moralization. Dear friends, Christ interposed himself in mortal battle between you and the devil himself, and sustained mortal wounds for you, and not only wounds, for he died a most ignominious death. Is it therefore just that anyone but you should undergo punishment and penance for his love? Indeed not. If two brothers are heirs to an inheritance, and have by some chance lost that inheritance, and one of them fights to regain the inheritance, and the other makes no effort, but wants to have it without any work at all, would this be just? Certainly not. This is how it is with you and Christ. Through sin we lost our inheritance of the celestial kingdom, and Christ won it by his death. So it is not just that anyone should win your right to this by acting on your behalf: rather you must do it yourself, if you desire to gain the everlasting kingdom. Which etc.

88. Of the devil's cunning, which leads many to their death[1]

The story is told of a certain prince who, being unable with all his forces to defeat his enemy, devised the following trick: he pretended to flee and abandoned his camp with all its provisions to the foe. Now in this camp he had left casks full of wine poisoned with the seed of a certain herb, and anyone who drank this wine at once fell asleep. He knew that the enemy were greedy and also famished; and when they came upon the wine they were overjoyed and drank all they wanted, then immediately passed out and were compelled to sleep. The prince then returned, and finding them in this state slew them all, just as he pleased.[2]

Dear friends, the devil employs this trick against many people he sees he cannot overcome: he pretends to flee and to be far away, while he allows them to sit at length in taverns in the hope of pleasant friendship and relaxation, so that when they are drunk he can lead them where he wants, now to murder, now to wantonness etc. Let us therefore beware of such a draught if we wish to come to life eternal. To which etc.

---

1 Other versions of the story are listed by Oesterley, p. 723; Tubach, no. 4336; Hope, pp. 531–2.
2 Cf. the stratagem of Croesus, Herodotus I.207.

89. Of the threefold state of the world

There was a knight with three sons who, on the point of death, bequeathed his inheritance to his first-born, his treasury to his second son, and to the third a precious ring which was worth more than everything he had left to the other two. He also gave rings to the older two sons; these were not precious rings, but they all looked the same.

After their father died the first son said: 'I have my father's most precious ring.' The second son said: 'No you don't. I have it.' The third said: 'It isn't right that you two should have it, because the oldest son has the inheritance, the second oldest his treasure. Therefore reason dictates that I should have his most precious ring.'

The first son replied: 'Let us put it to the test, and see which ring is most precious, and is superior to the others.'

'All right,' he said.

Without delay a number of people were brought in with a variety of infirmities, and the first two rings had no effect, but the youngest son's ring cured them all.[1]

Dear friends, the knight is our Lord Jesus Christ, who had three sons: the Jews, the Saracens and the Christians. To the Jews he gave the promised land, to the Saracens he gave the treasure of this world, in terms of power and riches, and to the Christians he gave a precious ring, namely faith, because through faith Christians can heal many infirmities and sicknesses of the soul, as is it written:[2] 'All things are

---

[1] Cf. the version of this story told at *Decameron*, Day 1, nov. 3. See also Oesterley, p. 724; Tubach, nos 2153, 4106; Hope, pp. 548–9.

[2] Mk 9.22.

possible to him that believeth.' Likewise:[3] *'If you have faith as a grain of mustard-seed etc.' Likewise:*[4] *'Without faith it is impossible to please God.'*

---

3 Mt 17.19; cf. Lk 17.6.
4 Heb 11.6.

90. Of freedom of choice[1]

There was once a kingdom which had a law that the older brother should divide up the inheritance, and the younger should choose his portion. The reason behind this was that it requires greater discernment to make the division than to choose one's portion, and the older son ought to be the wiser. There was also another law allowing a son born of a serving woman the same right of inheritance as freeborn sons.

Now it happened that an estate had to be divided between two brothers, one born of a maidservant and one born of a free woman, and the older brother divided it in the following way: he made one portion the entire inheritance, and the other portion his brother's mother. His brother thought: 'I ought to love my mother more than anything else.' Consequently he chose his mother, and forewent his inheritance, hoping to gain something through his brother's generosity. But he obtained nothing from him, so he went to the judge and accused his brother of denying him his inheritance. His brother answered this charge by saying that he had not deceived him, because it is the one who chooses, not the one who makes the division, who is assured of his portion.

Dear friends, God the Father had two sons, one by a maidservant, the other by a free woman; by the free woman he had Christ, who is of the same substance as the Father, and coeternal with Him; and by the maidservant he had man, because his body is composed of earth, and he is lesser, because created in time. Christ, the older son, divided the inheritance. How? Why, he put his mother, i.e., the earth and earthly things on one side, and on the other he put the heaven and heavenly

---

1 See Seneca, *Controversiae* VI.3.

things. He then gave the choice to man, which meant that if he chose his mother, i.e., the earth, he would forfeit his heavenly inheritance. And indeed by committing a mortal sin he spurned his heavenly inheritance and chose his mother, and he could not blame Christ, since the outcome lay not with the divider, but with the one who had the choice. So it is clear that anyone who prefers earthly pleasures and is living in mortal sin cannot claim eternal life either by grace or by right, or presume on his inheritance, except perhaps through some act of piety.[2] My counsel is therefore that we should not choose our mother, i.e., this world, because 'the whole world is seated in wickedness.'[3] Let us therefore strive to choose the heavenly inheritance.

---

2 An act of compassion on the part of the older brother, i.e. Christ.
3 1 Jn 5.19.

91. Of sloth and idleness[1]

King Polemius is said to have had three sons whom he loved dearly, so when he wished to dispose of his kingdom, he called all three of them and told them: 'Whichever of you is the laziest shall have my kingdom after I die.'

The oldest son then said: 'Father, your kingdom must therefore be mine, because I am so lazy that I sit by the fire and let my legs burn rather than move them out of the way.'

His second son said: 'Father, your kingdom must be mine. If I had a rope round my neck and a sword in my hand and was about to be hanged, I am so lazy I wouldn't reach out to cut the rope.'

The third son said: 'Father, I should be king, because I am lazier than either of them. While I am lying upstairs on my bed and drops of water fall on my face and on both of my eyes, I am so lazy that I cannot, and will not, move my head to right or left.'

When the king heard this, he bequeathed his kingdom to his third son, considering him the laziest of all.

Moralization. Dear friends, the king is the devil, who is king and father over all the children of pride, as Job says.[2] The first son is a good illustration of those who form evil unions, i.e., in adultery and fornication, which lead them to perdition. But they choose rather to be consumed or burnt in the fire of sin than to be sundered from these corrupt associa-

---

1 Cf. Herrtage, Text I.LVI, and Aesop's tale *The Father and his Three Children*. For cognate versions, see Gerd Dicke and Klaus Grubmüller, *Die Fabeln des Mittelalters und der frühen Neuzeit. Ein Katalog der deutschen Versionen und ihrer lateinischen Entsprechungen*, Münstersche Mittelalter-Schriften, 60, Munich: Fink, 1987, no. 281; also Oesterley, p. 724; Tubach, no. 372; Hope, pp. 540–1.
2 Jb 41.25.

tions. The second son signifies the man who, though he sees that he is encircled and bound in the fetters of his sins, by which he is soon to be hanged on the gibbet of hell, does not reach out to break them asunder, i.e., by using the sword of his tongue in confession. The third son represents the man who hears the doctrine of the joys of paradise and the punishments of hell, yet in his excessive indolence considers his condition, i.e., his sins, unimportant, and in his desire and lust for rewards does not forsake it to turn to the right or to the left, in order to abandon sin, if only through fear and terror of the torments of hell.

92. Christ chose to die that we might live

The story is told of a certain king who had a wife named Cornelia. It happened one day that under a wall in the king's castle two serpents were discovered, one male, one female. Hearing of this discovery the king asked his scholars and doctors what it signified, and they told him that the fact that the serpents were hiding there was a portent of the death of some man or woman. 'If the male serpent were killed,' they said, 'a man would die, and if the female, a woman.' Thereupon the king declared: 'Kill the male snake and let the female live.' He said he would rather die himself than have his wife die, and he explained why: 'If my wife lives,' he said, 'she might bear many sons who could succeed to my throne. But if she dies, the kingdom would have no heir.'[1]

Dear friends, the king is our Lord Jesus Christ, who rules us as king, and his wife is human nature, with which he was united in the Virgin's womb. But in this world, as in the house of this king, two serpents were discovered, namely those of the Old Law and the New. The female serpent was the kindness of divine mercy. The wife, i.e., human nature, could not have lived in God's favour,[2] but her spouse, i.e., Christ, chose death upon the cross that human nature might live. One can also interpret the serpents as flesh and spirit; thus the flesh, being male and unfruitful, must be slain.

1 The story is told of the father of the Gracchi at *F.D.M.* IV.VI.1; Pliny, *N.H.* VII.36. Other versions are listed by Oesterley, pp. 726–7, and Tubach, no. 4282.
2 *per gratiam*: Oest., K., L. If a *nisi* has dropped out ('except through grace') this would make better sense. *Per gratiam* regularly means 'by the grace of God,' i.e., by supernatural intervention. Human nature could not of itself have survived, had not the king/Christ sacrificed himself. But *per* is capable of a large variety of meanings in medieval Latin and it is possible that the text is sound.

93. Of the inheritance and the joy of a faithful soul

A powerful lord sent his two sons away to study so that they might work hard and gain the knowledge which would enable them to earn a living. After a short while he sent his sons a letter telling them to return home and they obediently went back to their native land. One of the brothers was very happy at returning home, and when he got back he was greeted with joy and appointed as heir. But the other brother was extremely annoyed at having to return. When he arrived back, his mother went to meet him and kissed him, and while she was doing so she bit off his lips; then his sister, following her mother, went to kiss him and bit off his nose; then his brother put out his eyes; and his father came up, seized him by his hair and tore off his skin.

Dear friends, the rich man is God, who sent his two sons, i.e., the body and soul, to study in the schools of this world and grow in good works, and so possess eternal life, i.e., their inheritance. The letter is death. This letter is despatched when man is dying. The [first brother], the soul, returns in joy to God and is welcomed with rejoicing and established in his inheritance. The second brother, who returns unwillingly, is the body; he is troubled at having to go back, and no wonder, because he is given a most wretched welcome. The sister and brothers who gnaw off his nose and eyes are toads and serpents. The father is the corruption of the earth, which consumes the hair and skin and flesh. Of his parents Job says:[1] *'I have said to rottenness, thou art my father, and to worms, my mother and my sister.' Let us therefore beseech our Lord etc.*

1 Jb 17.14.

94. The beautiful soul, once infected with the leprosy of sin, cannot regain its former beauty except through the deepest sighs and sorrows

There was a king who wished to travel to distant parts; but he had an only daughter, a girl whose beauty was more radiant than the sun, and he did not know to whom he might entrust her with confidence, so he kept her under close guard. Finally, however, he entrusted her to his private secretary, a knight whom he loved dearly, with orders to watch over her and keep her from going to a certain spring which rose in that part of the country. For if she drank from it, she would become a leper, because although its waters were deliciously sweet, this was the effect they had. So in order to give her back to her father when he returned from his travels as lovely as when he had received her, the knight kept the closest watch over her, reflecting that if he did not, he would then be certain to lose his position, and could not even dare to wait for the king's return. For some time he kept close guard over the girl, but at length she found her way to the spring in secret, drank of its water and was infected with leprosy.

When the knight realized what had happened he was horrified, and taking her with him fled into the desert. There he came upon a hermit's cell and knocked at the entrance. Finding a hermit inside, he told him the whole story, and the hermit gave him sound advice. 'Go to the mountain I will show you,' he said. 'There you will find a stone and near it a special stick. Beat the stone hard with the stick, beat it sharply and boldly until it becomes moist and you get a liquid from it. Anoint the girl with that liquid; smear it all over her and she will be healed and restored to her former beauty.'

The knight did as the hermit had told him and the king's daughter recovered both her health and her beauty.

Moralization. Dear friends, the king is our Lord Jesus Christ, who 'went abroad' because he wished to render to his Father what he had received from his Mother, the most pure Virgin Mary, namely, true humanity. And he will return on the Day of Judgement. His only daughter signifies our soul, which will be ten times brighter than the sun before it comes to eternal life. The knight is any sinner who embraces all the delights of this world, that is, sins which to him are sweet. The daughter became a leper, i.e., full of sin. Leaving the region signifies the sinner leaving all that is worldly and transitory. The hermit's cell is the Church, and the hermit a priest, and finding him there the sinner tells him the whole story, making a holy confession; and the priest gives him counsel and enjoins a penance on him. The mountain is the sinner's own body; the stone is his stony heart; the stick is heavy penance, i.e., the chastisement of his body by prayers, almsgiving and fasting; the moisture and liquid are the tears he will weep and his heartfelt contrition on the Day of Judgement. The only daughter is the soul, restored whole, in all its beauty and grace to its Creator etc.

95. Christ restored our inheritance of the heavenly kingdom

We read in the annals of Rome that there was a tyrant named Maxentius who wished to deprive the Roman citizens of their inheritances. Forced to leave Rome by the tyrant's ruthlessness, they fled to King Constantius of Britain. At length, when many had flocked there, they stirred Constantius up against the tyrant. 'King Constantius,' they cried, 'restore us to our kingdom!' Moved by their pleas, King Constantius armed himself, mounted his horse and overthrew the tyrant, and so gave the Romans back their inheritance.

Moralization. Dear friends, the tyrant is the devil, who was excessively cruel to humankind, in that he robbed the human race of its heavenly inheritance. In view of this humankind fled to King Constantine, i.e., to God, seeking his help; as the Psalmist says:[1] *'Take hold of arms and shield and rise up to help me'; for 'it is thou that wilt restore my inheritance to me'. God, the king, was moved by these words and armed himself, combining his divinity with human nature, and climbed upon his horse when he chose to be hung upon the cross, and so he laid the tyrant low and restored our inheritance to us.*

1 Ps 34.2; 15.5.

96. The present life is a life of pardon and grace

King Alexander placed a burning candle in his hall and sent heralds throughout his kingdom who proclaimed that anyone who had committed an offence against the king should come boldly forward, and as long as the candle was burning, the king would pardon the offence. But if anyone who had committed an offence did not come forward, as soon as the candle had burnt out he would die an evil death.

When they heard this proclamation, many people in the kingdom came to the king and begged his pardon, and the king received them kindly. But there were many who were unwilling to come and neglected to do so, and when the candle had burnt out the king had them forcibly brought to him and put to an evil death.[1]

Moralization. By King Alexander we are to understand Christ, who is King of Kings and Lord of Lords. He set up a burning candle, i.e., the present life, which passes like a burning candle. The heralds he sent out are preachers, who daily proclaim that if anyone sins against the king, i.e., Christ, he should come forth boldly as long as the candle is burning, that is, as long as the present life lasts, because Christ is exceedingly merciful. Hence David says:[2] 'His tender mercies are over all his works,' as is shown in his treatment of the robber etc. Now some hear this and come to the king and beg his mercy; these are those who abandon their sins, keep God's commandments and live like good Christians. These he receives kindly; and those who refuse to come we may take as bad Christians, i.e., robbers, usurers and other sinners. When the candle is extinguished, i.e., after this life, Christ will make them come before him on the Day of Judgement and die an evil death, i.e., suffer eternal death, when he says to them:[3] 'Go, you cursed, into everlasting fire.'

1 Cf. the similar tale, no. 98.
2 Ps 144.9.
3 Cf. Mt 25.41.

97. Of death

We read in the chronicles that twenty-two years after the foundation of the city, the Roman people set up a marble column in their forum, and placed on it an image of Julius Caesar.[1] On the head they inscribed the name of Julius because it had been erected in his honour. This same Julius Caesar had three warnings of his coming death, either at the time or before it. One hundred days before his death lightning fell on his image in the forum and obliterated the first letter of his name written there. And in the night before the day he died the windows of his bedroom flew open with such a violent crash that he thought the house was about to collapse. And on the very day of his death, as he was on his way to the Capitol, a letter was handed him informing him of his imminent death; and if he had read it straight away, he would have escaped death.

Moralization. Dear friends, this is how it is with us and God. In order that we may escape eternal death, God gives us three warning signs. The first is the obliteration of the first letter of our name. This letter which stands at the beginning of a name signifies abundance of wealth. For it is this that causes man to have a name in the world: no-one these days has a name unless he has wealth. This is clearly the case, for if anyone asks who is the greatest man in a town or city, the one who has most wealth is at once given pre-eminence, even if he is worthless. And this is how wealth gives man a name, because if he were not rich, his name would not have been mentioned. And because sometimes riches are the cause of eternal death, God gives man the first warning, because he wants to save such a person, and so he deprives him of the first letter of his name, i.e., riches, and makes him poor, so that he who

---

1 An astonishing anachronism, even by the standards of the *Gesta*. Traditionally, Rome was thought to have been founded in 753 BC.

had turned from him through wealth, should come to him again through poverty. The second sign Julius Caesar received was a loud din outside his bedchamber. This chamber is the human body. When man considers that he is handsome and strong, he at once falls into sin, for which eternal death is reserved for him; so God, wishing to rescue him from eternal death, sends a warning sign, i.e., a loud din assails his person, that is, He visits him with such severe sickness and infirmity that he thinks he is collapsing and dying, so that in this way those who had turned from God because of their beauty and strength might be rescued and repent because of sickness and infirmity. The Psalmist says:[2] *'Their infirmities were multiplied.' Saint Paul is an example:*[3] *'I will glory in my infirmities.' The third sign Julius Caesar received, was that he was handed a letter concerning his imminent judgement, and if he had read the letter, he would have escaped death. This is a sign God sends us sinners, who can be said to 'hand us a letter' concerning our death sentence when a healthy grace adorns our consciences,*[4] *that we may read of the sins by which we have merited everlasting death. And so, while we have the light and grace of the Holy Spirit, let us read that letter, i.e., recollect our sins willingly, and then verbally confess them to a priest, that by reading it in this way we may be able to escape eternal death, lest the unopened letter, i.e., our unclean consciences, may be opened after our death and made known to the whole world.*

---

2 Ps 15.4.
3 2 Cor 12.9.
4 *Le Violier* defines the letter as '*ce sont les bonnes inspirations et illustrations de nos consciences*'.

98. God can be conciliated in this life

We read that the ancient Romans had a custom that when they were besieging a fortress or a city, they would light a candle of a certain length, and as long as it kept burning, they were ready to make peace with the enemy, however great his offence had been. But once the candle burned out, they visited the enemy with the full force of justice, and refused to have mercy on anyone, even he were willing to surrender all his possessions.

Dear friends, this is how God treats sinners; for our hearts, the cities of our souls, are beset by vices and desires through the devil, the world and the flesh. In his mercy God appointed a time for men in which, if they wished, they could find the lighted candle, i.e., as long as life remained in their body, and, however great their sins, they could find mercy and be at peace and harmony with God. The whole of our life is allotted and granted to us that we may do penance and live; for the Saviour says:[1] 'I desire not the death of the wicked etc.' And as long as our soul remains in our body, let us ask for pardon and mercy and we shall obtain it. John 16:[2] 'Ask, and you shall receive.' Indeed, when our life ends in death, then will not be the time to ask for mercy, and even if we ask for it, it will not be given us. Let us therefore do penance while we are in this life.

---

1 Ez 33.11.
2 Jn 16.24.

99. Of Christ's valiant battle and his victory[1]

In the reign of Caesar there lived in his kingdom a noble and valiant knight who one day was riding through a forest when he saw a toad fighting a snake, and the toad prevailed and defeated the serpent. Observing this the knight went to the serpent's aid and dealt the toad such a serious wound that it turned and fled. But the knight received a nasty wound from the toad, and because of this he got down from his horse; but the toad's poison remained in his wound. He hurried home and was laid up with this wound for so long that he made his will and prepared for death. One day as he lay near his fire, all but despairing of his life, the snake he had rescued entered the room. When his servants saw it, they said: 'My lord, a snake has got in!' But when the knight saw it, he recognized it as the snake he had defended, and for whose sake he had been wounded and suffered so much. 'Leave it alone,' he told them. 'I don't think it will harm me.'

And as they watched, the snake went towards him and sucked the poison from the wound until its mouth was full of it. Then it sped outside and spat the poison from its mouth, then returned and made straight for the wound a second time, and a third, until it had drained all the poison. After this the knight gave the snake milk to drink, but no sooner had it drunk it than the toad which had wounded the knight came in and began to attack it, as if in revenge because the snake had healed the knight. Seeing this, the knight said to his servants: 'Friends, this is without doubt the toad I wounded while I was defending this snake and which has been the cause of all my pain. If it overcomes the snake it will attack me, so if you value my life, kill it this instant.'

1 Cf. Herrtage, Text I.II.

99. Of Christ's valiant battle and his victory   245

At these words the servants took swords and clubs and slew the toad, and the snake, as if to applaud him and thank him, entwined itself this way and that about his master's feet, before finally leaving. And the knight made a perfect recovery.

Dear friends, the emperor is our Heavenly Father; the knight is our Lord Jesus Christ; the toad is the devil; the serpent is man, and this is for two reasons: a serpent can symbolize man first, because of the venom of sin, and the antidote and image of Christ he bears. For man must fight against the devil, because: 'There is none other that fighteth for us, but only thou, our God.'[2] When the whole of humankind had been laid low through the sin of its first parent, Christ fought for us and overcame the devil, but he was seriously wounded, not only in one place, but in many, and fell ill, not in himself, but in his members. So if you[3] would please him, you must draw the venom from him, i.e., banish sickness and want from his people through works of mercy, as is written in Matthew c.3:[4] 'What you did to one of the least [of these], you did it to me.' And if the toad returns to harm you, you must fight manfully against it, and the servants of God, i.e., the virtues you received at baptism, will assist you; and thus you will overcome the devil and have life everlasting; to which etc.

---

2 See no. 1, note 7.
3 *homo ... fueris*: a sudden switch from third to second person.
4 Cf. Mt 25.40.

100. Christ does not with justice destroy a sinner at once, but mercifully awaits his repentance

When Diocletian was emperor, he enacted a law that any woman guilty of adultery should be put to death. It happened that a knight married a girl and had a son by her. As the boy grew up he was loved by everyone. Subsequently the knight went off to war and fought valiantly, but in this war he lost his right arm. In the meantime, while he was away, his wife committed adultery. On his return he discovered her adultery, and in accordance with the law was obliged to put her to death. He called his son and said to him: 'My dear boy, your mother has committed adultery, so according to the law I ought to put her to death. But I have lost my right arm and so shall not be able to kill her. I therefore command you to kill her.'

His son replied: 'The law commands us to honour our parents. So if I had to put my own mother to death, I would be acting contrary to the law and would bring my mother's curse upon myself. I refuse to obey you in this matter.'

And so, thanks to her son, the mother escaped death.[1]

Dear friends, the emperor is God the Father; the knight is our Lord Jesus Christ; and his wife is the soul. God the Father ordained that, if a soul that is subject to Christ commits adultery, it should suffer eternal death, i.e., suffer everlasting torments; and the soul is committing adultery whenever it commits mortal sin. God the Son went to battle against the devil, and in the battle lost his right arm, that is, all the severity that was his before the Incarnation. He therefore became as meek as a lamb, and does not desire our death. But God the Father ordained death. The Son replied: 'I took human flesh from my mother, therefore I cannot kill man.' Thus by contrition and confession the sinner can escape death and attain to life everlasting; to which etc.

1 Seneca, *Controversiae* I.4. See also Tubach, no. 4487, and Hope, pp. 552–3.

101. The world is steeped in evil and there is tribulation on every side[1]

The tale is told of a man named Ganter who wanted a life of never-ending joy. One day he got up and proceeded to walk the road alone until he reached a kingdom in which the king had recently died. The nobles of this kingdom, seeing how manly Ganter was, chose him as their king, and he was overjoyed at his election. When night came, servants took him to a bedchamber in which he saw a ferocious lion at the head of the bed, and at its foot a dragon; and on one side a bear, and on the other snakes and toads. 'What does this mean?' Ganter asked. 'Surely I haven't got to sleep in that bed surrounded by all these beasts.'

'Yes, my lord,' they replied. 'All the kings before you slept in this bed and were eaten by these beasts.'

'I like everything else,' said Ganter, 'but I find this bed and those beasts so loathsome that I will not be your king.'

So he left them and went to another kingdom, where, as had happened before, he was chosen as king. At night when he entered his bedchamber he saw a most beautiful bed covered with sharp razors. 'Do I have to sleep on this bed?' Ganter asked. 'Yes, my lord,' replied his servants. 'All the kings before you have slept in it and all have died in it.' 'Everything is fine,' Ganter replied, 'except this bed. And because of it I will not be your king.'

Next day he got up and travelled three days on his own, and as he journeyed he met an old man sitting at a fountain with a staff in his hand. 'Friend,' he asked Ganter, 'where have you come from?' 'From distant parts,' Ganter told him. 'Where are you going?' 'I am seeking three things,' he said, 'and cannot find them.' 'What are these three things?' Ganter replied: 'The first is plenty without

1 Cf. Herrtage, Text II.XLVI.

fail; the second is joy without sorrow; the third is light without darkness.'

'Take this staff,' the old man told him, 'and go on your way. You will see a lofty mountain ahead of you. At the foot of the mountain there is a ladder with six rungs. Climb it, and when you reach the sixth rung, at the summit of the mountain you will see a most lovely palace. Knock at the gate three times and the gatekeeper will answer you. Show him this staff and say: "The master of this staff commands you to let me enter." And once you gain admission, you will find there the three things you are seeking.'

Ganter carried out all the old man's instructions. When the gatekeeper saw the staff, he allowed him to enter, and there Ganter found the three things he had been seeking, and much else besides. And there he remained all the rest of his life.

Dear friends, Ganter represents any good Christian who must entirely spurn the world and seek three things, namely plenty without fail, joy without sadness, and light without darkness. They can never be had except in life everlasting, and that with great effort. O man, do as Ganter did: go on a journey of three days through prayer, fasting and almsgiving. If you chance to come to some kingdom, i.e., the things of the world, and the citizens, i.e., worldly vanities, choose you as king, i.e., dispose your heart to pride, consider your bed! The bed is human life, in which you will lie for a short time. But consider the lion, i.e., the devil ever ready to assail you, and the dragon, i.e., death, which awaits you at every turn, and the bear, i.e., your own conscience, which will condemn you, and the worms, i.e., your sins, which will accuse you! If you ponder these things carefully, you will soon be able to detach yourself from the world. 'Then he went to another kingdom etc.' It is the same with man: if he overcomes the devil in one place, the devil takes him to another kingdom, that of sin, the kingdom of the flesh, in which carnal delights and desires rule. If you yield to these you will become a son of perdition; therefore take heed of your bed! This bed is hell, in which the rich man lies, and it is full of razors, i.e., the most dire torments. If you consider this bed carefully, you will shun the delights of the flesh altogether. So if you wish to find these three things, ask the old man with the staff, i.e., our Lord Jesus Christ, who yields you the staff of his holy cross. The staff is penance, which will lead us to the way of salvation. As the Psalmist says:[2] 'Thy rod and

2 Ps 22.4.

101. The world is steeped in evil and there is tribulation on every side

thy staff etc.' But after this you must climb the ladder of a holy life, on which there are seven rungs, i.e., seven works of mercy through which you will attain to everlasting life.[3] But you must knock three times, i.e., undergo contrition, confession and penance; then the gatekeeper, i.e., divine goodness, will lead you into the eternal kingdom, and there you will find plenty without fail, joy without sadness, light without darkness. *To which light etc.*

---

3 The ladder in the tale has only six rungs, but the *moralisatio* adds one to correspond to the seven spiritual works of mercy; see no. 83, note 3.

102. Of the transgression of the soul and its wounds[1]

In the reign of Tiberius there lived a noble and very devout knight who had a lovely wife, but she committed adultery and refused to mend her ways. This caused the knight much heartache, and he decided to visit the Holy Land. 'My dear,' he said to his wife, 'I am going to the Holy Land. I trust you to act with discretion.' But no sooner had he gone abroad, than his lady fell in love with a clerk, an expert in necromancy, and slept with him. It chanced when they lay in bed together on one occasion that she said: 'If you do one thing for me, you could marry me.' 'What is it you want?', he replied. 'What can I do for you?' She said: 'My husband has gone to the Holy Land and does not much care for me. If you could kill him by some magic art all that I have would be yours.' 'I promise to do it for you,' said the clerk, 'but only on condition that you marry me.' 'I promise faithfully,' she told him. The clerk then made an image bearing the knight's name, and fixed it before his gaze upon the wall.

Meanwhile the knight was crossing a street in Rome when a learned master met him, looked closely at him, and said to him: 'Friend, I have a secret to tell you.' 'Tell me, master,' he said, 'what is it you wish to say?' He replied: 'Today you are going to die unless you let me help you. Your wife is a harlot and has arranged to have you killed.' When the knight heard this, he knew that what he had said of his wife was true, and he believed him. 'Good master,' he said, 'save my life and I will reward you as you deserve.' 'I will gladly save you,' he replied, 'if you do as I tell you.' 'Readily,' said the knight.

The master prepared a bath for him and told him to undress

[1] Cf. Herrtage, Text I.I.

102. Of the transgression of the soul and its wounds

and get into it. He then put a polished mirror in his hand and said: 'Look closely into the mirror and you will see things that will astonish you.' While the knight looked in the mirror the master sat near him and read a book.[2] 'Tell me,' he said, 'what do you see?' 'I can see a clerk in my house,' said the knight, 'who has fixed a wax likeness of me upon the wall.' 'What do you see now?' asked the master. He replied: 'He is picking up a bow and fixing a sharp arrow to it and aiming it at my image.' 'As you love your life,' the master told him, 'when you see the arrow flying towards the image, plunge your whole body beneath the bathwater, and stay there until I give you the word.'

So the moment the knight saw the arrow leave the bow he plunged completely beneath the water. When he had done this, the master said: 'Raise your head and look in the mirror.' He did so, and the master said: 'What do you see now?' 'The image was not hit,' he said. 'The arrow swerved to one side and the clerk is extremely annoyed about it.' 'Now what is he doing?', the master asked. 'Look in the mirror.' 'He is going closer to the image,' he said, 'he is putting another arrow in the bow and aiming to strike the image.' 'Do as you did before,' the master told him, 'if you value your life!' So, as soon as he saw the clerk bending the bow in the mirror, he plunged his whole body beneath the water. After he had done so, the master said: 'Look now, what now?' The knight looked in the mirror and replied: 'The clerk is really annoyed that he has not struck the image. He is telling my wife that if he doesn't hit it on the third attempt, he will lose his life right there in front of it. Now he is going so close to it that I don't think he can fail to hit it.' 'As you love your life,' the master said, 'as soon as you see him bend the bow, be sure to plunge your whole body beneath the water, and stay there until I tell you.'

The knight kept his gaze upon the mirror, and as soon as he saw the clerk stretch the bow to shoot, he plunged beneath the water. Then the master told him: 'Get up quickly and look in the mirror.' And when the knight looked, he laughed. 'My friend,' said the master, 'tell me, why are you laughing?' He replied: 'I see quite clearly in the mirror that the clerk has not hit the image, and the arrow rebounded and struck him midway between his chest and

2 *in libro legisset:* the master may have been reading out a magic incantation, or perhaps consulting some manual of instructions. Otherwise there seems little point in including this detail.

stomach, and he has died. My wife has dug a pit beneath my bed and buried him there.' 'Get up quickly,' said the master, 'put on your clothes and pray to God for me.'

The knight thanked him for saving his life, and after completing his pilgrimage returned to his own country. When he reached home, his wife met him and welcomed him with joy. For several days he pretended he knew nothing; then at length he sent for his wife's parents and said to them: 'My friends, the reason why I have sent for you is this. This daughter of yours, my wife, has committed adultery; and worse still tried to bring about my death.' This she denied on oath, so the knight began to relate the whole story of the clerk from beginning to end. 'If you don't believe this, come and see the place where the clerk is buried.' He took them into his bedchamber and there beneath his bed they found the clerk's body. The judge was then summoned and he sentenced the woman to be burnt to death. This was duly carried out, and the ashes of her corpse were scattered to the winds. The knight subsequently married a beautiful virgin, had children by her, and ended his days in peace.

Moralization. Dear friends, the emperor is our Lord Jesus Christ; the knight is man, his wife the flesh, which commits adultery whenever it commits a mortal sin. When man comes to know of this he must go to the Holy Land, i.e., to the heavenly kingdom, through works of merit. On the way a master meets him, i.e., a discerning confessor, who has to instruct the sinner. The clerk is the devil, who keeps man in his power through his fleshly desires. He sets up an image, i.e., uplifts the soul through pride and vanity. He takes the bow and arrow: the bow is this world, and its two ends are the pride of life and the concupiscence of the eyes. This is the bow that the avaricious man holds; the sharp arrow is pride, through which many are slain, as in the case of Lucifer and Adam, our first parent. Lucifer said:[3] 'I will ascend above the stars of heaven and be like the Most High.' But on the contrary the arrow rebounded and killed him. Adam desired what he should not have desired, and thus was slain; the image of the soul might well be of wax, because it perishes as wax does, i.e., 'melteth before the fire'.[4] What then are we to do to prevent the devil shooting us and killing us? Clearly we must get into the bath. This bath is confession, in which and

3 Cf. Is 14.13f.
4 Ps 67.3.

102. Of the transgression of the soul and its wounds

by which we must be cleansed of all the filth of sin. But we must keep the mirror polished; i.e., you must keep Holy Scripture in your hand, that is, you must gladly listen to sermons and edifying addresses, which will enable you to guard against dangers and ward off the arrows of the devil. How, pray? Thus: when through some temptation the devil's bow is drawn against you, plunge your whole body into the bath of confession, by considering all you have done, all the pleasures you have had and the temptations to which you have yielded, and the sin vanishes. And when you are cleansed and the devil is slain, i.e., vanquished, put on your garments, i.e., the virtues you received at baptism, and hasten to the house of your conscience and remove the body of the dead man, i.e., all your past deeds. Next send for your parents, i.e., the sins whereby your flesh wandered from the way of truth, and then burn your flesh in the fire of penance, until your bones, i.e., inveterate sins, are reduced to nothing, and thus blown away by the wind, i.e., your bitterness of soul. And you will be able to marry a virgin, i.e., the flesh purged of its vices by the fire of divine mercy and grace, and consequently beget offspring, i.e., virtues, through which you will win the eternal prize.

103. Of the need to do everything with harmony[1] and forethought

The emperor Domitian was very wise and perfectly just, for he allowed no-one to evade the course of justice. It happened once that as he sat at table a merchant came along and knocked at the gate. The gatekeeper opened the door and asked him what he wanted. 'I am a merchant,' he said. 'I have some useful things to sell to the emperor.' So the gatekeeper brought him in and he humbly paid his respects to the emperor.

'Friend,' the emperor said to him, 'what goods have you to sell?' 'Three wise precepts, my lord,' he replied. 'And how much do you want for each of these three precepts?' the emperor asked. 'A thousand florins,' he told him. 'But if your precepts are no use to me,' the emperor said, 'I lose my money.' 'My lord,' said he merchant, 'if my precepts do not prove of value to you, I will return the money.' 'Excellent,' said Domitian. 'Now tell me these precepts which you wish to sell me.'

'The first precept, my lord,' he said, 'is this: whatever you do, do it prudently and consider the consequences. The second is this: never leave a public highway for a byway. The third precept is this: never agree to stay as an overnight guest in the house of anyone where the master is old and his wife young. If you keep these three precepts, you will profit from them.'

The emperor gave him 1,000 florins for each of the precepts and had the first of them – 'whatever you do, do prudently etc.' – inscribed in his throne room, in his bedchamber, in all the places where he walked, and on the hand-towels on his dining table.

Soon after this, because of his severity, many of his subjects

---

1 *consensu*: here the word seems to mean 'consistency', acting in accordance with the same precepts. This story is listed by Tubach as no. 5334.

103. Of the need to do everything with harmony and forethought

conspired against him and plotted to kill him, and because they could not accomplish their ends by forceful means, they told his barber that if he cut his throat he would be rewarded. The barber took the money and promised faithfully to do it, but when he was about to shave the emperor, and was soaping his beard and beginning to shave him, he looked down and saw the towel around his neck, on which was written: 'Whatever you do, do it prudently, and consider the consequences.' And when he read it he thought to himself: 'I have been hired to kill this man today, and if I do it, I shall meet a terrible end, because I shall be condemned to a most ignominious death. As the writing says, whatever you do, it is well to consider the consequences.' And his hands at once began to tremble so violently that the razor fell from them. Noticing this the emperor said: 'Tell me, what is the matter?' 'Oh my lord,' he cried, 'have pity on me! Today I was bribed to kill you. But by chance, as God willed, I read the writing on the towel: "whatever you do, do prudently etc.", and I thought at once of the ignominious death I should face. That is why my hands began to shake.'

When he heard this, the emperor thought to himself: 'The first precept has saved my life. It was in a good hour that I bought it.' 'In future be loyal,' he told the barber. 'I forgive you.'

Now when the nobles realized that they could not kill the emperor by this means, they discussed among themselves how they might accomplish it. 'On such-and-such a day,' they said to each other, 'he will be leaving to go to another city. Let us hide that day along the byway he is going to take and kill him.' 'A good idea,' they all agreed. On the appointed day the emperor prepared to set out for the city in question, and when he had ridden on until he came to the byway his soldiers said to him: 'Lord, it would be better to take this byway than travel along the highway, because it is more direct.' The king thought to himself: 'The second precept was that I should never leave the public highway for a byway, and I will follow it.' So he said to his soldiers. 'I will not leave the public highway; so those of you who wish to take this byway, go ahead, and get everything ready for my arrival.' So they proceeded along the byway, and the king's enemies, in hiding along the track, thinking that the king was among them, rose up from their ambush and killed every one of them. The king heard the din, and said to himself: 'Now the second precept has saved my life!'

Realizing that their second plot had failed, the conspirators put their heads together to consider how they might kill the emperor. Certain of them suggested: 'On such-and-such a day he will stay in that man's house where all nobles are entertained, because there is nowhere else for them to stay. Let us bribe the owner and his wife, and kill him when he is lying in bed.' 'A good idea,' they agreed.

When the emperor arrived in the city he was put up in that very house, and had his host called to him. When he came, the man was obviously very old. 'Do you have a wife?' asked the emperor. 'Yes, lord,' he replied, 'I have.' 'Let me see her,' he said. And when she appeared, it was clear that she was very young, no more than eighteen years old. 'Quick,' the emperor told his chamberlain, 'prepare me a bed elsewhere, because I am not staying here.' 'Of course, sire,' he said. 'But everything is ready for you now. It isn't a good idea to sleep elsewhere; there isn't any more comfortable accommodation for you in the whole city.' But the emperor said: 'I tell you, I will sleep elsewhere.'

The chamberlain at once made the necessary arrangements and the emperor secretly went to another place, telling his soldiers: 'You can stay here if you want, but come to me in the morning.' And while the soldiers were all asleep, because of the bribe they had been given to kill the king as he slept, the old man and his wife got up and slew every one of them. When the king arose next morning he discovered that all his soldiers had been killed, and he said in his heart: 'Ah, if I had slept there I would have been murdered along with the rest. Now the third precept has saved my life!'

He had the old man with his wife and all his household hanged from the gallows, and as long as he lived he kept those three precepts in mind, and ended his days in peace.

Dear friends, the emperor stands for any good Christian, who has dominion over body and soul, and must govern his soul; the gatekeeper is free will, because there is no sin unless it be willed; the merchant who comes to the gate is our Lord Jesus Christ, according to the saying of Revelation:[2] *'Behold I stand at the gate and knock. If any man open it to me, I will come in to him and will sup with him.' For every day he sells you three precepts for your soul. The florins are spiritual virtues: the first precept, 'Whatever you do etc.,' means, whatever you do, it must first and foremost be for God, and not for worldly praise; as we*

---

2 Cf. Rv 3.20.

103. Of the need to do everything with harmony and forethought

read in Proverbs:[3] 'Remember thy last end and thou shalt never sin.' The second precept: 'Never leave a public highway for a byway.' The public highway is the way of the Ten Commandments to which you must always keep until death, and you must never walk the byway of a wicked life, as the heretics do. The third precept is: 'Never stay as an overnight guest in the house of anyone etc.' The old man is this world, and he has a young girl, i.e., vanity, for his wife. From day to day some new, unwholesome and empty vanity is conceived, so that, if you are a guest in the world, you should without doubt fear death, because no-one can serve God and the world. The nobles who conspired against the king etc. are demons, who are always striving to kill man spiritually, and if they cannot do so themselves, they speak with the barber, i.e., the flesh, which shaves off all the hair in the manner of a barber. The flesh through its will 'shaves off' the excellent virtues that man has received in baptism. But if man gave thought to his end, i.e., if he gave thought to the manner, the time and the place of his death, he would turn from all evil doing. Let us therefore strive to observe these three excellent precepts, and so we shall win the everlasting prize.

---

3 = Ecclus 7.40.

104. Of the remembrance of kindnesses[1]

There was a knight who loved hunting above all things. It happened one day when he went hunting that he was met by a lame lion, who showed him his foot. The knight got down from his horse and pulled a sharp thorn from its foot, then applied ointment to the wound and healed it. Subsequently the king of that country happened to be hunting in that same forest and caught the lion, and for many years kept it in captivity. Then the knight committed an offence against the king and sought refuge in that same forest, where he robbed and slew all who passed through it. But the king took him captive and sentenced him to be fed to the lion, and the lion was to be given nothing to eat so that he would be sure to devour the knight. Now the knight, who had been thrown into the pit, was terrified as he awaited the time when he would be devoured. But the lion inspected him closely and, recognizing him, greeted him fondly, and stayed with him for seven days without food. When the king heard of this, he was amazed, and had the knight hauled from the pit. 'Tell me, my friend,' he said, 'how can it be possible that the lion has not harmed you?' 'Sire,' he replied, 'I happened to be riding through the forest when that lion came up to me limping, and I removed a thorn from its foot and healed the wound. I suppose that is why he spared me.'

'Since the lion has not harmed you,' said the king, 'I will spare you. But in future strive to amend your life.'

The knight thanked the king, and thereafter wholly amended his life, and closed his days in peace.

[1] Cf. Herrtage, Text II.XVII. This is the well-known story of Androcles and the Lion, of oriental origin, which occurs in Aesop and Aulus Gellius (*Noctes Atticae* V.xiv). Other versions are listed by Oesterley, p. 728, and Tubach, no. 215.

104. Of the remembrance of kindnesses

Moralization. Dear friends, the knight who went hunting is a worldly man, who daily strives to acquire worldly goods. The lame lion is the whole of humankind, which was made lame through the sin of its first parent, but the thorn, i.e., original sin, was removed through baptism and healed with the unguent of virtues. The knight then rises up against the king, Almighty God, when he commits mortal sin and is stripped of the virtues he received in baptism. But the lion, i.e., humanity, is captured, when he is bound by God's precepts, and is cast into the pit of penance. And if the knight, i.e., sinful man, is cast into the same pit, every kind of evil will befall him; or rather every blessing, because he is able to win the salvation of his soul. To which may [God] bring us etc.

105. Of the inconstancy of everything good and especially of right judgement[1]

Theodosius was an extremely wise emperor. Having lost his sight he passed a law that a bell should be placed in his palace and anyone who had some complaint to make should pull the bell-rope with his own hand, and when he heard the bell ring a specially appointed judge would go down and administer justice. Now a snake had made its nest beneath the bell-rope, and soon after she produced young, and when they were able to get about she went one day with them for an excursion beyond the city. When the snake was absent, a toad got into her nest and took possession of it. The snake and her young then returned, and when she saw the toad occupying her nest she attacked it, but she could not overcome it, so the toad remained in possession of the nest. Thereupon the snake wound its tail around the bell-rope, gave a mighty tug, and rang the bell, as if to say: 'Come down here, judge, and give me justice! This toad is occupying my nest.'

Hearing the bell the judge went down, but seeing nobody there, went back upstairs. At this the snake rang again, and hearing the bell the judge came down, and when he saw the snake pulling the rope, and the toad occupying her nest, he went upstairs again and reported the whole matter to the emperor.

'Go down,' the emperor told him, 'and not only get rid of the toad, but kill it, and let the snake possess what is hers.'

His command was duly carried out. And one day after this the emperor was lying in his bed when the snake came into his bedchamber carrying a precious stone in its mouth. When the emperor's servants saw this, they told the king about it, but he cried: 'Don't trouble it. I don't think it will do me any harm.'

1 Cf. Herrtage, Text I.VII.

105. Of the inconstancy of everything good and of right judgement

The snake slithered up on to the emperor's bed and made its way towards his head. When it reached his eyes, it let the stone fall upon them, then immediately left the room. And no sooner had the stone touched his eyes than the emperor's sight was completely restored. Overjoyed, he conducted a search for the snake, but it could not be found. Thereafter he guarded the stone with care, and ended his days in peace.

Moralization. Dear friends, the king represents any worldly man, who is obliged to govern himself, and yet is blind to spiritual things, though he sees temporal things clearly enough. The bell that must be rung at certain times is the tongue of the preacher. The bell-rope is Holy Scripture, and when it is used the preacher must go down and make known the virtues and vices, explaining how through their virtues sinners can ascend to heaven, or enter hell through their sins. The snake that makes its nest under the bell-rope is the discerning confessor, who has to place himself under the bell-rope of Holy Scripture and bring forth young, i.e., virtues, in his nest, i.e., in the sinner's heart. If any of the senses is sullied, i.e., infected, by sin, he has to ring the bell with the rope of Holy Scripture, and then the judge, i.e., reason, must come down and by means of a proper confession examine the whole matter and administer correction. But it often happens that prelates and confessors are luke-warm and negligent and follow after worldly things, and thus those under their care remain in peril, because the toad, i.e., the devil, seizes their place. What then is to be done? Clearly, the confessor must return to the sinner bringing his young, i.e., virtues, with him. The snake has two young: he brings the venom of penance and the antidote of absolution for the soul's salvation, and he must fight against the devil by instructing the sinner as to how the devil must be resisted, and so banish him from the heart of the sinner. The snake then brings a stone etc.; even so the discerning confessor must give a stone, i.e., Christ, to the sinner through Holy Scripture, and through its virtue he can regain his spiritual sight and consequently win life eternal.

106. We must be on our guard against the devil lest he beguile us[1]

There were once three friends who went on a pilgrimage. During the pilgrimage it happened that all they could find to eat was a single loaf, and they were starving and said to each other: 'If this loaf is divided into three pieces, a single piece will not be enough to fill any of us. So let us consider how we can best divide up this loaf.'

'Let us sleep here on the wayside and dream,' one of them said, 'and whoever has the most amazing dream can have the whole loaf.'

'That's a good idea,' the other two said. So they lay down to sleep. But the one whose idea it was got up and ate the whole loaf while they were asleep, not leaving a single crumb for his friends. Then he woke them and said: 'Come on, get up, it's time for each of us to describe his dream.'

'My friends,' said the first, 'I had an amazing dream: I saw a golden ladder reaching down from heaven, and angels climbed up and down it and took my soul from my body up to heaven. When I was there I saw the Father, the Son and the Holy Spirit, and my soul was surrounded with such joy "that eye hath not seen, nor ear heard"[2] what I felt there. And that is my dream.'

The second said: 'And I saw demons that drew my soul from my body with instruments of red hot iron, and then manhandled

1 Cf. Peter Alfonsi, *Disciplina Clericalis* XIX. See also Robert Browning, *The Ring and the Book*, IX.1042ff., where a similar story is told of Peter, John and Judas, quoted from Sepher Toldoth Yeschu, whose *The Book of the Life of Jesus* was an early Jewish attack on Christianity. Other Classical and medieval versions are listed by Oesterley, pp. 728–9; Tubach, no. 1789; Hope, pp. 557–8.
2 1 Cor 2.9 quoting Is 64.4.

106. We must be on our guard against the devil lest he beguile us

me cruelly and told me: "As long as God reigns in heaven you will remain in this place."'

The third said: 'Listen to my dream. I dreamed that an angel came up to me and said: "Friend, would you like to see where your companions are?" "Yes," I replied, "for we have just one loaf to divide between us, and I fear they have gone off with it." "No, no," he said, "the loaf is just beside you. Follow me." He then led me to the gates of heaven and at his command I just put my head inside the gate when I saw you. It seemed to me that you had been snatched up to heaven and seated on a throne of gold, and had rich foods and the best wines set before you. "Look," the angel said to me, "your friend is blissfully happy and has all the food he wants, and he will remain here for eternity, because he who has once entered the heavenly kingdom can never leave it. Come with me now and I will show you where your other friend is." I followed him and he took me to the gates of hell, and there I saw you, just as you said, suffering the direst torments, and since formerly[3] you were given bread and wine[4] daily in plenty, I said to you: "My dear friend, I am sorry to see you suffering so!" And you replied: "As long as God reigns in heaven, I shall remain here, because this is what I have deserved. So, quick, off you go and eat the whole loaf, for you will not be seeing me or our friend again." After this revelation I left and ate the loaf as you said I should.'

Dear friends, these three friends should be understood as three kinds of men: the first, the Saracens and Jews; the second, the rich and powerful of this world; and the third, men of perfection, such as religious and other god-fearing men. The loaf of bread represents the kingdom of heaven. The bread, i.e., the heavenly kingdom, is divided among the three kinds of men according to their merits: some get more of it, some less. The first kind, the Saracens and Jews, are asleep in their sins and believe they will possess heaven. The Saracens believe this because of the promise of Mahomet, whose law they observe, and who promised them that they would reign in heaven. The Jews also believe they will win heaven because of the Law of Moses. This belief is just a dream. The second friend, who dreamed he was in hell, represents the rich and powerful of this world, who know of a certainty through preachers

---

3 *quotidie antea*: *antea* presumably means 'in your former life'.
4 *vinum*: Oest.; *vinum infernale*: K. K. (who omits *antea*) has the second friend being fed with copious amounts of the bread and wine of hell.

and confessors that if they die in sin without contrition, they will go down to hell and there be punished for eternity, and yet this does not hinder them, for they heap sin upon sin. And so it is written of the rich: 'Where are the mighty of this world, who would sport with their dogs and birds?' They have died and gone down to hell. The third friend, that is, the Christian who does not sleep in sin or in bad faith but is careful to perform good works, through the counsel of an angel, i.e., the gifts of the Holy Spirit, will so direct his life that he has bread, i.e., the heavenly kingdom. To which etc.

107. Of the remembrance of death and not delighting in temporal things[1]

There was a statue in the city of Rome of a figure standing upright with its right hand outstretched, and on its middle finger was the inscription: 'Strike here!' This statue had stood there like this for a long time, and no-one knew what was meant by 'Strike here!' Many people wondered about this and went to the statue often to look at the inscription, but when they went away again they had no idea what it meant.

Now there was a very clever clerk who had heard about this statue and was most anxious to see it. As he was looking at it and read the inscription 'Strike here!', the sun shone on the statue, and in the shadow it cast he could see the finger with the inscription 'Strike here!' So he at once got a spade and dug a hole about three feet deep there, and discovered some steps leading below. He was delighted at the discovery and went down the steps one by one until he came to a noble subterranean palace. He entered the hall and there saw a king and queen and a throng of nobles seated at table, and the hall was completely full of people, all of them dressed in the richest garments, but none of them spoke a single word to him. He then noticed in one corner of the hall a polished stone, the kind called a carbuncle, which was the sole source of light for the whole place; and in the opposite corner he saw a man with a bow and arrow in his hand ready to shoot at the stone. And on his brow was written: 'I am who I am. No-one can escape my bow, and least of

1 Cf. Herrtage, Text I.III. Warton compares Spenser, *Faerie Queen* II C.viii. The story was first told of Pope Gerbert (= Sylvester II, d. 1003) by William of Malmesbury. In that version, an accompanying page replaces the knife, and he and Gerbert escape alive. Other cognate versions are given by Oesterley, p. 729; Tubach, no. 2720; Hope, pp. 558–9.

all that carbuncle that shines so brilliantly.' Astonished at what he saw, the clerk entered a bedchamber, and there found some women of great beauty clothed in purple and pall[2] working at the loom, but they spoke not a word to him. He then went to the stables and found the most excellent horses and asses and other animals. He touched them, but when he did so they seemed to be of stone. After this he visited all the rooms in the palace, and discovered there whatever his heart desired. Then, as before, he went into the hall, and thinking about his departure he said to himself: 'I have seen marvels today, and found all that my heart desired. But no-one will believe my story about what I have seen, so I had better take something with me as proof.' Then, scanning the high table he saw some golden cups and beautiful knives, so he went up to the table and lifted one cup and one knife from it to take away with him. But as soon as he placed them in his bosom the figure standing in the corner with the bow and arrow took aim at the carbuncle, struck it, and shattered it in tiny pieces. At once the whole hall was plunged into darkest night. The clerk was utterly dismayed since because of the pitch dark he could not find his way out, and so he died a wretched death there in the palace.

Dear friends, the image that says: 'Strike here!' is the devil, who goes about 'seeking whom he may devour', and who has an outstretched hand, i.e., the power to deceive sinners. It says: 'Strike here!', i.e., it says to the avaricious man: 'Strike here!,' i.e., by seeking after worldly goods on the earth, and setting your heart on earthly things. The clerk who comes along after the others have gone away is a greedy or avaricious man, who is like the good cleric who strives day and night to fill himself with knowledge and to teach others, and will never be satisfied until he discovers things that are new; likewise the greedy man strives day and night upon the earth to acquire worldly goods; his eyes are never sated; and against such Seneca says: 'When other sins grow old, avarice alone is young.' Those who come to the statue are good Christians, especially religious, who look to the world for food and clothing and then depart, and have no concern for the devil's inscription. Such people escape peril. The clerk digs into the earth where the shadow of the finger indicated; even so the avaricious man takes a spade, i.e., his

---

2 *pallio*: there is ambiguity here: the ladies could be working at the loom making purple and pall, or dressed in these colours.

107. Of the remembrance of death and not delighting in temporal things

compact frame and his acquiescence in sin and his intelligence,[3] *and with these begins to dig up the riches of the world. And when he finds the steps he goes down them. The first step is pride, the second concupiscence of the eyes, the third concupiscence of the flesh. The avaricious man goes down by these and various other steps, and discovers a beautiful palace, as it seems to him, full of men and vanities, i.e., this world, in which palace and vanities wretched man takes such extraordinary delight. The man standing with the bow ready is death, which is always prepared to strike any of us down, as the writing says on his forehead: 'I am what I am,' i.e., death, 'and have long been in this world, which I entered through the sin of your first parent; and no-one, however rich, noble or mighty can escape my bow.' The carbuncle is man's life; as long as life remains in him, the carbuncle gives him light, i.e., lets him live, and yet the avaricious man believes in better things and expects to live for ever, and thinks he can hide in his bosom, i.e., his money box, his worldly goods, symbolized by the cup and knife. But death will come and with its arrow pierce his life with grave illness, and at once there is such total darkness that he loses all sensation, life and strength. And his body lies there dead and in a wretched state, for within three days it begins to stink. Then the devil seizes his soul, and his friends and relatives will get all the goods he acquired with God's curse, and the earth and worms will take possession of his body, and thus nothing is left for the sinner but eternal punishment. Let us therefore strive etc.*

---

3 *accipit ligonem*, i.e., *corpus condensum et assensum et intellectum* is the reading of Oest., K. and L. However, the translation in *Le Violier* (where the moralization is close to that in Oesterley) raises at least the possibility of corruption: '*print la besche, c'est assavoir la concupiscible volunté pour avoir et venir aux richesses*'. 'His appetitive will and intelligence' would make better sense here. (Perhaps we should read *consensum corporis et assensum intellectus*: the compliance of his body and acquiescence of his mind/intelligence.) The spade symbolizes the means by which the greedy man acquires worldly wealth.

108. Of faithfully keeping one's promise[1]

In the reign of a certain emperor there lived two thieves who had sworn each other an oath that neither would abandon the other in time of need, but that each would lay down his life for the other. They committed many crimes of theft and murder together. Now it chanced that, acting on his own in the other's absence, one of them was caught thieving and thrown into prison in fetters. When his partner, the other thief, heard of this, he went to him and said: 'My dear friend, tell me what to do, since we are bound by oath to one another.'

'As I see it,' his partner told him, 'I must die, because I was caught red-handed. But if you would just do as I tell you, I will always be beholden to you. I have a wife and family, but I have made no arrangements for them, nor for my possessions. If you would take my place here in gaol and await my return – and you can ask the judge's permission for this – I will go home, provide for my wife and family and put my affairs in order. I will return in due course and release you.'

'I promise faithfully to do as you ask,' the other replied. So he went to the judge and said: 'My lord, my friend has been taken and put in gaol. In my view he cannot escape death. Will you please grant me just one petition? Release him so that he can go home and make provision for his wife and family before he dies; and as security for him, I will remain here in gaol in his place until he returns.' The judge replied: 'Sentence will be passed on him along with others on such-and-such a day. But if he does not return on that day, how will you answer to that?' 'Lord,' he said, 'I will offer whatever surety you

1 Cf. Cicero, *Tusculanae Disputationes* V.22.63, and *De Officiis* III.10.45. This is very like the tale of Damon and Phintias, recounted by Valerius Maximus, *F.D.M.* IV.7 ext. 1. See also Oesterley, p. 729.

108. Of faithfully keeping one's promise

wish. If he does not come back, I will face death for love of him.' 'I will grant your petition,' the judge said, 'but on condition that I keep you in chains until he returns.' 'Very well,' the other replied.

The judge then put him in gaol and set free his partner, who went back home, made provision for his wife and children and household. But he stayed there so long that he failed to appear for the trial three days later in which all the other criminals were presented before the judge; and among them was his partner, who had so readily gone into gaol for him, and now appeared on behalf of his friend.

'Where is your friend,' the judge asked, 'who should have returned today and secured your release and saved you?' 'My lord,' he answered, 'I do not think he will fail to return.'

The judge waited some considerable time to see if he would come, but he did not. So he passed sentence and condemned him to be taken off and hanged. His orders were being carried out, and the thief was being taken off to the gibbet, when the judge told him: 'Friend, it is your own fault, not mine, that you are now to die. You said that your friend would come and secure your release.'

'My lord,' he replied, 'since I must die, please, I beg of you, grant me one petition.'

'What sort of petition?' demanded the judge.

'Before I die, allow me to shout three times.'

'Very well,' the judge agreed.

He then began to shout once, twice, three times at the top of his voice, and then scanned the whole horizon, and saw a man running very quickly towards him in the distance. 'Stay the execution!' he cried to the judge. 'Look, I can see a man heading this way. Perhaps it is my partner coming to set me free.' Hearing this the judge waited, and lo and behold!, the friend arrived. 'My lord,' he said, 'I am the man you want. I have arranged for the disposal of my property and made provision for my wife and friends. And meanwhile my friend has been in danger of dying in my place. Let him go free, because I am ready to face death for my crimes.'

The judge considered him carefully for a moment, then said: 'My friend, tell me how it is that you two are so loyal to one another.'

'My lord,' he replied, 'we swore an oath when we were children that we would be faithful to each other in all things, and this is the reason why he took my place until I had set my household in order.' 'Then if that is so,' replied the judge, 'I remit your death sentence.

Show your loyalty to me, and in future stay in my employment and I will provide you with all that you need.' 'My lord,' they said, 'from now on we promise you our utmost loyalty.'

So the judge received them into his favour, and everyone commended him for having shown them such compassion.

Moralization. Dear friends, the emperor is the Heavenly Father; the two thieves are the soul and the body, which were made friends through sin, but joined together in baptism such that each made a promise not to fail the other in his need, when they said: 'We renounce the devil and his vanities.'[2] *And after this they became allies in all they did; but one was captured without the other and tightly chained. When man commits mortal sin, the soul remains beneath the devil's yoke. The other friend, i.e., the body, hereupon gives himself up to his pleasures. But the good Christian, beloved of God, realizing that the soul is bound in sin, and consequently is in the devil's prison, has to offer himself up in his place, i.e., remain in the place of penance until the soul reaches his wife, i.e., conscience, and with her takes thought for his children and household, i.e., God's commandments and his own sins, recalling what he has done to contravene God's commandments, and how great his sin, and how long he has remained in sin; and he must atone to God for each and every sin. How, pray? Why, through prayer, fasting and almsgiving. Meanwhile the body must cry out three times: the first cry is bitter contrition, the second complete confession, the third full satisfaction. At these cries the soul, which has now set the house of its conscience in order, will immediately come to you in its proper form, and both, i.e., body and soul, will reign in the heavenly home, to which may our Lord bring us etc.*

---

2 A promise made at baptism and confirmation.

109. Those the devil enriches he finally lures into hell through their avarice[1]

There was a rich blacksmith who lived in a city by the sea. He was an extremely avaricious and wicked man, who had amassed a large amount of money, and he filled a trunk[2] with it and placed the trunk by the fire quite openly, so that no-one should suspect that it held any money. One day it happened that when everyone was fast asleep, the sea flooded into the house so that the trunk containing the money began to float about, and when the sea ebbed again, it took the trunk with it. The trunk floated many miles out to sea until it reached a city where there lived a man who owned and kept a public inn. This man got up early in the morning, and seeing the trunk floating on the water, brought it to land, thinking of it just as a piece of wood someone had cast out or abandoned. He was very kind and generous to paupers and pilgrims, and one day when some pilgrims were staying at his place, and the weather was extremely cold, the host decided to chop up the trunk with an axe, and after three or four blows he heard a strange sound; so he split the trunk in two and to his delight discovered the money. But he kept it safe in case the owner should come along and ask him to return it.

Meanwhile the blacksmith went from city to city searching for his money, and finally came to the city and the house of the innkeeper who had found the trunk. When he mentioned the loss of his trunk, the innkeeper realized that the money was his, and thought: 'I will now see if it is God's will that I give him back the money.' He then made three pasties: one he filled with earth, the

1 Cf. Herrtage, Text I.LXVI, and *Decameron*, Day 10, nov. 1. The story is listed by Tubach, no. 3613 (as 'the three pastries'). See also Oesterley, pp. 729-30.
2 *truncum: truncus* can mean the trunk of a tree, or, among other things, a trunk or chest. It could conceivably bear either meaning here.

second with the bones of skeletons and the third with the money he had found in the chest. Having done this he said to the blacksmith: 'We are going to eat three nice pasties, which are made of the finest meat. Whichever you choose will be sure to fill you.' The blacksmith picked up one after the other, and finding the pasty filled with earth the heaviest, chose that one. 'If I want more,' he told his host, placing his hand on the pasty full of bones, 'I can have that second one. You can keep the third pasty yourself.'

So the innkeeper said to himself: 'I can now see quite clearly that it is not God's will that this wretch should have the money.' He promptly called the poor and weak, the blind and lame, and in the presence of the blacksmith opened up the third pasty. 'Here is your money, you wretch,' he said, 'which I offered you to take, but you chose the pasties filled with earth and human bones, and that is good, because it was not the will of God that you should have your money back.'

Then before his eyes the innkeeper divided all the money among the poor, and the blacksmith left in confusion.[3]

Dear friends, the blacksmith represents any worldly man who strives to serve the world rather than our Creator. The trunk that is closed on every side represents the heart of any avaricious man, which is always closed to heavenly things; the money inside it symbolizes the works of merit that wretched man performs on occasion, compelled as he is through fear of God. The sea, which ebbs and flows, is this world, which snatches from the miser's heart whatever good he has done, not only[4] the virtues he received at baptism, but also the good thoughts of his heart. Matthew c.6:[5] 'Where thy treasure is, there is thy heart also.' The innkeeper who found the trunk is a good prelate or discerning confessor, who is bound to have a concern for sinners and to inquire into their hearts and deeds and discover how they may be brought to the path of righteousness. For man must follow the path which will enable him to find salvation, i.e., he must hasten to confession and be a guest in the

3 For the motif of the chests/caskets, cf. e.g. *G.L.* CLXXVI.87ff; Boccaccio, *Decameron*, Day 10, nov. 1; Gower, *Confessio Amantis*; and Shakespeare, *The Merchant of Venice*.

4 *non tamen:* Oest., K. I read *non tantum*. We are repeatedly told that mortal sin destroys the virtues received at baptism, and the world leads men to mortal sin.

5 Mt 6.21.

house of the Church, and obey its precepts. The confessor must then show him three pasties and ask him to choose one of them wherewith to quench the hunger of sin. The first pasty was full of earth, and signifies the world; if the worldly man chooses this one, he will find nothing else in this life but plain earth, i.e., a tomb scarcely seven feet deep, because everything that is in the world is either pride of life or concupiscence of the eyes or concupiscence of the flesh.[6] *Indeed 'the whole world is seated in wickedness.'*[7] *Therefore woe to them that choose the things of the world! Remember, O man, that you are dust and will return to dust. The second pasty was full of dead men's bones and signifies the flesh, i.e., carnal men, idle, gluttonous, wanton men, who devote all their effort to pleasing the flesh. It is these the Apostle reproaches:*[8] *'If you live according to the flesh, you shall die.' You will then find your works are like dry bones, which are good for nothing save burning. Therefore woe to them that choose this pasty, i.e., pleasures of the flesh! The third pasty was full of silver and solid gold, and this signifies the highest heaven where there is infinite treasure. There are comparatively few who reach out to take this pasty; as Matthew says, c.1:*[9] *'Broad is the way that leadeth to hell; strait is the way that leadeth to heaven, and thus few walk along it.' What then must we do? Why, we must summon the poor and weak, i.e., the just and holy, who in this life have passed through many tribulations and endured many miseries for God's sake. It is to them that Christ's words in Matthew c.25 will be addressed:*[10] *'Come, ye blessed of my Father, receive the kingdom that hath been prepared for you.' To which may He bring us etc.*

6 Cf. 1 Jn 2.16.
7 1 Jn 5.19.
8 Rom 8.13.
9 Cf. Mt 7.13f.
10 Cf. Mt 25.34.

110. Of the miraculous recall of sinners and the merciful consolation of those in distress[1]

In the reign of Trajan there lived a certain knight named Placidus who was the commander of the emperor's army. Placidus was very active in performing good works, but devoted to the worship of idols. He had a wife of the same religion who shared his feelings of compassion, and they had two sons whom he brought up in the magnificence befitting their high station. And because Placidus was constantly performing works of mercy, he was found worthy of enlightenment, and shown the way of truth.

Now one day when he was following the hunt he came upon a herd of deer, among which he saw one animal which was larger and more beautiful than the others, and it parted from the rest of the herd and sprang into the deepest part of the forest. So while the other huntsmen were occupied with the rest of the deer, Placidus focused his whole attention on this particular animal and strove to take it. He pursued it with all possible speed until finally the stag climbed to the summit of a steep rock. Placidus approached it and considered carefully how to take it. But as he gazed at it intently, he saw between its antlers the form of the holy cross shining more brilliantly than the sun, and the image of Jesus Christ, who, as formerly he had spoken through Balaam's ass, spoke through the mouth of the stag to Placidus. 'Placidus,' he said, 'why do you persecute me? For your sake I have appeared to you in the form of this animal. I am Christ, whom you worship in ignorance. Your alms have risen into my presence, and so I have come so that, through this stag which you are hunting, I too may hunt you.' (Others, however, say that it was the image of Christ, which appeared between the stag's antlers, that spoke.) When Placidus heard this he was absolutely terrified and fell from his horse to the ground. After an hour

1 Cf. Herrtage, Text I.XXIV.

110. Of the miraculous recall of sinners

he came to himself again, got up and said: 'Explain to me what you are saying and I will believe in you.' And Christ said: 'I am Christ, Placidus, who created heaven and earth, who caused the light to appear and divided it from the darkness, who appointed the seasons, days and years, who formed man from the dust of the earth, who for the salvation of humankind appeared on earth in the flesh, who was crucified and buried and rose again on the third day.'

Hearing this Placidus fell to the ground again, and said: 'Lord, I believe that you are the one who made all things and who convert those who err.' 'If you believe,' the Lord said to him, 'go to the bishop of the city and have yourself baptized.' 'Lord,' Placidus asked, 'do you wish me to tell my wife and children of this, that they also may believe in you, as I do?' 'Tell them,' the Lord said to him, 'that they like you may be cleansed. And come here tomorrow, that I may appear to you again and reveal to you more fully what will come to pass.'

Placidus then went home and told his wife all this in bed, and she exclaimed: 'My lord, I too last night had a vision and someone told me: "Tomorrow you and your husband and children will come to me." And now I know that it was Christ.'

So they went off in the middle of the night to the Bishop of Rome, who was overjoyed to baptize them. Placidus he named Eustace, his wife Theosbyta, and their two sons Theosbytus and Agapitus. Next morning Eustace went out hunting, as was his custom, and when he got near the place, dispersed his soldiers on the pretext that he was tracking game. At once he saw the apparition as before, and falling on his face to the ground he said: 'I entreat you, Lord, to reveal to your servant the things that you promised.'

'You are blessed, Eustace,' the Lord said to him, 'for you have received the baptism of my grace, you have now overcome the devil,[2] and you have now trampled on the one who had deceived you. Now your faith will be revealed, for because you have abandoned him the devil is arming himself against you furiously and will assault you in many different ways. For you must endure much in order to receive the crown of victory; you must suffer much in order to be delivered from the profound vanity of the world and humbled, and then be uplifted again with spiritual riches. Do not fail, therefore, and do not look back on your former high station,

---

2 *medidianum superasti*: Oest.; *modo eum qui te deceperat superasti*: K., G.L. CLVII.34; *modo diabolum*: L.

because you must show in your temptations that you are another Job. But when you have been humbled, I will come to you and restore you to your former glory. Tell me, then, whether you wish to endure your trials now, or at the end of your life.' 'Lord,' Eustace said to him, 'if it must be so, have the trials come to me now, but grant me the virtue of patience.' 'Be it so,' the Lord told him, 'for my grace shall keep your souls safe.'

And so the Lord ascended into heaven, and Eustace returned home and told his wife what he had heard. A few days after this a deadly plague seized his menservants and maidservants and they all died.[3] Then a few days later all his horses and cattle suddenly perished. Next, seeing all the losses he was suffering, some desperadoes broke into his home in the night and took everything they found, despoiling the house of all its gold and silver and everything else. Eustace and his wife and children, giving thanks to God, fled naked into the night. Fearing that people would ridicule them, they went to Egypt, and all that remained of their possessions was plundered by villains until there was nothing left. The emperor and the whole senate were deeply dismayed at the loss of such a valiant general, and especially so because they could find no trace of him.

As Eustace and his family travelled on they came to the sea and there found a ship on which they embarked. Now the ship's captain, seeing that Eustace's wife was beautiful, passionately desired to possess her. When they had completed the crossing, he demanded payment, and since they had no means of paying, he commanded that Eustace's wife be held in lieu of payment, because he wanted to make her his own. When he heard this proposal Eustace absolutely refused to agree, but as he persisted in his refusal, the captain signalled to his crew to throw him overboard so he could have his wife himself. Realizing what was afoot, Eustace sadly left his wife to them, and taking his two children went away in sorrow. 'Alas for me,' he said, 'and alas for you! Your mother has been given up to a foreign husband!'

He then came to a river which was so wide he dared not attempt to cross it with both his sons, so leaving one on the bank he carried the other across. When he had got across, he put the boy he was carrying on the bank and hurried back to get the other. But when he was about half way across, a wolf suddenly appeared and, snatching

---

3 Eustace's sufferings are clearly based on those of Job.

110. Of the miraculous recall of sinners

up the child he had just left on the bank, ran off into the woods. Despairing of him, Eustace made haste to reach the other. But as he swam, a lion came along and seized the other child and made off. Being in the middle of the river, Eustace could not give chase, and he began to weep and tear his hair out, and he would probably have drowned himself if divine providence had not held him back.

Now some shepherds saw the lion carrying a child and pursued him with their dogs, and, as heaven willed it, the lion let the child drop unhurt and disappeared. Moreover some ploughmen went after the wolf, shouting at it, and got the other boy from its jaws unharmed. Both the shepherds and the ploughmen were of the same village, and they brought the two boys up in their homes.

Eustace knew nothing of this, and as he went along weeping and wailing he said to himself: 'Ah me! Once I flourished as the green bay tree, but now I have been stripped of everything. Ah me! I used to have a multitude of soldiers around me, and now I am left on my own, and not allowed even to keep my children. Remember, Lord, that you told me that I should be tried as Job was; and lo!, you see me suffering more than Job. Though he was stripped of all he had, he still had dung to sit on, whereas I have been left with absolutely nothing. He had friends to share his suffering: for friends I have only the wild beasts who stole my sons. Job was left his wife: mine has been taken from me. Grant me a respite from my trials, Lord, and set a guard upon my mouth lest my heart be inclined to words of malice and I be banished from your sight!' With these words Eustace went on his way tearfully until he reached a village, where for fifteen years he earned his living tending the villagers' sheep. Now his sons had been brought up in the neighbouring village, and did not know they were brothers. Moreover, the foreign ship's captain took good care of Eustace's wife and did not sleep with her; on the contrary, he ended his days without ever touching her.

Now the emperor and the Roman people were under constant threat from their enemies; and remembering Placidus, and how valiantly he had fought against them, the emperor became more and more distressed at his sudden disappearance. He sent out many soldiers to different parts of the world, promising great riches and honours to anyone who could find him. Now two of these soldiers, who had once served under Placidus, came to the village in which he was living, and as he came back from the fields and saw them, he recognized them at once by their gait, and he groaned and became dejected when he thought of the high rank he had once had. 'Lord,' he said in his heart, 'these two men served with me once, and I never expected to see them again. Even so grant that I may see my wife again; for my sons, I know, have been devoured by wild beasts.' And a voice came to him saying: 'Only trust, Eustace, for soon you will have all your honours restored to you, and find your wife and sons again.'

When he met the two soldiers they did not recognize him at all. They greeted him and asked him if he knew of a stranger named Placidus, with a wife and two children. He declared that he did not know them, and at his entreaty they went to stay at his lodging. And when Eustace waited on them, recalling his former high station he could not hold back the tears, and went outside and washed his face, then returned and waited on them again. And as they watched him, one of them said to the other: 'How[4] similar he is to the man we are looking for!' And the other replied: 'He is very like him. Let us see if he has that scar on his head from the wound he received in battle.' So they looked at him closely, and seeing the mark, immediately knew that he was the man they were looking for. They leapt up and embraced him, and asked after his wife and children. He told them that his sons were dead and his wife a prisoner. All the neighbours ran up to witness this extraordinary happening, and the two soldiers regaled them with stories of their general's bravery and former renown. They then told him of the emperor's orders, and clothed him in the richest garments.

A fortnight later they reached the emperor, who, hearing of Eustace's approach, at once went to meet him and threw himself into his arms. Eustace told him all that had happened to him from beginning to end, and was immediately hurried off to the general's quarters and made to resume his former command. After counting up his forces he realized they were too few to engage the enemy, and gave orders for the levying of recruits in every city and village. Now it chanced that the area in which his two sons had been brought up was obliged to provide two recruits, and since all the local inhabitants thought these two young men the most suitable for military service, they sent them off to the general. When Eustace saw these two fine, upstanding young men he was greatly taken with them, and assigned them to places in the front line. He then set out to

---

4 *Quod*: Oest., K.; *Quam*: G.L. CLVII.95, L.

110. Of the miraculous recall of sinners

make war, and after they had subdued the enemy, he granted his army three days rest in the very place where his poor wife was living, and the two brothers were quartered in her house, though they did not know she was their mother.

Around midday, sitting and chatting together, they were telling each other about their childhoods, and their mother, who sat opposite them, listened most attentively to what they were saying.

'I cannot remember anything about when I was a baby,' the older son said to the younger, 'except that my father was a general and my mother was very beautiful. They had two sons, me and a younger brother, and he was very handsome too. Our parents took us and left our house in the night and boarded a ship, though I don't know where we were going. When we got off the ship, my mother somehow or other was left on board. Our father carried both of us, and wept as he went along, and when we came to a river he crossed it with my younger brother and left me on the river bank. As he was coming back to get me, a wolf came along and snatched my brother, and before he could get to me, a lion came out of the wood and seized me and carried me into the woods. But some shepherds tore me from the lion's jaws and brought me up in their village, as you know, and I could not find out what became of my father or my brother.'

When he heard this tale, his younger brother started to weep. 'By God,' he said, 'from what I hear I am your brother, for the people who brought me up told me that they snatched me from the jaws of a wolf!' They fell into each other's arms, and kissed each other, and wept.

Their mother, having heard all this, and considering all the circumstances they had related, one after the other, wondered at length if they could be her children. Next day she went to the general and appealed to him: 'My lord,' she said, 'I beg you to convey me back to your native land, for I am a Roman and a stranger here.' And as she spoke she saw the scar on his head that her husband had, and recognized him, and no longer able to contain herself, she fell at his feet and said: 'I beg you, my lord, to tell me of your earlier life. For I think you are Placidus, commander in chief of the army, who is now known as Eustace, for the Saviour converted him. And he endured one tribulation after another; and his wife, for I am she, was carried off to sea, but was preserved from all defilement. And he had two sons, Agapitus and Theosbytus.'

When Eustace heard this and considered her closely, he recognized that she was his wife, and wept for joy; and he kissed her, glorifying God, who consoles the afflicted. His wife then asked him: 'Where are our children, my lord?' 'They were taken by wild beasts,' he told her. And he explained to her how he had lost them. 'Let us give thanks to God,' she said. 'For I think that, as God has given us the joy of finding each other, he will also grant us that of finding our sons again.' 'I told you,' he said, 'they were devoured by wild animals.' She replied: 'Yesterday as I was sitting in my garden, I heard two young men recalling this and that about their childhood. I think they are our sons. Ask them, and they will tell you.'

So Eustace summoned them, and when he heard from them about their childhood, he realized that they were his sons, and embracing them, he and their mother bathed their shoulders in tears and kissed them repeatedly. The whole army was overjoyed that they had been found again, and that the barbarians had been vanquished.

When Eustace and his family returned to Rome, he found that Trajan had died, and an emperor named Hadrian, whose crimes were even worse, had succeeded him. Hadrian gave them a magnificent reception to celebrate both the victory Eustace had won and his reunion with his wife and sons, and held a sumptuous banquet. Next day he went in procession to the temple of the idols to offer sacrifice there for the victory over the barbarians. But seeing that Eustace would not offer sacrifice either for his victory or for his reunion with his family, he exhorted him to do so. Eustace told him: 'I worship Christ as God and I serve him and sacrifice to him alone.'

The emperor was enraged at this, and had Eustace with his wife and children put in the arena, and set a savage lion loose upon them. But the lion came up to them, and lowering its head as if in adoration, meekly went away again. The emperor then had a fire built under a brazen bull and ordered them to be shut inside it and burnt alive. So, as they prayed and commended themselves to God, the saints entered the bull and there gave up their souls to the Lord.

Three days later they were removed from the bull in the presence of the emperor and were found quite intact. The heat of the fire had not singed their hair or touched any other part of them at all. Christians took their bodies and buried them in a hallowed place, and there built an oratory. They suffered on 1 November, or according to some on 20 September, in the reign of Hadrian, which began around AD 120.

110. Of the miraculous recall of sinners

Moralization. Dear friends, the emperor is our Lord Jesus Christ; Placidus can be seen as any worldly man occupied with secular vanities who goes out to hunt for the things of the world with his knights, i.e., his five senses. Finally he comes upon a herd of deer, a sight which delights him greatly. These deer are sight, hearing etc., words of disparagement and vanities, and the other exterior senses. But note! The most handsome deer of all runs away and leaves the company of the rest, and Placidus pursues it with all his might. This deer is reason, which is the greatest power of the soul, and which man must follow in all his works with all his might if he desires to lead a holy life. The deer climbs a precipice; the precipice is justice, or rectitude, which reason always loves, and between the antlers of reason Placidus sees an image of the Crucified. The antlers are the Old Law and the New. In the Old Law many clear prophecies were made concerning Christ's coming and his death. In the New Law we can clearly see how he died, and what death he underwent for our salvation. So the deer tells us to despise the world and the things that are in the world, and to follow the footprints of Christ, as Placidus did. Should you say: 'I would gladly be instructed as to how I should follow the footprints of Christ,' then the story of Saint Eustace provides an example. First, renounce your wife and children. Your wife, who is extremely beautiful, is your soul, created in the likeness of God, and it is always ready to obey Christ if the flesh permits it. The two small children are will and action, which remain small as long as man remains opposed to God. So first you must overcome yourself, then cast all worldly things from you, if not in fact, then in intention, and this means you must put God before all else. Placidus next sets out and with his wife and children boards ship at night. So you too, my dear friend, must set out through contrition, with good intention and good works, and board the ship of Holy Church, and God will be merciful to you in all things. The ship's master is the prelate, who would gladly detain us, but has to keep our wife, i.e., soul, obedient to God's commandments. And if it chances that man wanders away from the ship of the Church, he can lose his two children, i.e., the good intention and the good works he previously performed for God, as Placidus did. Placidus gets into the river and carries his children, and the wolf seizes one and a lion the other. The river signifies this world, the lion the devil, the wolf our flesh. The devil seizes man's good intention from his heart, the flesh his good works. Reason says: 'It is good to fast and be vigilant in the performance of good works.' The flesh says: 'It is better to eat well and sleep long.' What then are we to do? If those two *things are taken from man, i.e., good intention and works of merit, then clearly the shepherds and ploughmen have to pursue them vigorously with their dogs. The shepherds are discerning confessors, who have to direct us and steer us from the path of perdition. The ploughmen are preachers, who have to plough the earth of our hearts with Holy Scripture, tear out the thorns of sins and plant virtues, uproot vices, and then maintain men in the service of God, so that they live in one city, that is, in such mutual love and harmony that the flesh does not oppose the spirit. The emperor then sends people to search for Placidus. Even so God sent to man first the patriarchs, and second the prophets, but man refused to acknowledge or recognize them, until the Son of Man came to us and redeemed us with his precious blood. So it is just that the accommodation our house offers should be cleansed through works of mercy, with no sin in it. And so our wife, i.e., the soul, will appear pure and lovely, with her two children, i.e., with its own will always serving God through works of mercy. And note that you must have a sign by which you can be recognized, as Placidus had. This sign must be the love of God and your neighbour, that you love God above all things, and your neighbour as yourself. And so you will become Commander of the Army, i.e., of all the senses, by subjecting them to the virtues, and after the martyrdom of mortification attain to life eternal. Which [reward] may He grant us etc.*

111. Of the care and vigilance we must exercise towards the flock entrusted to our care

A nobleman had a white cow of which he was very fond for two reasons: first, because she was white, and second, because she produced abundant milk. In his great love for her the nobleman decided that she should have a pair of golden horns, and then considered carefully to whom he might entrust the cow for its safekeeping. There was at that time a man called Argus who was absolutely truthful and had 100 eyes. So the nobleman sent a messenger to Argus asking him to come to him without delay, and when he arrived he told him: 'I am entrusting my cow with golden horns to your safekeeping, and if you guard her well, I will see you are amply rewarded. But if the horns are stolen, you will be put to death.' Argus took the cow with the golden horns and led her away. Each day he went out with her to pasture, and at night brought her back home.

Now there was an avaricious man named Mercury who was an extremely skilled musician, and he had a passionate desire to possess the cow. He often approached Argus hoping, by cajolery or bribery, to get hold of the horns. But Argus fixed the shepherd's crook he held in the ground in front of him, and said to it, as if it were his master: 'You are my master, and tonight I shall come to your castle. You will ask me: "Where is my cow with its horns?" And I shall reply: "Here is your cow, but it no longer has horns, for while I was sleeping some thief took them." You will reply: "You wretch, haven't you 100 eyes? How was it that all 100 eyes were asleep and a thief stole the horns? This is a lie!" And I shall die the death. If I say: "I sold it" My master will put me to death.'[1] He then told Mercury: 'Be on your way, you're certainly not having her.'

1 *infidelis ero*: Oest.; *filius ero*: K.; *filius mortis ero*: L.

So Mercury left him, but next day came along with the musical instrument at which he was so skilled. When he arrived, after the fashion of minstrels[2] he began to tell Argus tales, and sang him song after song until two of his eyes began to close, and then, as he continued to sing, two more of his eyes closed, and so it went on until all of them fell shut. As soon as this happened, Mercury cut off Argus's head and stole the cow with the golden horns.

Dear friends, the nobleman is our Lord Jesus Christ; the white cow is the soul created in God's image which, while it remains in purity of life, gives the milk of devotion and prayer. For these two reasons it is dearly loved by God; so he gave it horns of gold, because through both many men were saved after the death of Christ. The cow with its golden horns is handed to Argus, i.e., a prelate, and Argus, with his 100 sharp eyes, signifies a man who is provident and wise and entirely circumspect, who has to be ever watchful beside the flock committed to his charge. Hence Ezekiel tells the prelate, c.3:[3] 'If thou declare it not to him, nor speak to him, that he may be converted from his wicked way, and live, the same wicked man shall die in his iniquity, but I will require his blood at thy hand. But if thou give warning to the wicked man, and he be not converted from his wickedness and from his evil way, he indeed shall die in his iniquity, but thou hast delivered thy soul.' But alas! Many display the shepherd's staff, i.e., their power before the eyes of men that they may be seen and honoured by others; but it often happens that when some temptation comes from the devil, such as listening to melodious songs, i.e., to a woman,[4] which men often love to hear, they take such pleasure in them that they cease to be circumspect and vigilant, and while their wisdom sleeps they die a spiritual death, and through sin lose the cow, i.e., the soul, which they ought to be carefully guarding. So their heads i.e., the holy life they promised God to observe through works of merit, are taken from them. And Mercury, i.e., the devil, robs them of eternal life by taking the cow, i.e., their soul, off to hell.

---

2 *more historico*: Oest.; *more histrionico*: K., L.
3 Ez 3.18f.
4 *Le Violier*: 'la femme blandissant'.

112. Of the healing of the soul by the celestial physician, whereby some are cured and some not[1]

King Gorgonius had a lovely wife who conceived and bore him a son. As the boy grew he was loved by everyone, but when he reached the age of ten, his mother died and was given burial with all due honour. After this, on the advice of many of his counsellors, the king took another wife, who did not care for the son of his former wife, and regularly abused him. When the king learned of this, in his desire to please his wife, he ordered his son to leave the kingdom. During his banishment the son studied medicine and acquired such skill that he became a renowned and most accomplished physician. When the king heard how successful his son had been in his profession, he was overjoyed. Now it happened shortly after this that the king fell gravely ill, and he sent a letter recalling his son, asking him to come without any delay to heal him of his infirmity. When he received his father's request, his son went to him and restored him to perfect health, so that his fame spread quickly throughout the kingdom. Then his stepmother became mortally ill, and physicians were summoned from all parts, but they were all of the opinion that she must die. The king was overcome with grief at this, and asked his son to cure her, but he replied: 'I will not grant your request.' His father told him: 'I shall banish you from my kingdom.' 'If you do,' his son replied, 'you are doing me an injustice, father. You know perfectly well that it was at her prompting that you banished me from the kingdom before, and it was my absence that caused your sorrow and infirmity, and my presence is the cause of the queen's sorrow and infirmity. So I will not cure her. I will leave her and go.' 'She has the same illness that I had,' said his father. 'You healed me completely. Do the same for

---

1 Cf. Herrtage, Text I.LIII.

her.' His son replied: 'My dear father, it may be the same illness, but her constitution is not the same as yours. What I did for you, you considered acceptable and good, and when I entered the palace and you saw me, you were healed. When my stepmother sees me, she is annoyed; if I speak, it causes her pain; if I touch her, she is beside herself. And nothing is better for the sick than to give them what they want and to humour them.' So with these arguments the son avoided treating her, and his stepmother died.

Moralization. Dear friends, the king can be seen as our first parent Adam, who had a seat and a kingdom, namely paradise, and whom God appointed lord of the whole world. The Psalmist:[2] *'Thou hast subjected all things under his feet etc.' He married a beautiful wife, i.e., the soul created in the likeness of God, and by her had a son, i.e., Christ, who was, in respect of his humanity, one of his progeny. His wife, i.e., soul, died spiritually through the sin she committed. He at once took another wife, namely, the iniquity and misery into which he plunged, for which he was deprived of paradise and set in this world where he lived in sweat and toil. The Son of God, who was his offspring according to the flesh, came down from the heavenly kingdom because of our infirmity and iniquity, and became our physician. Now the perfect physician heals all infirmities, and the result was that his fame flew abroad in heaven, on earth and in hell. But our father Adam was gravely diseased both in body and soul because of the sin he had committed; in body, because he had lost glory and honour when he was banished from paradise; in soul, when he was separated from God and placed in hell. God indeed healed him completely and perfectly with his blessed Passion, but he would never cure his stepmother, i.e., the devil, to whom he was joined through sin. Why was this so, when they had the same sickness, since both had fallen ill through sin? My answer is this: Though both sinned, they sinned in different ways. The devil sinned without temptation and through his own wickedness, whereas man was tempted by the devil, and being formed of fragile matter fell into sin and sought the oil of mercy. So the physician, our Lord Jesus Christ, cured man, but not the stepmother, i.e., the devil. The stepmother is the reason why the Son of God is sent by many men into another country and banished by them; conversely the divine presence is the cause of the devil's death, because they are mutually incompatible.*

2 Ps 8.8.

113. Of the spiritual battle and our reward for victory[1]

King Adonias was extremely wealthy and took great delight in tournaments and jousting. Once he held a tournament and had it proclaimed that whoever came out best would receive a fitting reward from him. Hearing this proclamation all the nobles and lords came to the tournament. The king ordered that the knights be divided into two companies, so many on one side and so many on the other, and those in the first company placed all their shields and weapons in order in a place appointed for them. The king commanded that when one of the other company touched someone's shield with his lance, the one whose shield had been touched should at once come down to the tourney, and a maiden specially selected for this task should arm him. Then he should fight his opponent, and if he overcame him at the joust he would be crowned that day with the king's crown and be seated at the king's table.

Now on hearing this, one knight took a close look at all the shields and saw one with a device of three golden apples, and he conceived a great desire to possess it. So he touched that shield, and the knight whose shield it was promptly got the maiden to arm him, and came down to fight him. In the course of the sword-play he cut off the head of the knight who had touched his shield and received his due reward.

Dear friends, the king is our Lord Jesus Christ, who fought against the devil. First a tournament took place in heaven, i.e., a war between God and the devil, when Michael and his angels battled with the dragon; and afterwards on the earth on Good Friday. But to return to the point: God has three shields or standards, namely: power, which is the shield of the Father; wisdom, which is the shield of the Son; and goodness,

1 Cf. Herrtage, Text I.LIV.

which is the shield of the Holy Spirit. God placed these three shields in one ordained place, i.e., in human nature, when he created man in his own image and likeness. The first man lorded it over all the beasts – mark his power, which is the shield of the Father; the first man had knowledge of all things – mark his wisdom, which is the shield of the Son; the first man was created in grace and in the love of God and his neighbour – mark his goodness, which is the shield of the Holy Spirit. The Wicked One, obdurate in his evil, wishing to fight against God, approached man, to whom these three shields of the Three Persons had been given, and touched one: not the shield of the Father, saying: 'If you eat, you will be as powerful as gods'; nor the shield of the Holy Spirit, saying: 'You will be good and loving.' Rather he touched the shield of the Son, on which were the golden apples, i.e., the operation of the Trinity, saying: 'If you eat of this fruit, you shall be as gods, knowing good and evil.'[2] Therefore, since it was the shield of the Son of God that was touched, it was fitting that God the Father should send his Son to defeat the Wicked One for us. And God's Son was armed by a chosen virgin, i.e., the Blessed Virgin Mary, from whom he took human nature, with which he led us to everlasting life.

2 Cf. Gn 3.5.

114. Of the deliverance of mankind from the abyss of hell

There was once a king in whose realm there lived a poor man who every day went into a forest to gather wood to sell in order to have the means to buy his food and clothing. Now one day he went into the forest with his ass, and by chance, as he made his way between the thick branches, he fell and suddenly plunged into a pit from which he had no chance of escaping. In this pit there was a loathsome dragon, whose tail coiled round the whole circumference of the pit. The upper part of the pit was covered with scores of snakes, as was the bottom. Half way down there was a round stone, and once a day, every day, the snakes made their way to it and licked it. Then, in the same way, the dragon would lick it.

When the poor man witnessed this, he thought: 'I have been many days in this pit without any food, and if I cannot get any, I am going to die of hunger. I shall get to that stone and lick it, as the snakes do.' So he climbed up to the stone and began to lick it, and found it possessed all the flavours his heart could desire, and he was as refreshed as if he had had all the food in the whole world to eat.

A few days later there was such a violent and terrifying thunderstorm that all the snakes left the pit one after the other, and when not a single snake remained, the dragon started to fly out of the pit. Seeing this, the poor man held on to the dragon's tail, and the dragon carried him up out of the pit, and after taking him a considerable distance dropped him in safety. For some days he stayed where he was, not knowing his way out of the forest. Then some merchants came by and escorted him out of the forest, and set him on the right path. Overjoyed, he returned to his home town and told everyone what had happened to him. And soon after he ended his days.

Dear friends, the emperor is our Lord Jesus Christ, and the poor man signifies any man who has come naked from the womb of his mother, and who enters a wood, i.e., this world; and often he falls into a deep pit when he falls into mortal sin, and lies there in great peril because he is under the power of the dragon, i.e., the devil. The snakes who are with him in the pit are other venial sins by which man is poisoned as if by a snake; the round stone in the middle is Christ; as the Psalmist says:[1] *'The stone which the builders rejected etc.' In it is found all savour and sweetness, and to it we must have recourse in time of trouble, and lick it with devout prayer. The great thunderstorm is sincere confession made with contrition before a priest, and by this thunder, i.e., confession, all the snakes, i.e., sins and demons that we summon with our sinning, are terrified and driven away, and the dragon, i.e., the devil, is banished. The merchants are preachers and confessors, who daily win the souls that the devil is attempting to carry off. The poor man is then guided to the right road for the holy city of Jerusalem, to which may our Lord Jesus Christ lead us etc.*

---

1 = 1 Pt 2.7.

115. Of Christ's dying for our reconciliation

There was an emperor who possessed a forest in which there lived an elephant whom no-one dared approach. When he heard about this elephant, the emperor asked his philosophers and wise men about the nature of the elephant, and they answered him by saying that the elephant was very partial to pure virgins and delighted in their singing. The emperor therefore immediately sent men out to see if there were in his realm two beautiful and virtuous girls who could sing well. So two maidens of great beauty and virtue were found. On the emperor's orders these were stripped and made to enter the forest naked. One of them held a basin and the other a sword. They entered the forest, and as they went they began to sing a sweet song, and hearing this, the elephant came towards them and began to lick their breasts, and as the virgins continued to sing, the elephant fell asleep in the lap of one of them. Seeing him asleep in her friend's lap the other girl slew him with the sword, and the girl in whose lap he had been sleeping filled the basin with the elephant's blood. They then went back to the emperor, who was overjoyed, and at once had some beautiful purple clothing and many other things made using the blood as dye.

Moralization. Dear friends, the emperor is our Heavenly Father, and the elephant our Lord Jesus Christ, who before his incarnation was formidable; the two virgins were Mary and Eve, both of whom were naked of all sin. Mary was sanctified in the womb, and Eve was placed in paradise. Eve carried a sword, i.e., the sin she committed against God's commandments, and for which Christ, the true elephant, died. Mary had the basin, i.e., the virgin's womb in which Christ was conceived and his humanity was formed. The elephant licked the virgins' breasts, i.e., the Old Law and the New, which are the two breasts through which we can suck the milk of salvation. Christ licked both, i.e., he fulfilled both laws when he shed his blood, and with his blood our souls were richly adorned[1] *with all honour and joy, so that, if we wish, we may possess life eternal, to which may he bring us.*

---

[1] *facte purpurate*: literally 'empurpled', i.e., clothed in rich purple garments.

116. Of the love of God, who loves us all equally, until we disregard him through our sins[1]

King Pepin married a beautiful girl who conceived and bore him a handsome son, but died in giving birth. He married another, and by her had another son, and sent both sons to be reared in far-off parts. Now these two boys were alike in every respect. When, after they had been away some considerable time, the mother of the second son wanted to see her boy, she begged and begged the king to let her see him. The king granted her request, and dispatched a messenger to his sons. When they arrived, they were completely alike. Although the second was younger by about a year, he was nonetheless as big as the older son, as often happens, and by chance both of them so resembled their father in looks, in character and physique that the queen did not know which one was hers. She repeatedly asked the king which one was her own, but he refused to tell her, and at his refusal she wept bitterly. Realising the anguish he had caused her, he said: 'Don't cry. *That* is your son,' and he pointed at the son he had had by his first wife. She was overjoyed to hear this, and at once devoted all her attention to caring for him, and gave no attention to the other boy, who was really her own. Observing this, the king said: 'Why are you behaving in this way? I deceived you: that one is not your son, though one of them is.'[2] 'Why do you treat me like this?' she demanded. 'Tell me which is mine. I beg you.' 'I will not,' he replied, 'and my reason is this: if I told you the truth, you would love the one – your own son – and hate the other; but I want you to love and care for both equally. When they attain to their majority, I will reveal the truth to you, and then your joy will be complete.'

Thereupon the queen gave her unsparing attention to both boys

1 Cf. Herrtage, Text I.LV.
2 Presumably the two sons are absent during this conversation.

until they reached manhood, and when she found out from the king who her own son was, her joy was unconfined. And so she ended her days in peace.

Dear friends, the king is our Lord Jesus Christ; and the two sons are the elect and reprobates; the mother, who is the mother of the last son, is Holy Church; the mother of the first child, who died, is the Old Law that died with Christ's incarnation. God does not want Mother Church to know who is elect or reprobate, but wishes that she should nurture both in perfect charity, because if she knew, she would love one and hate the other, and thus there would be no peace and harmony. But on the Day of Judgement, when they reach the lawful age, then the truth shall be known as to who are elect and who reprobates. Then the Saviour will say to the elect, Matthew c.25:[3] *'Come, ye blessed of my Father etc.' But to the reprobates:*[4] *'Go, you cursed etc.'*

3 Mt 25.34.
4 Cf. Mt 25.41

117. Of the obdurate, who refuse to be converted, and their punishment through their appointed judgement[1]

The emperor Frederick enacted a law that if a virgin was raped, the man who freed her from the hands of her assailant could, if he wished, marry her. Now it happened that a certain overbearing lord carried off a girl, took her into a forest and deflowered her, which caused her to scream. A knight of noble birth and reputation happened to be riding through this forest, and hearing the girl he spurred on his horse, and when he got to her he asked her why she had cried out.

'My lord,' she said, 'for the love of God help me! This blackguard has carried me off and deflowered me, and now he means to do away with me!'

'My lord,' explained her assailant, 'she is my wife, and I have taken her in adultery. So I was going to kill her.'

'No, lord,' she said,' that is not true. I have never been anyone's wife, and I have never been defiled until today, by him. So help me, pray! You can still see on me the evidence of my lost virginity!'

The knight said to the man: 'I can see the evidence of her virginity upon her, which shows that you took her against her will and deflowered her. So I will take her from you.'

'If you try to free her,' the man replied, 'I will fight you for her.'

They immediately fell to fighting and after striking each other with mighty blows, the knight was victorious, though gravely wounded. After his victory, the knight said to the girl: 'Would you like to become my wife?'

'Gladly,' the girl replied. 'I wish it with all my heart, and I give you my pledge that I will.'

She did so, and the knight told her: 'You shall stay in my castle for a few days. In the meantime I shall go to my parents and provide

1 Cf. Herrtage, Text I.XLIX.

everything necessary for our marriage. Then I shall come back to you and we shall be married in great splendour.' 'My lord,' she replied, ' I am ready to obey you in all things.' So the knight bade her farewell and she went off to his castle.

While the knight was abroad making all the necessary arrangements for the wedding, the same overbearing lord came to the knight's castle, where the girl was, and knocked at the gate. She refused him entrance, but this lord then began to make her extravagant promises, and assured her that he would marry her honourably; and she accepted his assurances and let him in, and they slept together that night.

After a month the knight came back and knocked at the castle gate, but the girl did not answer him. Realizing that something was afoot, he cried out in bitterness of heart: 'My dear girl, remember how I saved you from death, and that you gave me your solemn pledge. Speak to me, dearest, and show me your face.'

Hearing his voice she opened a window and said: 'Here I am. What do you want? Tell me.'

'I am surprised that you can forget all I did for you,' said the knight, 'and the wounds I received for love of you. If you do not believe me, I will show them to you.' And with these words he removed his tunic. 'Look, dearest,' he said, 'these are the wounds I received when I saved your life. Open the door for me, and let me make you my wife.'

But she turned away from him and refused to open the gate. The knight then made a complaint to the judge and adduced the law in his own support, affirming that he had saved the girl's life and therefore claimed her as his wife. When he heard this the judge sent for her ravisher, and when he came, said to him: 'Did you ravish this woman, and did this knight courageously rescue her from your hands?'

'Yes, my lord,' he replied.

'Then according to the law, as he so wishes, she is his wife. Why then did you interfere with the wife of another man? First, you entered his castle behind his back; second, you dishonoured his bed; third, you have for a considerable time possessed his wife. What have you to say in your defence?'

The man was silent.

Turning to the woman, the judge said: 'Young woman, by law you are doubly the wife of this knight: first, because he rescued you

117. Of the obdurate, who refuse to be converted, and their punishment

from the hands of your assailant; second, because you gave him your pledge. Why then did you subsequently open the gate of his castle to someone other than your husband and let him in?'

She had nothing to say in her defence. So the judge immediately sentenced them both to be hanged. The hanging took place, and everyone commended the judge for pronouncing such a sentence.

Dear friends, the emperor who made the law is God; the ravished woman is the captive soul; her ravisher is the devil, who not only deflowers her by means of sin, but also desires to kill her for all eternity. But she cried out when she sought the oil of mercy, saying, in the words of Luke c.15:[2] *'Have mercy on me, son of David!', i.e., my conscience is sorely troubled by the devil. A knight, i.e., the Son of God, heard her cry as he rode by on the horse of his humanity. The Son of God came down into the forest of this world and joined battle with the devil on behalf of humankind, and in the battle received many wounds. Both were wounded in the exchange, Christ in the flesh, and the devil in himself; hence Isaiah says:*[3] *'The strong hath stumbled against the strong, and both are fallen together.' Christ arranged the betrothal by means of baptism, in which the soul makes a solemn pledge when it renounces the devil and all his vanities and promises to cleave to God. With the other virtues which man receives, he makes a castle to combat the devil, the world and the flesh. Meanwhile God goes up into heaven to prepare our nuptials, that we may be united with him in everlasting glory; as John says:*[4] *'I go to prepare a place for you.' But when the soul is in the castle of the body, then the ravisher, i.e., the devil, assails the girl, i.e., the soul, when he seduces her with worldly vanity; and he goes in to her, when she consents to sin and remains in it, and thus Christ is banished. But Christ returns daily to the door of your heart and knocks and says, in the words of the Song of Solomon:*[5] *'I stand at your gate and knock etc.' But the soul, obdurate in sin, does not acknowledge him; so Christ shows it the wounds that he suffered for us, so that we may at least incline our heart to him and open the window of our heart. But wretched man does not fear the Lord enough to open his heart, and on the Day of Judgement the Heavenly Judge will pass sentence against such, and condemn them to be hanged on the gibbet of hell etc.*

2 Cf. Lk 18.38.
3 = Jer 46.12.
4 Jn 14.2.
5 Cf. Rv 3.20.

118. Of deceit and cunning

There was a knight who spent some time in Egypt, and thinking to deposit his money there, he enquired if there was some honest person to whom he might entrust it for safekeeping. A certain old man was named, so he visited him to deposit 1,000 talents with him, then went off on pilgrimage. When his travels were over, he went back to the man to whom he had entrusted the talents and asked him for what he had deposited. But the old man, an inveterate rogue, declared that he had never seen him before. The knight was dismayed at this deception, and pleaded with him day after day and tried to wheedle him into returning the money. But the old swindler told him roundly not to speak to him any more of the matter, and not to bother him again. Dejectedly, the knight left him, and met an old woman dressed as an anchorite, with a stick in her hand, who was removing stones from her path in case they should hurt her feet. Seeing him weeping and perceiving that he was a foreigner, she took pity on him and called him to her and asked what had happened. He told her the whole story of how he had been swindled by the old man. 'Friend,' she said, 'if what you tell me is true, I have some sound advice for you.' 'As God is my witness,' he replied, 'it is quite true.' She said: 'Bring me a man of your own country who can be trusted in all he says and does.'

The knight did as she said, and when the man arrived the old woman told the knight to buy ten chests painted on the outside in the richest colours, bound with iron and fastened with locks of silver, and to fill them with stones. The knight did as she told him. When all was ready the woman said: 'Now find ten men to go with me and your friend and to carry the chests to the house of the man who swindled you. Let them go one after the other in a long line, and as soon as the first of them has entered and is standing there

118. Of deceit and cunning

with us, come in boldly and ask for your money. And I trust to God your money will be returned to you.'

The old woman then went with the knight's accomplice to the swindler's house and said to him: 'Sir, this stranger has been staying with me and wishes to return to his native land, but first he wants to leave his money, which is in ten chests, with someone honest and trustworthy, until he returns. So, for love of God and me, I beg you, keep it in your house; and because I have heard and know that you are honest and trustworthy, I do not want anyone else but you to keep watch over the money.'

As she was speaking these words, a servant suddenly appeared with the first chest, and when he saw it the swindler believed the old woman's story. Then the knight came in, as the old woman had told him to, and when the swindler saw him, fearing that if he demanded his money this new client would not trust him with the safekeeping of his own money, went up to him and said, in the most sycophantic fashion: 'My friend, where have you been? Come and take back the money you entrusted to my safekeeping so long ago.'

The knight happily took back his money, giving thanks to God and the old woman. Thereupon she said to the swindler: 'Sir, this gentleman and I shall go to get the other chests without delay. Wait for us to come back, and take care of what I have already brought.'

And so, with the aid of the old woman the knight recovered his money.[1]

Dear friends, the knight is any Christian, who as long as he lives in this world is a pilgrim, because every day he is on a journey towards death. Through sin he unwisely hands ten talents, i.e., the Ten Commandments of the Lord, to an old man; this old man is the world, which is so full of deceptions that if we delight in the things of the world and trust in the world, we discard God's commandments, and we wretched men can only with great difficulty win heaven, and never until we do so through sincere contrition, confession and penance. The old woman in the garb of a pilgrim is a clean conscience, which constantly removes the stones, i.e., evil works, from the path of your heart, lest your feet, i.e., good thoughts, stumble against them. Do you know how you are to recover what you have lost through sin? Why, you must take ten men,

---

1 Cf. the tale recounted in Peter Alfonsi, *Disciplina Clericalis* XV. For other versions, see Oesterley, pp. 730–1.

i.e., ten works of penance, from your homeland, *i.e.*, from your heart, so that for each commandment you have violated through sin, you fulfil one act of mercy or penance. For according to Saint Augustine no good goes unrewarded and no sin unpunished. Likewise you must have a well-bound chest, *i.e.*, a contrite heart, richly adorned with virtues, but full of little stones. These stones in your heart are meditation on the five wounds of Christ and the recollection of his Passion, which you must practise constantly to fight the devil, the world and the flesh. This is prefigured in 1 Kings,[2] when David slew Goliath with his shepherd's staff and his sling and five stones. David means 'of mighty hand'[3] and signifies Christ. His sling signifies the love that drew Christ from heaven to the world, and from the world on to the cross. The five stones are the five wounds; Goliath is the devil; and so he is finally slain by the five stones, *i.e.*, wounds. If therefore you keep these stones continually in the coffer of your heart, you will be able to regain the virtues you lost through sin, and so proceed with joy to your heavenly home, *i.e.*, to life eternal.

---

2 I Kgs 17. 48ff.
3 In fact the name David means 'beloved'.

119. Of all things living in this world, man is the most ungrateful for the benefits he has received[1]

A certain king had a seneschal as steward over his kingdom who was by nature so high-handed and proud that he tyrannized everyone, because his every wish was obeyed. Near the royal palace was a forest with abundant game, and this seneschal had a series of pits dug and covered with leaves so that the beasts would fall into them unawares and be taken. Now it happened that this seneschal was passing through the forest and in his extreme arrogance entertained the thought that there was no greater person in the kingdom than he. And as he rode on he fell into one of his pits and could not get out. That same day a lion had fallen into the pit, then an ape, and thirdly a snake. Seeing himself surrounded by these beasts, he cried out in terror, and his cries were heard by a poor man named Guido who was carrying wood from the forest on his ass, which was how he made a living. So he came to the pit and the seneschal promised him a rich reward if he would get him out.

'My friend,' said Guido, 'I have no means of livelihood if I cannot gather wood. If I forego it just today, I shall suffer a loss in income.' But the seneschal promised him faithfully that if he got him out he would make him rich. So Guido went back to the city and brought back a long rope with him, which he let down into the pit so that the seneschal could tie it around himself and be pulled up. But as he let the rope down the lion leapt upon the rope and was pulled up; and once out, it showed its gratitude to Guido and

1 Cf. Herrtage, Text I.LXV. This story is found, with variations, in a number of other works, including an Arabian fable book, *Calilah u Dumnah* (translated into English in 1570 and entitled *Donie's Moral Philosophie*); Matthew Paris, *Chronica Maiora*, under the year 1195; and Gower's *Confessio Amantis* V. For other examples, see Oesterley, p. 731; Tubach, no. 256; Hope, pp. 565–6.

then ran into the forest. Guido then let the rope down into the pit a second time, and this time the ape leapt upon it, and Guido pulled it up, and it ran off into the forest. Then Guido let the rope down again and the snake seized hold of it and Guido drew it out of the pit; whereupon the snake showed its gratitude to Guido, then slithered into the forest. The seneschal at once cried: 'Dear friend, blessed be the Most High, I am now free of those beasts. Let the rope down!' Guido did so. The seneschal tied the rope around himself and Guido pulled him out. They then pulled his horse out, and the seneschal immediately climbed on it and rode off to the palace. Guido went home, and seeing him empty-handed his wife was heartbroken. But he told her what had happened, and that he would be suitably rewarded for his help, and this cheered her.

Next morning Guido went to the castle and sent the porter to tell the seneschal that he was there. But the seneschal repeatedly denied that he had ever set eyes on him, indeed he said that if he did not go away he would have him severely beaten. When Guido came back and tried a third time, the porter beat him so savagely that he left him half dead. Guido's wife got to hear of this, and she brought him home on their ass. Guido was ill for a long time, and during his illness all his savings were used up. When he was well again and gathering wood one day, he saw in the distance ten asses laden with saddle bags, and a lion following them in the rear, and it led them straight towards Guido. Guido took a close look at the lion and at once remembered that it was the lion he had drawn from the pit. The lion came up to him, and with a paw gestured to him to go home with the asses and their loads. Guido did so; he led the asses home and the lion followed him until he got there. And when the asses had arrived safely, the lion wagged its tail in gratitude to Guido, then ran back into the forest. Guido had an announcement made in a number of churches to see if anyone had lost the asses, but no-one claiming to have lost them could be discovered. When Guido opened up the saddle bags he found they were packed with money, and to his immense joy he became a rich man.

The second day Guido went into the forest, but found himself without a cleaver for splitting the wood. Then he looked up and saw the ape he had pulled from the pit, which, by using its teeth and nails on the wood, broke it into such manageable pieces that Guido was easily able to load up his ass and return home.

The third day Guido returned to the forest, and as he was sitting

119. Man is the most ungrateful for the benefits he has received

getting his tools ready to use, he saw the snake he had drawn from the pit carrying in its mouth a stone of three colours: it was white on one side, black on another and red on the other. The snake opened its mouth and let the stone fall into Guido's lap, then went away. Guido took the stone to an expert who, as soon as he had seen it knew its virtue, and readily offered him 100 florins for it. But instead, through the virtue of the stone, Guido acquired many valuable possessions and was promoted to a command in the army.

When the king heard of this, he commanded Guido to appear before him, and wanted to buy the stone from him, threatening to banish him from the kingdom if he refused. 'Sire,' said Guido, 'I will sell the stone, but I make one condition: if you do not give me what it is worth, the stone will come back to me.' The king gave him 300 florins, and Guido took the stone from his box and gave it to the king. Admiring the stone, the king said: 'Tell me, where did you get this from?' So Guido told him the whole story from beginning to end: how his seneschal had fallen into the pit with the lion, the ape and the snake; how in seeking his reward he had been badly beaten by the seneschal; and of the gifts he had received from the lion, the ape and the snake.

When he heard this tale he king was incensed with the seneschal and said to him: 'What is this I hear of you?' The seneschal could not deny the charge. 'You scoundrel!' the king cried. 'You have shown abominable ingratitude to Guido, and it was he who saved you from dying, and you left him half dead. You wretch! Why, irrational beasts – a lion, an ape, a snake, – have rewarded him for his help, but you have rendered him evil for good. For that you will give everything you possess, your position as well, to Guido, and I sentence you to be hanged this very day.'

This judgement met with the approval of all the king's nobles, and Guido succeeded to the seneschal's office, and ended his days in peace.

Moralization. Dear friends, the king is God, who sees everything; the pauper is man, who has nothing of his own; Job c.1:[2] *'Naked came I out of my mother's womb, naked I shall return there.' God elevated man when he made him lord of paradise. The Psalmist:*[3] *'Thou hast*

---

2 Jb 1.21.
3 Ps 8.8.

subjected all things under his feet.' The pit into which he fell is the world, which is full of pits, i.e., perils, because *'the whole world is seated in wickedness'*.[4] In this world man has fallen into many pits: Genesis c.3:[5] *'In the sweat of thy face etc.'* The lion that fell into the same pit is the Son of God, when he assumed human nature and lived thirty years in great wretchedness. The Psalmist says:[6] *'I am with him in tribulation.'* This is the lion of whom Revelation says, c.8:[7] *'The lion of the tribe of Judah hath prevailed etc.'* Next the ape fell in, i.e., your conscience, which, like an ape, destroys those things that displease it, because it is always murmuring against sin. Likewise the snake fell into the pit, i.e., a prelate or confessor, who must go down with the sinner, i.e., grieve with him for his sins; as we read in Corinthians, c.6:[8] *'Who is weak, and I am not weak?'* And Guido drew out the seneschal with the rope; even so the Son of God has with the rope of his Passion drawn us from the pit of misery and from the power of the devil; but despite this, wretched man shows his ingratitude to God whenever he sins against God's law. Guido was beaten; even so man, when he commits mortal sin, does all in his power to crucify God a second time. But the lion, i.e., God, gave to Christ, as man, ten asses laden with packs, i.e., placed all the commandments under his authority, both old and new, in his dealings with man. And if we perform those commandments, we shall attain to everlasting riches. Guido cut up wood, i.e., your conscience spurs you to perform the works with which on the Day of Judgement you will be able to cover[9] body and soul, and for which you will obtain eternal rest. Because if you act against your conscience, you will be taken off to hell. The snake gave Guido a stone of three colours; even so the prelate and confessor through the instruction of Holy Scripture will be able to obtain the stone, i.e., Christ.[10] The stone was beautiful: black, and red, and white, as Christ was white, who is

4   1 Jn 5.19.
5   Gn 3.19.
6   Ps 90.15.
7   = Rv 5.5.
8   = 2 Cor 11.29.
9   *operari:* Oest.; *operiri:* K., L. 'Cover' in the sense of 'protect', 'defend' (cf. Ps 84.3, where *operio* means 'pardon'), implying the covering of vulnerable nakedness before the Judge.
10 *poterat:* Oest., K.; *poterit:* L. Cf. *Le Violier:* 'Le serpent ... est le prelat, lequel, par l'information de saincte et sacrée escripture, nous donne la cognoissance de la grace de Nostre Saulveur Jesus-Christ.'

119. Man is the most ungrateful for the benefits he has received

'beautiful above the children of men'.[11] He was likewise black because of his Passion, and red because of the blood he shed. So the man who carries this stone has unfailing plenty; and he should not sell the stone except for the price Christ demands,[12] i.e., contrition, confession and atonement. But ingrates will be hanged on the gibbet of hell, while the elect will obtain eternal life, which [may God grant] to us etc.

---

11 Ps 44.3.
12 *quantum Christus*: Oest., K.; *quantum Christus exigit*: L., *Le Violier*.

120. Of the subtle deceits of women[1]

King Darius was a most prudent king who had three sons whom he loved dearly. When he was near to death he bequeathed all he had inherited to his first-born; to the second he gave all he had acquired in his lifetime; and to his third and youngest son he gave three precious objects: a golden ring, a necklace and a valuable piece of cloth. The ring had the special virtue that whoever wore it on his finger found favour with everyone, and indeed obtained whatever he asked of them. The necklace had the special virtue that whoever wore it on his breast could gain anything his heart could possibly desire. The cloth had the special virtue that whoever sat on it and thought of somewhere he would like to go was at once there. These were the three precious objects Darius gave his youngest son in order to support him in his studies, and his mother was to keep them and give them to him at the proper time. Soon after this the king died and was buried with all honours. The two elder sons took possession of their legacies, and the third received the ring from his mother, to assist him in his studies. 'My son,' she said to him, 'learn all you can and beware of women, or you may lose the ring.'

Jonathan took the ring, began his studies and proved a good scholar. But one day he met a particularly beautiful young woman in the street, and was so smitten with her that he took her home with him. He used the ring continually, and found favour with everyone, and got whatever he wished from them.

His mistress was surprised that he lived in such luxury, though

[1] Cf. Herrtage, Text I.XLVI. Thomas Hoccleve (?1369–1426) composed a poem based on this story (printed in 1614 in Brown's *Shepheard's Pipe*). Cf. also the German legend of Fortunatus. The magic cloth/carpet is familiar from *The Arabian Nights*. For other cognates, see Oesterley, p. 731; Tubach, no. 2153; Hope, pp. 566–7.

120. Of the subtle deceits of women

he had no money, so one day, when he was in high spirits, she asked him how this could be; she told him there was nobody on earth she loved more than him, so he ought to tell her his secret. Not suspecting her of any mischief, he told her of the special virtue of the ring. 'But every single day you have dealings with other men,' she said, ' and you might lose it. I will keep it safe for you.' So he handed her the ring. But when straitened circumstances forced him to ask her to give it back, she brazenly declared that thieves had stolen it, and Jonathan wept bitterly when he heard this, because he had no means of livelihood. He went straight to his mother the queen and informed her of the loss of the ring. 'My son,' she told him, 'I warned you to beware of women. Here, take the necklace and guard it more carefully. If you lose it, you will lose something of unfailing honour and profit.' Jonathan took the necklace and returned to his studies, and lo and behold!, at the gate of the city his mistress met him, and welcomed him with joy. Jonathan lived with her as before, and wore the necklace on his breast, and had only to think of something and it became his. As before, he gave many banquets and lived a life of luxury, and his mistress wondered at this, because she could see he possessed neither gold nor silver. She suspected that he had brought some other precious object with him, and cleverly questioned him about this. So he showed her the necklace and told her of its virtue. 'You always have that necklace on you,' she said; 'in just an hour you could think of enough to suffice you for a year. So give it to me to look after.' 'No,' he said. 'I am afraid that you might lose the necklace as you lost the ring, and that would bring me utter ruin.' 'My lord,' she replied, 'I have learned a lesson by losing the ring, and I promise you faithfully that I shall guard the necklace so carefully that no-one will be able to take it from me.'

Believing in her sincerity, Jonathan handed the necklace to her, and when he had exhausted all the means he had, he asked her for it. As before, she swore it had been taken by some thief. When Jonathan heard this he was distraught. 'After losing the ring,' he said, 'I must have been mad to give you the necklace.'

He hurried off to his mother and told her the whole story. Deeply upset, she said to him: 'My dearest son, why did you ever trust a woman? Now you have been fooled by her a second time and everyone will think you are a simpleton. Now learn some sense, because I have nothing left for you except the precious cloth that your father gave you. If you lose that, there will be no point in coming back to me.'

Jonathan took the cloth and returned to his studies, and his mistress welcomed him back with joy as before. Unfolding the cloth he said to her: 'My dear, my father gave me this cloth.' And they sat down on it together. Jonathan thought: 'I wish we were somewhere far away where no-one has ever set foot.' And suddenly they were at the ends of the earth in a forest, far away from humankind. The girl was reduced to tears by this, but Jonathan vowed to heaven that he would leave her to be eaten by wild beasts if she did not give him back the ring and the necklace. This she promised to do, if it was possible. Then, because she asked him about it, Jonathan told his mistress of the virtue of the cloth, and that whoever reclined on it would at once be transported to any place he chose to go. She then sat down on the cloth and took his head in her lap, and as soon as he fell asleep pulled that part of it on which he was resting from underneath him. She thought: 'I wish myself where I was this morning.' Her wish was granted, and Jonathan was left asleep in the forest.

When he awoke and saw that both the cloth and his mistress were gone, he wept inconsolably and did not know where to go. But he got up and, fortifying himself with the sign of the cross, took a path which led him to a deep river which he had to cross, but its water was so brackish and hot that it burned the flesh of his feet down to the bare bones. Dismayed at this, he filled a vessel with some of the water and took it with him, and in due course began to feel hungry, and seeing a tree he ate its fruit, and instantly became a leper. But he also picked some of its fruit and took it with him. Then he came to another river and as he crossed it, its water restored the flesh to his feet, and he filled a vessel with its water and took it with him, and as he travelled on he began to feel hungry, and seeing a tree, picked some of its fruit and ate it; and just as he had been poisoned by the fruit he had eaten before, so he was cleansed of his leprosy by eating the fruit of the second tree. He picked some its fruit also and took it on his way. And as he proceeded, he saw a castle, and was met by two men who asked who he was. 'I am a skilled physician,' he told them. They replied: 'The king of this country lives in this castle and is a leper. If you can cure his leprosy he will give you riches in plenty.' 'Very well,' he said.

So they brought him to the king, and Jonathan gave him some fruit from the second tree and he was cured of his leprosy. He then gave him some water to drink from the second river, which restored his flesh to health, whereupon the king rewarded him lavishly. Jonathan then came upon a ship from his own city and so sailed home, where a rumour spread through the whole city that a great physician had arrived. His mistress, who had stolen his treasures, and who was mortally ill, sent for this physician. Jonathan was not recognized by anyone, but he knew his mistress, and told her that no medicine would be of any use to her unless she first confessed all her sins, and that, if she had cheated anyone of anything, she must give it back. She then brazenly confessed that she had cheated Jonathan of his ring, necklace and cloth, and left him in a desolate place to be devoured by wild beasts. When she had finished, he said to her: 'Tell me, lady, where are these three treasures?' 'In my chest,' she replied, and gave him the keys to the chest, and there he found them. Jonathan then gave her some of the fruit of the tree which had infected him with leprosy, and some of the water from the first river which had parted his flesh from his bones. As soon as she had eaten the fruit and drunk the water, her flesh was suddenly shrivelled and she was racked with internal pains, and with a pitiful cry she expired. Jonathan hurried off with his treasures to his mother, and the entire population was delighted at his return. From beginning to end, he told his mother the story of how God had delivered him from many terrible dangers. He then lived a number of years before ending his days in peace.

Moralization. Dear friends, the king is our Lord Jesus Christ; the queen is Mother Church; and the three sons are men living the world. The first I interpret as the rich and powerful of the world, to whom God gives the world to use as they will. The second is the wise of the world, who acquire whatever they have through their worldly wisdom. The third son is the good Christian, elect from eternity, to whom God gave three precious objects: the ring of faith, the necklace of his grace or hope, and the cloth of charity; and whoever wears the ring of faith will have the favour of God and the love of man in such abundance that he will obtain whatever he desires; as Paul writes:[2] 'If I have faith as a grain of mustard, I shall be able to say to this mountain: Go away! And it goes.' And if you have the necklace of hope upon your bosom, i.e., in your heart, think what you want, and if it is just, you

---

2 These are words that Christ addresses to his disciples: cf. Mt 17.19; Lk 17.6.

will obtain it. As the Lord says:³ 'Ask and you shall receive; seek and you shall find.' And in the Epistle to the Hebrews:⁴ 'We are saved by hope.' And if you have the cloth of charity, wherever you wish to be, your wish will be granted; Corinthians c.6:⁵ 'Charity seeketh not her own', but the things of Christ Jesus. And John says:⁶ 'God is charity.' But in his zeal for this world man often loses these three precious things through his mistress, i.e., his flesh, i.e., through carnal lust, for the flesh opposes the spirit. Jonathan's mistress drew the cloth from under him while he was sleeping. Even so the flesh often steals a man's charity from him through mortal sin, and while he is sleeping in sin, and as long as he remains in sin, banishes him from all God's grace and assistance. When Jonathan woke from sleep he wept bitterly. Even so you will have good reason to weep, after you have been woken from the sleep of sin, and find yourself without grace or virtues,. What then are you to do? Bestir yourself swiftly with works of mercy and sign yourself with the sign of the holy cross upon your breast, and you will find the way of salvation. Go on until you come to a stream, whose water separates the flesh from the bones. This is the water of contrition, and it must be so bitter that it separates the flesh, i.e., carnal pleasures, from the bones, i.e., the sins, wherewith you have offended God. And you must fill the vessel of your heart with this water, and as long as you are in this mortal body, you must feel contrition in your heart. Then you must go further on and eat the fruit of the tree. This fruit is repentance, by which the soul is nourished, but the body often turns black like that of a leper. You must gather this fruit and always carry it with you. When Jonathan went on, he came to a second river, by which his flesh was restored. This water is confession, which restores the virtues that have been lost. When he went further, he ate of the fruit of the second tree and was cured. This fruit is the fruit of penance, i.e., prayer, fasting and almsgiving. You must always carry some of this water and fruit with you, so that, if by chance you come upon a king who is a leper, you can cure him. This king signifies man, who is infected with sin, but who can be cured with the fruit of confession and the water of contrition. The two men who met Jonathan along the way, and took him to cure the king,⁷ are the fear of God and of hell, which causes man to turn

3 Cf. Mt 7.7f.
4 = Rom 8.24.
5 1 Cor 13.5.
6 1 Jn 4.8.
7 *ad curandum te*: 'to cure you'. The addressee is the good Christian,

120. Of the subtle deceits of women

from evil and do good. The ship that took Jonathan to his homeland is God's commandments, which bring you to everlasting joy. But first you must seek your mistress, i.e., the flesh that opposes the spirit, and you will find her in the bed of carnal lust. Give her some of the fruit of repentance with the water of contrition, and these will cause her flesh to rise, i.e., to be uplifted through sincere devotion to receive the yoke of penance. And thus you will be able to render your spirit to God together with the precious gifts, i.e., virtues, he gave you, and so reach the homeland of the heavenly kingdom; to which etc.

---

who has to go on a journey like Jonathan. But from this point there is a confusion of pronouns, as the preacher associates himself with the addressee, or counsels him *ex cathedra*. I have made some adjustments for clarity's sake.

121. Of worldly glory and luxury, which deceives many and leads them to destruction[1]

There was once a king who had two knights in the same city, one old, the other young. The old one was rich and married a lovely girl for her beauty. The young knight was poor and married an old woman for her money, and did not much care for her. Now it happened one day that the young knight was going through the courtyard of the castle belonging to the older knight, and his wife was sitting in a window at her leisure and singing sweetly. As soon as he saw her the young knight was captivated by her and thought to himself: 'It would be better for that young girl to be paired with me than with her husband, who is an impotent old man, and for my wife to be his.' And from that day on he was in love with her and sent her gifts of jewellery. The lady loved him passionately, and whenever she could she went to him, and did everything she possibly could to ensure that they would marry after her husband died. Now, by the window of the old knight's castle there was a fig tree on which a nightingale sat every night singing sweetly, and because of this the lady got up every night and went to the window, and remained at the window for some time waiting to hear its song. When her husband realized that she got up every night, he said: 'Dearest, why do you get out of bed every night?' She replied: 'A nightingale perches every night on the fig tree and sings so beautifully that I have to get up and listen to it.' When he heard this, the knight got up early next morning, took a bow and arrow, went to the fig tree and shot the nightingale; then he removed its heart and presented it to his wife. When she saw the nightingale's heart she wept bitterly. 'Sweet nightingale,' she said, 'you did what it was your nature to do, and I am the cause of your death!'

1 Cf. Herrtage, Text I.XVII.

121. Of worldly glory and luxury

She at once sent a messenger to the young knight telling him of her husband's cruelty in killing the nightingale. When he heard the news, the young knight was shaken to the core, and said to himself: 'If that cruel fellow knew how much his wife and I love each other, he would treat me even worse!' So he put on a double coat of armour, entered the castle and killed the old knight. His own wife died shortly thereafter, so he jubilantly married the wife of the old knight, and they both lived long and ended their days in peace.

Dear friends, these two knights symbolize the prophet Moses and our Lord Jesus Christ. Christ is the old knight who from the beginning of time married a young wife, i.e., the New Law. Moses is the young knight, because he was created in time, who espoused the Old Law. The tree on which the nightingale sang is the cross on which Christ hung. The nightingale is Christ's humanity, which sang sweetly when he entreated the Heavenly Father on mankind's behalf. But the Jews could not bear that the lady should rise from her bed, i.e., that so many should rise from the bed of sin and follow[2] Christ; so they destroyed his humanity and his heart, i.e., the love which he shows us, i.e., every Christian, that he may cease from sin and serve God faithfully. But Moses armed himself in a double coat of armour, i.e., he armed himself with ceremonies and with circumcision, and slew the lion,[3] and not only his own sins, but those of all the faithful slew him, from our first parent up to the advent of Christ himself; as it is written:[4] 'He bore our sins in his body.' What follows from this? Clearly that Moses, i.e., any faithful Christian who desires to enter the heavenly kingdom, must espouse the law,[5] as Matthew says:[6] 'He that believeth and is baptized, shall be saved.'

---

2 *insequebantur*: Oest.; *sequerentur*: L.
3 *leonem*: the introduction of a lion is surprising. *Le Violier*'s *'l'ancien chevalier'* (old knight) makes better sense. The old knight, the Old Law, is done away with by the New.
4 Cf. 1 Pt 2.24.
5 The New Law, that of grace.
6 Mk 16.16.

122. Of adulterous women and the blindness of prelates

A certain knight went to his vineyard to harvest his grapes and his wife, thinking he would be away some considerable time, having a lover, sent for him to come quickly. So he came and went to her bedchamber; but while they were in bed together, back came the knight, her husband, who had been struck in the eye by a vine branch, and knocked at the door. Trembling with fear she opened it, having first concealed her lover. The knight came in, and since his eye was painful, told her to get his bed ready so that he could lie down. But fearing that he might see her lover hiding in the room, his wife said to him: 'Why go to bed in such haste? Tell me what happened.' So he told her, and she replied: 'My lord, let me strengthen the eye that is sound with some medicine, in case you lose that one as well through contact with the diseased one.' So he let her, and as she bent her face over her husband's sound eye, as if to treat it, she gestured with one hand to her lover, who got away. When he had gone, she said to her husband: 'Now I am sure your sound eye will come to no harm. Into bed with you and rest!'[1]

Dear friends, the knight is a prelate of the church, who has to watch over Holy Church and govern the sheep entrusted to him. The adulterous wife is the soul, which often cleaves to the devil through sin. The knight is 'struck in the eye' whenever a prelate is blinded by gifts, for it is written in Wisdom c.6:[2] 'Gifts blind the eyes of judges.' So the soul must enter the chamber of a goodly life and cast from it all avarice and greed through penance. Then the knight must boldly knock on the door

1 Cf. the tale recounted by Peter Alfonsi, *Disciplina Clericalis* IX. For other versions, see Oesterley, pp. 731–2; Tubach, no. 1943; Hope, pp. 612–14.
2 Cf. Dt 16.19.

122. Of adulterous women and the blindness of prelates

of his heart, and his wife, i.e., soul, opens to him that he may receive God's glory. But alas!, often the eye that is sound, and with which we should contemplate God, is so clouded through carnal affections and worldly blandishments, through worldly vanities and desires of the flesh, that the prelate will not be able to see the perils that face him and his charges, and to correct them with penance. Let each of us therefore so direct his spiritual eyes towards God that he will be able to remove every veil of sin.

123. Young ladies should be kept from wantonness by their parents and not left to their own inclinations

A certain knight who was going to travel abroad left his wife in the safekeeping of her mother, his mother-in-law. After her husband had gone, his wife fell in love with a young man and told her mother of it. She at once lent her support and sent for the youth, but while they were at dinner the knight came back and knocked at the door. His wife got up at once, hid her lover in her bed, and then opened the door to her husband. He entered and told her to prepare him a bed because he was tired and wanted to sleep. His wife, in a panic, wondered what she could do. Observing her dilemma, her mother said: 'Don't make up the bed, dear, until we have shown your husband the sheet we have made.' And she held up a sheet by one corner as high as she could, and gave the other corner to her daughter to hold up, and they kept the sheet stretched out in front of him until the lover had got away. So the husband was fooled by the screen they had made. And when the lover had gone, the mother said to her daughter: 'Now spread the sheet that you and I have woven together on your husband's bed.'[1]

Moralization. Dear friends, the knight is any man who after baptism goes about like a pilgrim in the world, for, as long as we are here, we are pilgrims. The Psalmist says:[2] *'I am a pilgrim and the son of my mother.' But during this pilgrimage his wife, i.e., the flesh, often commits adultery because of her vices and desires. The knight knocks at the door when he recollects what sins he has committed against God,*

1 Cf. the previous tale and Peter Alfonsi, *Disciplina Clericalis* X. See also Oesterley, p. 732; Tubach, no. 4319; Hope, p. 614.
2 Cf. Ps 38.13: 'I am a stranger ... and a sojourner as all my fathers were'; and 68.9: 'I am become a stranger to my brethren and an alien to the sons of my mother.'

123. Young ladies should be kept from wantonness by their parents

and how great they were, and therefore he must knock, i.e., pray, fast etc., and do good works. And so he will be able to enter the chamber of a goodly life and go to rest in the heaven he is promised. But often when his wife, i.e., the flesh, realizes that her husband proposes to do penance, she is troubled, because she cannot happily endure penance. As soon as her mother, i.e., the world, realizes this, she holds up a sheet, i.e., the worldly vanities in which man takes such delight that he does not notice his own dangers, which is lamentable.

124. Women should not be trusted, and no secrets should be told to them, since when they are angry they cannot keep them hidden[1]

A certain noble knight had seriously offended a king whose vassal he was, and sent knights to the king to intercede for him. But only at length did they win him over, and only on condition that he should come to the palace on foot and on horseback simultaneously, i.e., half riding and half walking, and that he should bring with him his most trusted friend, a most excellent jester and his greatest enemy.[2] This distressed the knight, who began to wonder how he could possibly fulfil these conditions. Then one night, when he had offered hospitality to a pilgrim, he said to his wife in private: 'I know pilgrims carry ready money with them, so if you agree to it I am going to kill him and we shall have his money.' 'That is a good idea,' she said. So around first light, when the whole household was asleep, the knight got up, woke up the pilgrim and told him to be on his way. He then took one of his calves, cut it into pieces and put them in a sack. Next he woke his wife, gave her the sack and told her to hide it in some corner of the house. 'I have put the head and legs and arms in this sack. The body I have buried in our stable.' And with these words he showed her some money as if he had taken it from the dead pilgrim.

When the day was near when he was to appear before his lord, he set off with a dog on his right hand, his tiny son in his lap and his wife on his left, and when he was approaching the king's castle he placed his right leg over the dog's back as if he were riding, and walked on the other leg, and thus entered his lord's castle both walking and riding. The king and all his courtiers were astonished when they saw him.

1 Cf. Herrtage, Text I.XIV.
2 For the imposition of another seemingly impossible task, cf no. 64 and note 2.

124. Women should not be trusted

'Where is your most trusted friend?' the king asked him. The knight instantly drew his sword from its sheath and dealt the dog a nasty wound so that it yelped loudly with the pain and ran off. The knight then called it back and the dog returned. 'There he is, my most trusted friend.'

'You are right,' answered the king. 'Where is your jester?' 'Here he is, my tiny son. When I watch him playing he amuses me no end.'

'Where is your greatest enemy?' asked the king. The knight at once slapped his wife and said: 'How dare you look so shamelessly at my lord the king?' 'You accursed murderer,' she retorted at once, 'why do you strike me? Haven't you committed a dreadful murder in your own house, and killed a pilgrim for a handful of money?' The knight slapped her again and said: 'Accursed wretch, have you no thought for the disgrace you bring on your child?'

At this she flew into a rage. 'Come with me,' she told everyone, 'and I will show you the sack in which he put the head and arms of the pilgrim he killed, and the stable where he buried the body.'

So they went with her to see if she was telling the truth, and when they dug up the place she pointed out to them, they were astonished to discover pieces of calf's flesh. Then, when they perceived how cunning the knight had been, everyone praised him in the most fulsome terms, as was fitting, and thereafter he and his lord the king were united in a special bond of affection.

Moralization. Dear friends, the knight who lost the favour of his king is the sinner, who, to obtain the favour of his lord, sends people to intercede with God, i.e., men he loves, such as relatives and friends. But in order to atone to his lord, he must come to him on foot and on horseback; on foot, i.e., treading upon earthly and temporal things as despicable; and on horseback, by contemplating the things of heaven with all his heart's desire. But he must bring a dog too, on his right, as his most faithful friend, i.e., his good angel, or a priest, who has to keep watch over his soul, and who, despite being wounded and struck repeatedly with the sword of his sins, returns faithfully as his friend, and who will keep his secrets from the king's household. He must have a jester, i.e., his small son, in his lap, i.e., a good conscience which, if well governed, gives man much pleasure. On his left, as his most treacherous enemy, he must bring his wife, i.e., voluptuousness of the flesh, or the devil, who to his ruin discloses and reveals his secrets before the household and friends of the king, i.e., before all the angels and saints when the hour of his death is imminent. Then the wise knight will justly be praised for having tricked these foes as he did, by slaughtering a calf in private and burying it in a secret corner of the house, i.e., by scourging his own body in a secret chamber, or deeply cleansing the secrets of his heart with a tearful conscience; however, not by committing murder, i.e., exceeding due measure, but by persisting in fasts and prayer and other good works, through which he will regain the favour of his lord, which he had lost.

125. Women not only reveal secrets, but also tell many lies

There were two brothers, one of whom was a layman and the other a priest. The one who was a layman had often heard from his brother that women could not keep a secret and thought he would put this to the test with his own dear wife. So one night he said to her: 'Dearest, I have a secret, and I'd tell it to you if I were sure you would tell no-one. If you did, it would mean a lot of trouble for me.' 'My lord,' said she, 'have no fear, we are one body: your good is my good, and vice versa; your troubles are mine too.' 'When I went to the privy,' he told her, 'to obey the call of nature, a jet black crow flew out of my backside, and I was horrified!' 'You should be pleased,' she said, 'to have been delivered of such a painful thing.'

When the woman got up next morning she went next door and said to the lady of the house: 'My dear, can I tell you a secret?' 'Of course,' she replied. 'It is as safe with me as with yourself.' 'The strangest thing has happened to my husband,' she told her; 'he went to the privy in the night to obey the call of nature, and what do you think? Two jet black crows flew out of his backside, and I am very worried about it.'

Her neighbour then told another neighbour that there were three crows, and this third neighbour said there were four, and so it went on until the false rumour spread that sixty crows had flown out of him.

Disturbed at hearing the rumour, he called the townsfolk together and told them what he had done, and that he had wanted to test his wife and see if she could keep a secret. Some time after this his wife died and he entered a monastery, where he learned three letters, the first of which was black, the second red and the third white.[1]

---

1 This is unintelligible without the *moralisatio*, for which the last sentence seems to have been purposely added. Cf. the version of this story in La

Moralization. Dearly beloved, the man who proved the evil intent of women is the worldly man who labours with all his might to acquire worldly goods, and often, while he believes he can get away without causing offence, inclines to a thousand sins, as the man who inclines to pride inclines to many other sins that militate against the salvation of his soul; and this is the black crow that flies from his posterior, it is in fact sin; and so a man is slandered not only by his own wife, i.e., his flesh, but by other neighbours, i.e., by the five senses. Do therefore as he did. Assemble the people, i.e., all your deeds past and present, and cleanse yourself by means of confession, and then you will be able to enter the monastery of the good life and learn the three letters by means of which you will gain an eternal reward. The first letter is black, and is the remembrance of sins, which, like a gross and heavy burden torment and torture your bosom daily when you recall the pains of hell. The second letter is red, and is the remembrance of the rose-coloured blood of your Creator which he poured out on the cross for you, wretched sinner, in five rivulets, and gave abundantly in his compassion. The third letter is white, and is the desire for the joys of heaven and those who follow the Lamb of God in white garments wherever he goes. If we keep these three things firmly in our hearts we shall without doubt possess the everlasting kingdom.

Fontaine's *Les Femmes et le Secret*, VIII 6 (where eggs are substituted for the crows).

126. Women are never to be trusted and especially not in the keeping of secrets: an amusing example

Macrobius relates[1] that a Roman boy named Papirius once entered the Senate House with his father where a certain plan was discussed which was to be kept secret on pain of death. When the lad returned home, his mother asked him what it was that the consuls had forbidden anyone to speak of on pain of death. The boy replied: 'It is not permitted to reveal it to anyone.' This reply made his mother persist the more. She began to beg, to make him promises, then turned to threatening him with a beating to get him to reveal the secret. Finally, to satisfy her curiosity, yet keep his secret, he told her: 'The matter being debated is this: would it be better for one man to have several wives, or for one woman to have several husbands?'

No sooner had he said this than his mother revealed the secret to the other women of Rome, and next day on an impulse they all came in a crowd to the Senate with the petition that one woman should have two husbands rather than one man two wives. The Senate were alarmed to see such shameless hysteria in a sex normally so retiring, and wondered what this wild outburst on the part of the women might mean, and what this shameless petition might possibly signify, it being an omen of no[2] small significance. Seeing their puzzlement, the young Papirius told the senators how this had come about, and they applauded his subterfuge, and decreed that this boy, and no other, should always be present at their deliberations in future.

1 Macrobius (fl. c. fourth century AD), *Saturnalia* I.VI. The story is also told by Aulus Gellius (second century AD), *Noctes Atticae* I.23. For other cognates, see Oesterley, pp. 732–3.
2 *et ut parvae rei*: Oest.; *et ut non parvae rei*: Macrobius, *Saturnalia* I.VI.23.

Moralization. Dear friends, this boy is any pure man who leads a pure life, and who, with his father, i.e., a prelate, enters a council of wise men, i.e., religious, where the discussion is of salvation and spiritual wisdom, which wisdom is not to be expounded to all. But, while this is fitting for everyone, according to his status, he must not reveal to others what penance he has received from his own priest. And there are many other things that should not be related. The mother is this world, which persuades a man to abandon religion, and to disclose secrets, that is, not to keep them in his heart, but rather to give them up. And if she cannot persuade a man to do so in this way, then she determines to persuade him with threats, i.e., by tribulations and deprivation and other means. So do as young Papirius did! Fool the world by undergoing voluntary poverty, and show it that two women, i.e., the various vices of fleshly pleasure, should be handed over to the custody of reason rather than reason be trampled beneath the desire and pleasure of the moment. Without doubt, as far as the body is concerned, it prefers to choose that reason should be trampled on; but you must in no wise agree to this, rather the very contrary. So as a consequence young Papirius, i.e., the pure man, will be allowed to remain among the wise and to have virtues, i.e., he will always be able, among holy men and women, to hear the words of salvation and to win life everlasting. Which [may God deign] to grant us etc.

127. Of the justice and equity shown by Christ, the wisest judge, in his hidden judgements

There was an overbearing knight who for many years kept in his employ a servant who was both faithful and prudent in all he did. One day when he was passing through a wood with this servant on his way to market, he chanced to lose thirty silver marks in the middle of the wood. His servant knew nothing of this, but when the knight could not find the money, he asked him if he had come upon it. He at once denied any knowledge of it; he swore he knew nothing of it, and he told the truth. But when it could not be found, the knight promptly cut off one of his feet, left him there and went home.

A hermit lived nearby, and when he heard the servant's cries of agony, he ran swiftly to help him. He heard his confession, and realizing he was innocent, kindly took him on his shoulders to his abode. He then went into his oratory and reproached the Lord because he had not judged the man justly, and had allowed an innocent man to lose his foot. After he had prayed and wept at length, and taken the Lord to task somewhat for his false judgement, an angel of the Lord came to him and said: 'Have you not read in the Psalms:[1] "God is a just judge, strong and patient?"' 'That I have read many times,' he said, 'and believed it with all my heart, but either I have been in error today, or that wretch who has lost his foot has deceived me under the veil of confession.'

The angel replied: 'Do not charge the Lord with iniquity, for all his ways are truth and his judgements equitable. Recall to mind what you have read so often. "The judgements of God are a great deep."[2] Know then that man lost his foot for an old sin, because many years

---

1 Ps 7.12.
2 Cf. Ps 35.7.

ago he maliciously kicked his own mother out of a carriage with that same foot and subsequently never did worthy penance for it. The knight who is his master wanted to buy a warhorse, to amass more wealth to the defilement of his soul, and so it was by God's just judgement that he lost his money. There is an honest poor man who with his wife and children begged the Lord daily that he might deign to provide them with the necessities of life, and he found the money and offered it to his confessor to distribute among the needy. This man made enquiries everywhere, but honestly could not find who it belonged to. So he gave part of it to the poor man for God's sake, and distributed the remainder to other poor folk. Put a guard on your tongue, therefore, lest you reproach the Lord again in any way, as you have done, since he is a true, strong and patient judge.'

Dear friends, the knight can signify any good prelate, who must put on the armour of God that he may stand firm against the assaults of the devil. The faithful servant is one who is subject in all things, and obedient to, his prelate. The prelate has a treasure, i.e., souls to watch over, which he often loses through neglect. What then must he do? Clearly, he must diligently desire the soul's salvation, as long as he lives, and if he cannot find it, he should cut off his servant's right foot, i.e., chastise the rebel and cut him off from the Church until he knows that he has sinned. Do you know how? After the servant loses his foot he begins to cry out. Even so the sinner cries out in his confession, as the prophet says:[3] 'Cry, cease not, lift up thy voice like a trumpet etc.' Hearing his cries, the hermit, i.e., discerning confessor, has to carry him on his shoulders, that is, by instructing him, preaching to him, giving him penance and leading him into the house of the Church through works of mercy; and he has to intercede for him with the Lord, not reproaching him, but begging God with all his heart to save and watch over such a convert, who in a malicious frame of mind had once cast his mother, i.e., the Church, violently from him, when he was not keeping God's commandments. The poor man who found the money is Christ, who often keeps the soul from slipping down to hell, until the sinner rises again through penance, and so receives a cleansed soul from Christ, because without him we are not able to do good works. So, sinner, put a guard upon your mouth lest you presume to say anything against God! For God is a just judge, and mighty and patient; therefore do not say: 'Why did he make me and then leave me to fall?'

3 Is 58.1.

127. Of the justice and equity shown by Christ

Or this tale can be interpreted another way. The knight can be our first parent Adam, to whom God gave infinite blessings, because he made him lord over all creatures. The Psalmist says:[4] *'Thou hast subjected all things under his feet etc.' The faithful servant is reason, which rules over him. As long as he remains in purity of life, he has the riches of paradise, which God entrusted to him, for himself and his heirs. But Adam wanted to have more, when he sought to be*[5] *another god, and immediately lost the riches of paradise; and then he cut off his servant's right foot, because, seduced by Eve, i.e., by sensual means, not by reason, he scorned God's commandment; but he sought the oil of mercy by crying out in the valley of this world, when he gained his bread with his own sweat. Seeing his wretchedness, the Son of God came down from heaven and redeemed him with His own blood, and took him to God's house, when He despoiled hell. He bore our sins upon his own body when he died for us wretched men. The poor man who found the treasure is Christ, who won paradise not for himself but for all who love him. The hermit prayed to God; even so at his Passion, Christ, weakened by the flesh, began to be afraid, when he said:*[6] *'If it be possible, let this chalice pass from me', and he prayed for humankind. Let us strive therefore etc.*

---

4 Ps 8.8.
5 *ut ... non esset*: Oest., K.; *ut ... esset*: L.
6 Mt 26.39.

128. Of those who unjustly seize the goods of others: their judgement at the end will be severe[1]

In the reign of Maximian there lived two knights, one just and God-fearing, the other avaricious and wealthy, who was more anxious to please the world than God. The just knight possessed a piece of land bordering on the avaricious knight's land, and the avaricious knight longed with all his heart to have it. He approached the just knight time and time again and offered him all the gold and silver he wanted to sell him this piece of land, but he always refused him, and the avaricious knight went away unhappily and began to consider how he might cheat him out of the land. But it happened that the just knight died, and hearing of this, his avaricious neighbour had a document drawn up in the name of the dead man, stating that before he died the deceased man had sold him the land he wanted for a certain sum of money. Having done this he bribed three men to bear witness to this document, then went with them to the dead knight's house, found his signet ring, entered the room where he lay, cleared the room of everyone but his three witnesses, and in their presence put the ring on the dead man's hand, and pressing his thumb on the ring sealed his document with it. 'There,' he said, 'you are witnesses to this.' 'We are,' they agreed. And the knight took possession of the land, claiming it as his own.

When the son of the dead knight asked him: 'Why have you taken possession of my land?', he replied: 'Your father sold it to me.' 'No,' the son told him; 'you came to my father on many occasions and offered him money for it, but my father was never willing to sell it.'

So they both went to the judge. The avaricious knight showed him the purchase document sealed with the signet ring of the dead

[1] Cf. Herrtage, Text I.XXII.

man and produced the witnesses who testified to the fact. 'I know that this is my father's seal,' the son of the dead man told him, 'but I know that he never sold you the land. How you got hold of my father's signet ring, I do not know.'

The judge then separated the three witnesses and also the knight; he then summoned the oldest of the witnesses and asked him if he knew the Lord's Prayer, and made him say it in his presence from beginning to end; and he knew it perfectly. Then he had him put in a room on his own. Next he summoned the second witness and said to him: 'My friend, your companion was here before you, and the things he told me were as true as the Lord's Prayer. So if you do not answer my questions with the truth, I will have you hanged.'

The young man thought: 'My companion has told him everything, how the knight got the dead man's signet ring and put it on his thumb and sealed his document with it. If I don't tell the truth, I'm a dead man.' So he told the whole story in every detail. When the judge had heard his testimony, he had him kept apart from the others and summoned the third of them. 'My friend,' he said, 'the first of your companions told me things as true as the Lord's Prayer, and so has the second. So unless you tell me the truth, you will die an ignominious death.'

The fellow thought to himself: 'My companions have told him all the knight's secrets, so it would be best for me to tell the truth.' He proceeded to tell the judge every detail of what had happened. The judge then had him kept apart from the others and summoned the knight.

'You wretch,' he said fixing him with a stern look, 'your greed has blinded you! Tell me, how did the dead knight sell you the land you have taken possession of?' And the knight, not knowing that the witness had confessed, maintained that the land was justly his. 'Wretch,' the judge said, 'your own witnesses affirm that you took the signet ring after his death, put it on his thumb and sealed your document with it.'

At these words the knight fell to the ground and begged for mercy. But the judge told him: 'You shall have the mercy you have deserved.' And he had the three witnesses dragged at the tails of horses to the gallows and hanged there, and the knight likewise.

All the nobles of the kingdom commended the judge's sentence and the shrewdness he had shown in investigating the truth, and the judge gave all the knight's possessions to the son of the dead man, who gratefully thanked him for restoring his inheritance to him.

Dear friends, these two knights represent the devil and our first parent, whose son is the whole human race that sprang from him. His inheritance is paradise, which God gave him. Seeing this, the greedy knight, i.e., the devil, went to him, enticing him and tempting him to relinquish paradise through sin. And as long as he remained alive, i.e., in purity of life, he possessed his inheritance, i.e., paradise; but when he died through the sin he committed against God's command, he lost his inheritance, and the whole human race after him. How did he lose it? Thus: the document was drawn up when Eve consented to eat of the tree of life in defiance of God's command. It was sealed by Adam, who was the source of reason, and who was given a special command, when he ate and chose to follow his wife rather than God. A seal, as you know, leaves its impression on wax; even so God imprinted his image on Adam and appointed him lord of the world. Psalm [8.8]: 'Thou hast subjected all things under his feet.' Adam gave this impression, i.e., likeness, to the devil when he obeyed him, and this was done with his thumb after he died. The thumb unites the whole hand; if the thumb is lost the hand loses its strength. The thumb signifies reason, which God gave man so that he might choose good and reject evil; hence as long as man is governed by reason and reason prevails in him, he will be able to govern himself and others admirably. But the man who lacks reason, lacks virtue and spiritual strength. Now Adam our first parent had a knowledge infused in him by God above that of all other creatures, so that before his sin all creatures obeyed him; nonetheless, knowingly and with the thumb of reason he followed the devil, when the devil said to him:[2] *'You shall not die; rather if you eat you shall be as gods, knowing good and evil.' When the devil saw that he had been led astray and deprived of his heavenly inheritance, he wanted to exclude his son also, i.e., the whole human race. But if man is circumspect, he must approach the Heavenly King, as the patriarchs and prophets did, who cried out to God for relief: 'O Lord God, O Emmanuel, our king and lawgiver, the expectation of nations and their Saviour, come to save us, our Lord God!'*[3] *But the devil brings with him three witnesses, namely pride of*

---

2 Cf. Gn 3.4f.
3 This is one of the seven antiphons said each day at the Magnificat during Vespers from 17–23 December.

128. Of those who unjustly seize the goods of others

life, the concupiscence of the flesh and the concupiscence of the eyes,[4] *against whom we must proceed wisely. We must test the first witness by asking if he knows the paternoster, or Lord's Prayer; i.e., if he has done anything that bears evidence against him of the sin of pride. Let him humble himself in all things, in word and in deed, as truly as the Lord's Prayer is true, and he will appease the Heavenly King after the example of Christ, who was obedient to his Father even unto death. And if a man is afraid of the second witness, i.e., the concupiscence of the eyes, in which he so delights, let him make a sincere confession, as the second witness did, and he will be able to escape danger. And if a man is afraid of the third witness, i.e., the concupiscence of the flesh, let him make amends to God by the mortification of the flesh, i.e., through sincere repentance, as the third witness did, who acknowledged everything, and so with his two confederates was hanged on the gibbet. So too we must hang on the gibbet of penance, of which the Apostle says:*[5] *'My soul chooseth hanging', i.e., the hanging of penance. And if we do so we shall obtain life everlasting.*

---

4 Cf. 1 Jn 2.16.
5 = Jb 7.15.

129. The test of true friendship[1]

There was a king who had an only son whom he loved deeply. This son obtained leave from his father to see the world and make some friends for himself. For seven years he wandered the world and after that returned to his father, who received him with joy and asked him how many friends he had made.

'Three,' his son told him. 'The first I love more than myself; the second as much as myself; and the third little or nothing.'

His father replied: 'It would be a good idea to put them to the test before you need their help. Kill a pig, put it in a sack and go at night to the house of the friend you love more than yourself and tell him that you have accidentally killed a man. Say: "If the body is found in my possession I shall die a most shameful death. So I beg you, as I have always loved you more than myself, help me now in my hour of greatest need."'

The son did as his father suggested. But his friend answered him: 'Since you have killed him, it is right that you should pay for it. If the body were found in my possession I should probably be hanged. But because you were my friend I will go with you to the gallows, and when you are dead give you three or four yards of cloth for a winding sheet.'

On being told this he went to his second friend and put him to the test. But he refused him like the first. 'Do you think I am so stupid that I would put myself in such danger?,' he said. 'But because you were my friend, I will go with you to the gallows and console you along the way as best I can.'

So he went to the third friend and put him to the test; he said: 'I am embarrassed to ask you this, since I have never done anything

[1] Cf. Herrtage, Text I.XXXIII.

129. The test of true friendship

for you, and now I have accidentally killed a man etc.' His friend replied: 'I will happily do as you ask, and I will take the blame myself, and if needs be I will climb the scaffold in your place.'

It was therefore this man who proved to be his best friend.

Moralization. Dear friends, the king is Almighty God; his only son is any good Christian, who for twelve[2] years, i.e., the whole term of his life, has to go about the world and seek three friends. The first is the world, which he loves more than himself. Here is proof: for the world's sake man puts himself at the risk of death, now on the sea, now on the land, and often loses his life in order to possess temporal goods. Therefore he loves the world more than himself. And if you put it to the test in time of necessity, it will doubtless be found wanting; indeed if out of all your goods it gives you two or three yards of cloth in which to wrap your corpse, you are lucky. The second friend, whom you love as yourself, is your wife and sons and daughters, who at your death may well go to your grave weeping, but when your wife returns home, within a few days her grief subsides and she begins to love another. The third friend, for whom you have done little, is Christ, for love of whom we have done few good things, rather done many bad things, yet who at the hour of our death is our friend, if we are contrite and have made our confession; indeed, he endured death upon the cross for our sake.

---

2 In the tale the son is absent for seven years; but twelve signifies the span of man's existence.

130. A wise man is more valuable than a strong[1]

There was a king who advanced a certain poor man to great riches and entrusted to him the custodianship of a castle, and after such preferment he became extremely arrogant, and entered into a conspiracy with the king's enemies, turned traitor and let them into the castle. The king was deeply grieved at this and held a council to consider how to recover his castle. He was told that he could not regain the castle unless along with his riches, he possessed three things: courage, wisdom and love.

Now among his subjects there were three knights, one of whom was the bravest of all men, the second the wisest, and the third had a special affection for the king. These three knights were dispatched at the head of armies to attack the castle. The first and bravest of them advanced with a mighty army through a forest in which the king's enemies were, and engaged them in battle and fought valiantly. But a bolt from a crossbow struck him in the groin and he died. The wise knight entered the forest behind him and began to cite laws to the enemy, hoping to win them over in this way. But an arrow struck him in the midriff and he died. In view of this the third knight entered the forest and spoke to the enemy so diplomatically and so eloquently that they readily listened to him and allowed him to enter their lines. Indeed he made such progress with them that he gained entry into the castle, and his conduct impressed them so much that everyone in the castle joined forces with him, and in this way he won the castle for the king and set up his banner at its highest point.

When the king heard how clever he had been in taking the castle, he advanced him to a position of great wealth.

1 Cf. Herrtage, Text I.XVI.

Moralization. Dear friends, the king is our Lord Jesus Christ, who advanced the poor man, i.e., Adam our first parent, to a position of great wealth when he made him seneschal of paradise; but through sin he lost it. And few were found in the whole earthly kingdom who were able to take the aforesaid castle, i.e., win paradise. The three knights who were summoned signify three kinds of men: the first signifies the powerful, who believe they can win paradise through might and strength; and though they are worthy enough, the arrow of pride suddenly comes and kills them spiritually. The second knight signifies the wise of this world, who cite laws, men such as judges, men of the Church, advocates and temporal judges, who believe they can win paradise through wisdom. And as they cling to life, along comes the arrow of avarice, i.e., a purse full of money, and slays them, and they are spiritually dead. The third knight, who spoke mildly and without agitation, we may take as the simple Christian whose heart belongs wholly to God, and who does not trust in human vanity nor in his wisdom, but only in God; as the Psalmist says:[2] 'Blessed is the man who hopes in the Lord.' Such a man will assuredly win the castle of paradise; the which may God deign to grant us.

---

2 Cf. Ps 145.5.

131. Of the rich, to whom it is given, and the poor, from whom what they have is taken away, and how God rewards them for all eternity with the gift of a heavenly home

A certain king had it proclaimed that everyone might come to him, whatever their degree, and they would obtain of him whatever they asked. Some of the nobles and the rich asked for a dukedom, some wanted an earldom, some knighthood, others asked for gold and silver, and their requests were all granted. Then the poor and simple came to the king with their own requests. But the king told them: 'You have come too late: the nobles and lords have come before you and I gave them all I possessed.' This reply dismayed them, and moved by compassion the king said: 'My friends, I gave them only my temporal possessions. I kept my sovereignty because no-one asked for it. So I give you the power to be their lords and judges.'

When the rich heard what he had done they were greatly perturbed and went to the king and said: 'Lord, we are humiliated to hear that you have appointed the poor, our own servants, to be our judges and lords. We would rather die than be subjected to this.'

'My friends,' said the king, 'I am doing you no wrong. I gave you whatever you asked of me and kept nothing for myself except my sovereignty, which I have given to them. But I have some advice for you: if any of you has more than enough to live on, let him give some of his wealth to the poor, enough to enable them to live decently. I will take back my sovereignty from them, and it will remain mine, and in this way you will be saved from an oppressive subjection to them.'

And that is what happened.

Dear friends, the king is God, who is wealthy above all others; the herald who makes the proclamation is the preacher, who says:[1] *'Ask and you shall receive, seek and you shall find.' As soon as the rich and*

1 Cf. Mt 7.7f.

131. Of the rich and the poor

powerful of this world heard this cry, they went to the king as quickly as they could and asked for castles, cities, gold and silver, and obtained them; but Christ gave them only the things of the world, of which he kept nothing; Mt 4:[2] *'The foxes have holes, and the birds of the air nests, but the Son of Man hath not where to lay his head.' Then the poor came, and he had nothing to give them except sovereignty, and so he made them the lords and judges of the rich; as we read in Matthew:*[3] *'You who have left everything and followed me shall sit upon thrones, judging the twelve tribes of Israel.' We also read in Matthew:*[4] *'Blessed are the poor in spirit: for theirs is the kingdom of heaven.' When the rich heard of this, they were justifiably aggrieved that the poor, who were their servants in this world, should be their judges and lords in heaven. If therefore you desire to reign with them, do as they did! Give all the alms you can to the poor, that they may live, and then without a doubt you will reign with them for all eternity.*

---

2 Mt 8.20; Lk 9.58.
3 For the first part cf. Mk 10.28; Lk 18.28; for the second Mt 19.28; Lk 22.30.
4 Mt 5.3.

132. Of the envious, whose wicked lives infect the good[1]

There once lived in the same city four physicians, all skilled in medicine, but the youngest of them was so much more accomplished than the other three that he healed all the sick who came to him. This made the others jealous of him and they said among themselves: 'How can we get rid of him? Look, the whole world comes running to him and because of him we shan't be able to make any money.'

One of them said: 'Every week he visits the duke, some nine miles away, and he will be going to see him tomorrow. I will station myself outside the city at the three-mile mark. You be at the six-mile mark, and you at the nine-mile mark. When he reaches the three-mile mark I will meet him and cross myself; and you are both to do the same. He will ask the reason for this and we shall tell him: "You have become a leper." Then through his fear he will contract leprosy, because Hippocrates says: "The man who fears leprosy brings it upon himself with his fear." And once he becomes a leper no-one will go near him.'

And so it came to pass.

Dear friends, the three physicians who infected the fourth represent three vices that are prevalent in this world, namely pride of life, concupiscence of the flesh and concupiscence of the eyes; or they signify the devil, the world and the flesh. These are the physicians of reprobates, who cause the body to live amid pleasures, and the soul to reign in hell. The clever physician is any good Christian, as for example prelates and confessors, who have to care for us spiritually, to implant virtues and eradicate vices. But alas, alas!, often the spiritual physician is so infected with these three vices that he is not worthy to set his foot within

1 Cf. Herrtage, Text I.XX.

the Church, but only outside it, as in the case of simoniacs and others whose various sins are retained. Dear friends, if we wish to beware of these sins, let us walk away from them through works of mercy, and thus we shall be able to come to the eternal kingdom, which may God grant us etc.

133. Of spiritual friendship

A certain king had two greyhounds which, while they were chained up, showed great fondness for each other, but once let loose tried to devour each other. It distressed the king to observe this, because when he wanted to set them free and sport and course with them, they fought and had no thoughts of hunting. He sought advice on this and was told that he should get hold of a strong and savage wolf and let one of his hounds fight it, and when this hound was all but conquered he should let the other one loose to fight it. And when the first hound saw the help he had been given, they would subsequently always be firm friends. So this was done, and when the wolf was on the point of victory and the first hound was getting weaker, the other defended him and killed the wolf. And from that time on the hounds were the greatest of friends, whether chained or unchained.

Dear friends, the king is our Lord Jesus Christ; the two dogs chained together are the body and soul, bound together in baptism. And as long as they stay chained together, they love each other; but if through mortal sin they are set free, one immediately becomes the foe of the other; as the Apostle says:[1] *'The flesh lusteth against the spirit, and the converse.' What then is to be done? Clearly, the flesh must be subjected to penance and it will oppose the wolf, i.e., devil, and then the soul will be strengthened and will fight manfully with the flesh, and after this there will be love between them both in adversity and prosperity, and they will both be loved equally by the Lord, and because of his love they will obtain life eternal.*

[1] Gal 5.17.

134. Of the innocent death of Christ[1]

Seneca relates that there was once a law which required that every knight should be buried in his armour, and anyone who stripped the dead body of it should be put to death. It chanced that a city was besieged by a tyrannical king who set up ambuscades all round the city and killed so many of its people that they were in danger of annihilation, and very afraid, because they were no longer capable of resistance. While they were in this perilous situation, a noble, doughty and valiant knight came into the city and was deeply moved by the citizens' plight. The citizens approached him and said. 'Help us, Sire!' He replied: 'My friends, the only way you can be freed from this peril is "by a mighty hand".[2] And as you can see, I am not armed, so I cannot fight.'

'Sire,' said one of the citizens, 'a few days ago a knight was buried in this sepulchre here in the most splendid armour. Take his armour and deliver our city from its enemies!' The knight battled with the foe and was victorious, and so saved the city. He then put the arms back from where they had been taken. But certain rivals of his, jealous of the glory he had won in battle, accused him before the judge of breaking the law, because he had stripped the dead man of his armour.

'My lord,' he replied to the judge, 'of two evils the greater is the one to be avoided, and because I could not have protected the city from its enemies without armour, I took the armour and then returned it. Now when a thief or a robber takes things, he does not intend to return them, whereas I took the armour for the common good and then returned them. So I should be rewarded rather than be called to account. Similarly, if a house in a city catches fire, is it

1 Cf. Herrtage, Text I.IV.
2 Cf. Ex 3.19.

not better for that house to be destroyed without delay before other houses are burnt down and the whole city destroyed? The same is true in the present case: was it not better that I took the armour and saved your lives than if I had not taken them? For if I had not taken them you would all have perished.'

But his rivals cried: 'He is guilty of a capital offence!' So the judge granted their petition and sentenced the knight to death. The sentence was duly carried out, and his death was deeply mourned throughout the city.

Dear friends, the city is this world, which was besieged by the devil for a long time, and all those then living in the world were in danger of ruin, because they all went down to hell. This world was also surrounded by a wall of vices and desires. The brave knight who had no arms is our Lord Jesus Christ; as the Psalmist says:[3] *'The Lord is strong and mighty etc.' Seeing the world in danger, and the whole of humankind facing perdition, he went straight to the tomb, i.e., the womb of the Blessed Virgin, and there found the arms of our first parent, i.e., the humanity he assumed, and fought against the devil, won the victory, and delivered us from death. The Jews were jealous of him, and seeing this accused him before Pilate, saying:*[4] *'The Romans will come and take away our place etc.' The knight said: 'It is better for one house to be destroyed than a whole city.' Caiphas on the other hand said:*[5] *'It is expedient that one man should die and not the whole nation.' So Pilate handed him over to death, and at his death rocks were split asunder and there was darkness over the whole earth; but after his victory he put the arms back in the tomb again, i.e., his glorious body lay at rest in earth. Let us therefore strive to mourn his death in our minds, and to keep it in our hearts, and recall it to our memory, because he fought manfully for us and rescued us from the jaws of the devil, and for that we are obliged to love him above all things and for love of him to leave both our father and mother. Who ever heard of a man with an only son and heir permitting him to die, as the Heavenly Father did with his only Son our Lord Jesus Christ? And yet he died. Even so we too must willingly mortify the pleasures of the flesh and everything that displeases God through penance, and thus obtain life everlasting.*

3 Ps 23.8.
4 Jn 11.48.
5 Jn 11.50.

135. Of our conscience, and how, when it is anguished, we should have recourse to God through confession and good works

Augustine relates in *The City of God*[1] that Lucretia, a Roman lady renowned for her virtue, was the wife of Calatinus.[2] When Calatinus invited Sextus, son of King Tarquinius, to this castle, Sextus at once fell in love with the beautiful Lucretia. Waiting for an opportune time when the king and Calatinus were both leaving Rome, he returned to the castle and spent the night there. During the night, acting not as a friend but as a foe, he stealthily entered Lucretia's bedchamber, and laying his left hand on her breast, and with a sword in his right hand, he made himself known. 'Yield to me this instant,' he told her,' or you will die!' When Lucretia absolutely refused to yield, Sextus told her: 'If you do not do as I wish, I will cut your throat, then do the same to a slave and put his naked body next to yours, and the whole world will believe that Lucretia was killed in her bed because of her debauchery.' So, fearing the disgrace that would ensue, she was compelled to yield.

Having satisfied his lust, Sextus left, while Lucretia, grief-stricken, sent letters to her father and her husband, her brothers and nephews, the king and the proconsuls, asking them to come, and when they were all present she addressed them as follows: 'Sextus entered my house not as a friend but as a foe. Calatinus, you must know that the garments[3] of another man have been on your bed. But though my body has been violated, my heart is innocent. You may absolve me of guilt, but I will not acquit myself of punishment.' With these words she seized a sword hidden beneath her robe and

1 *De Civitate Dei* I.19; Augustine argues both for Lucretia's innocence and her possible guilt.
2 = Collatinus.
3 *vestimenta*: Oest., K.; an unfamiliar euphemism. Livy, I.58 has *vestigia* = 'impress', 'imprints', which makes better sense.

stabbed herself. Her friends then took the sword and swore by the blood of Lucretia to banish the whole family of Tarquinius from Rome and to eliminate it. And they did so, putting Sextus, the perpetrator of this outrage, to a miserable death.

Moralization. Dear friends, the noble lady Lucretia is the soul, cleansed by God and joined to God in baptism. Sextus is the devil, who strives with threats and bribes to violate the soul. He enters her house when man's heart, which is the house of the soul, consents to sin. He presses upon on her breast, when man consents fully, and so violates her, when through the heart's consent he completes his possession with the act.[4] After this, Lucretia, i.e., the soul, in grief calls her father and husband; even so, you too, dear friend, must call upon your father, i.e., confessor, and your husband, i.e., Christ, through works of mercy, and your friends, i.e., the saints, with sincere devotion, and lay bare your life through sincere contrition and confession, revealing how you have offended God, and how gravely; and then kill yourself with the sword of penance, i.e., root out your vices and sins and so let your body be conveyed to Rome, i.e., to Holy Church, to show, in what way,[5] publicly or secretly, and how greatly you have offended God. Then the devil and all his followers will be banished and retire in confusion, and you will remain saved in a life of goodness.

---

4 *manum per consensum actu complet*: see Corinne J. Sanders' discussion in *Rape and Ravishment in the Literature of Medieval England*, Cambridge: Boydell and Brewer, 2001, p. 162. Sextus's weight on Lucretia's breast is seen as the devil's pressure on the dwelling-place of the spirit, and the rape as the resulting consent and violation of the spirit. The heart acquiesces to sin and so is violated. However, L.'s *malum consensum* (a combination which occurs in the moralization of the next tale) yields good sense and may be the correct reading.
5 *in alia forma*: Oest.; *in qua forma*: K., L.

136. A shepherd of souls must be vigilant[1]

A thief went to the house of a wealthy man one night and climbing the roof listened through an opening in it to see if any of the household were awake. Wondering if something was afoot, the owner of the house whispered to his wife: 'Speak loudly and ask me how I acquired all the possessions we have, and don't stop speaking until I tell you.' So his wife said: 'My good lord, you were never a merchant, tell me, how did you get all this money you now possess?' 'Don't ask me this, you silly woman,' he replied. But she asked him time and time again and would not give up, and finally her husband, as if yielding under pressure, said: 'If you keep what I say a secret, I will tell you the truth.' 'As if I would tell anyone!', she answered him.

'I was a thief,' he told her, 'and I got everything I now have through thieving in the night.' 'Then I am surprised you were never caught,' his wife said. He replied: 'The man who was my master taught me a special word which I used to repeat seven times when I was climbing on people's roofs, and then I got down into the house on the rays of the moon, and took what I wanted. I climbed back up to the roof again by the same rays without any danger and went back home.' 'Please,' his wife said, 'tell me the word that gave you the power to do your thieving without any danger.' 'I will,' he said, 'but you must tell it to no-one, in case they rob us of all our possessions.' 'I would never do that,' she promised. 'It was this,' he said. '*Saxlem, saxlem.*'

His wife then fell asleep, but her husband only pretended to sleep, snoring loudly. Hearing his snores, the thief was delighted; he seized at a moon-ray, repeated the word seven times, then lost his

1 A very similar story occurs in Peter Alfonsi, *Disciplina Clericalis* XXIV. See also Oesterley, pp. 734–5; Tubach, no. 4778; Hope, pp. 574–5.

hold and fell through the skylight into the house with a resounding crash. He broke a leg and arm and lay there on the ground half dead. Hearing the crash, the owner asked him innocently how he had taken such a fall. The thief replied: 'I was fooled by the story you told.'

The owner then seized him and early next morning had him hanged.

Moralization. Dear friends, the thief is the devil, who climbs the roof of your heart through your evil thoughts and makes an opening through your evil consent to sin. The husband with the wife is a good prelate espoused to the Church, whose goods, that is, the virtues he received in baptism, the devil strives with all his might to remove. But the good prelate must be continually on his guard that he does not allow the thief to penetrate the house of his soul; as the Saviour said:[2] *'Watch, because ye know not at what hour the thief is to come.' And to combat his cunning he must take precautions for himself and his wife, i.e., the Church, in order to resist the devil, so that he falls from his heart and cannot harm him at all. Or this tale can be interpreted another way. The thief was the beautiful Lucifer, who tried with all his might to climb on high so that he might be another god, and to take God's honour from him; as he said to Isaiah:*[3] *'I will ascend into heaven and be like the Most High.' After this he climbed on a moonbeam, that is, through his beauty he fell down to hell, and broke his legs, i.e., he lost the glory and honour that God of his goodness had conferred on him, and was hanged on the gibbet of hell; from which etc.*

---

2 Cf. Mt 24.42; 2 Pt 3.10: 'the day of the Lord shall come as a thief'; also 1 Thes 5.2.
3 Cf. Is 14.13f.

137. Of the natural goodness of Christ and the compassion he naturally shows to sinners who turn from their ways, and how Christ accepts those whom the world rejects[1]

In his *Chronicles* Eusebius tells us of an emperor who governed the Roman people with the greatest impartiality, sparing no-one, but allotting punishment equal to the gravity of the crime to rich and poor alike. But because of this the Roman senators deprived him of his power and forced him to flee like a pauper. He went straight to Constantine and formed an alliance with him, and subsequently proved so valiant and wise that he was elected to succeed him as emperor. He mustered an army and laid siege to Rome, and since the Romans could not escape without being captured by him, they sent to him first their elders, then secondly their young men, and thirdly their womenfolk, who went barefoot and prostrated themselves before him begging his pardon. But they were unable to obtain this. Finally they sent his two parents, who lived in the city, and his mother exposed her bosom to him, showing him the breasts he had sucked. This stirred the emperor's natural affection, and, moved to compassion, he completely forgave their offences. Then he entered the city where he was received with honour.

Moralization. Dear friends, the emperor is Christ, who through sin was banished from his city, i.e., banished through sin from the heart of man and from this world, when the Jews put him to death. And when he was banished in this manner, he went to his Father, where he was elected as perpetual commander and as our judge on the Day of Judgement, for 'the Father hath given all judgement to the Son', John 22.[2] *We should therefore be very fearful as to how we should meet him on the Day of Judgement, when he will come with a mighty army of*

---

1 This is, *mutatis mutandis*, the story of Coriolanus. *F.D.M.* V.4.1. See also Oesterley, p. 735; Tubach, no. 1246; Hope, pp. 575–6.
2 = Jn 5.22.

angels. What then shall we do? Why, we should first send him elders, i.e., cry aloud to the patriarchs and prophets that they may plead with him on our behalf with bare feet, i.e., deep emotion; and second, young men, i.e., the Apostles, martyrs and confessors of the New Testament, and plead with him through works of mercy; and likewise women, i.e., holy virgins and widows; and above all let us ask the glorious Virgin Mother of God to intercede for us personally, and without doubt she will win eternal life for us, which may God deign to grant us.

138. Those whom we cannot overcome by severity, we should win over by kindness

There was a king called Medro who had an only son who was his heir, but this son disowned his father, who banished him for this. Consequently the son fled to the King of Persia, his father's rival and enemy, and told him he would be faithful to him until death, and was prepared if necessary to make war on his own father. At length war was declared between the two kings, and they fought each other.[1] It happened that King Medro was seriously wounded and bleeding heavily, and when his son saw this he ran to him at once and fought on his behalf against the King of Persia, his lord, and defeated him. Because of this his lord repudiated him for not abiding by his compact, and the son returned to his father, humbly begged his forgiveness, and was granted it. Thus peace was restored between them and the son regained his inheritance.

Dear friends, the two kings are God and the devil. Of the first Jeremiah says, c.4:[2] 'The Lord is the living God and the everlasting king.' Of the second Job says, c.45:[3] 'He is king over all the children of pride.' But the first king, i.e., God, has a son, i.e., the human soul, which turns from God and binds itself to the devil whenever it commits mortal sin. But assuredly, if the son recalls the bloody battle Christ fought for him against the devil in order to rescue him from the power of the devil, and as he ponders this humbles himself before God and asks pardon for his sins, then he can go to God without fear and win his inheritance of eternal life. As the Psalmist says:[4] 'It is thou that wilt restore my inheritance to me etc.'

1 *qui simul pugnaverunt*: this might mean that they fought each other in single combat to decide the issue.
2 = Jer 10.10.
3 = Jb 41.25.
4 Ps 15.5.

139. Of the wounds of the soul[1]

King Alexander was ruler of the whole world. He once gathered together a vast army and besieged a particular city in the vicinity of which he lost he lost many soldiers and other personnel without any sign of a wound. He was extremely puzzled by this and called his philosophers and said: 'Masters, how can it be that suddenly my soldiers are dying and show no signs of being wounded?'

'It is not surprising,' they told him. 'There is a basilisk on the city wall, and its gaze is infecting the solders and causing their deaths.'

'What remedy is there to defeat this basilisk?' Alexander asked.

They replied: 'Have a mirror placed on high between the army and the place on the wall where the basilisk is, and when it looks in the mirror it will see its own gaze reflected in it, and so it will die.'

And that is what happened.

Dear friends, so too the supreme remedy for pride is a consideration of one's own frailty and weakness, because if one asks why man is proud, the sure answer is that it is because he lacks the influence of virtue. So each of us must consider his own vanity, as it were in a mirror, and then return to a consideration of his frailty, scrutinizing his failings, and thus he will banish pride.

1 Cf. Herrtage, Text I.LVII.

140. Of the justice and equity to which we must always aspire in our present and future lives[1]

Among the many virtues he possessed, King Heraclius was pre-eminently just and could not anywhere or at any time be deflected by prayers or bribery from dispensing justice. Now it happened once that certain men accused a knight before him of causing the death of another knight. The substance of the charge was this: both knights went off to war, but there was no fighting. This knight returned without the other, and on this basis it was assumed that he had killed the other on the way home.

After hearing this evidence the king sentenced the knight to death, but as he was being led away, his accusers saw approaching them the knight for whose murder he had been condemned to death, and he was quite unharmed. So they took both of them back to the king. Angrily, the king said to the first knight: 'I order you to be put to death, because you have already been condemned.' And to the second knight he said: 'You too, because you are the cause of his death.' And to the third,[2] he said: 'And you also, because you were sent to execute the knight, and you did not.'[3]

Dear friends, the king is God, who is just in all his works. The two knights are the body and soul. The soul dies, seduced by the flesh, and so

1 Cf. Herrtage, Text I.LVIII. For other versions, see Oesterley, p. 735; Tubach, no. 4229; Hope, pp. 577–8.
2 Presumably the first knight is the one already condemned; the second, the knight he was supposed to have killed; and the third, a knight detailed to perform the execution. (Cf. Swan, who takes the second knight to be the accuser of the first; and the third to be the restored knight.)
3 Cf. Seneca, *De Ira* I.xviii.3; Chaucer, *Summoner's Tale* ll. 2025–6 ('and to another knight commanded he / "Go lede him to the death, I charge thee."')

by the just judgement of God his body is taken off to face the punishment of penance. But when he is subjected to penance, the soul is found to be alive, first, through Christ's Passion, and second, through penance. But both must die a temporal death. The third knight, who did not kill him, is a negligent prelate, who in accordance with God's command has to correct the sinner, root out vices and implant virtues; and if he does not do this, he will not escape eternal death; Ezekiel 3:[4] 'If thou declare it not to him, nor speak to him that he may be converted from his wicked way and live, and the same wicked man die in his iniquity, I will require his blood at your hand.' Let us pray therefore etc.

4 *et ipse impius in inquitate sua moreretur*: Oest.; cf. Ez 3.18: *ipse impius in iniquitate sua morietur*: L., V. ('the same wicked man shall die in his iniquity, but I will require etc.').

141. We must always listen to sound advice and reject what is not[1]

In the reign of Fulgentius there lived a certain knight named Zedekiah who had a very beautiful, but foolish, wife. This knight spent so much time at tournaments and jousting that he became extremely poor, and this caused him the deepest distress, and he walked up and down in despair, not knowing what he should do. Now in a room in his home there lived a serpent, and this serpent, observing his misery, was given a voice by God, as Balaam's ass was once, and it said: 'Why are you weeping? Do as I advise you and you will not be sorry. Give me some sweet milk to drink every day and I will make you rich.'

When the knight heard this he was overjoyed and he promised faithfully to do as he was asked. In a very short time he became extremely rich, and possessed great wealth and a fine son into the bargain. Now one day his wife happened to say to him: 'My lord, I believe that that serpent has great wealth in the room where it lives. I suggest we kill it and take its riches.'

So at his wife's bidding he took a hammer with which to kill the serpent, and also a bowl of milk. And when the serpent saw the bowl of milk it stretched its head out of its hole to look at the milk as it usually did, and the knight lifted the hammer to strike it. But the serpent saw this at once and withdrew its head, and the hammer hit the bowl. And immediately after this the knight lost his child and all the money he had. 'Alas!' his wife said to him, 'it was bad advice I gave you. But go to the serpent's hole and beg its pardon in all humility and perhaps you may win it over.'

The knight went to the room where the serpent lived and, weeping bitterly, begged its pardon and asked it to make him rich again.

1 Cf. Herrtage, Text I.LIX.

'Now I see that you are a fool,' the serpent replied, 'and you will remain a fool, for it is impossible for me to forget that great hammer blow, or for you to forget that that is why I killed your child and took away all your wealth. So there can never be any real peace between us.' This made the knight very wretched. 'I promise you faithfully,' he said, 'that I will never do any such thing to you in future, if only I can win your favour again.' 'My friend,' the serpent replied, 'a serpent's nature is to be cunning and venomous. Let what I have said suffice, because the memory of the hammer blow and your villainy is with me now. So away with you, or something worse may befall you.'

Heart-broken, the knight left him, and he said to his wife. 'Woe is me, that I ever took your advice!' And they lived in poverty for ever after.

Dear friends, the king is our Heavenly Father; the knight Zedekiah is the poor man, who came naked from his mother's womb, and who lost all the riches of paradise through the sin of his first parent, when Adam took the beautiful Eve to wife and through her counsel lost the joy of paradise. The serpent living in the chamber is Christ, contained in your heart by virtue of baptism, from whom man has received all good things: first, a son, i.e., a fair soul created in the likeness of God; second, he made man lord of the world; as the Psalmist declares:[2] 'Thou hast set him over all the works of thy hands'; third, paradise. But when our father Adam was deceived by Eve's counsel at the tempting of the devil, he lost everything, and even so every man who follows the counsel of his wife, i.e., flesh, will lose everything. The Apostle says:[3] 'If you live according to the flesh, you shall die.' At baptism you promised to give Christ milk, i.e., that of prayer, innocence and devotion. But you deal a savage blow to Christ when you commit mortal sin. And when he sees you do so, he takes your sons and daughters and riches from you, that you may mend your ways. As it is written:[4] 'Whom I love, I rebuke and chastise'. We must therefore rejoice rather than grieve at the rod of discipline.

2 Cf. Ps 8.7.
3 Rom 8.13.
4 Cf. Prv 3.12; Heb 12.6.

142. Of the snares with which the devil seeks to entangle us in manifold ways

There was an exceedingly powerful king who planted a forest which he fortified with a surrounding wall, and in this forest he put various different kinds of animals in which he took great delight. Now there was at that time a man who had been found guilty of treason, and as a result of his crimes he was dispossessed of all his property and banished from his homeland. He equipped himself with four different breeds of dogs and abundant nets so that he could capture and kill the king's beasts in his forest. The names of his dogs were: Richer, Emulemin, Hanegiff, Bandin, Crismel, Egofin, Beanus and Renelin.[1] With these dogs and his nets he accounted for all of the king's animals. When the king heard of this he was angry; he called his son and said: 'Arm yourself, my dear son, and take some soldiers and kill this traitor, or chase him from the realm.'

'I am ready to do so,' he replied. 'But from what I have heard from a number of people this fellow is so strong that I ought rather to hide myself for a while with a girl who is of surpassing wisdom, and speak with her, and so prepare myself for battle.'[2]

'If the girl is wise,' his father said, 'and if with her aid you can defeat our adversary, I will reward her with great honours.'

So the son armed himself, and without anyone knowing entered the castle where the girl lived, and she received him with great joy. He stayed with her some time. Then he left the castle and within a

---

1 Names of apparently Saxon origin, which led some scholars to conclude that the origin of the *Gesta* was Germany. Oesterley (p. 262), however, contends that the names are English in origin.
2 Oesterley's text implies that the son already knows such a girl. K. and L., however, have the father direct him to the castle of Varioch, where he will find a wise girl.

week engaged his father's foe, and after fighting him valiantly and cunningly, cut off his head. After this he returned to his father, who made him king in his place.

Dear friends, the father is our Lord God; the forest is this world, or the Church; the world was fortified by God's commandments according to the law of Moses; the Church was fortified by Christ's Passion, and by the teachers, preachers and confessors of his mercy.[3] *The treacherous knight, who was banished, is the devil, who was cast from his kingdom, and who schemes every moment to destroy the Church and all Christians. He equips himself with dogs and nets; just as hunters lie in wait for wild beasts leading a simple existence,*[4] *so that when they leave the caves of the goodly life in which they were living, they have nets with which they catch them.*[5] *When men leave the caves of a goodly life, demons then have nets ready, i.e., the pleasures of the world and the flesh, and they throw them in front of them and capture them. The Psalmist says:*[6] *'The wicked shall fall in his net etc.' Note therefore that the hunter is the devil, and he has four kinds of hunting dogs: some of them to hunt down spiritual beasts, and others for other quarries. The two first dogs, i.e., Richter and Emulemin, run after deer and bears, i.e., riches and pleasures, by which many are induced to do wrong, because riches often turn a man from the path of wisdom, and because of their great wealth they want to have positions of power and to impose their own will. So let us use our power wisely as a means of justice, 'let our strength be the law of justice',*[7] *which is to say, let all we will or can do be wholly just. These two dogs, i.e., riches and pleasure, or power, course together, and draw many after them and lure them to sin; thus Scripture says:*[8] *'The heart rejoices greatly when it sees the deer heading towards the net'; so too does the devil when he sees man heading towards mortal sin, and consequently all hell rejoices*

---

3 *misericordie*: Oest.; *misericordia*: K., L.
4 *simplici vita*: this seems to qualify *venatores*, but in the context it makes better sense to take it with *bestiae*. Men (= wild beasts), while leading a good/simple life, are safe, but once they leave the cave of this life they are ensnared.
5 *capiunt eas. Sic et cum enim*: Oest.; *capiunt eas: Cum enim*: K., L.
6 Ps 140.10.
7 Wis 2.11.
8 I am unable to find this quotation in Scripture.

142. Of the snares with which the devil seeks to entangle us

greatly. Then the hunter, i.e., devil, lets another pair[9] loose, namely Hanegif [and Bandin], i.e., receive and give. These two dogs chase abbots and pastors, who have the power to confer livings; they give in order to receive, because what they should give to decent men and good clerics they give to fools and ill-natured men in return for their goodwill and praise, which is contrary to Scripture, where it is said:[10] 'Give to the good, and receive not a sinner.' So Hanegif, i.e., receive and give, draws many into the net, i.e., hell, and the other dog, Bandin, draws judges and advocates into the net, because contrary to justice they work by means of their trickery. Job says:[11] 'They rashly provoke God, because if the party in the right gives them nothing, they accept a full purse from the party in the wrong, with the result that the former cites decrees and decretals, and thus they create discord, in defiance of the truth';[12] hence Habakkuk says:[13] 'The law is torn in pieces', because the outcome will be a wrong judgement. Against such men the Psalmist says:[14] 'The labour of their lips shall overwhelm them', i.e., plunge them into the depths of hell; 'in miseries they shall not be able to stand'. Then another dog, Crismel, is let loose to chase hares, which are swift and pass quickly over the mountains; these are those appointed in the Church, such as priests, rectors, chaplains, monks and mendicant friars, who ought to use reason in order to pass to the mountains of the exalted life, i.e., to cast off the burdens of earthly things and despise the world. But alas!, many are so tempted by this dog that he leads them to the devil's net just as he wishes, because they trust in things in which they are deceived. As when the rector of a church or a parish priest takes 200 or 300 marks annually out of the goods of the Church, when, after receiving enough for his own simple needs, he should give all that is left over to the poor, but which he now lays out on worldly vanities and earthly display, and, what is worse, on wantonness and gluttony. Then

---

9 It is clear from what follows that Hanegif forms a pair with Bandin, and the two are unleashed together.
10 Ecclus 12.5.
11 I cannot trace this quotation.
12 *quia si pars una eis vult dare aliquid, accipiunt de parte altera bursam plenam, dum illam trahant ad se*: Oest.; *quia si pars vera eis nihil vult dare, accipiunt de parte falsa bursam plenam, ita quod illa trahat ad se decreta & decretalia*: K., L.
13 Hb 1.4.
14 Ps 139.10f.

another dog is loosed; he is called Belin,[15] *and his quarry is merchants and usury, on account of which many fall into the devil's net, because they buy and sell at a profit of 30 per cent or more. The Psalmist says:*[16] *'Usury and deceit have not departed from their streets.' Then another dog is loosed, who is called Beanus, i.e., wantonness, through which many clerics and lay people, rich and poor, lowly and great, young and old fall into the devil's net. So God, seeing the whole human race being ruined and held captive in the devil's net, sent his son to the castle of the wise girl*[17] *armed with a double coat of armour, i.e., that of his divinity and his humanity, and on the eighth day after he was born, i.e., when he was circumcised, he advanced against the devil and then, i.e., on Good Friday, he declared war and won the victory, and thereby delivered us from the vices and the nets of the devil and brought us to life everlasting.*

15 Belin is not mentioned in the tale.
16 Cf. Ps 54.11.
17 Surprisingly the girl is not identified. But she is presumably the Virgin, whom Christ leaves to fight the devil on the eighth day after his birth, i.e. after his circumcision.

143. Of the fear of the last judgement[1]

There was a king who enacted a law that, when someone's death was imminent, trumpets should be sounded in front of his house in the morning before sunrise, and he should at once clothe himself in black and go to receive judgement. This king held a great banquet and invited all the nobles of his kingdom, and duly all arrived. At this banquet there were all kinds of excellent musicians whose sweet melody provided excellent entertainment for the guests, but the king gave no sign of satisfaction or pleasure; his face was sad and he continually sighed and groaned. His guests were surprised at this but did not dare inquire the reason for his sadness. However, they requested the king's brother to ask the cause of his great unhappiness; and this he did, telling the king that everyone at the banquet was surprised at his great sorrow and was anxious to know the reason. 'Go home,' the king told him. ' You will know the reason tomorrow.' So he did.

The king then ordered his trumpeters to go and stand in front of his brother's house next morning and sound their trumpets, then to bring him to him as the law prescribed. They obeyed, and when the king's brother heard the trumpets sound early that morning before his house, he was absolutely terrified. He got up, clothed himself in black and went to the king, who had a deep pit dug, and a fragile chair with four flimsy legs suspended over it, and made his brother take off his clothes and sit upon it. When he was placed on this chair, the king ordered a sharp sword to be hung above his head by a thread of silk; he then ordered four men, holding razor-sharp swords, to surround him, one in front, one behind, the third on his right and the fourth on his left. When they were in position,

1 See *G.L.* CLXXVI.82ff. (Barlaam and Josaphat); also Oesterley, p. 736, and Tubach, no. 4994 ('Sword of Damocles').

the king told them: 'When I give the word, plunge your swords in him, on pain of death!' He then had trumpets and all kinds of other musical instruments brought, and a table was laid and all sorts of foods were placed upon it, and he said: 'My dearest brother, why are you so miserable and so sad at heart? Here you have the most exquisite food, the most melodious music. Why are you not happy and enjoying yourself?'

'How can I be happy,' he replied, 'when this morning I heard the trumpets sound before my house as a sign that I was to die, and now I have been placed on a rotten, flimsy chair like this? If I make the slightest movement the chair will break and I will fall into the pit and never be able to get out of it. If I raise my head, the sword above it will fall and pierce my head to the brain and kill me. And I am surrounded by four executioners armed with swords who are ready to kill me at one word from you! All things considered, if I were lord of all the world, I could not be happy.'

The king replied: 'I will now answer the question you asked me yesterday, about why I was not happy. I am, just as you are now, seated on a frail and perishable chair, because I inhabit a body that is frail, with four flimsy legs, that is, composed of the four elements; and beneath me is the pit of hell. The sharp sword above my head is divine justice, ready to separate my soul from my body; the sharp sword before me is death, which spares no-one, and will come before it is expected, and how it will come, or when, I have no idea. Behind me is another sword ready to strike me, and that is the sins that I have committed in this world, which are ready to accuse me before the Tribunal. On my right is another sword, the devil, who 'goeth about seeking whom he may devour'[2] and is ever ready to take my soul and lead it down to hell. On my left there is another sword, the worms that will eat my flesh after I die. And when I consider all these things I can never be happy. If you have been in such fear of me today, a mere mortal, should I not fear my Creator much more? Be off with you, then, and do not ask me such questions again.'

His brother got off the chair and thanked the king for his life, promising faithfully to amend his ways in future, and all who were present commended the king for the answer he had given him.

2 1 Pt 5.8.

144. Of the present state of the world[1]

The story is told of a certain king whose kingdom suddenly underwent such a change during his reign that good turned to evil, truth to falsehood, strength to weakness, and justice to injustice. Wondering at this change the king asked his four wisest philosophers what had caused it. After sober deliberation they went to the four gates of the city, and each of them wrote upon them three reasons.

The first wrote: 'Power is justice; therefore the land is without law. Day is night; therefore the land is without a pathway. Battle is flight; therefore the land is without honour.'

The second wrote: 'One is two; therefore the kingdom is without truth. Friend is foe; therefore the land is without trust. Evil is good; therefore the land is without piety.'

The third wrote: 'Reason is banished; therefore the land is without a name. A thief is set above us; therefore the kingdom is without money. The gnat[2] wants to be an eagle; therefore there is no discrimination in our homeland.'

The fourth wrote: 'Will is our counsellor; therefore the kingdom is ill cared for. Money passes judgement and sentence, therefore the kingdom is ill governed. God is dead, therefore the whole kingdom is full of sinners.'

Dear friends, as to the first saying, ['power is justice']: once the world was ruled by justice according to the laws of God and the king, but now it is ruled by power. Note the moral significance of this – and its truth – for once justice prescribed that God was to be loved above all things etc. But in the kingdom of the soul, power holds such sway that

1 Cf. Herrtage, Text II.XXXVII.
2 *corobola*: Oest. The word is corrupt. Graesse and Trillitzsch translate it as 'snail' (*cochlea*). See below n. 15.

man, out of a certain perversity, acts as he does against the inclination of his own will, which is naturally more inclined to good than to evil. The second saying ['day is night'] is also true, because once clerics showed laymen the way to the eternal home through good example, but their excellent character has changed, and they have all fallen by the wayside, 'all are become unprofitable together, and there is none that doeth good'.[3] This is clearly true of the pope, who once gave benefices to worthy clerics for God's sake, spurning gifts, as Peter did when he answered Simon Magus:[4] 'Keep thy money to thyself, to perish with thee!' The same is true of religious, who used to show the way to a good life through poverty, because they heeded the saying that a monk with a halfpenny is not worth a halfpenny. The same is true of priests, because as Jerome says: 'Whatever you keep besides a simple garment and food from the altar is not yours, but theft from the poor.' It is sacrilege, for all these, monks, canons, nuns or priests have turned day to night, and 'narrow is the way that leads to the heavenly home'[5] and few walk along it, because they are blind. The third saying of the first philosopher: 'Battle is flight', is literally true, because once, if one lord had a grievance against another, they would fight; but now honour is gone. They refuse to fight, but daily one will enter the land of another to plunder and thieve and commit other crimes; they refuse to fight, because they buy the swiftest horses so that they can flee. It is spiritually true, because once men overcame temptations and conquered their adversaries, i.e., the flesh, the world and the devil, and won great merit[6] with God, and received honour for this. But today, when they ought to fight, they give in and flee.

The second philosopher said: 'One is two etc.' What is the reason? It is that there is no truth today in the world, except that heart and tongue, which should be one, are now at variance, because whatever man declares with his tongue, his heart denies. Note, in consequence, that today sealed letters are worthless, oaths given are not kept etc.; and this was not so once, because if one person said to another simply: 'I will do this for you,' the other would believe him. And it is spiritually true, because the soul, which should be in charity and at one with God, is separated from him through sin. The second saying: 'Friend is foe etc.' What reason is there for this other than that there is no fidelity

3 Rom 3.12.
4 Acts 8.20. *in perdicione*: Oest., K.; *in perditionem*: V., K.
5 Cf. Mt 7.14.
6 *nuncii*: Oest.; *meriti*: K., L.

144. Of the present state of the world

in the world? Certainly he who should be a friend is now a foe; and now Christ's saying is proved true:[7] *'Son will rise up against father.'* I believe there is now no friend so good that he would not become a foe for money's sake. It is also spiritually true, because in the Gospel we are called Christ's friends, for as Christ says:[8] *'I will not now call you servants, but friends.'* But today we have become foes, because we have surrendered the Lord's castle, i.e., our heart, to the devil. The third saying: *'Evil is good etc.'* Why is it that today such cruelty and avarice prevails in the world? Of course, it is for no other reason than that what is an evil has become a good, namely money. That money is evil is proved by the philosopher who says that gold and silver are nothing but the dregs of the earth; and when these dregs became so beloved, godliness disappeared. However, as a wise man testifies,[9] nothing is more wicked than the love of money. What is a spiritual sin, which is the greatest evil in existence, has today become a good, for there are few who do not sin; and the prophet rails against such, saying:[10] *'Woe to you that call evil good and good evil!'*

The third philosopher said: *'Reason is banished'*. Why is it that today Christians are not called by that name? There is no other reason than that reason has been banished[11] among men. Man was, with reason, called a Christian after Christ, but men do not employ reason, because *'man, when he was in honour, did not understand etc.'*[12] For in his wantonness he is like a pig, in his pride like a lion, in his jealousy like a dog, in his deceitfulness like a fox, and so he does not deserve to be called either a man or a Christian, because he has completely forsaken the life of Christ. It is spiritually true, because if man possessed reason, he would love God above all things. My proof is that what is good must be loved, and what is more good must be loved more, and what is most good must be loved most of all; and it is agreed that God is the greatest good, a greater good than which cannot be conceived,[13] so if man possessed reason he would love him more than all else. The

---

7 Cf. Lk 12.53; Mt 10.21, 35.
8 Cf. Jn 15.15.
9 1 Tm 6.10.
10 Is 5.20.
11 *licenciam – licenciata*: reason has 'leave of absence', it has been granted leave.
12 Ps 48.21.
13 This recalls the words of Anselm's 'ontological argument' to prove the existence of God.

second saying: 'A thief is set above us.' Why is it that money etc.?[14] There is no other reason than that our officials are thieves, I do not mean actual thieves, but one thing I observe from experience is that earthly lords are poor and their stewards have plenty. I also observe that country villagers and other poor folk have only a small amount, and the rich an abundance. What can the reason for this be other than that there are thieves? Dear friends, if one man took five marks or as many florins from another, would he not be adjudged a thief? But how much these officials take from the principal sum is known only to their confessors; so the real thieves are not hanged. As witness the philosopher who laughed as he watched a judge leading a thief to the gibbet, and when the judge asked him why he was laughing, he replied that a big thief was leading a little one. It is spiritually true of those who for some small pleasure steal from God and subject to the devil souls which he won with his blood. The third saying,[15] about the gnat: in Latin, *culex cupit tam alte volare sicut ipsa aquila.* [*'The gnat wants to fly as high as the eagle.'*][16] Therefore there is no discernment, for those who ought to cultivate the land, today want to be lords over it, for as soon as they have one pair of leggings and spurs and a horse, they want to go about on horseback and be called 'Squire' John, and so on. It is also true of those citizens whose parents were tanners or cobblers, yet who behave like knights. Today there is little discrimination in the world. You may also apply this, as you please and know best, to women. This is spiritually true of nuns, monks and clerics. Observe how they go about etc. today.

The fourth philosopher said: 'Will is our counsellor. Therefore the kingdom is ill cared for.' What is the reason for the land being ill cared for? Why, none other than that the counsel of its lords is evil; for once counsellors were accustomed to give counsel in accordance with justice, whereas now they give it in accordance with their will. Consider, as you please and know best, their reasons for doing so. It is also spiritually true: whatever reason dictates for our eternal salvation, the will wants the opposite. The second saying: 'Money passes sentence etc.'

14 The second statement of the third philosopher was that 'A thief is set above us, therefore the kingdom is without money.'
15 *corobola*: corrupt. Swan believed that the true reading was *parabola* ('parable', 'illustration'; *Parabole* = the Book of Proverbs).
16 This proverbial saying was in none of the manuscripts examined by Oesterley, and seems to be an addition made by the editors of the printed editions.

144. Of the present state of the world

What is the reason that justice is sold in this way? It is none other than money; because if you come to a trial and have money to give, though your cause is less just,[17] *the judge will pronounce in your favour; he does not consider whether you are guilty, because 'gifts blind the eyes of judges'.*[18] *It is also spiritually true of your judgement at confession; because if you want to gain pardon for big sins easily and to placate your judge and confessor, offer him money, and though he has no authority, he will absolve you and impose a penance. Note also that this is literally true of these officials, and of the Roman Curia, which 'does not want a sheep without wool'. The third saying: 'God is dead etc.' Certainly things could not be as they are if God were still alive, as before his Incarnation, when to punish the sin of wantonness he drowned the whole world except for eight souls. Note how men in those times used to keep themselves from sin: they did so through fear of God at least, if not love, because they knew he punished everything! But now he is considered by us as if dead, and we do not think of the future judgement, or of hell, or everlasting punishment, or the everlasting kingdom etc. There: you have heard twelve reasons why the world is seated in evil. Cease therefore, dear friends, to act wrongly! 'Learn to do well,' Isaiah c.68.*[19] *'Then you shall know the truth, and the truth shall make you free.'*[20] *Which may God grant us.*

---

17 *causam in justitiam*: Oest.; *causam minus justam*: K., L.
18 Cf. Dt 16.19.
19 = Is 1.17.
20 Jn 8.32.

145. Of the way of salvation, which our Lord God revealed through his son

Albert relates[1] that in the time of Philip there was a way between two mountains of Armenia that had been disused for a long time, and then it chanced that because of the pollution of the air no-one could use the pass without choking to death. The king asked his wise men the reason for this great bane, but none of them could tell him the truth. Finally he summoned Socrates, who told him that he should construct a building equal in height with the mountains. When the king had done so, Socrates had a mirror of steel made with a pure and polished surface, so that every part of the mountain would be reflected and seen in it. Socrates then entered the building and saw two dragons, one on the mountain, the other in the valley, and facing each other they opened their jaws in turn and inhaled the air. As he was observing them, a youth on horseback, not knowing of the danger, tried to travel through the pass, and in a moment fell from his horse and died. Socrates immediately hastened to the king and told him all he had witnessed, and subsequently the dragons were captured by guile and slain, so the pass became safe for all who went through it.

Dear friends, I see these mountains which were elevated above the whole surface of the earth as the nobles and the powerful of the world, who are raised up above the common people, whether the laity or the clergy; for the Psalmist says:[2] *'The mountains ascend etc.' Between*

1. Albert of Stade, who was originally a Benedictine and became abbot of the Benedictine monastery of St John at Stade near Hamburg in 1232, wrote a chronicle beginning at the Creation and ending in 1256. He became a Franciscan in 1240.
2. Cf. Ps 103.8: 'The mountains ascend, and the plains descend into the place which thou hast founded for them.' God is praised for his mighty works and providence.

145. Of the way of salvation

these mountains is the pass used by the people, because the whole world is governed by those on high. On these mountains two dragons customarily lie hidden, i.e., two vices, namely pride and wantonness, by whose poison the whole world is infected, according to the saying of John c.2:[3] *'All that is in the world is either pride or wantonness.' The power of these dragons is unknown to us, and so those who use the public pass in which the dragons lurk are suddenly overtaken by their poison and die. But before we sense the danger, we must direct our gaze at a pure and polished mirror, i.e., the Saviour, whom Wisdom c.7 calls:*[4] *'The brightness of eternal light, and the unspotted mirror [of God's majesty].' Likewise we must construct another building; this building is a life purified by penance and adorned with virtues, from which we must see what perils face us. And when the youth, i.e., man, devoted to vanity, falls from the horse of virtue and dies a spiritual death, Socrates, i.e., the good prelate, must go without delay to the King of Glory and devoutly pray to him on his charge's behalf that he may take precautions for his hazardous journey, and choose the way of salvation and eternal glory, and so possess life everlasting. Which etc.*

---

3 Cf. 1 Jn 2.16.
4 Wis 7.26.

146. Princes and other grandees must be boldly rebuked for their misdeeds

Augustine relates in *The City of God*[1] that with a single galley the pirate Diomedes robbed and captured many people at sea. At the command of Alexander he was pursued by a large fleet and at length taken captive and brought before Alexander, who asked him: 'Why do you infest the sea?' Diomedes at once replied: 'Why do you infest the earth? Because I do it with one galley, I am called a robber; whereas you who oppress the world with a great armada of vessels are called an emperor. If my fortune were kinder I would become a better man. You are the opposite: the more fortunate you become, the worse you are.' 'I will change your fortune,' Alexander replied, 'that your wickedness may not be ascribed to fortune, but [your fortune] to your merits.'[2]

And so Alexander made Diomedes a wealthy man, and he turned from being a robber into a prince and a zealot for justice.

Dear friends, the pirate at sea with one galley is a sinner who is in the world and has one life, yet he never ceases through sin to destroy and plunder the virtues he received at baptism. But Alexander, i.e., the prince, or prelate, has to bring such a one to the path of righteousness with his ships, i.e., the admonitions of Holy Church. But let the prelate or prince be careful to judge himself first, that he may not be found worse than the one he wishes to reprove, because if he is, he will be punished the more severely. At length the pirate becomes a zealot for

1 *De Civitate Dei* IV.4.
2 *Fortunam tibi mutabo, ne malitia tuae fortunae, sed meritis adscribatur*: Oest., K. The meaning of this sentence (which does not appear in Augustine) is not quite clear. L. omits *sed*: 'lest your wickedness be ascribed to the merits of your (ill) fortune', and this seems to be the text translated by *Le Violier* and Graesse.

justice, and through the grace he has won the sinner comes to an excellent end, and then there is 'more joy upon one sinner that doth penance, than upon ninety-nine just, who need not penance etc.'[3]

---

3 Cf. Lk.15.7.

147. Of the bane of sin that poisons the heart

There is a story that the enemies of a certain king planned to assassinate him, and because he was powerful, they decided to kill him with poison. So some of them, dressed in humble clothing, came to the city in which he lived. There was a spring there from which the king often drank, and they saturated its waters with poison. Not knowing of this the king drank the water as he always had, and died.

Dear friends, the king is Adam, the first man, to whom all physical creatures were subject. The Psalmist:[1] *'Thou hast subjected all things under his feet.' Demons tried to kill the king with poison, which they poured into the spring. The spring is the human heart, because just as streams of water issue from the spring, so the heart of man pours virtue and governance into all his members. Poison was introduced into this spring when through temptation our first parent thought to act contrary to God's command, and succumbed to it, and then drank death from the spring; and after him almost countless men died, until Christ came and saved us from the spring. Its streams still shower down upon us, because by reason of that sin we are always ready to sin, as Genesis says, c.3:*[2] *'The imaginations and thoughts of man are prone to evil from his youth.'*

1 Ps 8.8.
2 Cf. Gn 8.21.

148. Sin will be punished in one place or another

Aulus Gellius says of Arion[1] that he was very rich, and when he wanted to travel from one country to another hired a vessel, but the sailors decided to kill him for his wealth. However, he got them to allow him first to sing in honour of the dolphin, which takes delight in men's singing. And when he was cast overboard, a dolphin took him on its back and carried him to land. While the sailors believed him dead, he was on dry land and accused them before the king.[2] They were then brought before the king and condemned to death.

Dear friends, so it is now, if any man richly endowed with virtues means patiently to cross the sea of this world to God. The sons of the devil will come and take away his reputation and temporal goods, and harass him with other troubles. And in the midst of this he must certainly be on guard, seeking help from God in devout prayer, and so he is carried to the land of which the Psalmist says:[3] *'Let my portion, o Lord, be in the land of the living'; and his enemies will be consigned to everlasting torment.*

1 *Refert Agillus de Amore*: Oest.; *refert Aulus Gellius de Am(m)one*: K., L. The story is treated at length by Aulus Gellius, *Noctes Atticae* XVI.19. See Herodotus I.23f; also Oesterley, p. 736; Tubach, no. 1726; Hope, pp. 584–5.
2 Periander, King of Corinth.
3 Cf. Ps 141.6.

149. Of vainglory, which is attended by many evils

Valerius relates[1] that a certain nobleman asked a wise man for advice as to how he could immortalize his name. The wise man replied that he would do so if he killed someone famous. So he killed Philip, the father of Alexander the Great, to make a name for himself. But soon afterwards he himself died a miserable death.

Dear friends, through their evil deeds some noblemen and worldly potentates acquire a name for falsehood, and without doubt because of that name they will do all in their power to destroy the Lord God. Such people will therefore die an evil death when they are buried in hell.

---

1 *F.D.M.* VIII.14 ext. 4. The nobleman is Pausanias, who murdered Philip of Macedon in 336 BC. The sage is Hermocles.

150. Of the dew of celestial grace

Pliny relates[1] that there is a land in which neither dew nor rain falls, which results in extreme aridity and lack of water, because there is only one spring there and its water is deep below. When people want water, they go to the spring with every kind of musical instrument, and walk around the spring playing sweet melodies, and in response to the music the water rises to the mouth of the spring and flows in abundance. And having obtained their water in this fashion the people go their way.

Dear friends, the dry land is this world, which makes man arid in prayer and devotion and steals the dew of heavenly grace from him. The spring is God; Ecclesiasticus c.6:[2] '[The word] of God on high is the fountain of wisdom.' Let us therefore go to that spring with musical instruments, i.e., with devout prayers, that our voices may be sweet in the ear of our beloved God, and the water of his grace will come to us; which etc.

---

1 This story does not appear in Pliny's *Natural History*. On the strange characteristics of springs and fountains see II.103 and XXXI.2.
2 Cf. Ecclus 1.5.

151. Of the sinful soul made leprous through its sins, and how it is cured

In the country of a certain king[1] there lived two knights, one of whom was avaricious and the other envious. The avaricious knight had a beautiful wife whom everyone loved, while the envious knight had a wife who was extremely ugly and was hated by everyone, but he possessed a piece of land that bordered on that of the avaricious knight, and his greedy neighbour longed above all things to have it. He approached him often and asked him if would sell him the land and made many offers, but the envious knight replied that he did not want to sell his inheritance for gold or silver. However, in his envy he began to wonder how he could tarnish the beauty of the avaricious knight's wife, and said to him: 'If you want to possess my land, I won't ask any money, just that your wife should spend one night with me.' The avaricious knight agreed to this and told his wife, who at first rejected the idea out of hand, but was at length persuaded by her husband and agreed. But before he slept with her, the envious knight lay with a leprous woman, then he went to his neighbour's wife and had intercourse with her as often as he pleased. He then informed her that she would catch leprosy, and told her that he was envious because his own wife was so exceptionally ugly while she was so beautiful; and this was why he had marred her beauty. When she heard this, she was aghast, and weeping bitterly she told her husband, who was extremely angry and said to her: 'Take my advice. There is as yet no sign of leprosy on you. Near the frontiers of our kingdom there is a large city which has a university. Go there and make yourself available to all-comers, and the first one to go with you will catch your disease and

---

[1] He begins as a king (*rex*), but continues as an emperor (*imperator*). I have called him a king throughout.

151. Of the sinful soul made leprous through its sins, and how it is cured

you will be completely cured of your leprosy.'

So she did as he said, and the king's son came along, fell in love with her, got her go home with him and begged her to yield to him. But she refused. 'God forbid,' she said, 'that I, a poor woman, should become the prince's mistress!' But he pressed her again and again to agree. She thought: 'This is the king's son. If he caught leprosy it would be a terrible disaster.' So she explained that if he lay with her he would catch leprosy. But he would not give up, and he lay with her and caught the disease. Next day, realizing that she was cured, she hastened back to her own city, first telling him: 'If you should catch leprosy, come and stay with me and I will do everything I can to provide you with all you require.'

Not long after this the king's son became a leper, and he was so ashamed that, unknown to anyone, he went off that night to his mistress and stayed with her. She explained the situation to her husband: 'This is the man who was infected by me,' she told him, 'as a result of which I myself was cured of leprosy.' Her husband was alarmed to see how badly infected he was, but he had a bedroom made ready for him, and there the prince lived in isolation, while his wife tended him in person. He remained there for seven years.

Now it happened that in the seventh year there was an unendurable heat wave, and the leper had by his bed a large pitcher of wine for his refreshment, and a snake who lived in the garden got inside this pitcher, bathed in the wine, and after bathing lay at the bottom of it. The leper suddenly woke from sleep and, feeling very thirsty, picked up the wine pitcher and unwittingly swallowed the snake. The snake subsequently began to gnaw at his entrails so violently that the leper shrieked and groaned with the pain. The lady felt the keenest pity for him, and his agony lasted for three days without ceasing. On the fourth he vomited, and together with the vomit and the poison inside him he threw up the snake. At once the pain stopped, and as the days went by the symptoms of leprosy gradually disappeared. After a week his flesh was free from all signs of the disease and like the skin of a child. This brought great joy to the lady, who dressed him in the richest clothing and gave him a noble war horse on which he rode back to his kingdom. There he was received with all honour, and after his father's death he became king, and ended his days in peace.

Dear friends, the two knights, one greedy and one envious, represent the devil and the first man, i.e., Adam. The devil was envious and had an ugly wife, i.e., an image deformed through pride, because it was created in radiant beauty but made ugly through sin. The avaricious knight, i.e., Adam, had a beautiful wife, that is, a soul created in the likeness of God, Genesis c.1.[2] *Seeing that man was formed in such a way that he might possess a place in heaven, the devil was very envious of him, and carefully considered how he might defile his wife, i.e., soul. Adam was greedy, because he was not only not content with the bounty God had given him, i.e., paradise, but he wanted to be as another god; and seeing this the devil went to Eve and said: 'If you eat of the tree of life, you will be as gods knowing good and evil', Genesis c.1.*[3] *The devil first infected himself with leprosy, i.e., sin, and went to the innocent Eve, who committed mortal sin when she broke God's commandment; and so man became a spiritual leper, for which he was cast from the kingdom of paradise into the wide world outside. The king's son, i.e., the Son of God, seeing man, whom he had formed, in misery, partook of man's nature when he came down from heaven and assumed our flesh, and consequently by his Passion cured us of all the leprosy of sin; and he bore our sins in his body,*[4] *and became unsightly at his Passion. Isaiah c.18:*[5] *'We have seen him without beauty or comeliness.' And there follows: 'We have thought him as it were a leper, as one struck by God and humiliated.' So we have been saved by the death of Christ and will be able to go safely to heaven, if we wish, but Christ in heaven makes trial of us daily; he knocks at the door of our heart, as he himself bears witness, Song of Solomon c.11:*[6] *'I stand at the gate and knock; if anyone open to me, I will sup with him.' But let us note carefully that we must open the door of our heart to him by the seven works of mercy, and receive him with all joy, and place him in a special chamber apart from men, that he may always stay with us. And just as the leprous son thirsted, so Christ thirsted upon the cross, and said:*[7] *'I thirst.' What did he thirst for? Not wine, but the salvation of our souls. When the Jews heard this they gave him vinegar mixed with gall. And lo!, he swallowed the poisonous serpent for our salvation and vomited up all*

2 Gn 1.26.
3 Cf. Gn 3.5.
4 1 Pt 2.24.
5 Cf. Is 53.2, 4.
6 Cf. Rv 3.20.
7 Jn 19.28.

151. Of the sinful soul made leprous through its sins, and how it is cured

the poison of the sin of our first parents; and thus, on the war horse of his divinity and humanity, on the day of his Ascension he went up to heaven with a multitude [of the heavenly host].[8] *And so the tale ends.*

---

8 *cum multitudine*: missing from *Le Violier*. The preacher is perhaps imagining a host of attendant angels. See the moralization of no. 155, where the preacher pictures a host of patriarchs, prophets and saints acclaiming Christ at his Ascension.

152. Christ delivers us from eternal peril and the assaults of demons

There was a prince named Cleonitus whose people in a certain city were surrounded and under siege. Wishing to advise them as to their most useful expedient, he commanded one of his soldiers to go to the scene of the siege and to taunt those besieging it. He ordered him to write a cunning secret message upon his missiles:[1] 'Be strong in the Lord, and steadfast under siege. I, Cleonitus, am coming in person and will raise the siege.'

Moralization. Dear friends, the prince is Christ; the people besieged in the city are sinners in this world, who are besieged by the devils, and if we are not warned from on high, they will destroy our souls. The soldier who is sent is a preacher: Paul's Epistle to Timothy:[2] *'Labour as a good soldier!' This soldier looks in outward appearance to sinners like an adversary, because he has the lance and arrow of his taunts, and he has sharp words to say, now in reproach of gluttons, now of lechers, and so on; but he is most certainly our friend, because the chastisements of love are worth more than the kisses of flattery.*

1 i.e., on the darts he was to shoot into the beleaguered city.
2 2 Tim 2.3.

153. Of temporal tribulation, which at the last shall be turned to everlasting joy[1]

Antiochus, who was King of Antioch, the city named after him, had a most lovely daughter, and when she came of age and became even more lovely, many sought her hand in marriage, offering unbelievably large dowries. As her father was considering to whom he should best give her in marriage, he was unaware that there burned within him a depraved lust and a flame of perverse passion for his daughter, and he began to love her more than a father ought. He wrestled with this madness, battled with his sense of shame, but was overcome by his desire. One day he went into his daughter's room and told everyone there to remain outside, as if he was going to have a private conversation with his daughter. But goaded by his mad lust, and though she fought back for a long time, he tore her girdle of her virginity[2] from her and deflowered her. As the girl was wondering what she should do, her nurse suddenly came in to her, and when she saw the tears in her eyes, she asked: 'Why are you so distraught?' 'Dear nurse,' the girl replied, 'two noble names have just died in this room.' 'My lady,' said the nurse, 'why do you say so?' The girl answered her: 'Because I have been most wickedly violated before my wedding day.' When the nurse heard this and saw what had happened, she nearly lost her senses. 'And what devil has had the great audacity to dare violate the bed of a queen?' she

[1] The story of Apollonius, Prince of Tyre, is very ancient (there is an anonymous romance of Greek or Latin origin, the *Historia Apollonii Tyri*, generally dated to the third century AD) and is the basis of Shakespeare's *Pericles*. See Oesterley, p. 737; Tubach, no. 306; Hope, pp. 587–92; see also, for a survey of the Apollonius tradition as a whole, Elizabeth Archibald, *Apollonius of Tyre: Medieval and Renaissance Themes and Variations*, Cambridge: Brewer, 1991
[2] *nodum virginitatis*: her virgin knot, i.e. hymen.

asked. The girl told her: 'It was impiety that committed the crime.' 'Why do you not tell your father?' asked the nurse. 'Where is my "father"?' the girl replied. 'If only you knew! I can never call him "father" again! Death is my only remedy.'

When the nurse heard her talk of seeking relief in death, she recalled her to her senses with some soothing words, and persuaded her to abandon her resolution. Meanwhile her impious father was hypocritically playing the role of dutiful father before his citizens, when inside the walls of his house he exulted at being his daughter's husband. And in order to secure for himself permanently his impious enjoyment of his daughter's bed, he decided on a new form of wickedness as a way of getting rid of the suitors who were asking her hand in marriage. He asked them a riddle, and told them: 'He who finds the answer to my riddle shall have my daughter in marriage. But if he fails, he will lose his head.' Because of the extraordinary and unrivalled beauty of the girl, a large number of kings from every part of the world came, and if any through his learning chanced to supply an answer to the riddle, he was beheaded, as if he had said nothing at all, and his head was suspended over the gate, that all who came there might see these dreadful faces and be deterred from agreeing to such conditions. All of this the king had done so that he could continue his unchaste relationship with his daughter.

After a short time, while Antiochus was carrying on in this perverse fashion, a young prince of Tyre named Apollonius, an exceedingly wealthy and well-educated man, came sailing by and put in at Antioch. He went before the king and said: 'Hail, king!' 'A blessing on the parents of the bridegroom!'[3] the king replied. 'I ask your daughter's hand in marriage,' said the youth. When the king heard these unwelcome words, he looked closely at the youth and asked him: 'Do you know the conditions?' 'I do,' replied the youth, 'and saw evidence of them at the gate.' 'Then hear my question,' said the king angrily. 'I am impelled by wickedness, I feed on mother's flesh, I seek my brother, my mother's husband, and cannot find him.' Having been given this riddle, the youth withdrew for a time from the king and, calling on all his knowledge, with God's aid he found the solution. Returning to the king he said: 'My good lord, you set me a question, now hear the answer. "I am impelled

---

3 If the text is sound, the king is being ironic: he is not going to allow anyone to have his daughter.

153. Of temporal tribulation

by wickedness". You told no lie: for consider yourself! "I feed on mother's flesh." Consider your daughter!' When the king heard the youth's answer to his riddle,[4] fearing that his sin might become public knowledge, he fixed him with an angry look and told him: 'You are far from the truth, young man. None of what you said is true, and you deserve to be beheaded. But you shall have the space of thirty days: consider it again, and return to your native land. If you find the solution to the riddle you shall marry my daughter. If not, you shall lose your head.'

Dismayed, the youth gathered his company together, boarded ship and made for his home in Tyre. After he had left, the king summoned his steward, whose name was Thaliarchus, and said to him: 'Thaliarchus, you are the most faithful guardian of my secrets. Know that Apollonius of Tyre has discovered the answer to my riddle. So board ship this moment and go in pursuit of him, and when you get to Tyre, find him and kill him either with the sword or with poison. On your return you will be handsomely rewarded.'

So Thaliarchus took arms and money and went to the young prince's country. But Apollonius got there before him. He went home and consulted all the books in his library, but could find no answer to the riddle other than the one he had given to the king. So he said to himself: 'Unless I am mistaken, King Antiochus has an incestuous love for his daughter.' And as he pondered the matter he thought: 'What are you doing, Apollonius? You found the answer and did not receive his daughter as your reward. It must be that God has brought you home to save you from death.' Without delay he had ships made ready for sailing; he loaded them with 100,000 bushels of corn and a huge weight of gold and silver and rich garments, and at the third hour of night boarded ship with a few of his most faithful friends and put out to sea. Next day when his fellow citizens looked for him, he could not be found, and it was a cause of great sadness that a prince so beloved of his land was nowhere to be seen. The whole city went into deep morning, and indeed the citizens felt such love for him that for a considerable time the barbers stopped

---

4 The third and hardest part is not explained. The riddle is less cryptic in Shakespeare's *Pericles* (I.i.65ff.): 'I am no viper, yet I feed / On mother's flesh which did me breed. / I sought a husband, in which labour / I found that kindness in a father. / He's father, son, and husband mild; / I mother, wife, and yet his child: / How they may be, and yet I two, / As you will live resolve it you.'

working, public entertainments were banned, the baths were shut and no-one went into the temples or taverns. While all this was happening, Thaliarchus, who had been dispatched by King Antiochus to kill Apollonius, arrived in Tyre. Seeing everything shut up, he said to a boy: 'Tell me, on your life: why is this city in such deep mourning?' The boy replied: 'My dear sir, don't you know? How can you ask? The city is in mourning because Apollonius, prince of this country, after returning from visiting King Antiochus, is nowhere to be seen.' Overjoyed to hear this Thaliarchus went back to his ship and sailed to Antioch, where he went before the king and told him: 'My lord king, joyful news! Apollonius has fled in fear of you.' 'He can flee,' the king replied, ' but he cannot escape.' And he immediately published the following edict: 'Whoever brings before me Apollonius of Tyre, who has defied my authority, shall receive fifty talents of gold. If he brings me his head he shall have 100.' In response to this not only Apollonius's enemies, but also his friends, seduced by their greed for money, made haste to pursue him. They searched for him at sea and on land, in the forests, and in every nook and cranny, but he could not be found. The king then ordered a whole navy to be got ready to pursue the youth, but while the ships were being fitted out, Apollonius arrived at Tarsus; and as he walked along the seashore, he was seen by one of his own servants, a man named Elinatus, who had arrived there that very hour. Elinatus went up to him and said: 'Hail, King Apollonius!' Apollonius acknowledged his greeting, but did so as the great are wont to do, and turned his back on him. The old servant was deeply offended and greeted him again. 'Hail, King Apollonius! Pray return my greetings and do not despise poverty when it is adorned by an honest nature. For if you knew what I know, you would take care.' 'Then tell me, if you please,' Apollonius replied. 'You are proscribed,' he said. 'And who proscribes one who is a prince of his own country?' Apollonius asked. 'King Antiochus,' he said. 'For what reason?' 'Because you wanted to be what her father is,' Elinatus told him. 'And what is the price on my head?' 'If anyone takes you alive, fifty talents of gold; if he produces your head, he will get 100. So I advise you to flee and be on your guard.' With these words Elinatus made to leave, but Apollonius asked him to come back because he wanted to give him 100 talents of gold. 'Have this much of my poverty,' he told him, 'for you have earned it. And cut off my head and present it to the king, and then he will be overjoyed. Here, the 100 talents

153. Of temporal tribulation

of gold are yours, and you are innocent of any wrongdoing, because I am paying you to bring joy to the king!'

'Lord,' replied the old man, 'far be it from me to take money for an office of such a kind! Among good men friendship is valued more highly[5] than money.' And bidding him farewell, he went on his way.

As Apollonius was walking along the same stretch of shore, he saw a man named Stranguilio[6] coming towards him weeping and with a doleful expression on his face. Apollonius went straight up to him and said: 'Hail, Stranguilio!' 'Hail, Lord Apollonius!' he replied, then added: 'Why are you walking about here looking so troubled?' Apollonius told him: 'Because I sought the hand of a king's daughter, who was in truth his wife, and wanted to marry her. So I have been seeking asylum, if it can be had. I cannot hide myself in my own country.'

'Lord Apollonius,' Stranguilio replied, 'our city is very poor and could not entertain someone of your rank. What is more we are suffering a dire famine because of the failure of our corn, and there is no longer any hope that our citizens will survive. A cruel death is staring us in the face.'

'Give thanks to God,' said Apollonius, 'who has caused me in my flight to land upon your shores! I will give your city 100,000 bushels of corn, if only you conceal my flight.' When Stranguilio heard this, he prostrated himself at Apollonius's feet and said: 'Lord Apollonius, if you help my starving city, not only shall we conceal your flight, but if need be, we will fight to save you.'

So Apollonius mounted the tribunal in the forum before all the citizens of the place and said: 'Citizens of Tarsus, you are suffering from a lack of corn and oppressed by famine. I, Apollonius of Tyre, can provide relief; for I think you will remember the help I am giving you and will conceal my flight. Know this: it was not the malice of Antiochus that made me flee, rather it was the hand of providence that brought me here in my travels. So I will give you 100,000 bushels of corn at the price I paid for it at home, which was eight pence a measure.'

When the citizens heard that they could buy corn at eight pence a measure they were overjoyed; they thanked Apollonius and at once began to prepare the corn for use. Then Apollonius, loath

5 *comparanda*: or 'cannot be bought'.
6 What Elinatus, the prince's servant, is doing so far from home in Tarsus, and how Apollonius knows Stranguilio, are not explained.

to lay aside his princely dignity and seem to be acting more as a tradesman than a benefactor, gave back the proceeds of the sale for the use of the city. As witness to his great kindnesses to them, the citizens erected a chariot in their forum in which the figure of Apollonius stood, holding corn in his right hand and trampling it with his left foot; and on its base they put the inscription: '*Apollonius of Tyre made a gift to the city of Tarsus which saved its people from a cruel death.*'

A few days after this, on the advice of Stranguilio and his wife Dionysiades, Apollonius decided to sail to Pentapolis in Etruria, where he could remain hidden and enjoy more comfort and tranquillity. So he was escorted to the shore with great pomp, and bidding everyone farewell he boarded a ship. For three days and nights the winds were favourable, but as soon as he left the coast of Tarsus, the sea changed; for in a few hours the north and east winds blew violently and the heavens burst open and poured down torrential rain. The Tyrian crew was carried off by the storm, and the vessel's timbers burst asunder. Then westerly winds churned up the deep, and hail fell and pitch black clouds overshadowed them, and the winds kept blowing so furiously that death stared them all in the face. Everyone on board seized hold of planks, but in the darkness of the storm they all perished. Apollonius, however, clinging to a single plank, was washed up on the coast of Pentapolis; and standing on the shore, gazing at a sea which was now calm, he said to himself: 'Ah, how treacherous the sea is! I would rather fall into the hands of the cruellest king! Where am I to go? What country shall I make for? What friend will help me, an unknown stranger?'[7]

As he spoke these words he saw a young man approaching him, a hardy fisherman wearing dirty sackcloth. Compelled by his need, he threw himself at his feet, and weeping copiously said: 'Take pity, whoever you are, on a man who has been shipwrecked and lost everything, one born not of humble but of noble family! And that you may know whom you pity, I am Apollonius of Tyre, the prince of my homeland. I beg you, save my life!'

When the fisherman observed the young man's comeliness, he was moved to pity; he raised him to his feet and took him to his

7 The passage describing the shipwreck is composed in strikingly elevated language, and full of rhetorical devices. The rhythms in more than one place suggest an original in verse, and indeed in *H.A.T.* this section is in verse.

own home, and placed whatever he could find before him. Then, to show his charity the more fully, he took off his shabby cloak and divided it into two halves, and gave one to the young stranger. 'Take what I have,' he told him, 'and go to the city. There perhaps you will find someone to take pity on you. If you do not, return here to me, and whatever poverty can afford must suffice. We can fish together. But one word of caution: if you are ever restored to your former dignity, do not despise the meanness of this poor cloak.' 'If I do not remember your kindness,' said Apollonius, 'may I be shipwrecked again and not find another like yourself to help me!' And with these words he took the path shown him by the fisherman and entered the gates of the city. And as he was wondering where he might find help, he saw a naked boy running along the street; his head was anointed with oil and bound with a cloth, and he was shouting at the top of his voice: 'Listen, everyone, pilgrims and slaves, listen! Anyone who wants to wants to wash, go to the gymnasium!' When Apollonius heard this, he took off his cloak, got into the bath and swam about in the water. And as he looked at the people there he tried to find someone of his own degree, but could not, until suddenly Altistrates, king of the whole country, entered with an entourage of servants. As he was playing ball with them, Apollonius bowed to the king, caught the ball as it flew by him, then struck it skilfully and quickly back to the king.

'Leave me,' the king told his servants. 'This young man, I suspect, is a match for me.'[8]

Hearing himself praised, Apollonius confidently approached the king, and taking some oil, anointed his person skilfully and with practised hand. Then warming him in a most pleasant bath, he left. After the young man had gone, the king said to his friends: 'I swear to you, in all truth, that I never enjoyed a bath more than I have today, and it was through the kindness of a young man whose name I do not know.' And he nodded to one of his servants and said: 'That young man who was so attentive – find out who he is.' The servant followed Apollonius, saw him wearing the shabby cloak, and returned to the king and told him: 'The youth has been shipwrecked.' 'How do you know?' asked the king. 'He said nothing,'

8 *mihi comparandus est Appollonius: Appollonius ut audivit*: Oest., K., L. I suspect dittography, and that the text should read: *mihi comparandus est.' Apollonius, ut audivit*. The king does not know who Apollonius is, as what follows makes clear.

the servant replied, 'but it is clear from his clothing.' 'Go quickly, then,' said he king, 'and tell him that the king invites him to come to supper.'

When Apollonius received this invitation, he accepted and went back with the servant to the king. The servant went in before him and said to the king: 'The shipwrecked youth is here, but is ashamed to come in because of his shabby cloak.' The king at once commanded that he should be dressed in decent clothing and come in to supper. Apollonius entered the dining hall and reclined in the place assigned him opposite the king. First a breakfast was brought in, and then a regal banquet. But while all the others ate, Apollonius did not; with tears in his eyes he kept gazing at the gold and silver that adorned the king's table. 'Unless I am mistaken,' one of the guests said to the king, 'this young man is envious of your royal wealth.' 'Your suspicion is ill-founded,' the king replied. 'He does not envy my wealth, rather he is sad for all that he himself has lost.' Then with a smile on his face he turned to Apollonius and said: 'Young man, eat with us, and hope that God will send you better fortune.' Suddenly, as he was speaking these charming words to Apollonius, in came the king's daughter, who was now a young lady, and she kissed her father, then all his guests in turn. Having kissed each of them she returned to her father and said: 'Father dear, who is the young man sitting in the place of honour opposite you, who is so sad?' 'My sweet,' he replied, 'he is a young man who has been shipwrecked and who was most courteous to me today in the gymnasium, so I invited him to supper. Who he is I do not know. But if you wish to know, ask him. It is fitting that you should know the truth, and perhaps, when you know, you will take pity on him.'

Thus encouraged, the girl went to the young man and said: 'Dear friend, your looks prove your noble birth. If it does not distress you, tell me your name and circumstances.' 'You ask my name,' he replied. 'I lost it at sea. My nobility? I left it in Tyre.' 'Speak more plainly,' the girl said, 'so that I can understand.' Apollonius then told her his name and all that had befallen him, and when he finished speaking, he began to weep. Seeing him weeping, the king told his daughter: 'My sweet, you did wrong to ask the young man his name and circumstances, for you have renewed his past miseries. But since you know the truth, dear child, it is right that you should now show him the generosity of a princess.' Responding to her father's wish, she turned to the youth and said: 'You are now one of us, Apollonius. Lay aside your

153. Of temporal tribulation

grief and my father will make you wealthy.' With a sigh, and in all humility Apollonius thanked her. The king then said to his daughter: 'Bring your lyre to cheer the banquet with your singing.' So the girl had her lyre fetched and began to play it with surpassing sweetness. Everyone applauded her and said: 'No-one could play or sing more sweetly!' Only Apollonius was silent. 'Apollonius,' the king said, 'this is unseemly behaviour. Everyone praises my daughter's playing. Why do you alone find fault with it?' 'Gracious king,' he replied, 'permit me to speak my mind. Your daughter has begun to learn the art of music, but has not yet mastered it. Have someone hand me a lyre, and you will hear the difference at once.' 'Apollonius,' the king replied, 'I see you have every kind of skill!' He commanded that a lyre be given to him, and Apollonius left the room and crowned his head with a garland. He then took up the lyre and re-entered the dining room, and played before the king so beautifully that all present thought it was not Apollonius, but Apollo playing. The guests at supper with the king declared that they had never heard or seen a better performance. And when the king's daughter heard him, she fell in love as she gazed at the youth, and said to the king. 'Father, let me choose a reward for the young man.' The king agreed, and turning to Apollonius she said: 'Master Apollonius, of my father's bounty receive 200 talents of gold, 400 pounds of silver, rich garments, twenty menservants and ten maidservants.' She then told her attendants: 'Bring what I have promised.' And in the presence of the king's friends, the doors of the dining room were opened and everything was brought in at the princess's behest. This done, they all rose, took their leave and departed.

'Gracious king,' Apollonius said, 'who pity the unfortunate, and you, princess, lover of study and friend of philosophy, farewell!' He turned to the servants whom the princess had given him and told them: 'Take up these gifts of mine, men, and let us go and look for lodgings.' This saddened the girl, who feared she would lose her beloved, and she turned to her father and said: 'Gracious king and best of fathers, do you wish Apollonius, whom today we have made rich, to leave us, and risk being robbed of our gifts by criminals?' So the king quickly assigned him rooms where he could stay in comfort. His daughter, aflame with love, spent a restless night, and early next morning she entered her father's bedroom. When he saw her he asked: 'What is it? Why are you up at such an unusually early hour?' 'I cannot sleep,' she told him. 'So I beg you, dearest father, have me taught by our young guest, so that I can learn music and other things.'

The king was delighted to hear this, and had the young man brought to him. 'Apollonius,' he said, 'my daughter is most eager to acquire your skill. So I would like you to teach her all you know, and I will reward you handsomely.' 'My lord,' he replied, 'I am ready to do as you wish.' So he taught the girl everything that he himself had learned, but by and by her passionate love for the youth made her ill. Seeing how her health had deteriorated, her father urgently summoned physicians, who felt her pulse and various parts of her body but could find nothing wrong with her.

A few days later three young nobles, who had long been asking for the girl's hand in marriage, came to the king and greeted him together. Regarding them, the king asked: 'Why are you here?' They replied: 'Because you have so often promised to give us your daughter's hand in marriage. That is why we have come together today. We are your subjects, we are rich and born of noble families. So make your choice: which one of us will you have as your son-in-law?' 'You have called upon me at an inconvenient time,' the king told them. 'My daughter is devoted to[9] her studies and because of her passion for them has become unwell. But lest I seem to you to be delaying my decision too long, write down your names on pieces of paper and the amount of dowry you are offering. I will pass them on to my daughter and she can then choose which of you she wants.' When they had done this, the king took the pieces of paper, read them and sealed them, then gave them to Apollonius. 'Take these, Master,' he said, 'and hand them to your pupil.'

So Apollonius took them to her, and when she saw the man she loved, she cried: 'Master, what can you mean by entering my chamber alone?' Apollonius answered: 'Take these pieces of paper which your father has sent you and read them.' The girl opened the documents, read the names of her three suitors and threw them to the floor. Looking steadily at Apollonius, she said: 'Master Apollonius, are you not sad that I must be given in marriage to another?' 'No,' he replied, 'for anything that does you honour will be a boon to me.' 'Master,' she replied, 'if you loved me you would be sad.' And so saying, she wrote down her answer, sealed the papers again and handed them to Apollonius to deliver to the king. This was what she wrote: 'My king and dearest father, since you have kindly

---

9 *studiis vacat*: conceivably this might also mean 'is unable to pursue her studies'.

153. Of temporal tribulation

allowed me to reply to you, I do so. I wish to marry the one who was shipwrecked.'

When the king read what his daughter had decided, but not knowing which of the suitors she meant, he turned to the youths and asked: 'Which one of you has ever been shipwrecked?' One of them, named Ardonius, said: 'I have.' 'Plague take you!' said another. 'I know you. You are the same age as I. You have never been beyond the city gate! Where were you shipwrecked?' So the king, being unable to find out which of them had been shipwrecked, turned to Apollonius and said: 'Take these documents and read them. Perhaps you know something I do not. You must understand, as you were there with her when she wrote this.' Apollonius took the documents and quickly glanced through them, and blushed when he realized that he was the one she loved. 'Apollonius,' the king insisted, 'have you discovered who this shipwrecked person is?' In his embarrassment Apollonius said little.[10] And when the king realized that his daughter meant Apollonius, he told the others: 'When I have time, I will come to you.' So they said their farewells and left him. He then went in to his daughter and asked her: 'Whom have you chosen to be your husband?' In tears she threw herself at his feet and said: 'Dearest father, I want the shipwrecked Apollonius.' Seeing his daughter's tears, the king raised her from the floor and spoke as follows: 'My sweet child, you need not worry, since you have chosen the one I chose myself as soon as I saw him. And as I am a loving father,[11] I shall appoint a day for your wedding without delay.'

The following day all the king's friends from neighbouring cities were summoned to him. 'Dear friends,' he announced, 'my daughter wishes to marry her teacher Apollonius. I therefore beg you all to celebrate, because my daughter is to be wedded to a wise man.' So saying, he fixed the day for the wedding.

His daughter soon conceived, and while she was carrying the child in her womb, it happened that she was walking along the seashore with her husband Apollonius when she saw a splendid

---

10 Swan interposes a *moralisatio* here (which is preserved in L., and translated by Graesse) which commends keeping a close guard on the tongue.

11 *ut eum vidi; quia et amando factus sum pater:* this might conceivably also mean 'as soon as I saw him, through my love for him I became (as) his father'. Altistrates has, as it were, adopted the shipwrecked Apollonius.

ship. Apollonius knew that it was from his own country, and calling to the captain he asked: 'Where are you from?' 'From Tyre,' he replied. 'That is my own country,' Apollonius told him. 'Then you are a Tyrian?' asked the other. 'I am.' 'Do you know a prince of that country,' asked the captain, 'by the name of Apollonius?' He continued: 'I beg you, if you see him, tell him to celebrate and make merry, because King Antiochus and his daughter were both killed by a lightning bolt, and all the wealth of the kingdom of Antioch awaits his possession.'

When he heard this Apollonius was filled with joy, and he said to his wife: 'Will you please allow me to go and take possession of the kingdom?' When she heard his request she burst into tears. 'O my lord,' she said, 'if you were to go away on a long journey you would have to hurry back for the child's birth; and now you are by my side, yet you propose to leave me! However, if you wish to do this, let us go together.' She went to her father and said: 'Father, rejoice and be merry: that cruel King Antiochus and his daughter have received God's judgement and been struck by lightning, and his wealth and kingly power await our possession. So please allow me to go there with my husband.' Delighted at the news, the king had ships drawn up along the shore and filled them with every kind of provision. And while this was being done he instructed Ligozis, his daughter's nurse, and a midwife to sail with her to assist at the birth of her child. Having given them leave to depart, he escorted them to the seashore, kissed his daughter and son-in-law, and they set sail.

When they had been at sea a few days a mighty storm blew up. The princess meanwhile, in giving birth to a daughter, was so ill that she almost died, and her attendants wept and wailed for grief. Apollonius, hearing their cries, ran to her room, and seeing his wife lying there, to all appearances dead, he tore his clothes from his breast, and in floods of tears threw himself upon her body and cried: 'Dear wife, daughter of Altistrates, what shall I say to your father?' He had scarcely uttered these words when the helmsman told him: 'A ship cannot carry a dead body. Have the body cast into the sea so that we can escape its curse!' 'What are you saying, you cur?' Apollonius cried. 'You want me to throw this body into the same sea that received me when shipwrecked and destitute?' He called his servants and told them: 'Make a coffin and bore holes in it; seal it with bitumen and put a tablet of lead inside, then close it up.' When the coffin was finished, he told them to adorn the prin-

153. Of temporal tribulation

cess's body with all her regal finery. They duly placed the girl in the coffin, and put a quantity of gold at her head, and Apollonius kissed her corpse, bathing it in his tears. He then gave instructions for the upbringing and care of the infant, that he might have at least a granddaughter to show the king, if not his daughter; and amid loud cries of mourning he ordered the coffin to be cast overboard.

On the third day the sea washed up the coffin on the shores of Ephesus, not far from the house of a certain physician named Cerimon, who that same day went for a walk along the coast with his pupils. He saw the coffin lying there washed up by the waves, and said to his servants: 'Take up that coffin with great care and carry it to my house.' They did as he commanded, and when the physician opened it up he found a beautiful girl, arrayed in all her regal finery, lying there in the semblance of death. Astonished, he said: 'Sweet maid, why have you been abandoned like this?' He saw the money placed beneath her head and beneath it the tablet with writing on it. 'Let us find out what is written on the tablet,' he said. And when he opened it he discovered the inscription: 'I beg whoever finds this coffin to take ten pieces of gold for himself and spend another ten on a funeral. For the body it contains has left many a tear and bitter sorrow for those that gave it birth. And if he does not act as compassion requires of him, may he die and have no-one to give him burial!' Having read this message, Cerimon said to his servants: 'Let us bury the body as compassion requires. And I swear to you as I hope to live that I shall spend more on the funeral than mourning demands.' He at once told them to prepare a funeral pyre, but while it was being constructed and set in place, up came one of the physician's pupils, who, though he was only a youth, possessed the wisdom of old age. As he regarded the lovely corpse when it was laid on the pyre, his master observed him and said: 'You have come at the right moment; for I have been waiting for you this hour. Take this phial of ointment and pour it upon the corpse as a final funeral offering.' The youth approached the body, drew the garments on her breast aside, and poured the unguent on her. And as he smoothed it over her whole body with his hand he felt signs of life in her heart. He was amazed; he felt her pulse, checked for breath from her nostrils, pressed his lips to hers, and could feel that her life was still struggling with death. He said to the servants: 'Put torches at the four corners of the pyre, and do it slowly and carefully.' This was done, and the blood which had coagulated was liquefied. As soon as he observed this the youth told his master: 'The girl you say is dead is alive, and that you may believe me, I will give you proof.' So saying he picked up the girl and put her in his own bedchamber; there he poured warm oil on her breast, and soaked a piece of wool with it and laid it on her body. In this way the blood which had congealed inside gradually became more liquid, and life began to spread to her vital organs. Once the blood was running freely through her veins, she opened her eyes and drew breath and said: 'Whoever you are, touch me only as is proper, for I am a king's daughter and the wife of a king.'

When the young man heard her speak he was overjoyed, and went to his master's chamber and said: 'A miracle, master! The girl is alive.' 'I commend your skill,' he replied, 'I applaud your art and I admire your wisdom. See what diligent study can achieve, and never be ungrateful to your art. And take your payment. For this girl brought with her a great deal of money.'

Cerimon then commanded that the girl be given fresh garments, wholesome food and the best medicines. A few days later, having been apprised that she was of royal blood, he called his friends to him and in their presence adopted her as his daughter. Tearfully she begged him that no man should touch her, so he sent her with some women servants to live among the priestesses of Diana's temple, that her chastity might be preserved.

In the meantime Apollonius sailed on in his great grief. Under God's guidance he put in at Tarsus, and disembarking he made for the house of Stranguilio and Dionysiades. After greeting them he told them of all that had befallen him. 'To my great grief my wife has died,' he said, 'but my daughter has been preserved, and that is reason to be glad. So, since I trust you, I am going to take back the kingdom I had lost, which awaits my possession. But I shall never go back to my father-in-law, whose daughter I have lost at sea; I would rather work as a merchant! I entrust my daughter to you. I wish her to be brought up with your daughter Philomatia, and to be known as Tarsia. Moreover I want my wife's nurse Ligozis to take charge of your daughter as well.' So saying he handed Stranguilio the child and gave him gold and silver and rich garments, and swore never to shave his head or cut his hair or nails until he had given his daughter in marriage. They were amazed at the severity of this oath, but promised to bring up the girl with every care. Apollonius then boarded his ship and sailed away to distant parts.

153. Of temporal tribulation

When the young Tarsia completed her fifth year, she was sent to school to study the liberal arts with her foster parents' daughter Philomatia, who was the same age. When she was fourteen years old she returned from school to find that her nurse Ligozis seemed suddenly unwell, and sitting next to her she asked her the reason for her illness. 'Listen, my dear daughter,' her nurse said. 'Who do you think are your father and mother, and what country are you from?' 'My home is Tarsus,' the girl replied, 'my father is Stranguilio, my mother Dionysiades.' The nurse groaned and said: 'Listen, my daughter, and I'll tell you the true story of your birth so that after my death you may know what you must do. Your father's name is Apollonius, and your mother was Lucina, the daughter of King Altristrates. She breathed her last while giving birth to you. Your father Apollonius had a coffin made and put her in it in her royal apparel and cast her into the sea. He put twenty gold pieces beneath her head so that wherever she was washed up, they could be used for her funeral. The ship struggled on, tossed by the winds, with your father in mourning and you in your cradle, and came to this city. So Apollonius of Tyre entrusted you, as he did me, to Stranguilio and Dionysiades, your foster parents, and made a vow not to shave his head or cut his hair or nails until he had given you in marriage. Now this is my advice: if after my death these foster parents, whom you call your parents, ever do you any injury, go to the forum and there you will find a statue of your father. Take hold of it and cry out: "I am the daughter of the man whose statue this is!", and the citizens will remember your father's kindnesses to them and will avenge your wrong.'

'Dear nurse,' Tarsia said, 'as God is my witness, if you had not told me this, I would never have known the truth about my birth.' And while they were speaking together, the nurse gave up the ghost. So Tarsia buried her nurse's body and mourned her death a whole year. Then she resumed the clothing appropriate to her status and went back to school to study the liberal arts, and, when she returned from school she never ate anything until she had visited her nurse's monument. She would take a flask of wine with her, enter the monument and remain there while invoking the names of her parents. One day at this time Dionysiades happened to cross the forum with [her and][12] her daughter Philomatia. Now

12 The Latin does not make it clear that both Tarsia and Philomatia are with Dionysiades.

all the citizens who saw them commented on Tarsia's beauty and grace. 'Happy the father whose daughter Tarsia is!' they said. 'But the one holding her hand is ugly, hideous!'

When Dionysiades heard Tarsia being complimented and her daughter insulted, she was beside herself with anger. She sat down on her own and thought to herself: 'It is now fourteen years since her father left here. He won't come to fetch his daughter back and hasn't sent a single letter to her. I think he's dead. Her nurse is dead, too, so I have no-one to stand in my way. I will kill her and dress my daughter up in her precious things.' As she was thinking these thoughts, a bailiff named Theophilus[13] came by from the farm. She called to him and said: 'If you want a reward, kill Tarsia!' 'What has that innocent young girl done?' the bailiff asked. 'She is utterly wicked,' Dionysiades told him, 'so you should not refuse to do this for me. Do as I say. If you do not, it will be the worse for you.' He said: 'Tell me how this is to be done, mistress.' She replied: 'It is her custom, as soon as she leaves school not to eat a meal until she has visited her nurse's monument. Let her find you there waiting with a dagger. Grab her by the hair and stab her, then throw her body into the sea, and I will give you your freedom and a handsome reward into the bargain.' So the bailiff took a dagger and went off unhappily to the monument. 'Woe is me!' he said to himself. 'Is shedding the blood of an innocent maiden the only way I can earn my freedom?' When the girl was on her way back from school and entered the monument with the flask of wine, as she was accustomed to do, the bailiff lunged at her, and grabbing her by the hair threw her to the ground. As he attempted to stab her, Tarsia cried out to him: 'Theophilus, what have I done to you or anyone that I should die?' 'You have done no wrong,' said the bailiff. 'It was your father, who left you such great wealth and your royal jewellery.' 'I beg you, sir,' the girl pleaded, 'if there is no hope left, let me call upon my God!' 'Do so,' said the bailiff. 'And God knows that I am killing you under duress.'

Then as she was praying, some pirates came by and seeing that the girl was in mortal danger, and there was a man with a weapon ready to stab her, they shouted: 'Spare her, cruel savage! She is our prey: you shall not triumph!' When he heard them Theophilus

---

13   Theophilus is known to Dionysiades and also to Tarsia. It seems that Stranguilio has a farm somewhere.

153. Of temporal tribulation

fled behind the monument and hid on the seashore, whereupon the pirates seized the girl and made for the coast. The bailiff then went back to his mistress and told her: 'Your order has been carried out. I suggest that you put on mourning clothes, as I shall, and let us shed some feigned tears in front of our fellow citizens and say she died of a mortal illness.' When Stranguilio heard what had been done he was seized with fear and horror. 'Give me some mourning clothes,' he said, 'that I may mourn her, for I too am involved in this vile crime. Ah, what am I to do? The girl's father saved this city when it was in the grip of death, he suffered shipwreck for the sake of this city, he lost his property and endured privation, and we have given him evil in return for good. A savage lioness has devoured the daughter he gave us to care for! Ah, I have been blind! Now I must mourn the innocent, who am shackled to a wicked and deadly serpent!' Lifting his eyes to heaven, he said: 'God, you know I am innocent of Tarsia's blood. Require it of Dionysiades!' Then glaring at his wife he said: 'You enemy of God and reproach of mankind, you have killed the daughter of a king!'

Dionysiades duly dressed herself and her daughter in mourning garments, and made a pretence of grief before their fellow citizens. 'Dear friends,' they said, 'we cry out to you because the hope of our eyes, Tarsia, whom you know, has died a sudden, painful death, and left us only suffering and bitter tears. But we have given her a fitting burial.' The citizens then made haste to the place where, because of his goodness to them, Apollonius's form had been sculpted in bronze, and there in recognition of her father's kindness they erected a sepulchre of bronze for the young virgin Tarsia.

The pirates who had kidnapped the girl came to the city of Machilenta[14] and there she was left among other slaves to be sold. Hearing of her beauty, a godless and debauched pimp resolved to bid for her. But Athenagoras, the prince of that city, observing her noble bearing, beauty and intelligence, offered ten gold pieces for her. 'I will give twenty,' the pimp said. 'I will give thirty,' said Athenagoras. 'Forty,' countered the pimp. 'Fifty,' said Athenagoras. 'Sixty,' said the pimp. 'Seventy,' said Athenagoras. 'Eighty,' said the pimp. 'Ninety,' said Athenagoras. 'I will give 100 gold pieces on the nail,' the pimp said, and added: 'If anyone offers another ten, I will give ten more.' Athenagoras said to himself: 'If I have to match

---

14 In *Pericles* this is Mytilene.

this pimp's bids to buy the girl, I shall have to sell a lot of slave girls. I shall let him buy her, and when he prostitutes her, I will go to his brothel and be the first to get to her and take her virginity, and it will be the same as if I had bought her.'

So, to cut a long story short, Tarsia went with the pimp to a room in his house where he had a golden, gem-encrusted statue of Priapus. There he told her: 'Girl, worship him!' 'I would never worship such a thing,' she said; then she added: 'Sir, are you perhaps from Lampsacus?' 'Why do you ask?' said the pimp. 'Because the Lampsacans worship Priapus,' she replied. 'Wretched creature,' he said, 'don't you know that you have entered the house of a money-grubbing pimp?' At this the girl threw herself down at his feet and cried: 'Oh sir, have pity on my virginity! Do not defile my body by putting it to such a shameful purpose!' 'Don't you know,' the pimp asked her, 'that to the pimp and the hangman prayers and tears mean nothing?'

He then sent for the overseer who looked after his girls and told him: 'Have this girl dressed in precious clothing, appropriate to her age, and put this notice up: "The man who takes Tarsia's virginity shall pay a half pound of gold. Thereafter she will be publicly available for a single gold piece."' The overseer did as he had been told, and two days later a crowd arrived at the brothel with the pimp at its head and a band playing. But first to enter, with his head veiled, was Prince Athenagoras. When she saw him, Tarsia cast herself at his feet and cried: 'Have pity on me, sir, for the love of God! I adjure you in God's name not to deflower me! Quell your lust! Listen to the tale of my misfortunes and consider with care the truth about my birth!' And after she had recounted to him all of her adventures, the prince was ashamed and overcome with compassion. He said to her: 'I have a daughter like you myself, and dread a similar fate for her.' So saying he gave her twenty gold pieces and said: 'Here, you have more than the price put upon your virginity. Tell those who come to you what you told me, and you will be freed.' In floods of tears the girl replied: 'I thank you for your pity, but do not tell anyone what you have heard from me.' 'I will not,' Athenagoras replied, 'save my daughter, when she comes to your age, lest she should suffer a similar misfortune.' He then left her with tears in his eyes. As he went out another client met him and asked: 'How did you get on with the girl?' 'It couldn't have been better,' he replied, 'but she was very upset.' The young man went inside and the girl closed the door as she had before.

153. Of temporal tribulation

'How much did the prince give you?' he asked. 'Forty gold pieces,' she told him. 'Here,' he said, 'take a whole pound weight of gold.' And the prince heard this[15] and told him: 'The more you give, the more she will weep.' The girl took the money, then threw herself at his feet and told him of her misfortunes. Perplexed,[16] the youth said to her: 'Stand up, lady. We are humans and all of us subject to misfortunes.' And with these words he left, and as he did so he saw Athenagoras laughing, and said to him: 'A great man like you! Have you have no-one to give your tears to but me?' And they swore not to tell anyone about their conversation, and waited for the arrival of other clients. Many came and gave her money, but they all left in tears. In due course Tarsia offered the money to the pimp. 'Look,' she said. 'Here is the price you set on my maidenhead.' The pimp told her: 'See that you bring me as much every day.' Next day, however, learning that she was still a virgin, he angrily summoned the overseer and said: 'Take her off and deflower her yourself.' The overseer said to her: 'Tell me, are you a virgin?' She replied: 'As long as God pleases, I remain a virgin.' 'Where did you get all that money?' he asked her. 'I burst into tears,' she replied, 'and told the men of my circumstances, and asked them to take pity on my virginity.' And she threw herself at his feet and cried: 'Have pity on me, sir! Help me, I am a king's daughter held captive, do not ravish me!' 'The pimp is a grasping man,' he told her. 'I don't know if you can remain a virgin.' 'I was educated in the liberal arts,' she said, 'and I can play a musical instrument. Take me to the forum and there you will hear how eloquent I am. Suggest questions to the people and I will answer them all. By demonstrating my skill at this I shall earn money every day.' 'Very well,' he agreed.

All the people flocked to see the girl and she began to demonstrate her learning and eloquence. She had them ask her questions, all of which she answered lucidly, and so in this way she received a great deal of money from the people. Athenagoras watched over her as if she were his only daughter and made sure that she remained a virgin; indeed he commended her to the care of the overseer whom he won over with many gifts.

15 He has presumably been listening at the door.
16 *Apoziatus*: Oest., K.; *apportatus*: L. I read *aporiatus*. The youth is not named in *Le Violier*, and there seems little point in naming him at this late stage, when he is never to reappear.

While all this was going on, Apollonius returned after fourteen years to the house of Stranguilio and Dionysiades in Tarsus. When Stranguilio saw him he ran with all haste to his wife Dionysiades and told her: 'You said Apollonius was shipwrecked and had died. Look!, here he comes to ask us to give him back his daughter! Well, what are we going to say about her?' 'You wretched man,' she said, 'let us both put on mourning garments and shed some tears, then he'll believe our story that his daughter died a natural death.' As they were doing this, Apollonius walked in, and when he saw them dressed in the garments of mourning, he asked: 'Why do you weep at my return? Those tears are not for yourselves, I think, but for me.'

The wicked woman replied: 'Would that another, and not I or my husband, could tell you what I am to tell you! Your daughter Tarsia has unexpectedly died!'

When Apollonius heard this his whole body shook, and for a long while he stood rooted to the ground. At length he came to himself again, and fixing his gaze on Dionysiades he said: 'Woman, if my daughter is dead, as you say, have her money and clothing disappeared with her?'

'Some is left,' she replied,' but the rest has gone.' 'Trust us,' they told him; 'we believed you would find your daughter when you came back. But to convince you that we are not lying, we have evidence to prove it, for our fellow citizens, mindful of your kindness to them have contributed to set up a monument to your daughter's memory on the shore nearby, which you can see for yourself.' Believing his daughter dead, Apollonius told his servants: 'Take these things to my ship. I shall go to my daughter's sepulchre.' And there he read the inscription written above it, and was almost beside himself with grief, and cried: 'Ah, cruel eyes, that behold my daughter's grave and can shed no tears!' With these words he hurried away to his ship and told his men: 'Cast me into the depths of the sea, I beg you. I long to breathe my last among the waves!' Then, while they were returning to Tyre with favouring winds, the sea suddenly changed, and they were tossed about by violent storms. But they all prayed to God to save them, and put in at the city of Machilenta, where his daughter Tarsia was. The helmsman and all the crew gave a great shout of joy. 'What is this sound of merrymaking that assaults my ears?' Apollonius asked him. 'Cheer up, sir!' the helmsman told him. 'We are celebrating a feast day.' Apollonius gave a groan and replied: 'Everyone can celebrate this feast day but

153. Of temporal tribulation

me. My men must be content with my pain and misery!'[17] I give them ten gold pieces. Let them buy what they wish and celebrate the feast day; but if anyone calls me or tries to divert me, I will have his legs broken.' So his purser [purchased the] necessary provisions and brought them back to the ship.[18] And since Apollonius's vessel was more magnificent than all the rest, his crew celebrated the feast in greater style than the other crews.

Now Athenagoras, who had fallen in love with Tarsia, happened to be walking on the seashore nearby, and he saw Apollonius's ship and said to his friends: 'Look, I like that ship, for I can see it is beautifully made.' And when the sailors heard him praising their ship, they said to him: 'Lord, climb aboard, please!' 'Gladly,' he replied, and went on board and reclined at table with them, and putting ten gold pieces on the table he said: 'There. Your invitation shall not go unrewarded.' 'We thank you, lord,' they replied. When the prince saw that all the guests were at table, he asked: 'Who is the master of this vessel?' The helmsman answered: 'He is in mourning. He is lying down below and wants to die, for he has lost his wife and daughter abroad at sea.' 'I will give you two gold pieces,' Athenagoras told a servant named Ardalius. 'Just go down and give him this message. "The prince of this city desires your company. So leave this gloom and come up into the light."' The young Ardalius replied: 'I cannot mend my broken legs with your two gold pieces. Ask someone else. He has commanded that if anyone calls him his legs are to be broken.' 'This command applies to you,' Athenagoras said, 'not to me. I will go down to him myself. Tell me his name.' 'Apollonius,' they told him, and when Athenagoras heard the name, he said to himself: 'Apollonius is what Tarsia called her father!'

So he went down to him, and when he saw his long beard and unkempt hair, he said softly: 'Hail, Apollonius!' Thinking he was being called by one of the servants, Apollonius turned with an angry look, but saw a complete stranger, a distinguished and handsome man, and was silent. 'I know you are surprised,' the prince said, 'to hear your name on the lips of a stranger. But know that I

17 *H.A.T.* reads (c.39): *Sufficit enim servis meis poena, quod me tam infelicem sortiti sunt dominum* ('For it is sufficient punishment for my servants that they have been allotted such an unfortunate master!')
18 *Dispensator itaque necessaria tulit et rediit ad navem.* In view of what follows, it seems likely that the purser/steward goes ashore to make purchases for the feast. This sentence is not in the text of *H.A.T.*

am prince of this city and my name is Athenagoras. I came down to the shore to see the ships, and I saw how much more beautifully made yours was than the rest, and I liked the look of it. I was invited on board by your crew, so I came on board and took my place at table with them. I asked them who the master of the vessel was, and they said he was in deep mourning. So I have come down to you to bring you up from the darkness into the light. After your grief, I hope God will give you joy!'

Apollonius raised his head and said: 'Whoever you are, sir, go in peace. I am not worthy of a place at the feast, and I do not wish to live any longer.' Perplexed, Athenagoras went back to the upper deck of the ship and said: 'I cannot persuade your master to come back into the light. What can I do to dissuade him from his thoughts of death?' He then called one of his servants and told him: 'Go to the pimp and ask him to send Tarsia to me. She is clever and has a way with words, perhaps she will be able to persuade him that a man like him should not end his life in such a way.'

So the girl came to the ship, and Athenagoras said to her: 'Come here to me, Tarsia. Now you will need all the skills you have learned to comfort the master of this ship, who is sitting below in the dark, for he is in deepest mourning for his wife and daughter. Go to him and get him to come back into the light, for perhaps through you God will turn his grief to joy. If you can do this, I will give you thirty gold pieces, and as many silver pieces, and I will redeem you from the pimp for thirty days.' When she heard this the girl went down to Apollonius resolutely and greeted him humbly. 'Greetings, whoever you are! I wish you happiness: know that it is an innocent virgin who greets you, who has kept her virginity and chastity through her many misfortunes.' She then began to sing and sang so melodiously and sweetly that Apollonius was entranced. The words of her song[19] were as follows:

> *I move among harlots and yet I know no harlotry,*
> *Like a rose I am, that cannot be harmed by its thorns;*[20]
> *A pirate snatched me from death as a sword was poised to strike me.*[21]

19 Twelve dactylic hexameters, the 2nd and 9th, as they stand, unmetrical.
20 I read *sic rosa de spinis nescit violarier ullis*, the reading of a Latin copy of the tale (1595) quoted by Swan.
21 *Corruit et raptor gladium ferientis ab ictu*: text and meaning uncertain.

153. Of temporal tribulation

> *Sold to a pimp I still preserved my chastity.*
> *My heartache would cease, my tears would dry,*
> *No-one would be happier than I if I could know my parents!*
> *For I am of royal stock and a king's daughter*
> *And trust, if God so wills, to be happy again one day.*
> *So dry your eyes now,*[22] *chase dull cares away!*
> *Let heaven see your face, lift up your heart to the stars!*
> *For God is the Creator, Ruler and Author of mankind,*
> *And he will not permit your tears to be shed in vain.*

At these words Apollonius lifted his eyes, and when he saw the girl he groaned and said: 'Ah me, wretch that I am, how long shall I have to fight this grief? I thank you for your wisdom and generosity of heart. Accept as my reward that I will remember you, if I can find happiness and consolation in the power of my kingdom.[23] Perhaps you are, as you say, of royal birth and will be reunited with your parents. Now take these 100 gold pieces and leave me. Do not call me: my grief is still fresh, and in hearing of your misfortunes I am overwhelmed with grief anew.'

The girl took the coins and was about to leave the ship when Athenagoras asked: 'Where are you going, Tarsia? You have failed in your purpose. Could you not take pity on a man who wants to kill himself and help him?' Tarsia replied: 'I have done all I could. He gave me 100 gold pieces and asked me to leave.' 'I will give you 200,' said Athenagoras. 'Go down and give him back the coins he gave you, and say: "It is your well being I want, not your money."'

So Tarsia went below again, and sat by Apollonius. 'If you are resolved to persevere in this wretched state, allow me to have a few words with you. If you can answer my riddles, I will go; if not, I will give you back your money and leave you.' Not wanting to take the money back, but loath to deny what the clever girl proposed,

---

H.A.T. (41) has *piratae me rapuerunt gladio ferientes iniquo* (pirates abducted me, striking with the cruel sword). *Le Violier* has '*Je suis comme le couteau tombé des mains du frappant.*' I adopt the reading of the 1595 version: *corripit et raptor gladii ferientis ab ictu*.

22 *Fuge lacrimas*: unmetrical. I read *Fige*, with the 1595 Latin version.

23 *ut memor tui sim; quando laetari licet, regni mei levabor*: Oest. The text of H.A.T. makes better sense: *ut merito, quandoque si laetari mihi licuerit, te regni mei viribus relevem*. ('If I can ever be happy again, I will console you as you deserve with the resources of my kingdom.')

Apollonius replied: 'There is no relief for me in my misery except weeping and lamentation, but lest I should deny myself the pleasure of listening to your wisdom, tell me your questions and go. I beg you, leave me time for my tears.'

'Hear me,' Tarsia said.

> *There is a house in the world, that, closed to us, re-echoes.*
> *The house itself resounds, but the guests within are silent.*
> *And both move swiftly along, the guests and the house together.*[24]

If you are a king, as you say, you ought to be cleverer than I, so solve the riddle.'

Apollonius replied: 'Here is proof that I did not lie. The house that resounds throughout the world is a wave; the silent guest is the fish who moves along with its house.'

She continued:

> *Tall child of the lovely forest, I am borne swiftly along,*
> *Attended equally by a countless throng of companions,*
> *I run over many paths but leave not a single footprint.*

Apollonius answered her: 'If it were permitted, I would reveal much to you that you do not know, as I answer your riddles. But I wonder that someone of your tender years should be endowed with such amazing wisdom. The tree with its accompanying throng that passes swiftly over many paths and leaves no trace is a ship.'

The girl continued:

> *Through all the building*[25] *it*[26] *passes and does no damage.*
> *There is great heat in the centre which no-one seeks to remove.*
> *The house is not*[27] *naked itself, but fit for guests that are naked.*
> *If you would cast off your grief,*[28] *you might enter the heat unharmed.*

---

24 This is no. XII of Symphosius's *Aenigmata*, a collection of 100 riddles, each of three hexameters, generally thought to have been composed in the fourth–fifth centuries AD. The following riddle is no. XIII. The third is based on no. LXXXIX.

25 *Per rotas et aedes*: unmetrical. I read *per totas aedes* (1595 version).

26 I take *ille* to refer to *ignis*.

27 *Non est nuda domus*: Oest., Graesse, Trillitzsch and *Le Violier* translate as if there is no negative. See Apollonius's reply. The negative can perhaps stand: the house is covered, but those inside it are naked.

28 *luctum*: Oest.; *lucrum* L. *Le Violier* clearly translates *lucrum* ('if you wish to profit). For *poneres*, I read *ponas*, metri gratia. The second half of the line is unmetrical.

153. Of temporal tribulation

'I would be entering a bath,' Apollonius answered, 'where heat rises up everywhere through the wainscot.[29] A house is naked in which there is nothing, it suits a naked guest, and the naked man will perspire.'

After posing these and other similar riddles, the girl flung herself upon Apollonius, and opened her arms and embraced him. 'Hear my prayer and respect a maiden's entreaty!' she said. 'It is wicked for a man of such wisdom to wish for death. If God of his grace restores to you the wife you long for, if you can find the daughter you say is dead, and she is safe, then you should live on in hope of that joy!'

But these words roused Apollonius to anger, and he got up and kicked out at the girl. This drove her backwards, and falling she tore the skin of her cheeks, from which the blood streamed. In her distress she began to weep. 'Oh God, Creator of the heavens,' she cried, 'look upon my misery! I was born amid the wind and the waves of the sea; my mother died in the pains of childbirth and was denied burial in earth; she was clothed in her royal robes by my father and put in a chest with twenty gold pieces and committed to the sea. It was my evil fate to be entrusted by my father to two godless creatures, Stranguilio and Dionysiades, together with my royal jewellery and garments, and they condemned me to die at the hands one of their servants. At the last I asked if I might pray to God before he killed me, and he agreed. Then pirates suddenly appeared and I was seized, and the man who would have killed me took flight, and I was brought to this place; and may God, when it pleases him, restore me to my father Apollonius!'

When he heard all these clear proofs of her origin, Apollonius cried out at the top of his voice: 'O merciful Lord, who look upon both heaven and hell and reveal all secret things, blessed be your name!' And with these words he fell into the arms of his daughter Tarsia and kissed her jubilantly, and wept for joy. 'My sweetest only daughter,' he said, 'half of my soul, for your sake I will not die! I have found the one whose loss made me wish for death!' Then he gave a loud shout: 'Quickly, servants, come quickly, my friends, come quickly, everyone, and celebrate with me the end of my misery! I have found the girl I had lost, my only daughter!'

---

29 *per tabulas*: Oest. Meaning uncertain. *H.A.T.* (42): *per tubulos* (through pipes).

When they heard his cry, his servants came running, and Athenagoras led the way; and going down below into the hold of the ship they discovered Apollonius weeping for joy upon his daughter's neck. 'Here is my daughter,' he told them, 'the daughter I have been mourning, the half of my soul! Now I will live!' And they all wept with him for joy. Then Apollonius got to his feet, cast off his garments of mourning and dressed himself in the most elegant clothing, and all exclaimed: 'Lord, how like you your daughter is! If there were no other proof, her likeness would be proof enough that she is your daughter.' Then Tarsia kissed her father twice, a third and a fourth time, and said: 'Father, blessed be God who has graciously permitted me to see you, live with you and die with you!' Then she told him how she had been bought by the pimp and placed in a brothel, and how God had preserved her chastity. And Athenagoras, fearing that Apollonius might give his daughter in marriage to someone else, threw himself at his feet and said: 'I adjure you by the living God, who has restored you to his daughter, not to give your daughter's hand in marriage to anyone else but me.[30] I am prince of this city, and it has been by my aid that she has remained a virgin, and through my mediation that she has come to recognize you as her father again.'

Apollonius replied: 'I cannot refuse you, for you have done much for my daughter, so it is my wish that she be your wife. Now it remains for me to take my revenge upon the pimp.'

Athenagoras went straight into the city and summoned the citizens. 'Let the city not perish,' he told them, 'because of one godless person. Know that King Apollonius, the father of Tarsia, has come here. Look! His fleet has brought a great army that is hastening to destroy the city because of a pimp who set up his daughter Tarsia in a brothel.' His words were greeted by an uproar, and there was such a great commotion that everyone present, men and women, wanted to rush off without delay to see King Apollonius and beg his mercy.

'If you are to prevent the destruction of the city,' Athenagoras told them, 'I advise you to take the pimp to him.' The pimp was promptly seized, and with his hands bound he was taken off to the king. Apollonius, clad in regal robes, his hair shorn, placed a

---

30 Athenagoras has already said that he has a daughter, so he must be a widower.

153. Of temporal tribulation

crown upon his head, climbed the tribunal with his daughter and addressed the citizens. 'Here you see the virgin Tarsia, who has today been rediscovered by her father, and this avaricious pimp did everything he could to bring about her corruption and her everlasting shame, and could not be persuaded to abandon his purpose by her civility, her pleas or her money. So, avenge my daughter!' With one voice they cried: 'Lord, let him be burnt alive and all his money be given to the girl!' The pimp was at once brought forward, placed upon a fire before everyone and burnt to a cinder.

'I grant you your liberty,' Tarsia told the overseer, 'because it was through your kindness and that of your fellow citizens that I have remained a virgin.' Along with his liberty she also gave him 200 gold pieces, and when all the other girls were assembled before her she gave them their liberty, and said: 'Whatever you have done with your bodies hitherto, you are now free to forget.'

Apollonius said to the people: 'I thank you for kindnesses to my daughter and me, in token of which I now bestow on you fifty pounds of gold.' The citizens all bowed their heads to him in gratitude, and erected a statue of Apollonius in the centre of their city, and inscribed upon the base: '*To Apollonius of Tyre, preserver of our homes, and to the most holy Tarsia, his virgin daughter.*'

After a few days, to the great joy of all the citizens, Apollonius gave Athenagoras his daughter's hand in marriage, then with his son-in-law and daughter and all his retinue he set sail for his own country by way of Tarsus. But he was warned in a dream by an angel to go to Ephesus and enter the temple of the Ephesians with his daughter and son-in-law; there he was to relate in a loud voice all the misfortunes he had suffered from his youth, and how he had later come to Tarsus and avenged his daughter. When Apollonius woke he told all this to his son-in-law and daughter, and they said: 'Sir, do whatever seems good to you.' He then commanded his helmsman to sail for Ephesus. Disembarking there, he set out with Tarsia and Athenagoras for the temple where his wife lived a holy life among the priestesses, and at his request the temple gates were opened. When his wife heard that a king had arrived with his daughter and son-in-law, she put royal gems upon her head, dressed herself in a purple robe and entered the temple with a guard of honour. She was very beautiful, and because of her special devotion to chastity everyone declared that there was never a virgin so lovely as she. When Apollonius saw her he did not recognize her at all, but together with his daughter and son-in-law threw himself at her feet; for her beauty was so dazzling that all who saw her thought she was Diana herself. Apollonius set down precious gifts in the temple, then began to speak as the angel had instructed him: 'I was born and raised a king, I come from Tyre and my name is Apollonius. Having attained to fullness of knowledge, I solved the riddle of the evil King Antiochus in order to marry his daughter. But he had deflowered her and continued in his godless ways, and attempted to kill me. I took flight and lost all I had at sea. Then I was most graciously received by King Altistrates, who proved so well disposed to me that he gave me his daughter in marriage. Then, after Antiochus's death, I took my wife with me to succeed to the throne. My wife gave birth to this daughter of mine at sea, but died in childbirth. I enclosed her in a coffin with twenty gold pieces and cast her into the sea, so that when she was found she might have a fitting burial. I entrusted this daughter of mine to people who proved utterly godless, then left for the upper regions of Egypt. After fourteen years I came back to ask for my daughter and they told me that she had died. Believing this to be the case, I went into mourning, and wore black garments, and wanted to die. But then my child was restored to me.'

While he was relating these and other facts, his wife, the daughter of King Altistrates, rose and, seizing him in her arms, tried to kiss him. But Apollonius, not knowing that she was his wife, pushed her away indignantly. 'O my lord,' she said tearfully, 'half of my soul, why are you acting in this way? I am your wife, the daughter of King Altistrates, and you are my husband and lord, Apollonius of Tyre. You are my teacher, the one who instructed me; you are the shipwrecked man whom I loved, not out of carnal desire, but for his wisdom!'

When Apollonius heard this, he recognized her instantly, and fell upon her neck and shed tears of joy. 'Blessed be the Most High,' he said, 'who has restored to me my wife and daughter!' 'Where is my daughter?' his wife asked. 'This is your daughter Tarsia,' he said, bringing her forward. And she kissed her; and to great rejoicing the news spread through the whole city and surrounding regions that King Apollonius had found his wife in the temple.

Then, with his wife and daughter and son-in-law, Apollonius boarded ship and sailed for his native land, and when he arrived in Antioch he received the kingdom that had been awaiting him.

153. Of temporal tribulation

After appointing his son-in-law Athenagoras to rule there in his stead, he set off for Tyre. Next he went with his son-in-law, wife and daughter and a royal army to Tarsus, and commanded that Stranguilio and Dionysiades should be seized and brought before him, and said before all the people: 'Citizens of Tarsus, have I ever been unfriendly to any of you?' 'No, lord,' they said to a man. 'We are ready to die for you. This statue was set up because you saved us from death.' Apollonius then said: 'I entrusted my daughter to Stranguilio and his wife Dionysiades, and they would not give her back to me.' 'My good lord,' the wretched Dionysiades cried, 'did you not read what was written on her monument?' Apollonius then had his daughter appear before them all, and Tarsia cursed her and said: 'All hail! Tarsia gives you greeting, recalled from the dead!'

When the unhappy woman saw her she trembled all over, while the citizens were amazed and overjoyed.

Tarsia then commanded the bailiff to appear, and told him: 'Theophilus, you know me. Answer me clearly: who compelled you to murder me?' He replied: 'My mistress Dionysiades.' At this the citizens seized Stranguilio and Dionysiades, dragged them outside the city and stoned them. They wanted to kill Theophilus too, but Tarsia saved him from death. 'If he had not allowed me time to pray,' she told them, 'I would not now be defending him.'

Apollonius stayed there three months making gifts for improvements to the city, then sailed to the city of Pentapolis, where, full of joy, he went to the palace to see Altistrates. The king was now old, but he saw his daughter and granddaughter with her royal husband, and they all lived together happily for a whole year. Then, having reached his allotted span, he died, leaving half of his kingdom to Apollonius and half to his daughter.

After all this had come to pass, Apollonius was walking by the sea one day when he caught sight of the fisherman who had taken him in after he had been shipwrecked, and gave orders for him to be arrested and brought before him. When the fisherman was seized by the soldiers he thought he was going to be executed. Then Apollonius entered the palace and ordered him to be brought before him. 'This is my matchmaker,[31] the one who helped me after I was shipwrecked and showed me the way to the city.' And he

---

31 *paranymphus*: literally 'best man'. In sending Apollonius to the city, where he met Altistrates and his daughter, the fisherman had been instrumental in his marriage.

told him: 'I am Apollonius of Tyre.' He ordered that 200 gold pieces be given to him, and menservants and maidservants, and made him one of his attendants for the rest of his life. Then Elinatus, who had told him of Antiochus's plot, fell at Apollonius's feet and said: 'Remember, my lord, your servant Elinatus!' Apollonius grasped his hand, raised him to his feet and made him a wealthy man, installing him as his attendant. After this, Apollonius's wife bore him a son, whom he appointed king in place of his grandfather Altistrates.

Apollonius lived eighty-four years with his wife and ruled Antioch, Tyre and the Tyrians in peace and prosperity. He wrote an account of his adventures in two volumes, one of which he placed in the temple at Ephesus, and the other in his own library. When he died he went straight to everlasting life, to which etc.

154. Of the heavenly home

Gervase relates[1] that because of the presence of a holy image of Christ in the city of Edessa, no heretic can live there, no worshipper of idols and no Jew; neither can barbarians attack that place. If ever an enemy army approaches, an innocent young child, standing on the gates of the city, reads an Epistle, and on the same day that the Epistle is read, the barbarians are either appeased, or unmanned and flee.

Dear friends, this city is the city of which it is said in Revelation:[2] *'I saw the holy city of Jerusalem coming down out of heaven adorned as a bride for her husband.' This city is built of living stones, i.e., holy martyrs and others who are devoted to, and pleasing to Christ. Because of the presence there of the holy image of Christ no idol worshipper or heretic or barbarian dare go there or invade the place. Or the city can signify our body, in which, because of the presence of the holy image of Christ, i.e., the soul imparted to it and cleansed from original sin through baptism, no heretic, i.e., no wile or vanity of the devil, can live, since in baptism we have firmly promised to cleave to God and renounced the vanities of the devil; for man was fashioned and created in the image of the Holy Trinity, as we read in Genesis c.1:*[3] *'Let us make man to our image and likeness.' So the devil cannot live in him after baptism, unless man wills it. Nor can barbarians invade the place. The barbarians are mortal sins that, through the presence of divine grace, cannot invade our soul. And if, because of the fragility of our condition and the temptation of the flesh, the soul is invaded*

1 *O.I.* III.XXVI. Gervase of Tilbury (fl. c.1200) was a canon lawyer, statesman and writer.
2 Cf. Rv 21.2.
3 Gn 1.26.

by some mortal, or at any rate unusually grave sin, an innocent boy, i.e., the gnawing of conscience, must repel the invading enemy army with the epistle of confession, and after confession by atonement for sins. And so, the same day that the boy standing on the gate, i.e., at the beginning of a godly life, reads the epistle of correction and confession, the barbarians invading the conscience and hampering our good works are always 'either appeased, or unmanned and flee'. But they are never appeased, because as they witness our good works they are all the more goaded into a fury of temptation and go wild. And if through a lapse of the flesh we fall into the net in this present life, we shall never succeed in placating the devil and stop him from tempting us thereafter. Therefore the barbarians must be unmanned and vanquished by us and made to flee; for it is foolish to serve the devil, who is not appeased by any servility; rather we must cleave to God, who has given life and an eternal reward to those who serve him; to which may he bring us etc.

155. Of the manner of fighting against the devil through Christ's Passion

On the borders of the bishopric of Ely in England, as Gervase relates,[1] there is a castle called Cathubrica, and just below it is a place they call Wandlesbury, because the Vandals, while laying waste parts of Britain and savagely killing the Christians, pitched their camp there. The place where they pitched their tents, near the summit of a hill, is a circular area of level ground enclosed by ramparts, through which there is only one entrance, like a gateway. It is commonly said, and has been rumoured since time immemorial, that if a knight ventures on to this area of land at dead of night in the light of the moon and calls: 'Let the foe come forward!', at once a knight comes to meet him from the opposite quarter. He is ready for battle, and as their horses clash he either unseats his opponent or is unseated himself. The knight can only ride alone through the opening of the rampart, but he is not hidden from the view of anyone watching from outside.[2] To attest the truth of this, I will now give an account of an incident that actually happened and was common knowledge, and which I heard from the inhabitants and natives of the place.

In days past there lived in Great Britain a knight called Albert

1 *O.I.* III.LIX (p. 26, ed. F. Liebrecht [1856]; and see note 49, pp. 126ff.). Our text is very close to that of Gervase.
2 *et ab exteriori adspectu alicuius foris non artatur*: translators offer various interpretations of this passage (which Swan typically omits). Gervase has *ab exteriore conspectu sociis non arctandis*, which makes it clear that, while the knight must enter the field of battle alone, his companions are not prevented from watching from outside. (L.'s text, however, suggests that the sentence ends not after 'outside' but after 'to attest the truth of this', and this might explain why the author stresses that the knight can be observed.)

who was a valiant warrior and adorned by every virtue. One day he entered the aforementioned castle as a guest, and after supper, as is the custom among the nobility in the cold of winter, the members of the rich man's family sat by the fire and busied themselves telling the stories of olden times. At length one of the people born there gave an account of the remarkable occurrence referred to above. The doughty Albert, wishing to test the truth of what he had heard, chose a noble squire as his companion and went to the place with him. Clad in a coat of mail, Albert approached the place that had been described to him, climbed the hill, and leaving his noble attendant behind, proceeded alone on to the level area. He gave a shout, asking for an opponent to appear, and at his call another man, seemingly a knight, and armed, apparently, as he was, met him swiftly from the opposite quarter. In short: they raised their shields, levelled their lances at each other and charged.[3] Both knights were hit and shaken under the impact, but the other knight's lance was broken when he made an ineffectual thrust at Albert, and Albert then gave his foe such a mighty blow that he unseated him. He fell, but rose again at once as he saw Albert trying to lead his horse away by the reins[4] as his prize. He picked up his lance and threw it at him, using it like a javelin, and dealt Albert a ghastly wound as it pierced his thigh. Our knight, however, in his joy at victory either did not feel, or pretended not to feel the wound he had sustained. His adversary then vanished, and leaving the field as victor Albert handed the horse he had won to the squire. It was a huge animal, but sprightly and agile, and most handsome in appearance.

When the renowned Albert returned, the whole household came out to meet him and marvelled at what had occurred. They were delighted at the defeat of the knight he had unseated, and commended the prowess of the illustrious lord. When he removed his iron greaves, however, he saw that one of them was filled with coagulated blood. Everyone was horrified at the wound, but Albert dismissed their fears with contempt. All the people stirred themselves and came running, and even those who had been fast asleep were woken as the cries of admiration increased. As proof of Albert's triumph, the horse, held by the reins, was displayed to

3 There are enough dactylic sequences in this passage to suggest that the author is reminded of some poem.
4 *per luta:* Oest., K., L. ('through the mud'). I have translated *per lora* (Gervase).

155. Of the manner of fighting against the devil through Christ's Passion

public view, with its wild eyes, high-arching neck, dark black mane and the knight's saddle on its back. But at first cockcrow, the horse, leaping about, snorting and drumming the ground with its feet, broke the thongs that held it, and regaining its natural freedom, took flight, and though pursued, it soon disappeared. But our noble knight had a perpetual remembrance of his cruel wound, for every year, at the very same moment on the same night, the wound broke open again on the surface of his flesh. It then came to pass, a few years after this, that the illustrious knight went overseas, and after many a fierce battle fighting against the heathen he died and rendered up his soul to the Lord.

Moralization. Dear friends, the valiant warrior is our Lord Jesus Christ, who is a warrior and King of Kings and Lord of Lords, and who, to fight with his adversary, i.e., the devil, left the castle of the citizens of heaven and entered this world. For the human race could not have been redeemed had not the Son of God entered the world to fight against the devil. Before Christ's nativity none of the saints, however righteous, could enter the kingdom of heaven; so the Son of God, at the decree of God the Father, learning of this remarkable fact from the inhabitants of hell, who had entered limbo many thousands of years before, chose one of his noble squires, entered this world in his company, and entrusted his horse to him before the combat. For when Christ wished to be born of the Virgin Mary, with the aid of the Holy Spirit he took flesh from her most pure blood, and this flesh he appointed as his squire. When the warrior entered the field and looked for his adversary, the devil, he cried out for him to appear, and lo and behold!, another warrior, i.e., the devil, armed proudly like a knight, came to meet him from the opposite direction. Our Lord dismissed all who were with him, and entered the field alone save for his horse, i.e., his humanity; and when the time of his Passion was approaching and the Jews arrested him and crucified him, he had no-one with him, because the disciples, as the Gospels attest, left him and fled. He was in the garden alone, alone at his arrest, alone on the cross, alone in all his sufferings and bodily anguish, so that the saying of Isaiah was fulfilled:[5] 'I have trodden the wine press alone, of the Gentiles there is not a man with me.' Without a word they raised their shields, levelled their lances at each other, and the horses[6] etc. For when Christ raised up human nature, which he had

5 Is 63.3.
6 *equi*: in the tale the subject is the knights (*equites*).

come to redeem from the fall of their first parents, he raised the shield of his humility, and shattered the spear of pride of the wicked devil, and struck his adversary so mightily so that he unseated him, and plunged him to the deepest depths of hell. But in this battle, i.e., in his Passion, our knight Jesus Christ fell, through the treachery of Judas, through all the derision he suffered, and the sentence of death upon the cross; but he quickly got up, because on the third day he rose again, as he himself bore witness:[7] 'I will go before you into Galilee.' Then Christ's adversary drew his lance on Good Friday and ran it through the thigh of our most noble king, dealing him a ghastly wound. But Christ in the joy of victory did not feel the blow, or pretended not to, and his adversary disappeared; for while Christ was dying on the cross, the devil came to him to see if he had any strength left, because he thought him a mere man. When his adversary disappeared in defeat, our knight entered the field of the world in victory, and surrendered the horse he had won, i.e., his body and soul, on the day of his Ascension, to God the Father. And while he was leaving the world in glory on Mount Olivet and returning to his Father, a crowd of his friends gathered, a host of all the patriarchs and prophets and other saints, in joy at the victory he had won, and, still enclosed in the limbo of hell, they each cried: 'You have come, beloved! etc.'[8] They marvelled at the happening, and rejoiced at the fall of the defeated warrior who was their adversary, and commended the bravery of the illustrious victor. But the warrior knight kept the wounds he had sustained in his triumph as a sign of his victory, and at the Last Judgement he will show them to the just as a reward, and to the wicked as punishment. The household was horrified at his wound, i.e., all the elect marvelled at the severity of the wound and at Christ's Passion, thanking him; but the Lord disdained to fear, because he had manfully fought against the world, the flesh and the devil, and mightily overcome them. A devout throng of people was aroused and gathered, people who before had had no compassion for Christ, but seeing his wounds and pondering in their heart his bitter suffering, those who had been overwhelmed by the sleep of oblivion and ignorance were woken as the cries of admiration increased. Witness to this triumph is the horse, i.e., the bloody body of Christ, on which, as

---

7 Mt 26.32; Mk 14.28.
8 *Advenisti, desiderabilis*: part of the Easter antiphon, the *canticum triumphale*, which expresses the joy of the souls in limbo. It continues *quem expectabamus in tenebris* ('whom we awaited in darkness').

155. Of the manner of fighting against the devil through Christ's Passion

Isaiah says:[9] *'from the sole of the foot unto the top of the head there is no soundness therein'. He was displayed to the public view of all the faithful in remembrance of the triumph. But at first cock-crow the horse leapt about, snorting and drumming the ground with his hooves etc. Cock-crow signifies the hour of Christ's death, i.e., the ninth.*[10] *This was then, according to the gentiles, the hour of midday, we understand; but to all of us it was night, since the prophet says:*[11] *'It is vain for you to rise before the light', because all those who were born before Christ went down to hell. Therefore Christ leapt up wildly when he rose and ascended into heaven, and will snort to the terror of all the damned on the day of the Last Judgement, and drum the ground with his feet, i.e., cause men to rise up from the earth when the sound of the trumpet rings out at the last: 'Rise up, you dead, and come to judgement!' Then he will say to the just:*[12] *'Come, possess you the kingdom prepared for you from the beginning of time!' But the reprobates will wait for that terrifying sentence, when he tells them:*[13] *'Go, you cursed, into the everlasting fire.' From which etc.*

9 Is 1.6.
10 *nonam*: i.e. the ninth hour. According to the Jewish system of timekeeping, which began the day at sunrise, this would mean around 3 p.m. According to Mark, the crucifixion took place at the third hour, and in the Synoptic Gospels there was darkness from about the sixth until the ninth hour. However, in John, Christ is still with Pilate at the sixth hour. The precise timing is uncertain.
11 Ps 126.2.
12 Cf. Mt 25.34.
13 Mt 25.41.

156. Of the cause of the destruction of Troy

Concerning the Trojan War Ovid relates that Helen was abducted by Paris, and that there was a prophecy that the city of Troy would not be subdued until Achilles was dead. When his mother heard of this, she hid him in a room, in female clothing, among the ladies-in-waiting of a certain king.[1] Learning of this, Ulysses loaded a ship with merchandise, including women's ornaments and splendid armour, and went to the castle where Achilles was living in seclusion with the young ladies. As soon as Achilles saw the ship laden with jewellery and armour, he went on board with the young ladies to buy some of the merchandise. But when Ulysses carefully picked up some weapons and invited him to inspect them, Achilles seized a spear and brandished it, and so the truth was revealed. Ulysses took him prisoner and escorted him to Troy, where the Greeks finally prevailed. After Achilles's death, Troy was captured and the hostages of the opposing side were set free.

Moralization. Dear friends, Paris signifies the devil, Helen the soul or the whole of humankind in the clutches of the devil; Troy signifies hell, Ulysses Christ, Achilles the Holy Spirit; the ship laden with merchandise is the Blessed Virgin Mary adorned with virtues; the arms of Achilles are the cross, the nails, the spear and crown etc. Before Christ's death Troy, i.e., hell, was all powerful and kept our fathers of old in captivity. But when Christ died on the day of Good Friday, hell was captured and surrendered the captives it held.

---

[1] Lycomedes, King of Skyros.

157. Of the punishment of sinners who do not make amends for their sins in the present life

There was a certain emperor who possessed a shrewd gatekeeper. He insistently begged his master to let him be gatekeeper to the whole city for one month and receive a denarius from every hunchback, everyone with one eye, or scabies, impetigo or a hernia. The emperor agreed and confirmed his appointment with his seal. The gatekeeper assumed his office and stood at the gateway to the city to note all those entering and leaving and to see if he could make any profit out of his new position. One day a hunchback wearing a fine hood entered the gateway, and the gatekeeper went up to him and asked for a denarius in accordance with the decree the emperor had made. But the hunchback refused and would give him nothing. The gatekeeper then laid hands on him and tried to take his hood from him, and as he lifted his hood from his head he found he had only one eye. He at once demanded two denarii of him. The hunchback refused to give him the money and decided to run away, but the gatekeeper pulled him back by the hood, and lo and behold!, his head was uncovered and seen to be mangy. So he immediately asked for three denarii. This only made the hunchback struggle the more determinedly, and as his arms were exposed, it was clear that he was covered in scabs. So the gatekeeper demanded a fourth denarius. And as the hunchback resisted him, he removed his cape, and as it fell he was seen to have a hernia. So he asked him for a fifth denarius. And thus it came about that the man who had refused to pay a just fine of one denarius had against his will to pay five.[1]

Moralization. Dear friends, this emperor is our Lord Jesus Christ, and the gatekeeper is a prelate or discerning confessor, who has to stand at

---

1 Cf. the story related by Peter Alfonsi, *Disciplina Clericalis* VI. See Oesterley, p. 738, and Tubach, no. 4892.

the gate of the city, i.e., to proclaim the word of God and his commandments. This city is the world, which has only one gate of entry, i.e., the belly, for men and beasts have one entrance into life.[2] But there are many gates of exit: some die by the sword, some by fire, some suddenly, some are killed by wild beasts, for there are many different ways of dying. But before man leaves this world through the gate of death, if he has any imperfection he must of necessity pay the gatekeeper a denarius. We should interpret the hunchback, the man with scabies etc. as a sinner, full of vices and wanton desires, and in particular one who is embroiled in the seven mortal sins, who must pay a denarius for every one of them: that is, the miser must pay the denarius of generosity, the glutton that of temperance, the wanton that of chastity, and so on: each sinner must pay for his sins in the opposite coin. For he must of necessity pay either here or elsewhere, and what he can pay here in one day, elsewhere he will hardly be able to do in a year. So pay what you owe, and you will be able to pass safely through the shining gateway to life eternal. Which etc.

---

2 *unus introitus hominum et jumentorum*: see no. 63, note 4.

158. Of the soul's immortality

At Rome an incorrupt corpse was discovered that was taller than the city wall, and on it were inscribed the following verses:

*Here in death lies Pallas, the son of Evander,
slain by the spear of the warrior Turnus.*[1]

At his head was a burning candle, which neither water nor wind could extinguish until a hole was made with a needle and air was let in beneath the flame. The giant's wound was four and a half feet long. He had been killed after the sack of Troy and lain there for 2,240 years.

Dear friends, this giant is our first father Adam, who was formed innocent of corruption, except through sin. He was taller than the wall of the city, which stands for the world, and he was taller, because according to the Psalmist:[2] *'Thou hast subjected all things under his feet etc.' He was seriously wounded when in defiance of God's command he ate the fruit of the forbidden tree; not only was he wounded, but the whole of the human race was so deeply pierced by the wound of perdition that neither in heaven nor on the earth, nor among angels nor among men could anyone be found who could heal it, until the Son of God came*

---

1 *Filius Evandri Pallas quem lancea curvi*: *curvi* ('bent', 'crooked') makes no sense and is surely corrupt. The couplet is elsewhere quoted (e.g. Martinus Polonus, *Chronicon* XII.67) with *Turni* for *curvi*. Turnus, who killed Pallas, was the King of the Rutuli. The first verse is a dactylic hexameter, and the second (*morte sua jacet*: Oest.; I read *morte sua jacet hic*) should probably be a pentameter (though K. and L. have another hexameter), making an elegiac couplet, which would be appropriate for an epitaph.
2 Ps 8.8.

down from his kingly abode to the depths of our mortality, and with the rose-red blood of his Passion perfectly healed humanity's savage wound. The burning candle at his head, that could not be extinguished by either water or wind, is the pain of hell, where he had been without the vision of God for 4,000 years; and neither water, i.e., the prayer of some saint, nor wind, i.e., fasting, could free him from this punishment, nor extinguish it, until the flame, i.e., divine mercy, with the needle of Christ's most bitter Passion, went down to hell by virtue of its power, a soul with all honour,³ and took him with him to the joys of paradise, where he will enjoy the bright vision of God for all eternity, unless he willingly subjects himself to sin and chooses to undergo torment.

---

3 *anima cum dignitate*: if *anima* is right, it seems to be nominative in apposition to *flamma* (flame).

159. Of the invention of vineyards

In his book *On the Causes of Natural Things*[1] Josephus relates that it was Noah who discovered the wild vine, i.e., *labrusca*, which is so called because it came from the edges [*labra*] of fields and the roadside. And since it was bitter, he took the blood of four animals, viz. the lion, the lamb, the pig and the monkey, mixed it with earth and made a compost which he placed at the roots of wild vines, and in this way the wine was sweetened by their blood. After this Noah became intoxicated with wine, and as he lay naked was mocked by his younger son. He then gathered all his sons together and told them that he had used the blood of the abovementioned animals for the instruction of mankind.

Dear friends, through wine many men have become lions in their wrath, and at the time have no discernment; some become lambs in their timidity; some monkeys in the attitude of curiosity they assume and their foolish mirth; for everything the monkey sees done in front of him he also wants to do, but he makes a muddle of it. If you want to catch a monkey, get some shoes made of lead, and when it sees you taking them off and putting them on, and tying them tightly, it will do the same. Then, when it tries to run away, it is crippled by their weight and can be captured. And this is true of many men, who, when they try to do things in a drunken state, can hardly do any properly, but, like the monkey, make a disastrous muddle of them.

---

1 If Josephus did write such a work it has not come down to us.

160. How the devil prevents us from doing good[1]

It frequently happens that Satan's angels transform themselves into angels of light and nurture in human hearts something inspired by the devil. An illustration of this is given by the following most remarkable instance.

When Valentine was Bishop of Arles, there was on the borders of the diocese a castle whose mistress habitually left church after the Gospel and before the solemnities of Mass, because she could not endure the consecration of the Lord's body. Although her husband, the lord of the castle, had known of this for many years and had carefully investigated the matter, he could not discover the reason for this impudent behaviour. But one feast day, after the Gospel ended and the lady was leaving, she was detained against her will by her husband and his servants, though she struggled with them; and as soon as the priest uttered the words of consecration, she was lifted on high by a diabolical spirit and flew away, taking down to hell with her part of the chapel, and was never seen again in those parts. And the part of the tower against which the chapel rested still remains to attest the truth of this story.

Dear friends, the castle in the tale signifies the world, and the lady[2] of this castle is the worldly man, who is so wholly devoted to the world that when through divine inspiration he begins some good work, he cannot complete it because of the worldly vanity to which he is devoted, and so often loses his life because of worldly things. For since the devil is the perpetual foe of the human race, he more often stops us from completing some good work than induces us to begin it; for he is aware that when the

1 See *O.I.* III.LVII. See also Oesterley, p. 738; Tubach, no. 1059; Hope, p. 597.
2 *dominus*: Oest., K., L. I read *domina* with *Le Violier* (*la dame*).

160. How the devil prevents us from doing good

victory is finally won the palm of glory is given for fighting manfully. But the lord of this castle is a discerning confessor, who, when he sees his lady, i.e., the sheep entrusted to him in the Church, erring, and refusing to obey the Church's commands, and leaving church after the Gospel, i.e., a brotherly admonition – that is, when the priest and your confessor reveals to you, and instructs you in the way[3] of salvation, and you in your error scorn to listen – then, through his servants, i.e., the censure of the Church and public excommunication, he will assuredly bring you to obedience against your will. But if you can still not endure the words of consecration, i.e., the salvation of your soul, you will be uplifted by a diabolical spirit and fly to the depths of hell, where there will be weeping and gnashing of teeth. The words of our salvation are the words of preaching and salutary exhortation that are spoken daily, and especially on feast days. But there are some who are so filled with the diabolical spirit that it is only when they hear the bell for the sermon that they lie on their bed to rest, and who only begin to sleep when they have spent the whole night in frivolity and wantonness and other kinds of revelling, so that Job rightly says of them:[4] 'They have turned night into day.' And there are some who, when they rise in the morning, do not hasten to church to hear Mass or to ponder the sermon that is preached, rather they hurry there to do business transactions or indeed to listen to tales. And there are some who, while physically present in church, allow the concerns of their heart to wander outside and do not focus them on appeasing God. There are others who enter church and begin to hear Mass, but once the Gospel is read, just like the lady in the tale, leave the church so as not to hear the sermon, and position themselves by the walls around the graveyard, so that when the sermon is over, at the sound of the bell they may run back to the church then quickly return home. These people, who show such grievous intransigence, the discerning confessor, after first administering an admonishment, as we said before, must remove from the bosom of the Church and, as long as they are unrepentant, commend to the devil, lest he himself, by condoning their sins, be adjudged guilty by the Lord, when he says to them:[5] 'Go, you cursed, into the fire etc.'

---

3 *vitam*: Oest., K.; *viam*: L.
4 Jb 17.12.
5 Mt 25.41.

161. One must always be grateful to God for his goodness[1]

In the kingdom of England there is a hillock in a wooded dell which, at its top, is about the height of a man, and which knights and other huntsmen used to climb when they were exhausted with heat and thirst and in search of some sorely needed relief. Due to the nature of the place and their circumstances, each of them left their companions at a distance and climbed the hillock alone; and, though alone, he would say, as if he were speaking to someone: 'I am thirsty.' And suddenly, out of the blue a cupbearer stood at his side, splendidly attired and with a smiling face, and offered him in his outstretched hand a large horn decorated with gold and jewels, such as some people still use today instead of a cup. The horn was full of some unknown liquid, but its taste was most delicious, and when he had drunk it all the heat and tiredness left his body so completely that no-one would have believed he had been engaged in strenuous activity, rather that he was eager to find some work to begin. And after he had finished the drink the cupbearer offered him a spotless napkin with which to dry his mouth; then, having performed this service, he vanished without waiting for a reward or allowing himself to be questioned. This had happened over a very long period, since time immemorial, and to men of old it was a well-known and daily occurrence. Then at length a knight came to that place to hunt, and asked for a drink, and took the horn, and did not give it back to the cupbearer, as custom and courtesy required, but kept it for his own use. When the knight's lord discovered the truth about this, he punished the thief and presented the horn to Henry the Elder, King of England, so that he should not be considered a party to the crime.

1 See *O.I.* III.LX. See also Oesterley, p. 738, and Tubach, no. 2604.

161. One must always be grateful to God for his goodness

Dear friends, the wooded dell represents the kingdom of heaven and the hillock is this world, since in the world 'there are creeping things without number', as the Psalmist says.[2] *The hunter is man, who daily hunts in this world; and each day that passes is another stage on his journey as he climbs the hill to hunt death. But when in the course of his hunting he finds nothing except the reptiles of tribulation and the beasts of diabolic temptation, in the heat of his spiritual desire and his thirst for reward, let him approach the horn of the oil of mercies, which, from the fountain of its goodness, 'giveth to all men abundantly and upbraideth not'.*[3] *By the horn we are to understand the Son of God, who, with solemn devotion, smiling face and hands stretched wide, bounteously offered that saving nectar of sweetest flavour from his most holy wounds upon the altar of the cross for the redemption of the whole human race. This precious horn was adorned with gold when, after the many torments he had endured, and the wounds inflicted by his scourging, the glorious body of our Saviour was covered with rose-red blood 'from the sole of the foot unto the top of the head', as Isaiah attests.*[4] *The horn was decorated with gems when his glorious head was pierced with the cruel wounds of a thick crown of thorns. The cupbearer gives us the napkin of confession and pardon with which to wipe away our sins; so we must restore to him a spotless vessel, i.e., a heart that is contrite and humble and cleansed of its sins, and give him eternal thanks for that sweet cup. If we do not do so the Judge of the living and the dead will demand the horn from us on the Day of Judgement, and to our shame he will display it in the sight of everyone, and will hang us on the gibbet of hell to suffer everlasting torment. From which etc.*

---

2 Ps 103.25.
3 Jas 1.5.
4 Is 1.6.

162. We should be wary of cursing

Gervase of Tilbury relates[1] in his work dedicated to the Roman emperor Otto[2] a story which is quite extraordinary but full of sage advice and which serves as a caution to the unwary.

There is in the bishopric of Girona in Catalonia a towering mountain whose sides are precipitous and in parts impossible to climb, and on its summit there is a lake whose waters are black and fathomless. It is said that there is a demon's abode there, an extensive building like a palace, whose gate is shut, but this dwelling, like the demons themselves, is usually hidden and invisible. If anyone throws a stone or some other hard object into the lake, the demons are at once offended and a storm breaks out. On one part of the mountain there is perpetual snow and permanent ice. There is an abundance of crystal there, and there is never any sun. At the foot of this mountain is a river whose sands contain gold, and this gold is extracted from its sands and is commonly called gold-dust. On the mountain itself and in the area around it silver is mined, and it is rich in much else besides.

In a cottage near this mountain there lived a farmer who one day, while busying himself with domestic matters, was annoyed to hear the continual and unrelenting wailing of his little daughter, and finally, as people do when they are irritated, he told her to go to the devil. His rash curse at once found ready ears, and in a moment his daughter was seized and carried off by a host of demons. Seven years after this, as a native of the place was travelling towards the foot of the mountain, he saw a man going by at a great speed and crying out pitifully: 'Ah me! What shall I do? This great weight is crushing me!' And when he asked him why he was so wretched, the man answered

1 *O.I.* III.LXVI.
2 Otto IV.

162. We should be wary of cursing

that he had for seven years now been going across the mountain, because he had been consigned to the demons, who used him daily as their chariot. And to convince him that this incredible story was true, he gave him incontrovertible proof. He told him that a neighbour's daughter, whom he knew, had been similarly consigned to the devil, and the demons had tired of bringing up the girl, and would happily restore her to the one who had consigned her to them if he would look for her on the mountain. The traveller was dumbstruck, not knowing whether to keep silent about this incredible story or speak of it; but he decided to inform the girl's father about his daughter's situation. When he reached the man he found him bemoaning the daughter he had lost so long ago. He asked him why he was so upset, and after receiving confirmation of what had taken place, he told him what he had heard from the man whom the demons were using as their chariot, as related above, and said it would be advisable for him to go to the appointed place and adjure the demons, calling on God as his witness, to restore his daughter to him.

When the girl's father heard this news, he was thunderstruck; then, considering what was the best way to proceed, he decided to do as the traveller suggested. He went up the mountain and ran along the side of the lake, and adjured the demons to give him back his daughter. At length there was a sudden gust of wind and his daughter stood before him. She was tall in stature, with wild eyes, and her flesh scarcely covered her bones and sinews. She was a terrifying sight, quite unable to speak, and in understanding and intelligence scarcely human at all. Her father was astonished at the child who had been restored to him, and, uncertain whether he should keep her and look after her, he went to the Bishop of Girona, related the whole sad story to him, and anxiously asked him what he should do. The bishop, being a pious man who instructed the flock entrusted to him by good example, brought the girl forward before all the people, and revealing every detail of the affair, taught those under his charge in a sermon that they should not in future consign anything of theirs to the demons, because our 'adversary the devil, as a roaring lion, goeth about seeking whom he may devour',[3] and some that are given to him he slaughters or keeps imprisoned without hope of redemption; and some, consigned to him for a time, he torments and tortures.

3 1 Pt 5.8.

Not long after this, the man was freed whom the demons had been using as their chariot because of a similar curse his father had uttered,[4] and since, when he had been carried off he had been of keener and more mature discernment than the girl, he was able to explain with greater accuracy and clarity what went on among the demons. He affirmed that near the abovementioned place, in a subterranean cave, there was a vast palace, whose entrance is a gateway, and all was covered in darkness there. Here the demons flocked and greeted each other after they had traversed every part of the world, and reported to their superiors what they had done. But entry into this palace is permitted to none save themselves and those who have become the demons' property under the yoke of perpetual damnation.

Dear friends, we can learn from the foregoing that when we are hindered in our doings by obstacles that occur, we should not at once call on the devil or ask any help from him, and should not consign any of our family to him even if they have done some wrong, because when someone is consigned to him in the body, the devil strives the harder and opposes the good works which he might then do in spirit, hoping to possess some part of his soul. The devil cautiously lies in wait for him to seize the poor soul that is infected with sin and to draw it to everlasting pain and damnation in the lake of misery and the quagmire of sin, for there is perpetual snow and continual ice there, as Job attests, who says:[5] 'It passeth from the snow waters to excessive heat', and vice versa, and there is an abundance of crystal there, and the sun is never present. Crystal signifies a mirror reflecting the most brilliant form of the Trinity, a mirror without flaw, I say, at which the army of holy angels rejoices to gaze, but which at no time shone forth with compassion in hell. There, there is the penance of crystal, i.e., a perpetual abundance of unendurable fire, in which the man's daughter, i.e., the damned soul of the sinner, is handed over to be tormented not just for seven years, but for everlasting punishment.

4 *consimili patris imprecatione*: Oest., K., L. *Imprecatio* can mean 'prayer' or 'curse'. Graesse has the man freed 'by the decree of the Heavenly Father', *Le Violier* 'by the prayers of his beloved father'. Both suggest a slightly different reading. Swan fancifully attributes the man's release to his own faith and discretion.
5 Cf. Jb 24.19.

163. Of inordinate fear

King Alexander had an only son called Celestinus whom he loved dearly. He thought to himself: 'It would be good to have my son educated.' So he sent for a certain philosopher and said: 'Master, if you take my son as your pupil I will reward you.' The philosopher replied: 'Sire, I am ready to do your will in all things.' And he went off with the boy and took great care of him. Now it chanced one day that he went with his pupil Celestinus to a meadow and there they both saw a mangy horse lying on the ground. Near this horse were two sheep tethered to each other, which were grazing. It happened that these two sheep were grazing so near the horse, one on his right side and one on his left, that the rope by which they were tethered passed continually over his back until gradually it reached the scabby patch on the mid point of his back. And when the horse felt the rope on the wound on his back, he sprang to his feet. But this made the pain worse, and he began to run about wildly in his torment and carried the two sheep off with him, and the more they weighed down on him, the harder the rope chafed his wound and increased the pain.

Near this meadow was a miller's house, and maddened by the pain the horse entered the house with the sheep. There was no-one in the house, but a fire was burning which the horse scattered in all directions. This set the whole house ablaze, and as a result the horse and the sheep were burnt to death.

At this the teacher said to his pupil Celestinus: 'My dear boy, you have witnessed the beginning of this incident and its development. Now compose me some verses on the subject, without any errors, and determine who is responsible for the burning of the house. If you fail to do this, I promise you that you shall be severely punished.'

As soon as his master had gone, Celestinus set to work on this, and he tried hard, but he knew very little about writing verses and as a result became disheartened. In a flash the devil stood before him in the likeness of a man, and said: 'Why so sad, my son?' 'It would be no good telling you,' Celestinus said. 'You can tell me what is wrong with confidence,' the man replied, 'and I will put it right.' 'I have to compose some verses about a mangy horse and two sheep or I shall be severely punished,' Celestinus told him, 'and I have no idea how to do it.' 'I am the devil in human form,' the man told him, 'and an excellent versifier. Don't worry about your teacher, just promise me you will be my faithful servant. I will compose some verses for you that are better than those of your teacher.' And he proceeded to recite the following verses:

The rope that bound two sheep chafed a mangy horse's backbone.
In pain the horse sprang up, with the two sheep hanging from him.
He carried his dangling burden to the nearby house of a miller,
And scattering the fire with his hooves was burnt with the house to a cinder.
The owners were not inside, but they must bear all the losses.[1]

The boy was overjoyed to be given these verses and hurried home. 'My son,' his teacher said, 'did you read these verses somewhere or write them yourself?' 'I wrote them,' he replied, and recited the verses as set down above. When the master had heard them he was amazed and said: 'Tell me, my son, who composed them for you?' 'No-one,' he said. 'Unless you tell me the truth,' his teacher replied, 'I shall beat you until the blood runs!'

In fear, the boy told him the whole story of how he was bound to the devil from start to finish. His teacher was horrified, and persuaded the boy to repent, to confess himself with great contrition and to renounce the devil. Subsequently Celestinus became a holy man, and after living a good life he rendered up his soul to God.

Moralization. Dear friends, the king is our Lord Jesus Christ, handed down to us in the keeping of prophet and prelate to instruct us in good works, who often goes about the meadow, i.e., the world. He sees the mangy horse lying there, that is, the sinner embroiled in his sins, and the two sheep tied to him, i.e., the prelate of the church and the preacher,

[1] Two elegiac couplets followed by a pentameter.

163. Of inordinate fear

who must be tethered to each other by the rope of charity. The prelate of the church is bound to welcome preachers, such as Friars Minor and Friars Preachers.[2] *Because of the great love which binds them together, these two often touch on a place which pains the sinner, that is, the preacher in his sermon touches on their sins, but we observe that some who are stung by the prelate or preacher do not reform. Like the horse, they at once begin to kick back, to complain that they are supporting both, withholding*[3] *offerings everywhere and paying tithes as alms under sufferance. But what happens then? The horse drags both sheep to the mill, i.e., the sinner often behaves improperly towards both, whenever he harms them by word or deed, and he burns them in the fire of detraction, when he impugns their reputation.*

Or the tale can be interpreted in another way. The mangy horse is the whole human race infected through the sin of its first parent; the two tethered sheep are the two Testaments, because the Ten Commandments are set forth in both laws. Note that the two great Testaments are tethered together by these two laws. The horse, i.e., the sinner, is stung when he feels pain from each of these laws; but often the sinner kicks back, just as Dathan and Abiron[4] murmured against God and so perished. Thus if the whole human race is stung with repentance at Christ's Passion, it must return to the mill with the two sheep, i.e., with the two Testaments; that is, it must go back to the Church and there burn itself in the grace of divine love, for what the Old Law said figuratively is stated expressly in the New, because the Old Law was not totally destroyed, but burnt in the grace of the Holy Spirit; for what the Old Law said figuratively is set forth clearly in the New. The New Law was also burnt in the fire of the Holy Spirit, as Solomon attests:[5] 'I will send you the Holy Spirit etc.', i.e., the fire of love.

Or there is another interpretation. The mangy horse in the field is the sinner in the world; the two tethered sheep are the body and soul which are bound together in baptism so that they should be of one will, and the flesh should not oppose the spirit. But wretched man often drags himself body and soul to the mill, i.e., to hell, where all bear their individual losses, i.e., all the faculties now absent through sin that

---

2 i.e., Franciscans and Dominicans, two mendicant orders devoted to preaching.
3 *detrahendo*: this might also mean 'denouncing' the system of offerings.
4 See Nm 16.1ff., 26.9.
5 Cf. Jn 15.26, 16.7.

were among the virtues they received at baptism.[6] Thus each man will bear his own penance: if his eyes have seen an illicit sight, or his ears heard slanderous words, and so on, each must be punished in his own way. You must then 'compose verses': this means that you must tether soul and body to righteousness through works of mercy; and you must do this not at the suggestion of the devil, but under the instruction of a good prelate, and consequently lay hold of everlasting life, to which etc.

6 *Le Violier*: 'mais le pecheur sonnant au molin d'enfer les traine, dont ils bruslent pour l'absence de sens entre les vertus, parquoy il portera sa penitence.'

164. Of the perversity of the world

We read in a certain book of a conversation between Peter and Jesus in which Peter said: 'I saw five men whom I thought mad. I saw one eating the sand of the sea so greedily that it poured from both sides of his mouth. I saw another standing over a pit full of sulphur and pitch, from which there came an unbearable stench, and he was striving with all his might to draw that stench into his mouth. I saw a third man lying on a blazing furnace, but its heat was not enough for him, so he was trying to catch the sparks as they flew from the furnace and swallow them. I saw a fourth man sitting on the pinnacle of a temple trying to catch hold of the wind, and he kept his mouth permanently open, hoping that the wind would pass into it. I saw a fifth man doing his utmost to take into his mouth every single one of his members, and he was devouring them, and laughing continually at the other men. Many people saw these five men and wondered how they could do such things.'

Dear friends, the first man, who was eating the sand of the sea, we may take to be the avaricious man. Ecclesiastes c.4:[1] *'There is one, and he hath not a second, no child, no brother, and yet he ceaseth not to labour, neither are his eyes satisfied with riches, neither doth he reflect, saying: "I labour; but for whom, I do not know; and I defraud my soul of good things."' An example of this is the rich man who said:*[2] *'I will pull down my barns etc.' The second man, who stood above a pit full of sulphur, can be compared with the gluttonous and dissipated. Philippians c.3:*[3] *'And now I tell you weeping, that they are enemies of the cross of Christ, whose end is destruction, whose god is their belly.'*

1 Cf. Eccles 4.8.
2 Lk 12.18.
3 Phil 3.18f.

Such people are so devoted to and intent upon their drunkenness and gluttony, that if God were to allow them to live in this state they would never seek to enter heaven. According to Boethius, in Book IV of The Consolation of Philosophy,[4] *those who find the greatest happiness in pleasure will be given the cup of grief and the sand of tribulation to drink in hell, for it is impossible for them to satisfy their bellies here and their souls there, and pass from one delight to another delight. The third man, whom Peter saw lying on a blazing furnace, and for whom the heat was not enough, and who in addition to this swallowed the fire, can be compared with those who possess themselves of riches and other honours, but even this is not enough for them, and they strive with all their might to rob the poor, and they will take from them all they have, either through usury or other illicit means of extortion. Of these Job says, c.20:[5] 'Thou hast taken away the pledge of thy brethren without cause, and stripped the naked of their clothing.' Proverbs, c.18:[6] 'You who heap up riches etc.' The fourth man, who stood on the pinnacle of the temple, signifies those who do all their good works that they may be seen by men, like the hypocrites who do all the evil they can under an appearance of good. Amen I say to you, they have received their reward.[7] Hence Job says, c.21:[8] 'They take the timbrel and the harp etc.' For when the Pharisees and those like them wished to do some good work, such as give alms or the like, they positioned themselves at the end, or a corner of some public road where men pass,[9] in order to be seen, and proclaim the fact with trumpets and harps. The fifth man, who was devouring his own limbs, signifies those who denigrate all the good works of men of the Church and the holy doctors, who are zealous followers of holy doctrine, and as they devour them understand them as perversely as they possibly can, and never cease from their slander.*

4 Cf. *De Consolatione Philosophiae* III.7: even pure pleasures can turn to gall.
5 = Jb 22.6.
6 Cf. Prv 28.8: 'He that heapeth together riches by usury and loan, gathereth them for him that will be bountiful to the poor.'
7 Mt 6.2.
8 Jb 21.12. The wicked often prosper in this world, but will be judged in the next.
9 See Mt 6.5.

165. Another example of the perversity of the world

We read in the *Lives of the Fathers* that an angel showed a holy man three men struggling to do three foolish things. The first man was making a bundle of faggots, and because it was too heavy for him to carry, he kept adding more wood to it. The second was laboriously drawing water from a deep well with a vessel with as many holes as a sieve, but he never stopped trying to fill it. The third was carrying a beam in his chariot and was trying to enter a barn, but the door was so tiny and narrow that he could not get in; but he never stopped beating his horse and goading it on, so that eventually they fell into a deep pit together.

'What is your opinion of these three men?' asked the angel. 'They are three fools,' the holy man replied. The angel told him: 'The first man you saw symbolizes people who commit sins and believe that they can bear them from day to day to their end; and daily they add more and more until they can bear them no longer, and suddenly death comes and carries their soul off for punishment and sinks them into the bottomless pit. The second man you saw, who was drawing water from a deep well to no effect, symbolizes those people who perform good works yet gain no profit from them, because they are full of holes, in other words sins, and whatever good they do is wholly destroyed by sin. The third man, who carried the beam, symbolizes the mighty of this world, who think to enter the gate of heaven with their pride of life and worldly pomp. But they are barred from entry until they fall down into hell,' from which etc.

166. Of the game of chess[1]

The chessboard has sixty-four points divided into eight rows, namely a man and wife, bridegroom and bride, clergy and lay, rich and poor. Six pieces are used in playing this game. The first is the Rook, which is of two kinds, white and black. The white plays on the right side, the black on the left. Its characteristic is as follows: when all the pieces have been put in their places, whether noble or commoner, they have goals to which they can advance; but the Rooks alone, when they are shut in, do not have the power of going forward unless the way is opened up for them by the noble or common pieces. The Rook always moves straight ahead and never uses the corner of the board whether moving forwards or backwards; and if it moves sideways and takes a piece from the other side, it becomes a thief. *Likewise, dear friends, the poor man has*

---

1 *De ludo schacorum.* What follows is an incomplete, occasionally muddled, and muddling, account of an early form of chess. Much is unclear, and the text may be partly to blame. In his *Regiment of Princes*, Hoccleve quotes as one of his sources *The moralized game of Chess*, a popular didactic work by Jacobus de Cessolis, a thirteenth-century Italian Dominican, who used the pieces and moves of chess to describe the ideal estates of society. Caxton also used it as the basis of his *The Game and Playe of Chess* (1474), one of the earliest printed books in English. See Herrtage, pp. 460–1, where a *Moralitas de Scaccario*, attributed to Pope Innocent III (d. 1316), is reproduced, which possibly provided the basis of this story. See also the *moralisatio* to Herrtage, Text I.XXI. For a recent discussion of chess allegories in the Middle Ages, notably that of Cessolis, see Oliver Plessow, *Mittelalterliche Schachzabelbücher zwischen Spielsymbolik und Wertevermittlung – Der Schachtraktat des Jakobus de Cessolis im Kontext seiner spätmittelalterlichen Rezeption*, Münster: Rhema, 2007. See also Oesterley, pp. 738–9; Tubach, no. 962; Hope, pp. 600–1.

nothing but the path of poverty to tread, by which he passes directly to the Lord of all the poor, Jesus Christ, and takes the place of the queen alongside the King of Kings. But if he murmurs about his condition and leaves that path and regresses, he becomes a thief, and seizes whatever he can, and cares nothing for the queen's throne.[2]

The second kind is the Alphinus,[3] which moves over three points; in its proper place, the one which is black is placed to the right of the King, and the white one to his left; and they are not called white and black because of their colour, but with reference to their situation. For the one on the right, which is black, moves towards the right and takes up a position in an empty black space before the Farmer,[4] while the characteristic of the one on the left is that it moves in two directions: one to the right into an empty white space, the other to an empty white space on the left. And so they move from third square to third square, keeping their proper position on the board, so that if they are black, they are always in a black square, and vice versa, and they always move diagonally. *Dear friends, these bishops that walk up and down represent the worldly wise, who have three attributes: intellect, reason and courage. These ought to direct them upwards towards God through the performance of works of mercy, but they go downwards through their eloquence and human deceit, and they move sideways over three points, which signify: gluttons, who live in daily drunkenness; thieves, who illegally plunder and make off with the property of others; and the proud, who glory in their lineage, in beauty and the abundance of their wealth. All these move diagonally, deviating from the path that is straight, and at length are seized by the King, i.e., the devil, and cast down into hell by God's righteous judgement.*

The third kind is that of the Knights, of which the one on the right is white, and the one on the left black. The white Knight makes three moves from his proper position, one towards the right in the black square before the Farmer, the second in a black and empty space before the Weaver;[5] the third towards the left in the place of the Merchant.[6] When this piece stands near the King it can move

---

2 As e.g. in no. 165, the *moralisatio* is here included in the tale.
3 The Bishop.
4 Wynnard Hooper (who in 1876 revised Swan's 1824 translation) believed this to be the Rook's pawn.
5 The Bishop's pawn?
6 The King's pawn?

six squares; when it is in the middle, eight. The same applies to the left. When the black and the white move towards the King, the one is placed before the Queen on the left, the other before the King on the right. *Dear friends, so too knights, when they go to war and seek the battlefield, must be valiant and brave in the fight, and surround the king like a wall and defend him. For we are all knights and must fight against the devil on the battlefield of this world, and defend our king, in other words our soul, because our adversary is strong when he tempts us and prompts us to do wicked and unlawful things, but weak if we mean to overcome him. So, as Paul says,[7] we must resist him, strong in faith, and not be afraid. For when they first take up arms, valiant and experienced knights are wont to tremble, to go pale and to bleed from the nose, which attests rather to their bravery than to any failing. For he who at the beginning shakes with fear of battle is likely to be all the more steadfast and not to turn his back when he returns to battle, and when it comes to the point where the horror of death, which he has only contemplated before, is now staring him in the very face. For we are all terrified by the threat of future death; would that it were only that of temporal death! We must therefore take up the arms of faith without fear and, holding the shield of our good works before us, fight valiantly, that we may boldly overcome the second death, that which is eternal, of which Boethius says:[8] 'You lie quite unknown in death ... now a second death awaits you.' When these knights move to the confines after the battle, as if they had taken fresh heart and courage they leap forward eight squares and when they meet with the enemy overthrow them. The same is true of every man who thinks of himself with humility and is in no way proud; he will hereafter leap over the eight squares of the eight beatitudes, because every man who humbles himself shall be exalted.*

The fourth kind is that of the Commoners, all of which have one and the same way of moving forwards. From the square in which they are placed they can advance to the third, because there they are, as it were, safely within the territory of the King. But when they move beyond the King's territory they content themselves with one square, and always go up the board in a straight line. They never turn back, but as they progress they seek to win through their valour what the noble pieces possess from the beginning by virtue of their dignity. If they are aided by the Knights and other

---

7 In fact Peter: 1 Pt 5.9.
8 Boethius, *De Consolatione Philosophiae* II.vii (verses 21, 26), speaking of fame and mortality: the mighty lie as low as the humble.

166. Of the game of chess

noble pieces and reach the line of squares occupied by the opponent's noble pieces, they win by their valour the power that belongs naturally to the Queen. But note that, as the Commoners move forward, if they meet an opposing piece, noble or common, they can take him and kill him in a corner on the right or left. But the Commoner never moves to right or left out of a straight line unless he possesses the power of a Queen. *Dear friends, these Commoners symbolize people of different rank and of either sex, among whom kings, mighty nobles and other aristocrats are set in order to rule them and make them perfect. When they do not perform their offices according to law and reason, they lose the privilege of their nobility and take on the office and rank of commoners. For we were all born and begotten of one parent, Adam, and only those pre-eminent in virtues are rightly accorded the name of 'kings' and 'nobles'. But when commoners, i.e., simple, ordinary people live according to the precepts of their discerning confessors, and are obedient to the commandments of the Church, and lead their lives in a proper and upright manner, they are rightly given the names of holy kings and nobles in heaven by virtue of the perfection of their lives. No-one therefore should despise commoners, for we read that, full of virtues and graces, they have attained to imperial power and the supreme pontificate. A giant named Arius, who was swollen with pride at his wealth in his magnificent kingdom of India, and was a completely godless king, went to the dwelling of Apollo to ask him if anyone was more fortunate than he. From the hidden depths of the sanctuary a voice rang out and said that a commoner named Aglaus was: he was exceedingly poor in material things, but rich in spirit, though he was of advanced age and had never passed beyond the boundaries of his land. Thus Apollo prized Aglaus's rude cottage with its assured tranquillity above the wealthy giant's gloomy palace with all its anxieties. He prized a few clods of earth possessed without fear above the rich coast of Lydia with its many terrors. This poor Aglaus had been a most virtuous man, for the lowlier a man's birth, the greater he is in virtue, and the more glorious and renowned does he become. Virgil, of Lombard origin, was born of a humble family in Mantua, but through his wisdom was renowned as the greatest and most excellent poet. When someone accused him of inserting some verses of Homer in his work, he replied that it required great strength to strike Hercules's club from his hand.*[9]

9 According to Petrarch, *Rerum Memorandarum Libri* II.45, Virgil was deflecting a criticism of plagiarism with a witticism: it takes a great poet to steal from a poet as great as Homer.

The fifth piece in the game of chess is called the Queen, and she moves from white to black and is placed next to the King, and if she leaves the King she is captured. When she moves from the black square in which she was first placed, she can only go forward from one square to the next, and diagonally, whether forwards or backwards, whether she takes a piece, or is taken. If it be asked why the Queen is exposed to warfare when the condition of a woman is weak and frail, the answer is, if we wish to know, that she is following the custom of those women who, when the men go to war, are taken to the camp with them – the womenfolk, wives and all the rest of the household together. This is the practice of the Tartars, and though they do not use the bow, and cannot destroy the foe by physical strength, they can impede their progress. It is to support the King and show her love for him that the Queen follows him into battle. *Dear friends, this queen symbolizes our soul, which by virtue of our good works will be crowned queen in heaven. This queen is white and black: it is white through confession and absolution, when its servant, the body, makes a sincere confession and is absolved, and by atoning for its sins it becomes such a dazzling white that it will seem ten times brighter than the sun. But it becomes black through the disfiguring soot of sins. It must stand beside the King, and if it does not, it is captured and dishonoured. For our soul was implanted into our body so that through its redemption and salvation, the angelic host, which suffered great loss at the fall of Lucifer, may be restored to wholeness again, and that it may be set as a queen next to the King of Glory. But when it leaves the side of the King, under whose care it is directed and guided, it is captured and for mortal sins it has committed offered as a sacrifice to hell, and there it is inextricably swallowed up. Though this queen, our soul, cannot do battle outside our bodies, it can prompt them from within to perform good works, because our soul, i.e., reason, should steer our body, as a rider his horse, towards the virtues, and teach it not to transgress the commandments of the Church, but to move in a straight line from the square of one virtue to the square of another. So the queen should proceed at a slow pace on the chessboard and not make leaps; and she must stay within her proper bounds. Dinah, Jacob's daughter, preserved her virginity as long as she stayed quietly in her brother's house, but as soon as she left it in her desire to see other parts, she was led astray by the son of Sichem.*[10] *Seneca says that women with ugly*

10 Gn 34.2.

166. Of the game of chess

faces are fickle and unchaste: it is not that they lack the inclination, but a seducer.[11] *Solinus*[12] *says that, apart from women, few animals desire intercourse when pregnant. Women should therefore present a gloomy countenance to all men who see them, so that they are not importuned by others and accused of incontinence. Ovid says:*

> They may consent, or not, but they love to be propositioned.[13]
> All beauties play the game: if she's chaste then nobody asked her.[14]

The sixth piece used in this game is called a King. The King is the most important piece, as is shown by the nature of his movement and progression. For when he stands on the fourth white square, if he himself is black, he has a Knight to his right in a white square, and a Bishop and a Rook in a black square. On the left side he occupies the opposite position. Since the King, as we said, has more dignity and power than the other pieces by reason of his rank, it is not becoming for him to remove himself far from his royal throne, so when he begins to move from his white square, he moves, like the Rooks, to right and left, but in such a way that he cannot be placed in a black square next to a Rook in a white one. But he can be placed in a white square next to the aforesaid Rook in the corner square, where the guardians of the city are positioned, and thus in this move he has the nature of a Knight.[15] He makes these two moves after the manner of the Queen. *Dear friends, this king is our Lord Jesus Christ, who is King of Kings above all in heaven and on earth, as is shown by the nature of his movement and progression. For as he advances, all the choirs of the holy angels accompany him worshipping him as their Lord, and he has his rook and bishop and other chess pieces with him, and directly occupies every space in the whole universe, as the Psalmist attests, who says:*[16] *'If I ascend into heaven, thou art there; if I descend into hell, thou art present.' At length he takes his queen with him, i.e., his pious Mother of Mercies, our Lady Mary. For her sake he makes a movement of mercy towards the square of the commoners, i.e., people living in the world, and thus*

11 Seneca, *Controversiae* II.1, in fact says the opposite: ugly women are often chaste, perforce.
12 For Solinus, see no. 36, note 6, above.
13 *Ars amatoria* I.345.
14 *Amores* I.VIII.43.
15 The move known as 'castling'?
16 Ps 138.8.

merits the glorious name he was given by the prophet[17] *when he declared him to be the 'Father of mercies, and the God of all comfort'. For while none of the saints or the elect could rescue us from the misery and damnation caused by the sin of the first man, the King himself in his mercy deigned to move from his celestial abode to the miserable square of this world to make the flock and number of his people whole again, and delivered it from its bondage to the devil, for which let us give him thanks for all eternity.*

17 Paul: 2 Cor 1.3.

167. Of heeding good counsel

An archer caught a little bird called a nightingale, and as he was about to kill it, the bird was given the power of speech and said: 'What good will it do you to kill me, young fellow? You won't be able to fill your belly with me. But if you were to let me go, I would give you three rules, and if you kept them faithfully, you would profit from them greatly.' Astonished at hearing the bird speak, the archer promised to let it go if it told him these three useful rules.

'Then listen,' the nightingale said. 'The first rule is this: never strive to lay hold of something that is unattainable. The second is this: never grieve over what is lost and irrecoverable. The third is this: never believe what is unbelievable. Observe these three rules and it will go well with you.'

The archer let the bird go as he had promised, and as the nightingale flew away through the air it sang sweetly, then, having finished, it said to him: 'Hard luck, young fellow. You made the wrong decision, and you have lost a great treasure today, because in my bowels is a pearl bigger than an ostrich's egg.'

When he heard this the archer was deeply vexed that he had let it go, and he spread out his net and tried to catch it. 'Come into my house,' he said to it, 'and I will show you every kindness. I will feed you with my own hands and allow you to fly about as you wish.'

The nightingale replied: 'Now I know for certain that you are a fool, because you have not profited from what I told you. You are grieving over something that is lost and cannot be recovered. You cannot catch me, yet you have tried to do so with your net. Also you believed there was a huge pearl in my bowels, when the whole of my body is not the size of a ostrich's egg! You are a fool, and you will always remain a fool.' With these words it flew away and the archer went back home a sad and sorry man, and never saw the nightingale again.[1]

Moralization. Dear friends, this man signifies any good Christian, who has been cleansed of original sin at baptism, and in that baptism received some sharp arrows, i.e., virtues with which to fight the devil, the world and the flesh. He captured the nightingale, i.e., our Lord Jesus Christ, when he renounced the devil and all his vanities. The nightingale sang with marvellous sweetness when Christ poured forth his prayer for humankind to his Heavenly Father, but the wretched sinner thought to kill the nightingale, i.e., our Lord Jesus Christ, whenever he thought to commit mortal sin. As the Apostle says:[2] *'They crucify the Son of God again', with all their power. But listen carefully, for God has given you three rules, and if man keeps them faithfully, he can profit greatly from them. The king*[3] *is the Trinity, in which there are three persons and one God, which is something we shall never be able to understand while we are in this mortal body, as the Apostle tells us:*[4] *'We see now through a glass in a dark manner, but then we shall see him as he is.' Nor does faith have any merit when human reason can furnish proof. Likewise in the Gospel when the woman asked:*[5] *'Say that these my two sons may sit etc.', the Saviour replied to her: 'You know not what you ask.' Likewise, when someone asked about the end of the world, Peter replied to him:*[6] *'It is not for you to know the times or moments etc.' Of course, they were at a loss to comprehend the matter, which was beyond their grasp.*

Alternatively this tale can be taken to refer to those who seek after honours and riches. An example of this was Lucifer, who sought after something which it was impossible for him to attain; for he said:[7] *'I will ascend even to the third heaven.' What followed then? He fell down into hell. The same was true of our first parent, who by eating the apple*

1 This story is told by Barlaam, *G.L.* CLXXVI.97ff., to illustrate the foolishness of idol worshippers. Cf. Peter Alfonsi, *Disciplina Clericalis* XXII. See also Oesterley, p. 739; Tubach, no. 322; Hope, pp. 602–3.
2 Cf. Heb 6.6.
3 *Rex iste*: Oest., K., L. There is no king in the tale. *Le Violier*: 'Les trois commandemens sont la credence des trois personnes de la Trinité.'
4 Cf. 1 Cor 13.12.
5 Mt 20.21f.
6 This is Jesus speaking, after his death, and before his Ascension. Acts 1.7.
7 Cf. Is 14.13.

167. Of heeding good counsel

had wished to become a god, and for that was expelled from paradise and brought death on himself and us all. I advise you therefore, all you who are rich and powerful in the world: do not strive to lay hold of something that is unattainable, such as worldly goods and earthly honours, which can never truly be possessed except with the loss of the soul. As the Apostle says:[8] *'He who would become rich falls into the snares of the devil.' And even though you do obtain many goods, if you optimistically hope to have joy of them, you will be cheated of that hope. An example is provided by the rich man, who said:*[9] *'I will pull down my barns', and the same night died.*

The second rule is: Do not grieve over what is lost and irrecoverable. Dear friends, you must know that by 'what is lost' we are to understand bodily health and riches, which God takes from the man whom he loves, according to the saying:[10] *'He scourgeth every son of his whom he loveth.' But when people become blind, lame or deprived of some limb, or robbed of their riches, their grief is unbelievable, and they do not offer thanks to God; just as Esau grieved bitterly that he had been deprived of his father's blessing, and yet was unable to obtain it.*

The third rule was: Do not believe what is unbelievable! Dear friends, in that way many have been deceived by the devil, the world and the flesh. The devil suggests many things, and makes false promises that are unbelievable, as he did to our first parent, who believed the devil when he said:[11] *'If you eat of the tree, you will be as gods.' He believed, and was deceived and so was banished from paradise. The devil's promise was unbelievable for two reasons: first, because it was a lie; second, because God had told Adam:*[12] *'In what hour soever thou shalt eat of the tree, thou shalt die.' Some, however, now believe the devil so readily that they at once follow him and consent to sin, and say: 'The egg is so precious etc.' The egg signifies the world, which is round. The world says to man: 'It is good in our youth to enjoy the world, because though we fall into sin while doing so, then it is "bigger than an ostrich"',*[13] *i.e., God's mercy is greater than our wretchedness.*

8 Cf. 1 Tm 6.9.
9 Lk 12.18.
10 Cf. Heb 12.6.
11 Cf. Gn 3.5.
12 Cf. Gn 2.17.
13 The analogy with the tale here is not clear, but the concluding message is that though God's mercy is boundless, this should not be taken as a licence to sin.

In reproof of such the Psalmist says:[14] '*Have no mercy on all them that work iniquity.*' *Let us therefore strive etc.*

---

14 Ps 58.6.

168. Of eternal damnation[1]

Barlaam[1] says that a sinner is like a man who, in fear of the unicorn, stepped backwards into a pit. As he was falling, he grabbed hold of a sapling that grew up from the bottom, and as he looked down, he saw at the foot of the tree a noisome abyss and a terrifying dragon coiled around the tree waiting with open jaws for him to fall; and two mice, one white, one black, were gnawing away constantly at the roots of the tree, and he could feel it swaying. Also four white vipers were making their way up to the ledge on which he had set his foot, and infecting the whole place with their poisonous breath. Then lifting up his eyes he saw a stream of honey dripping from the branches of the tree, and forgetting the danger that threatened him on all sides, he abandoned himself totally to relishing its sweetness. And when a friend held out a ladder to him so that he could get out, he was so delighted with the honey that he delayed his escape, and the tree collapsed and he fell into the mouth of the dragon, which plunged down into the abyss and there devoured him. And thus, alas, he died a wretched death.

Moralization. Dear friends, this man is a sinner; the unicorn is death, which always stalks man; the pit is the world; the tree is life, which every hour of the day and night is eaten away by a white mouse and a black mouse; its base, from which the vipers come, is the human body with its four kinds of humours, which, if they are combined irregularly, destroy the body's framework. The dragon is the devil; the pit is hell;

1 This is an apologue from *Barlaam and Josaphat*, a medieval romance erroneously attributed to John Damascene. See *G.L.* CLXXVI.114ff. Ultimately the story goes back to the Panchatantra, a pre-fifth century BC Indian collection of animal tales, and has been made applicable to Christian theology by the addition of a ladder (penance).

the sweet taste of the tree's bough is the pleasure of sin, by which man is seduced, so that he does not consider the danger; the friend is Christ, or a preacher; the ladder is penance, and when man delays his submission to it, when his life fails he falls at once into the mouth of the devil, who snatches him off to hell and devours him.

169. Of the twelve laws, and how a man should live

Pompeius Trogus relates[1] of the noble knight Ligurius[2] that he induced all the inhabitants of a state to swear that they would keep certain just and beneficial laws, which at first seemed harsh, until he brought back an answer from the god Apollo, who he pretended was the originator of these laws. After this he went off to Crete where he lived in perpetual exile. But when he was on the point of death, he ordered that his bones should be taken back to his country lest the people, thinking that they were freed from their oath, might abandon their observance of the laws.[3]

These laws were twelve in number. In the first, he laid down that the people should obey their rulers, and the rulers should protect their subjects and keep the wicked in check. In the second, he urged everyone to be parsimonious and frugal, in the belief that the best soldiers were those who displayed moderation rather than drunkenness. In the third law he ordained that things should be valued not according to their monetary worth, but according to their merit. In the fourth law he decreed that gold and silver were the most worthless of all things. In the fifth he divided the administration of the state among the orders, giving to the kings all power in war, to the magistrates the right to pass judgement and punish all crimes, to the senate the custody of the laws, and to the people the power to appoint and elect the magistrates. In the sixth he divided the land equally between everyone, and made

1 = Justinus 3.2–3.
2 = Lycurgus, the traditional founder of the Spartan constitution, of unknown date.
3 According to legend, Lycurgus brought about his own death and ordered his ashes to be thrown into the sea, in case they were taken back to Sparta and the citizens, having proof of his death, would think their oath was no longer binding.

all estates equal, so that no one man would be more powerful than another. In the seventh he commanded everyone to eat together in public, so that no-one might give anyone else cause for extravagance. In the eighth he determined that young men should wear only one garment all the year round. In the ninth he commanded that poor boys should be employed in the country, not in the life of the city, so that they could spend their first years in hard work, not in frivolity. In the tenth he decreed that girls should be married without a dowry. In the eleventh he required that wives should not be chosen for their wealth. In the twelfth he determined that the greatest honour should be given not according to wealth, but to seniority. And whatever he ordained by law, Ligurius was himself the first to observe, as an example to others.

Dear friends, this noble is our Lord Jesus Christ, who entered a certain city, i.e., this world, and made the people swear an oath, i.e., promise firmly at baptism to keep his laws, i.e., the Ten Commandments, until he came to judge them. But when he died, he put not only his bones, but his whole body in the sea, i.e., in the earth. – The first law demanded obedience to rulers etc., that is, Christians should always be ready simply to obey prelates and heads of the Church in all things without any excuse or argument, and that the rulers, i.e., prelates who have undertaken the duty of guarding souls, should direct their charges to the way of salvation and surpass them in their lives through their good example; for 'it is a disgrace for the teacher to be guilty of the sin he reproves'.[4] – The second law urged everyone to practise frugality and forbade simony and other violations, recommending parsimony, and forbade them to indulge in carnal gluttony and drunkenness, to which many people are devoted and dedicated these days, and so shorten their lives. He intended us, and urged us all to observe fruitfulness in good works and generosity in almsgiving, and ordained this by a law, in which he established the eight works of mercy; for whatever prelates or other rich men of the Church possess beyond the simple necessities of life, they are bound to distribute as alms to the poor, otherwise, as Saint Jerome attests, it is robbery and sacrilege in God's eyes. – The third law ordained that things should be valued not according to their monetary worth but by a proper consideration of their merit: that is, the more merit you possess, the more your worth. God does not consider

---

4 Part of an often quoted distich of the late Latin writer Dionysius Cato, the first verse of which is *quae culpare soles ea tu ne feceris ipse* ('what you are wont to reprove, be sure not to do yourself').

169. Of the twelve laws, and how a man should live

gifts so much as the heart and the intention of the giver, and so he will make your reward great or small according to the merits of your heart. For nothing is hidden from his eyes that is not known to him, nothing is concealed that is not revealed to him, for he sees everything. – The fourth law established that gold, i.e., the wealth of this world, was regarded by God as more worthless than any other substance in the whole world. But he accepts the prayers and pities the misfortunes of the poor; as we read of the rich banqueter[5] who had no regard or sympathy for the poor Lazarus, covered in sores; then after he lay buried in hell and begged for a drop of water from Lazarus's finger, he did not get it, but was subjected to flames and perpetual torments, and is scorched for ever, while Lazarus for his patience was placed by the angels in Abraham's bosom. – The fifth law gave power to kings etc. This signifies that princes and prelates have to judge those under them; but they must beware of being corrupted by bribes to give false judgements, because if they are, at the Last Judgement the Judge of the living and the dead will pay them back in the same measure with which they have meted, i.e., justice or injustice.[6] For the judges of modern times take bribes from anyone, poor or rich, and are so blind to justice that they can scarcely see the way of equity and righteous judgement; rather, whoever gives more will have the stronger case and obtain a more favourable sentence even if it is contrary to justice. – The sixth law divided land up equally among everyone, that is, from all eternity God has bestowed his grace equally upon all men according as he sees them progress; as it says in the Gospel:[7] 'Ask and you shall receive.' And elsewhere it says:[8] 'Whatsoever you shall ask the Father in my name, believe that you will receive it, and it shall be done for you.' For Christ has an abundance of riches, and when he is petitioned by us in a worthy manner, he will be most generous in his giving, for he can give more than our mind can conceive of asking. – The seventh law was to prevent riches becoming a cause of extravagance. It therefore ordained that meals should be taken in public, because many have perished on account of their riches, and riches are the reason that many people so often lapse into dissipation and commit other mortal sins. This was why Solomon prayed to the Lord:[9] 'Give me neither riches nor beggary.' – The eighth law required youths to have only one garment all the year

5 Lk 16.19ff.
6 Mt 7.2; Mk 4.24; Lk 6.38.
7 Cf. Mt 7.7; Lk 11.9.
8 A conflation of Mt 21.22 and Jn 14.13.
9 Prv 30.8.

long. What are we to understand by this garment but simply charity, which covers a multitude of sins? With this garment we can please God, who loves fraternal charity in us above all things. Charity, according to the Apostle,¹⁰ 'dealeth not perversely, seeketh not her own, envieth not etc.' Even so if we are rooted in charity we must not seek our health and salvation alone, but we must take thought for the salvation of our brother, and direct him to the path of righteousness through our exemplary lives and godly admonition, lest he be lost like a sheep wandering from the shepherd; let him rather find the pastures of heavenly life through the garment of charity. – The ninth law made provision for poor lads etc., i.e., that, according to their merits, they should be taken into the field of the Church for their advancement, because God chose the poor in this world, making them his heirs, when he said:¹¹ 'Blessed are the poor [gloss: not all the poor, but the poor in spirit!] for theirs is the kingdom of heaven.' And the Psalmist says:¹² 'This poor man cried, and the Lord heard him etc.' And who is that poor man? [gloss: poor in spirit.] The poor man labours in the field, i.e., in this world, for we are God's farmers, and are born from youth to labour, as the bird is to fly, Job c.9,¹³ and in the Lord's vineyard, i.e., the Church, we undertake the labour of penance, and after we have come to an agreement and are hired, we shall receive, according to the merits or demerits of our labour, either glory or punishment for eternity from the steward and master of the estate, Jesus Christ. – The tenth law decreed that virgins should be married without a dowry, i.e., good Christians should espouse Christ without a dowry, i.e., without love of the world. There are many who embrace chastity of their own free will and despise earthly things so that afterwards they may receive their reward in heaven. – The eleventh law decreed that men choose suitable wives, i.e., that we should employ in his service souls that are pleasing to God. Nothing pleases God so much as a pure soul that is wholly devoted to him. – The twelfth law ordained that everyone should win honours and riches according their merit; but let princes and prelates and others in authority see that they themselves perform works of merit before they instruct others; as we read of Christ in the Gospel:¹⁴ 'Jesus began to do and to teach.'

10   1 Cor 13.4f.
11   Mt 5.3.
12   Ps 33.7.
13   = Jb 5.7.
14   = Acts 1.1: i.e. Jesus put actions before words.

170. Of calling the sinner to the way of repentance

A gambler met St Bernard riding by, and said to him: 'Father, I will gamble with you and stake my soul against your horse.' St Bernard at once got down from his horse and replied: 'If your throw is higher than mine, my horse will be yours. But if my throw is higher, your soul will be mine.' The gambler agreed and immediately picked up three dice and threw a score of seventeen, and having done so took hold of the horse's rein as if he had already won it. St Bernard said: 'My son, an even higher score is possible from three dice.' And taking the dice he threw a score of eighteen, one higher than the gambler. As soon as he saw this, the gambler submitted to the authority of St Bernard, and after a life of sanctity came to a happy end and passed to the Lord.[1]

Dear friends, the gambler is a worldly man who is devoted to and subject to vanities; St Bernard is a discerning prelate or confessor, who has to play with such a man with extreme prudence, revealing to him the life that is the game and the joy of the soul. He has to wager his horse, i.e., subject his heart and soul to labours, in order to lead the sinner to the way of truth; as the Apostle says:[2] 'As Christ hath laid down his life for us, so we too ought to lay down our lives for the brethren.' For we are all brothers and of one father, Adam. Therefore it is right that we should love one another. The three dice are Father, Son and Holy Spirit, who have many spots,[3] i.e., infinite joys, which must be revealed and related to the sinner; as we read in the Gospel:[4] 'In my Father's

---

1 A conflation of two tales in the Life of St Bernard, *G.L.* CXVI.143ff. and 157ff. For other versions, see Oesterley, p. 740; Tubach, no. 2239; Hope, pp. 604–5.
2 Cf.1 Jn 3.16.
3 *puncta*: the spots on the face of a die denoting the score.
4 Jn 14.2.

house there are many mansions.' Indeed, there are so many joys therein that 'eye hath not seen, nor ear heard, nor can the thought of man express the things which God has prepared for them that love him'.[5] There is rest without toil, life without death, joy without grief, and, in short, all fullness of joy. To which etc.

---

5 Cf. 1 Cor 2.9, quoting Is 64.4.

171. Of excessive love and loyalty, and how truth delivers us from death[1]

Peter Alfonsi relates[2] that there were two knights, one of whom lived in Egypt and the other in Baghdad. Messengers frequently passed between them and the Egyptian knight told the knight of Baghdad what was happening in Egypt, while his friend obliged him with news from Baghdad. In this way a firm friendship grew up between the two of them, though neither had ever seen the other.

One day as the knight of Baghdad lay on his bed he thought to himself: 'My colleague in Egypt has behaved in a very friendly fashion towards me, and I have never set eyes on him. I shall go and visit him.' So he hired a ship and went to Egypt, and when his friend heard he had arrived he went to meet him and joyfully took him back to his home. Now this knight had a very beautiful girl living in his house, and as soon as the knight of Baghdad saw her, he was captivated by her eyes and fell so passionately in love that he became ill. When the knight of Egypt became aware of this, he said to him: 'My dear friend, tell me, what is the matter?' 'There is a girl in your house I long for with all my heart and soul,' he replied, ' and if I do not have her I shall die.' So his friend brought all the women of his house before him except the girl in question. And when the knight of Baghdad looked at them, he said: 'I care little or nothing for all these. There is another one I cannot see here, and she is the love of my life.' Finally he was shown this girl, and when he saw her he said: 'Dear friend, she alone means life or death to me.' The knight replied: 'And I tell you this: I have

1 Cf. Herrtage, Text I.XLVII. See also Oesterley, p. 740; Tubach, no. 2215; Hope, pp. 605–6.
2 This is the second fable in his *Disciplina Clericalis* (early twelfth century). It is also the basis of Boccaccio's story of Tito and Gisippo, *Decameron*, Day 10, nov. 8.

brought her up in my house from her childhood so that she could be my wife, and with her I should possess riches untold. But I am so fond of you that, sooner than let you die, I will give her to you in marriage together with all her riches that I would have received myself.' When the knight of Baghdad heard this he was overjoyed. He married the girl, and with her received great wealth, and went back with his wife to his home in Baghdad.

Soon after this the knight of Egypt became so very needy that he possessed neither a house nor anything else, and he thought: 'I am poor. Whom should I go to? Who better than my friend in Baghdad, whom I helped to make so rich, so that he can help me in my hour of need?' He boarded a ship and went to Baghdad, arriving in the city where his rich friend lived after sunset. He thought: 'It is night. If I go to my friend's house now, he will not know me because I am so badly dressed, and have no-one with me – I, who used go about with a crowd of servants and had so many possessions.' He said to himself: 'I shall first rest tonight, then go to him tomorrow.' He looked around him, saw a churchyard, and noticed that the door of the church was open, so he went inside to spend the night there. But as he lay there and tried to sleep, two men were fighting each other in the street, and one of them killed the other; the murderer then fled into the churchyard and got away on the other side. Immediately a great cry went up in the city. 'Where is the murderer? Where is the villain who killed this man?' 'Here I am,' said the knight. 'Take me to the gallows and hang me.' So they laid hands on him and shut him up all night in gaol. Next morning the city bell was rung, the judge passed sentence on him and they took him off to hang him. Among those who followed him was his friend, the knight whom he had come to see. When he saw him being led away to the gallows, he said to himself: 'That is my friend from Egypt who gave me my wife and all those riches. And now he is going off to be hanged while I remain alive!' So he cried out at the top of his voice: 'Friends, do not kill an innocent man! The man you are leading off to his death is innocent! I am the one who killed the man, not he!' At this they laid hands on him and took both of them off to the gallows. When they were near the gallows, the man who was really guilty thought: 'I am guilty of this crime. If I allow these innocent men to die, it must be that God will take vengeance on me some day. It would be better for me to suffer a brief pain here than to endure eternal

171. Of excessive love and loyalty, and how truth delivers us from death

pains in hell.' So he shouted: 'Friends, for the love of God do not kill innocent men! Neither of them has shown by any sign, or word or deed that they had the slightest reason to kill the man who was murdered. I am the one, I killed him with my own hands. So kill me and let the innocent go free!' When the people heard this they were amazed; they seized him and took all three of them before the judge. When the judge saw them he asked in surprise: 'Why have you come back?' They then told him all that had happened from start to finish, and the judge said to the first knight: 'Friend, why did you say that you had killed the man?' He replied: 'I will tell you the truth, without a word of a lie. In my own land of Egypt I was rich and had an abundance of everything. Then I became so poor that I possessed neither a house nor any lodging nor anything else. In my humiliation I came to this country to see if I could get some help. So I said that I had killed the man because I would rather die than live. And I still beg you, for God's sake, to kill me.' The judge then addressed the knight of Baghdad. 'And you, my friend: why did you say that you had killed the man?' 'My lord,' he answered, 'this knight gave me my wife, a girl whom he had brought up to be his own, along with untold wealth, and through him I became rich in every way. So when I saw such a dear friend being taken off to the gallows, one who has given me so much, and to whom I am so indebted, I shouted out: "I am guilty of the man's death, not he." For I would willingly die for love of him.' The judge then said to the murderer: 'Why did you say that you had killed the man?' He replied: 'Lord, I spoke the truth. It would have been a grave sin if I had allowed the innocent to die and remained alive myself. So I chose to tell the truth and suffer punishment here rather than that the innocent should be condemned though guiltless, and I be punished in hell or elsewhere.'

'Because you have told me the truth,' the judge said, 'you have saved these innocent men. From henceforth strive to amend your life. Now go in peace.'

When they heard his verdict, everyone applauded the judge for having shown such mercy to the guilty man because he told the truth.

Dear friends, the emperor[3] is the Heavenly Father, and the two knights our Lord Jesus Christ and Adam our first father. Jesus Christ stayed in

---

3 There is no emperor in this story, but the author seems to have felt obliged to include one.

Egypt, according to Scripture:[4] 'I called my son out of Egypt.' Adam our first father was formed in the region of Damascus. There was the closest friendship between the two, and they sent messages one to the other, when the Father spoke to the Son and Holy Spirit, saying:[5] 'Let us make man to our image and likeness.' Then the knight travelled to Baghdad, i.e., Adam went to paradise, and stayed in the house of our Lord Jesus Christ; and in that house he saw a beautiful girl, i.e., the soul, whom he desired. God gave her to him along with infinite riches and made him lord of the world, in accordance with the words of the Psalm:[6] 'Thou hast subjected all things under his feet etc.', and he set out into this world with his wife. After this the other knight, i.e., our Lord Jesus Christ, became needy and poor; as he said:[7] 'The foxes have holes and the birds of the air nests; but the Son of Man hath not where to lay his head.' He came into this world, where two enemies were fighting, i.e., the flesh and the spirit. Christ entered the temple, i.e., the womb of the Blessed Virgin, as is written:[8] 'The temple of God is holy, which you are.' The one killed the other, i.e., the flesh killed the spirit. The cry went up in heaven and on earth over the killing of the spirit, when Adam sinned. Many pursued him, i.e., the Jews went after him with clubs and swords and lanterns, and he, like the knight, answered for the sin of another: 'Leave them alone, I am he, let them go!' He at once offered himself to die on the cross for humankind. The second knight, who offered to die for his friend, represents the Apostles, who died for the name and the truth of Christ. The third man, who said: 'I am guilty etc.' signifies the sinner, who has to speak the naked truth in confession: 'I am the one who sinned, who did evil; I committed the crime.' And if you do the same, on the Day of Judgement the Judge will doubtless commute the sentence passed against you, so that you will obtain eternal life. To [which] etc.

4 Hos 11.1.
5 Gn 1.26.
6 Ps 8.8.
7 Mt 8.20; Lk 9.58.
8 1 Cor 3.17.

172. The constancy of a faithful heart[1]

There was once a king[2] of England in whose kingdom there lived two knights, one called Guido, the other Tyrius. Guido fought many wars and was victorious in all of them. He was deeply in love with a beautiful girl of good family, but he could not win her as his wife until he had endured many fierce battles for love of her. At length, after one particular battle, he won her and married her in great pomp. On the third night after their wedding he got out of his bed after cockcrow and looked closely at the sky, where among the stars he saw quite clearly our Lord Jesus Christ, and he was saying: 'Guido, Guido, you have often fought battles for the love of a single girl. It is now time for you to strive to fight manfully against my enemies for love of me.' So saying, Jesus Christ vanished. Guido realized that it was God's will that he go to the Holy Land and avenge Christ on the infidels. He said to his wife: 'I believe you have already conceived a child of mine. Bring it up until I come back, for I plan to go to the Holy Land.' When she heard this she got up from the bed like a mad woman, picked up a dagger which lay at the head of the bed and said: 'My lord, I have always loved you and it was for love of you that I waited so long to be married to you, so that you would fight all those battles and your fame be spread through the whole world. I have already

---
1 This is the story of Guy of Warwick, a highly popular verse romance of around 1300 based on an Anglo-Norman original. Lydgate composed a version in verse (c.1450). For a survey of this tradition, see Velma Bourgeois Richmond, *The Legend of Guy of Warwick*, New York: Garland, 1996. See also Oesterley, pp. 740–1; Tubach, no. 2390; Hope, pp. 606–9.
2 Like the king at the beginning of no. 173, this king plays no part in the tale.

conceived a child: do you mean to leave me now? I will kill myself first with this dagger!' Guido leapt up and took the dagger from her hands. 'Dearest,' he said. 'Your words distress me. I have made a vow to go to the Holy Land. And now is the best time for me to fulfil my vow, rather than when I am old. Be patient. With God's help I shall soon be back.' Comforted by his words, she gave him a ring and told him: 'Take this, and whenever you look at it on your pilgrimage, think of me, and I will wait patiently until you return.' Having said his farewell to her Guido took the knight Tyrius with him, and for many days his wife wept and was inconsolable. When the time came, she gave birth to a most handsome son and brought him up with every care.

Guido and Tyrius travelled through many countries and fought many battles for the love of Christ. At length the kingdom of Dacia was laid waste by the infidels, and Guido said to his companion: 'Dear friend, you must go to that country and aid the king with all your might against the infidels, because you are a Christian. I will go to the Holy Land and fight against the enemies of Christ; then I will return to you, and we can go back to England in joy.' 'Your will and mine are one,' Tyrius said. 'I will go to that kingdom, and if you live, come back to me and we can go home again.' Guido replied: 'I give you my word.' So they embraced one another and wept bitterly at their parting.

Guido went to the Holy Land and Tyrius to Dacia. Guido fought many battles against the Saracens and the heathen, and was victorious in every one, so that his fame quickly spread through the whole world. Tyrius too drove all the infidels from the kingdom of Dacia, and fought many battles in which he was victorious. The king loved him and honoured him above all others, and he was so popular with all the king's subjects that the king gave him great riches. But there was at that time in Dacia a powerful baron called Plebeus, who was jealous of Tyrius because he had so suddenly been advanced to wealth and honour; so he accused him of treason to the king, alleging that he meant to take the kingdom from him. The king believed him, because he was a mighty and valiant man, and took all Tyrius's honours and riches from him, so that Tyrius was reduced to such dire poverty that he had scarcely enough to eat. He was in deep distress, abandoned as he was and so poor. He wept bitterly and said to himself: 'Woe is me! What am I to do?' Then one day, as he was walking alone in his sorrow, Guido, in the guise

172. The constancy of a faithful heart

of a pilgrim, met him. When Tyrius saw him he did not recognize him. Guido knew Tyrius at once, but decided not to reveal his identity to him. 'My friend,' he said, 'where are you from?' Tyrius replied: 'I am from distant parts, but have spent many years now in this kingdom. I had a companion who went to the Holy Land, but whether he is alive or dead, or what has happened to him, I have no idea at all.' Guido said: 'For love of your companion, allow me to rest in your lap so that I can sleep a while, for I am weary from my journey.' So Tyrius let him. And as Guido slept in his lap, Tyrius saw his mouth open and a white weasel come out of it, which made its way towards a nearby mountain. Then, after it had remained there for a time it came back and re-entered Guido's mouth. After this Guido woke up and said to Tyrius: 'My friend, I have had a strange dream. I dreamed that a weasel came out of my mouth and went on to that mountain, and then came back into my mouth again!' 'Friend,' Tyrius replied, 'what you dreamed I saw with my own eyes. But what the weasel did on the mountain, I have no idea.' 'Let us both go to the mountain,' Guido said, 'for maybe we shall find something of use to us there.' So they went to the mountain and – lo and behold! – they discovered a dead dragon whose belly was full of gold, and a brightly polished sword bearing the following inscription: *'With this sword the knight Guido shall vanquish the adversary of Tyrius.'* Guido was overjoyed at finding the dead dragon and said to Tyrius: 'My friend, I will give you all the treasure, but I will keep the sword for myself.' 'My lord,' Tyrius replied, ' I have not deserved such a gift from you.' Guido said: 'Open your eyes and look at me. I am your friend Guido.'

At these words Tyrius looked at him closely and then recognized him. He fell to the ground with joy, then wept bitterly and said: 'I have reason enough to live on,[3] now that I have seen you once again!' 'Up with you, quickly!' Guido told him. 'You should be happy that I have come, not weep. I will fight your adversary and then we will go to England together with all honour. But above all, see you tell no-one who I am.' Tyrius got to his feet and fell on Guido's neck and kissed him. He then went home with the gold, while Guido went and knocked at the gate of the king's palace. The gatekeeper asked him why he was knocking, and he told him:

---

3 *sufficit mihi de cetero vivere*: this might also mean 'I have lived enough now I have seen you again', i.e. I am content to die.

'I am a pilgrim lately come from the Holy Land.' He was let in immediately and presented to the king, at whose side the baron was sitting who had robbed Tyrius of his honours and riches. The king asked him: 'Is there any peace now in the Holy Land?' 'Lord,' Guido replied, 'there is now lasting peace, and many have been converted to Christianity.' The king continued: 'Did you see that English knight Guido who fought so many battles there?' 'My lord,' Guido replied, 'I have seen him often and eaten with him.' The king asked: 'Did you hear[4] any talk of the Christian kings?' 'Yes, my lord, they speak of your person. They say that Saracens and other infidels occupied your kingdom for many years, and that at the instigation of a knight named Plebeus you deprived a noble knight of all his honours and wealth, and did so unjustly. That is what is said about you there.'

When Plebeus heard this, he said: 'You are a false pilgrim if you tell such lies. If you are man enough to defend him now, I will fight you, because that Tyrius meant to rob our lord of his kingdom.' Guido said to the king: 'My lord, since he says I am a false pilgrim and the knight Tyrius is a traitor, with your permission I will fight him and prove in single combat that he is lying.' 'I consent,' replied the king. 'In fact I would have you do this without delay.' Guido said: 'Then give me arms, my lord.' 'Whatever you need,' the king replied, 'you will find ready.'

The king then appointed the day for their duel, and fearing that the pilgrim Guido might meanwhile be slain by some underhand means, he called his young daughter to him and said to her: 'My child, as you love your own life, watch over this pilgrim with care, and provide him with all he needs.' So she took the pilgrim to her own room, bathed him and fulfilled his every wish. The day of the battle arrived. Early in the morning Plebeus stood fully armed at the door and cried: 'Where is that lying pilgrim? Why does he delay so?'

Hearing him, Guido armed himself and they proceeded together to the field of battle, where they exchanged blows so fierce that Plebeus would have expired had he not had something to drink. 'Good pilgrim,' he said, 'let me have just one drink of water.' Guido replied: 'If you promise me faithfully to extend the same courtesy to me if I need it, I agree.' 'I promise you faithfully,' Plebeus said,

4 *mentis*: Oest., K.; *mentio*: L.

172. The constancy of a faithful heart

and went for some water, which he drank until he was full; he then at once charged at Guido with every ounce of his strength, and they fought each other manfully until now Guido became thirsty. 'Friend,' he said, 'show me the same courtesy now that I showed you, for I am unbelievably thirsty.' But Plebeus replied: 'I vow to God you shall taste nothing but my right arm.' At this, Guido, defending himself as best he could, edged towards the spring, and when he was close enough, leapt in and drank all he wanted. Then he got out and rushed upon Plebeus like a raging lion, and Plebeus took flight. Observing this, the king had them separated and made them rest that night, so as to be ready for battle the next day. The pilgrim went to the princess's chamber, and she provided him with every comfort; she bound up his wounds, and after he had supped, settled him down on a strong wooden bed, where, tired from the battle, he fell fast asleep.

Now Plebeus had seven strong sons, and he called them and said: 'Dear boys, you are my sons, and I tell you, if that pilgrim is not killed tonight, I shall be a dead man. I have never seen a more valiant man.' 'Father,' they replied, 'he shall be dispatched tonight.'

Around midnight, when all were asleep, they got into the princess's chamber, which overlooked the sea and was washed by the waves below. 'If we kill him in his bed,' they said one to another, 'we are dead men. We will throw him into the sea together, bed and all, then everyone is bound to say that he ran away.' So they picked him up as he slept and threw him into the sea, and he was so fast asleep he knew nothing about it.

That night a fisherman was out at sea and heard the splash made by the bed, and when he saw it in the moonlight he was amazed and shouted: 'In God's name, who are you? Tell me, so I can help you before you drown!' Hearing the shouting, Guido woke from his sleep, and seeing the stars in the sky above, wondered where he was; then realizing that he was in the water, he cried to the fisherman: 'Friend, help me and I will reward you. I am the pilgrim who was fighting a duel yesterday. But how I came here I have no idea.' When he heard this the fisherman helped him into his little boat, took him home with him and gave him a bed to sleep in.

Plebeus's seven sons went back to their father and told him that Guido had drowned, so he need have no more fear. Plebeus was overjoyed and got up early next day and armed, then went to the gate of the palace and cried: 'Bring that pilgrim out so that I can take my revenge on him!' When the king heard him he told his daughter to wake Guido and prepare him for battle, but when she went to his bed she could not find him. Weeping bitterly she cried: 'Alas, my treasure has been taken from me!' And when she told her father, the king was dismayed, and when his servants could not find the bed itself they were astounded. Some said he had run away, others that he had been murdered. Meanwhile Plebeus kept shouting at the gate: 'Bring out your pilgrim, for today I shall present his head to the king!' And while everyone in the palace was trying to find out where the pilgrim had gone, the fisherman appeared before the king and told him: 'Sire, you need not be alarmed. Last night while I was at sea fishing I found the pilgrim; he had been cast into the sea. So I picked him up and took him to my home and have left him sleeping there.' The king was overjoyed at this news, and sent a messenger to Guido telling him to prepare himself for battle. When Plebeus heard that he was not dead, he was terrified and asked the king for a stay of battle, but the king refused him a truce of even an hour. So both men went to the field of battle and exchanged blows twice, and with his third stroke Guido severed Plebeus's arm, then his head, and presented it to the king. The king was delighted that the pilgrim had won such a glorious victory, and when he learned that it was Plebeus's sons who had cast him into the sea, he had them hanged. The pilgrim then took leave of the king, who offered him many gifts if he would remain with him, but he would not agree to this. So the king gave him a large quantity of gold and silver, which Guido in turn gave to his friend Tyrius, whom Guido and the king then restored to his former dignity and loaded with riches. Guido then bade the king farewell. 'Dear friend,' the king said to him, 'in God's name, one thing I beg of you: tell me what your name is.' 'Sire,' he replied, 'my name is Guido – that Guido of whom you have often heard.' When the king heard this he fell upon his neck and promised him a large part of his kingdom if he would stay with him. But Guido would not hear of it, and kissing the king he left him.

Guido went to England and made his way to his own castle, where sitting before its gates he found a large gathering of poor folk, and among them, in the garb of a pilgrim, sat his wife, the countess, who attended to their wants every day and gave a denarius to each of them, saying: 'Pray for my lord Guido, that before I die I may have the joy of seeing him, and that he may succeed in returning

172. The constancy of a faithful heart

to me; for he went to the Holy Land so long ago.' Now it happened that day that her son, who was seven years old, was following his mother about among the poor in splendid attire. And when he heard his mother name Guido to some poor person, he asked: 'Mother, is it not my father you are commending so earnestly to these poor people?' 'Yes, my son,' she replied. 'The third night of our marriage, after I had conceived you, he left me and I have not seen him since.' Then as she walked along the rows of poor folk, she came to her husband Guido and gave him her alms, quite ignorant of who he was. And he bowed his head, so he should not be recognized. As she went about among the other poor people her son followed her, and Guido lifted up his eyes and saw his son, the son he had never yet seen, and could not contain himself. He took his son in his arms and kissed him, and said: 'My darling child, may God give you the grace to please him!' But when the countess's handmaids saw the pilgrim kiss the boy, they called him over and told him he was not to remain there any longer. Guido then approached his wife and asked her for a place in the forest where he could always stay, and, believing him to be a pilgrim, for the love of God and her husband she built a dwelling for him where he lived for many years. And when the hour of his death was near, he called his servant and told him: 'Friend, go quickly to the countess and give her this ring, and tell her that if she wishes to see me, she should come to me without a moment's delay.' His messenger hurried to the countess and showed her the ring, and as soon as she saw it she cried out: 'This is my lord's ring!' She went as fast as she could to the forest, but before she could get to him Guido died. She fell upon his dead body and cried aloud: 'Woe is me, all my hope is gone!' And with many a sigh and groan she said, 'What use were the alms I gave every day for my lord's sake? I saw my lord receive alms from my own hands, and did not know him! And you, Guido, you saw your own son before you, you touched him, kissed him and never revealed yourself to me or him. What have you done, O Guido, Guido! I shall never see you again!' She then gave his body a magnificent burial and mourned his death for many a day.

Moralization. Dear friends, this knight represents God, who fought many battles. First, in heaven when he expelled the demons, as it is written:[5] *'There was a great battle in heaven.' Then on earth; and*

5 Rv 12.7.

many times, for example when he cast the Pharaoh and his army into the sea; and on Good Friday; and all this he did for love of a girl, i.e., the soul. Then he took Tyrius with him, i.e., assumed manhood, in order to banish the infidels, i.e., sins, from his kingdom and set virtues in their place. He appointed Tyrius, i.e., Moses, to lead his people to a life of righteousness. Then Guido came from the Holy Land, when the Son of God came down from heaven and found Tyrius i.e., the whole of humankind, wandering along the way of perdition, because all those who had come before him had gone down to hell. He slept in our lap when he assumed our humanity from the Virgin's womb. The weasel came out and made its way to the mountain etc., i.e., John and the other prophets prophesied about his coming, and went to the mountain, i.e., entered into the world, preaching the word of God, as is attested of John:[6] 'Behold, I send my angel etc.' After this he returned to Christ, when he said:[7] 'Behold the lamb of God!' And Christ found the dragon dead, i.e., the Old Law crushed by its rituals,[8] and discovered in it the treasure, i.e., the Ten Commandments, which he gave to man, together with the sword of power,[9] which he kept for himself, as it is written:[10] 'I will not give my judgement to another.' With this sword he killed the tyrant Plebeus, who robbed Tyrius, i.e., man, of his honour and riches, when he[11] made our first father transgress. He fought bravely on the field of this world and was armed with the armour of humanity by a virgin, i.e., Blessed Mary. The seven sons of Plebeus are the seven mortal sins which caused him to come down from heaven. And he was cast into the sea of this world, where the fisherman, i.e., the Holy Spirit, descended upon him and remained always with him, and finally he vanquished the

6 Mal 3.1.
7 Jn 1.29.
8 *legem antiquam conculcatam per cerimonias*: Oest., K. *Conculcare* ('trample on', 'tread down') is used rather frequently in the Old Testament, often of people, but also of sanctuaries and holy places that are trodden underfoot. (Interestingly, L. has *occultantem cerimonias*; and *Le Violier*: *'l'ancienne loy qui couvroit les ceremonies.'*)
9 *cum gladio potestatis diem latuit, quam sibi retinuit*: if the text is sound it could conceivably mean that Guido kept the sword in order to avenge Tyrius, but told no-one about when he was going to do it. But I have followed the version in *Le Violier* (omitting *diem latuit*), which seems more convincing.
10 Cf. Is 48.11.
11 The tyrant Plebeus is the devil (as explicitly stated in *Le Violier*), who caused Adam to sin.

devil and presented his victory to the king, i.e., the Heavenly Father, and so passed to his own country, i.e., heaven, and left us the ring of his faith, by which we shall be enabled to reach our everlasting home. When Guido reached his homeland he was not recognized. Even so the Son of God entered heaven; and his relatives, namely some of the holy angels, had no idea who he was. They said:[12] *'Who is this that cometh from Edom, with dyed garments from Bosra?' But we must kiss our Father, i.e., pour forth prayer to him, because he is our Father; for it is written in Deuteronomy:*[13] *'Before you were, he was your father etc.' Let us therefore strive to follow our father Christ with works of charity, and consequently we shall attain to everlasting joys.*

12 Is 63.1.
13 Cf. Dt 32.6.

173. Of the burdens and troubles of the world and the joys of heaven

It happened one day that a king[1] went to a fair and took with him a wise master together with his pupil. As they stood in the market place they saw eight packages set out for sale. The pupil inquired about the first of these, and asked his master what was the value[2] of its contents, i.e., poverty and tribulation for the sake of God. 'The kingdom of heaven,' his master replied. 'That is a great prize,' said the pupil. 'Open the second and let us see what is inside.' The master said: 'It contains meekness. "Blessed are the meek."'[3] 'Meekness is a wonderful and godlike virtue,' the pupil replied. 'What is its worth?' The master said: 'Pure gold cannot be given for it, nor silver paid in exchange for it. I want earth. I desire nothing but earth for it.' 'There is a vast area of earth between India and Britain,' the pupil replied, 'and it is without inhabitants. Take as much of it as you please.' 'No,' said the master. 'That is the land of the doomed, which devours those who live in it. The men there die. I want the land of the living.' The pupil said: 'What concern is it of mine that they die? You too must die, however unwillingly. Do you want to live for ever? "Blessed are the meek, for they shall possess the earth." What does the third package contain?' 'Hunger and thirst,' the master told him. 'And what is their value?' asked the pupil. He replied: 'It is called righteousness. "Blessed are they who hunger and thirst after righteousness, for they shall be filled."' 'Then you shall be filled, and bring forth righteousness, if you admit of no negligence. What does the fourth contain?' The master told him: 'Tears, weeping and wailing, floods above and floods below.' 'Tears and grief are not usually bought,' the pupil said, 'but rewarded,

1 See n. 2 of the previous tale.
2 *precium*: price, value, worth.
3 The words of the beatitudes are much used in this tale. Mt 5.

173. Of the burdens and troubles of the world and the joys of heaven

because this is the price saints choose to pay. "Blessed are they that mourn, for they shall be comforted." What does the fifth bag contain?' 'Something precious – mercy, and I think that it will please you. In a word, I desire mercy for mercy, eternity for time.' 'You are no good at selling your wares,' the pupil told him. 'You will never receive eternity in exchange for time unless mercy pleaded for you, and that you will obtain in proportion to your faith. "Blessed are the merciful, for they shall obtain mercy." But in this life we have an abundance of poverty, misery and tribulation. Undo the sixth package, for perhaps it contains something better.' 'It is quite full,' the master said, 'but, like purple, does not like the eyes of the world. It must be seen in a private chamber and there its value shall be settled.' 'Well, we have inspected it; what is its value?' 'Purity of heart, a precious thing. Here you will find vessels of gold and silver: piety, goodness, mercy, charity and joy in the Holy Spirit. Here you will find rich garments, such as readings, meditations, prayers and contemplations, and the true judgements of the Lord, which are justified in themselves and far more desirable than gold and precious stones.' '"In keeping them,"' said the pupil, '"there is a great reward."'[4] Ask therefore what you will.' 'To see God,' replied the master. '"Blessed are the pure in heart,"' the pupil said, '"for they shall see God." Open the seventh package.' 'It contains peace,' the master told him. 'Are you going to sell me your peace?' asked the pupil. The master replied: 'It does not befit my poverty, nor does it accord with your righteousness or become one of your wealth, that you should receive anything from me without payment. But through your generosity I already have an abundance of all things. So what more do I need? I am a simple man of lowly birth and made of clay, formed of the dust of the earth; my lowliness disgusts me, and I do not want any longer to hear the reproach: "You are earth, and to earth you shall go." I would rather be told: "You are heaven and to heaven you shall go."'[5] I long for the lot of the sons of God. I desire to be a son of God.' 'I have spoken the truth,' the pupil said, 'I abide by it and do not doubt it. "Blessed are the peacemakers, for they shall be called the sons of God." If therefore you show a son's love, you will possess your father's inheritance. Only the last package is left. Open it.' The master said: 'There is nothing in it

4 Ps 18.10ff.
5 Cf. Gn 3.14f.

but persecution and hardship for righteousness's sake.' 'And what do you want for that?' 'The kingdom of heaven,' replied the master. 'I have already given you that as the reward, or price of poverty.' 'Indeed,' said the master, ' but month follows month, week follows week. You are mistaken: I want it this week, this month. In the meantime, I will wait.' 'I admire your shrewdness in bargaining,' the pupil replied. 'Now listen, O good and faithful servant, "because thou hast been faithful over a few things, I will place thee over many. Enter thou into the joy of thy Lord."'[6]

---

6 Mt 25.21, 23; cf. Lk 19.17. This is a very curious tale, and one in which pupil and master sometimes confusingly change places.

174. No-one can alter the teaching of nature; and of the punishment for ingratitude

An emperor rode off to hunt one afternoon and it chanced that as he was passing through a wood he came across some shepherds who had caught a snake and tied it firmly to a tree, and the snake was hissing horribly. Out of pity the emperor set it loose and laid it in his bosom to give it warmth. But as soon as the snake was warm, it began to bite him and shoot its poison into him. 'What are you doing?' cried the emperor. 'Why do you repay goodness with evil?' The snake, like Balaam's ass in former times, was endowed with the power of speech and replied: 'What nature teaches no-one can alter. You did what you had to do, and I acted according to my nature. You showed me all the kindness you could, and in return I gave you all that I had. I offered you poison, because I had nothing but poison to give you, and I shall always be the enemy of man, since it was because of man that I have been punished and cursed.'

And as they continued to argue, they called a philosopher to judge between them and give a just verdict. The philosopher said: 'What I know of this affair comes only from your account and from hearsay. If I could see precisely what it is that you are telling me about, I could pass judgement. I want the snake to be tied to the tree exactly as it was tied before, and the lord emperor to be free of him. Then I will pass judgement on you both.' When his instructions were carried out, the philosopher said to the snake: 'Now you are bound. Free yourself if you can, and go.' 'I cannot,' said the snake, 'because I am tied so tightly I can scarcely move.' The philosopher replied: 'Then you will die, and rightly so, because throughout history you have always been disagreeable to man and always will be.' He then turned to the emperor and said: 'My lord, you are now free. Squeeze the poison from your bosom and be on your way. In future never commit so great a folly again, because the snake can only do what nature has taught it to do.' When he heard this, the emperor thanked the philosopher for the sound judgement he had given, and went on his way.

Moralization. Dear friends, this emperor represents any good Christian or man of the Church, such as a good prelate, who has to hunt continually for the salvation of souls, and so he has to pass through a wood. This wood is the world, in which he finds the tethered snake. The snake is the devil, who through Christ's Passion was so tightly bound that he can do nothing except by permission, i.e., unless man, who has free will, permits him to tempt him and gives in to him. But wretched man, not thinking of the future, sets the devil free and puts him in his bosom whenever he succumbs to mortal sin and takes pleasure in it. So what does the devil do? Of course he injects his poison into the man's heart; and what the devil's poison does is to add sin to sin and heap evil upon evil. Many people of today are infected with this poison. When some commit the sin of wantonness, they are not only incontinent in private, but urge others by their bad example to commit a like sin. Others receive the most evil poison that is poured from the devil's jaws, i.e., that of slander, in such copious amounts that, when they see they are poisoned, they do not cry for aid by making their confession, but for others also to come to drink this poison and give it to others. The Psalmist says of these slanderers:[1] *'The venom of asps is under their lips.' And elsewhere:*[2] *'Their tongue is a sharp sword.' This poison is so detestable that scarcely any evil can be compared with the poison of detraction; hence Ambrose says: 'For those who rob others of their good name are worse than those who violently seize their goods; they can restore their goods to them, but never their good name. "A good name is better than precious ointments."'*[3] *Our enemy is always striving to pour the poison of sin into us, because his nature is evil, and therefore he cannot do good, and there has been enmity between the devil and man from the beginning. But the sinner sets the devil free when he actively commits the sin suggested to him by temptation. And having set him free, he warms him in his bosom when the sin is repeated and the sinner through habit continues to sin, which is grievous, and at the last the devil takes him off and plunges him into the abyss of despair. The shepherds who tied the snake up are the prophets, patriarchs, Apostles*

1 Ps 139.4.
2 Ps 56.5.
3 Eccles 7.2.

174. No-one can alter the teaching of nature

and other teachers and preachers of the Church of the present time, who with the bonds of their tongue tie him so tightly that he has no power at all, and who through their holy lives and works of mercy, and with the Lord's Prayer, wrest all his power from him. But wretched man, who does not fear God, does not fight against the devil or bind him, but rather sets him free by committing mortal sins, and takes him to his bosom and warms him, and then is filled with the poison of sin in body and soul. If therefore you desire to be freed, call a philosopher to you, i.e., a discerning confessor, who has to judge between you and the devil, and who knows how to distinguish between what is leprosy and what is not, and between the different varieties of sins, and open your heart to him. But no-one will be able to pass judgement unless the devil is first bound. And how is he to be bound? Clearly, by a triple chain, that of contrition, confession and penance, because as the Psalm bears witness:[4] *'a contrite and humbled heart, O God, thou wilt not despise'. For God does not desire the death of a sinner, but rather that he should be converted and live.*[5] *Therefore the sinner has this triple chain, and whenever some sin is suggested to him, he must fasten it to the devil's neck and so compel him to stop. This adversary, who goes about us like a raging lion, 'seeking whom he may devour', is therefore the foe of the whole human race, because he lost the place in heaven from which he and his partners fell through sin, and wants man through repeated sin to lose his place in the same way, and not to win heaven's favour. He will therefore at the last, in our presence, lay bare all our sins, however tiny, that have not been destroyed through confession. So let us take the second strand of this chain and tie it to his neck, that thus we can lead captive through confession one who is working continually for our humiliation. Then the confessor will give us a saving remedy with the third strand of the chain, i.e., penance and atonement, and say: 'You are now freed from the devil. Go in peace: that is, sin no more!' Let us pray therefore etc.*

4 Ps 50.19.
5 Cf. Ez 18.23, 32.

175. Of the strangeness of the world and its wonders, together with an interpretation of them

Pliny relates that there are some men with the heads of dogs, who speak by barking and clothe themselves in the skins of animals. These signify preachers, who should clothe themselves in the skins of animals, i.e., wear the sackcloth of harsh penance in order to give good example to others. Likewise in India there are certain men who have just one eye in their foreheads above their nose,[1] and eat the flesh of animals. These represent men who have only the eye of reason, and that they use in their forehead, but not in their will.[2] In Lybia there are some women without heads who have their mouths and eyes in their breasts. These represent men who wish to behave with heartfelt obedience, and have minds that are not frivolous, and who consider well beforehand in their hearts all that they must perform outwardly in action. In the East, near the earthly paradise, there are men who eat nothing because their mouths are so small that they drink through a reed. They live on the scent of fruits and flowers, and a bad odour kills them instantly. They represent people of the cloister, who must be especially abstemious in taking food and drink, i.e., have a small appetite, and partake of food with a straw, i.e., with prudence. Such men must live spiritually on the odour of fruits and flowers, i.e., of good doctrines and virtues, and so provide others with a model of chastity and austerity. But they are quickly destroyed by a bad odour, i.e., sin, because as soon as sin is committed, man dies unto Christ. There are also men in the same region without noses, and with rounded faces, and whatever they see they think wholly good. These symbolize fools who so lack

1 Pliny, *N.H.* VII.2.
2 *quo in fronte utuntur et non voluntate:* Trillitzsch expands this to explain that the eye in the forehead indicates outward, as opposed to inward, reason.

175. Of the strangeness of the world and its wonders

the nose of discernment that everything they see and do seems to them good. There are also men there who have noses and lower lips so long that they cover the whole of their face when they sleep. These symbolize the righteous, who below, i.e., towards the world, possess a large lip of reflection, as they regard the vanity of the world and its slander and deceit. But with the lip of watchfulness they protect their whole face, i.e., their whole life through constant meditation, lest they sleep in sin.

In Scythia there are men with ears so large that they can cover their whole bodies with them. These symbolize people who willingly hear God's word, and through it can keep their souls and bodies free from sin. There are also some who walk about like cattle, and these signify people who honour neither God nor his saints, but walk from sin to sin like cattle and irrational beasts, to whom the Psalmist says:[3] 'Do not become like the horse and the mule etc.' Likewise there are horned men with snub noses and goats' feet. These are the proud, who show the horns of pride everywhere, and have but a small nose of discernment with respect to their salvation, but a goat's feet for running after excess, for the goat can run very fast and is adept at climbing. The same can be said of the proud.

In Ethiopia there are men with only one foot, but who run with such speed that they can hunt wild animals. These are people who have but one foot of perfection with respect to God and their neighbour, namely that of charity, and such people move swiftly towards the kingdom of heaven.

In India there are pygmies three feet tall who ride on goats and do battle with cranes. These symbolize men whose good lives are short: they begin well, but do not persevere and do not fight manfully against cranes, i.e., the stains of sin. In India there are also men with six hands who go about naked and are hairy and live in rivers. These men with six hands symbolize those who strive zealously to obtain eternal life; the Psalmist says:[4] 'My soul is continually in my hands'; and in their nakedness they symbolize sinners who are stripped of virtues, and who live in the river of this life. There are also men there who have six fingers on each hand and six toes on each foot. All week they keep themselves free from

3 Ps 31.9.
4 Ps 118.109.

the contagion of sin, and the seventh day they celebrate everywhere as a feast and regard as wholly sacred. And there are women with beards that reach down to their breasts, but their heads are bald. These symbolize just men who keep to the level path of the Church's commandments, and are diverted from it neither by love nor hatred.

In Ethiopia there are men with four eyes, and these represent people who fear God, the world, the devil and the flesh. One eye they direct to God by living justly, that they may please him; the second to the world, that they may flee it; the third to the devil, that they may resist him; and the fourth to the flesh, that they may chastise it.

In Europe there are men who are handsome, but who have a crane's head and neck and beak. These symbolize judges, who, like cranes, must have long necks so that they may first consider prudently in their hearts the judgements they are to deliver through their mouths. If all judges were such, there would not be so many bad judgements.

176. Of spiritual medicine

A boy was born with his body divided from the navel upwards, so that he had two heads and two breasts, and each had its own organs of feeling, and while one ate or slept the other did not. After living two years, one half of him died, while the other half survived for three days.

Also, as Pliny tells us, there was a tree in India whose flowers had a sweet smell and its fruits a delicious taste. Near this tree lived a serpent called Jacorlus who utterly loathed the smell of this tree, and in order to destroy its flowers and fruits, it crept to the roots of the tree and infected them with its poison. But a gardener saw this and took an antidote[1] known to that country, put it on the tip of a pole and dripped it over the ends of the branches of the tree. It swiftly expelled the poison infecting the roots and enabled an otherwise barren tree to bear fruit.

Moralization. Dear friends, the boy signifies any man, who is composed of two parts, i.e., soul and body, each of which has its own activities: Galatians c.2:[2] *'The works of the flesh are uncleanliness, fornication, wantonness, and idolatry; the works of the soul are joy, peace in the Holy Spirit, patience, longanimity and the like.' These activities are opposed to each other: when one is sleeping or eating, the other always does what opposes it, because 'the flesh lusteth against the spirit'.*[3] *When the soul rests from its activities, then the flesh does not rest, indeed it is anxious to perform its own evil and perverse deeds, and so one part of man is dead and the other alive, for the flesh performs the works of death, and the soul desires the works of life. As Matthew*

1 *tyriacam*: see no. 23, note 1.
2 Cf. Gal 5.19ff.
3 Gal 5.17.

says, c.5:[4] 'By their fruits you shall know them.' Before sin the tree brought forth sweet fruits, as a wise man says:[5] 'My flowers are the fruit of honour and riches.' These fruits the ancient serpent could not endure, and he injected his poison into its roots when he put sin in our first parent. Then the tree became so diseased that it could not bear its sweet fruits, because man could not enter heaven, however meritorious his works, and for many thousands of years wandered like an outcast away from his true inheritance, and having been banished, lived in exile until a wise gardener, i.e., the Heavenly Father, dripped theriac over a branch of this tree. This branch is the Blessed Virgin Mary, of whom Isaiah says:[6] 'There shall come forth a rod out of the root of Jesse.' And likewise Virgil says in his second Eclogue:[7]

> Now the Maiden[8] returns, the reign of Saturn[9] returns,
> Now a new race is sent down from the height of heaven,
> Smile[10] on the birth of the boy, when first the race of iron
> Shall cease, and a golden race rise up over the whole world.

Theriac was put on this branch when the Son of God was sent by his Father, working with the Holy Spirit, into the Virgin's womb, and when Christ was born of the Virgin. Through the medicine of the healing theriac the diseased tree recovered its former sweetness, of which 'it giveth to all men abundantly and upbraideth not';[11] as is written in Isaiah:[12] 'All you that thirst, come etc.'

4 = Mt 7.16.
5 Ecclus 24.23. *ut dicit sapiens*: Ecclesiasticus, an apocryphal wisdom book, was called in Greek 'the wisdom of Jesus Ben Sira', whose Greek form is Sirach. The book was written in Hebrew, but the Church recognizes the canonicity only of the Greek text.
6 Is 11.1.
7 = Eclogue IV.6–9. Virgil pictures the advent of an age of peace. The identity of the child is unknown, but early Christians saw in the virgin and the child a prophecy concerning the Messiah.
8 The maiden is Astraea, or justice, the last of the immortals to leave the earth when men became corrupt.
9 i.e., the good days of old, when Saturn reigned.
10 Lucina (Diana), named in the following verse (10), is asked to look kindly on the new child that is to be born. The Latin is incorrectly quoted. The dative *nascenti* is governed by *fave*, which occurs in the next verse: *casta fave Lucina*.
11 Jas 1.5.
12 Is 55.1.

177. Of persecution

King Assuerus held a great banquet for all the princes and people of his kingdom, and gave orders for his Queen Vashti to be presented at the feast so that the people might see her beauty. But she refused to come in, so the king stripped her of her royal title and raised Esther to the throne in her place. After this the king elevated a certain Haman to pre-eminence in the kingdom, and made all the princes subject to him. But while all the others bent the knee to Haman, the king's uncle Mordecai alone refused to do him homage, whereupon Haman indignantly ordered him and all his family to be put to death. With the authority of the royal seal he decreed that all the Jews in Assuerus's kingdom should be annihilated, and erected a towering gibbet on which to hang Mordecai. But in the meantime two men planned an attempt on the king's life. Mordecai denounced them and brought them before the king, who ordered that they should be put to death, and that Mordecai should be clothed in purple, given a crown and be led about the city on a royal horse, while Haman went before him with his troops singing his praises. After this had taken place, Mordecai told the queen that Haman had condemned her and all the people of her nation to death, whereupon Esther imposed a fast on all the people, while she mortified herself with fasting and prayer. Then she had a banquet prepared to which she invited the king, and she also commanded Haman to be present. During the feast she begged the king to spare her life and the lives of her people, and told him that they had all been condemned to death by Haman. In a fury the king ordered Haman to be hanged on the very gibbet he had himself intended for Mordecai, and furthermore appointed Mordecai as his successor. Mordecai then destroyed all Haman's kin, and so by God's dispensation an innocent people were delivered and an evil seed utterly extinguished.

Moralization. Dear friends, the king is our Lord Jesus Christ, who sprang from the root of Jesse. He held a banquet for the princes and peoples of his kingdom, because he gave his body and Holy Scripture as a banquet for many princes of the world and the faithful of his kingdom. He called Queen Vashti to the banquet wearing her crown, because he invited the synagogue, delivered from the law and the philosophers, to the heavenly feast. But she refused and was deprived of her royal estate, and the captive Esther was placed on her throne, because Judaea, refusing to believe, was cast out of Christ's kingdom, and a gentile girl, a prisoner of the devil, was led into the king's bedchamber to share[1] his heavenly kingdom. Haman, who was advanced to honour by the king, is the Jewish people, which was exalted by God in respect of its royal power, its priesthood and divine worship, and he sought to eradicate the queen's offspring, because the Jewish people sought to extinguish the spirit of the Church. Haman also built a gallows[2] for Mordecai, and was himself hanged on the same gallows, because the devil is signified by the gibbet of the cross. The two traitors who conspired against the king are two unbelieving peoples, namely the Jews and the Gentiles, who urged that Christ should be killed, and whom Mordecai accused, because the Christian people condemned their actions. The former were killed by the king, the latter damned by Christ. Mordecai was clothed in purple and crowned, and led through the city on a royal horse, because the Christian people are honoured by the learned throughout the whole world; for their community is the horse of Christ the King, which he rides through the world. Haman and his soldiers shouted his praises, because the Jewish people as well as the Gentiles, like it or not, celebrate the special glories[3] of the Christian. The queen called the king to her feast, because the Church invites Christ to the solemn rites of his body. She also commanded Haman to be present, because Christ in his preaching offers his feast to all faithful people. Haman, who built the gallows for Mordecai, is also the antichrist, who threatened the people with the punishment of death for their faith, and was hanged on the same gallows and himself received the punishment of death. Mordecai was made a prince by the king, because the faithful people, when judge-

1 *concors*: Oest., K.; *consors*: L.
2 *eculeum*: properly a wooden rack in the shape of a horse, used as an instrument of torture. At Est 5.14 it is a beam (*trabem*), and at 8.7 a gibbet (*cruci*).
3 *preconia propria*: Le Violier: 'aucunes choses'.

177. Of persecution

ment is passed, are made lord of all their master's goods.[4] *An 'evil seed' is exterminated, because the generation of the wicked is then damned, while the queen's people are set free and their sadness is turned to joy, because the generation of the righteous shall be blessed, and enjoy great happiness and exultation.*

---

4 Cf. Mt 25.21ff.

178. Of foresight, the mother of all riches

A king wanted to know how best to govern himself and his kingdom, so he called to his presence a man who surpassed all others in wisdom and said to him: 'My friend, give me a rule whereby I may govern myself and my kingdom.' 'Willingly, my lord,' he replied, and at once drew on the wall a king with a crown on his head. This is how he was depicted: the king was sitting on his throne, dressed in purple, and he held in his left hand a ball and in his right a sceptre, and above his head was a burning light. On his left was a beautiful queen, crowned and clad in a rich garment embroidered in gold; on the other side were counsellors sitting on chairs and before them was an open book. In front of them, and below the king, was a knight on horseback, decked out in his armour, with a helmet on his head, a lance in his right hand and a shield in his left as protection; a sword hung at his right side; he had a cuirass on his upper body, buckles on his breast, iron greaves on his legs, spurs on his feet, iron gauntlets on his hands, and his steed was seasoned in warfare and wore rich trappings. Below the king were depicted his deputies, one seated like a knight on a horse, with a cloak and hood made of different animal skins, with a rod outstretched in his right hand. Beneath the king's deputies there were also the people, depicted as follows: there was one man dressed like any other man,[1] who held in his right hand a mattock for digging the earth, and in his left hand a stick for driving herds of cattle; at his belt he had a sickle for reaping corn and pruning vines and trees. On the king's right side before the knight, an artisan was depicted, life-sized, with a hammer in his right hand, and in his left an axe, and at his belt he carried a mason's trowel. Before the people there was

---

1 *in specia humana*: 'in human form/guise'. I take this to mean that he was wearing ordinary, everyday clothes.

178. Of foresight, the mother of all riches

also a man who held some pincers in his right hand, and in his left a great, long sword; and at his belt a writing slate and an inkhorn with ink; and over his right ear he carried a writing pen. Also before the people there was a man with a balance and weights in his right hand, and a yardstick in his left hand, and at his waist he carried a purse containing various pieces of money. Before the queen there were also physicians and spicers,[2] who were depicted as follows: one man was seated on a master's chair holding a book in his right hand, a jar and spice box in his left, and carrying at his belt iron probes for examining ulcers and wounds. Next to him was a man depicted as follows: he was holding his right hand aloft to invite passers-by into his inn; his left hand held a fine loaf of bread, and above him was depicted a cask of wine; at his waist he carried some keys. Also on the left, before the knight, there was a man depicted as follows: he had in his right hand some large keys and in his left a yardstick, and at his belt he carried a purse full of coins. Also before the king was a man with shaggy, dishevelled hair; in his right hand he had a little money and in his left three dice; and at his belt he carried a box full of letters.

The king considered this picture, and studied it with such care that he found it contained much wisdom.

Dear friends, this king is any good Christian, especially a prince or prelate, and both of them must be placed on a throne clad in purple, which symbolizes the power of grace and beauty of character with which the Christian heart and soul must be adorned; and especially that of the prince or prelate, who must be clothed in the garments of the virtues more richly than all his subjects, so that his body glitters with its golden apparel; and he must have a crown upon his head, which manifests royal dignity in a king, which is the glory of the people, and which directs the eyes of all his subjects towards him, and they obey him. In his left hand he holds a globe, which shows that the king is the administrator and guardian of all his subjects; in his right hand he holds a sceptre, demonstrating the rigorous justice with which he checks the wicked, whom love of virtue does not keep from doing wrong. Above the king's head is a burning lamp, which symbolizes the king's mercy. Likewise the queen on his left is charity, and she is lovely of soul, for a

---

2 *pigmentarii*: these supplied both spices for cooking and drugs for medicinal purposes.

woman espoused to King Jesus Christ should be modest and chaste; second, she must be pure and noble; third, she must be wise and discerning, and moderate in speech and character. Likewise there are counsellors, i.e., judges, sitting on chairs; they are prelates and preachers who must keep the commandments of the Lord, and open their books, i.e., Holy Scripture, to the people. The knight is a good Christian, who must be armed with virtues. The knight who is to be armed is bathed, so that he may lead a new life, and he also spends the night in prayer, asking heaven for the grace that he cannot have by nature; the same is true of the good Christian. And the knight must be bathed in the water of confession and pour forth many a prayer. The knight needs many qualities: first he must be wise; so too the Christian must learn wisdom to fight the devil; second, the knight must be faithful to his lord; even so the Christian to his Lord Jesus Christ; third, the knight must be benevolent; so too, even more obviously, must the Christian; fourth, he must be bold; so must the Christian be, to fight sin; fifth, the knight must be merciful; so too the Christian; sixth, the knight must vigilantly watch over the people; so too the Christian must do all he can by word and deed to keep others from sin, and prelates especially must do this. Then there are the deputies, and one of them is a knight on horseback etc. This knight is a judge who must be seated on the horse of justice and clothed in the cloak of mercy with a hood of different kinds of animal skins. The hood signifies integrity, based on the many counsels of the saints and examples of the fathers in giving their judgements. The rod he holds is outstretched to poor and rich alike. Likewise the people before the judge, and the man dressed like any other man etc. These three represent the whole of agriculture. It is said that the first farmer was Cain, the first-born of Adam; and it was necessary for man to till the earth, that she, who is our mother and of our bodily nature, who gives us a common beginning and who at the end of our life a common home, should give us food in the middle of our life in response to our labour. The farmer must personally observe many rules: first, he must acknowledge God and give a tithe to Him who has given him everything; second, he must keep to the law, and carry out his lord's business more conscientiously than his own; third, farmers must not fear death, but love life; fourth, they must labour and have done with idleness. The farmer has three particular jobs: the first is to cultivate the land, thus in his right hand he carries a spade with which to dig the ground; the second is to feed his cattle, so he holds a rod with which to steer his beasts; for a shepherd must show not only skill, but virtue, as

178. Of foresight, the mother of all riches 485

did Abel, the first shepherd, who offered God the firstling of his flock, and gave him the best sheep he had; third, it is his job to clear thickets, plant trees and set vines; even so the good prelate must be virtuous, offer works of merit to God, clear the thickets from the hearts of sinners with good doctrine, plant trees, i.e., virtues and set the vines of holy preaching. The sickle at his belt signifies the judgement in his heart, the right judgement and wisdom to cleanse sins. And the artisan before the knight with the hammer in his right hand symbolizes all those who work iron, silver and bronze with a hammer. In his left hand he has an axe, the symbol of all those who work in wood, like shipwrights and carpenters. At his belt he carries a trowel, the symbol of all stonemasons. All these must possess three qualities: the first is fidelity and loyalty; second, they must have wisdom, and trustworthiness, lest one should envy another or harbour some suspicion against him; third, they must all have unshakable strength, especially the ships' captains. Then the man holding pincers in his right hand and a sword in his left, and with a writing tablet at his belt: he represents all clerks working in cloth and wool and linen, for weavers of cloth, cutters and trimmers,[3] for example. The pen and writing tablet denote all notaries, whose work is to assist the judge, to compose documents and do much reading. It is the duty of all these to show honesty in three ways: first, honesty of life to prevent all sin; and primarily in the words they speak, so that they are not deceitful either in word or deed; second, they should be just and observe justice before everyone; third, they should show integrity of character in the face of discord, trustworthiness in the face of deceitfulness and amiability in the face of envy. Likewise the man with a balance and weights in his right hand: the balance is the symbol of assayers and moneychangers. In his left hand he has a yardstick, which denotes measurers of woven cloth and other things; at his belt he carries a purse containing various sorts of money etc. All these must shun avarice, which is idolatry; second, they must beware of contracting heavy debts; third, they must return without delay any deposit that is entrusted to them, when it is requested. Then, below the queen there is a man seated on a master's chair etc. His book is the symbol of doctors and physicians, and the teachers of all the liberal arts. All these must possess a variety of cures to treat a variety of illnesses, and the [works of the] particular authorities on them, such as Hippocrates, Galen and

---

3 *doleatores*: meaning uncertain. *Doleator* can be an alternative form of *dolator*, a hewer (usually of wood or stone). There seems to be a notion of 'dressing' or 'smoothing'.

so on. The urn signifies apothecaries and chemists. Second,[4] they must live chastely, display a virtuous character in their words and deeds, regularly visit the sick and restore people's health. Third, the spicers must take great care in mixing their medicines. Then the man with his right hand extended etc., which signifies that all the goods his guests have deposited with him are secure and in a safe place. These [innkeepers] must first avoid gluttony and drunkenness, that through their example all who come to them display temperance of life. Second, they must give their guests a warm welcome, inviting[5] them in kindly, and speaking to them agreeably and pleasantly. Third, they must do those things that give the host a good name: first, they must inform those whom they have received as guests about the dangers of the highways; second, when they leave the inn they should escort them;[6] and third, both inside and outside the house they should defend their guests' lives and reputations and all their property as they would their own. Then, on the left side, the man who has the keys etc.: he represents the guardians of the city. In his left hand he holds a yardstick, signifying the officials of the city or community, who are set in authority. The belt signifies toll-gatherers and all those who receive the community's money. These must be devoted to the common good, they must be provident and conscientious, and fear and honour God. And the man with the shaggy hair etc. signifies men who are wasteful and squander their goods. In his left hand he has three dice, which signify gamblers and whoremongers. At his belt he has a box full of letters, and this symbolizes merchants who go hither and thither about the world etc.

---

4 *Secundo*: the spicers are grouped under the heading of doctors and physicians etc. First, they must know the cures for all manner of ailments etc.; second, they must lead chaste lives etc.
5 *imitatione*: Oest., K.; *invitatione*: L.
6 *conducere in domo*: Oest.; *in aliam domum*: K., L. I read *conducere, in domo et extra domum*.

179. Of gluttony and drunkenness

Caesarius[1] says of the abominable vices of gluttony and drunkenness, that gluttony is an immoderate and shameful bodily appetite for eating and drinking. Its daughters are impurity, buffoonery, improper mirth, loquacity and a dulling of the intellectual faculties. In gluttony there are five stages of sin: the first is hankering after costly and luxurious food; the second is taking great pains over its preparation; the third is eating it before the proper time; the fourth is eating too greedily; and the fifth is eating too much. It was gluttony that overcame the first man in paradise and brought about his downfall; it was this that robbed Esau of his birthright; it was gluttony that induced the people of Sodom to sin so grievously; it was this that overthrew the children of Israel in the desert. As the Psalmist says:[2] 'As yet their meat was in their mouth, and the wrath of God came upon them.' The iniquity of Sodom came about because the people had too much bread and an abundance of everything. The man of God, Abdon,[3] who was sent to Bethel, was eaten by a lion because he broke his fast. The rich man who dined magnificently every day is buried in hell.[4] It was Nabuzardan, 'the prince of cooks',[5] i.e., gluttony, that destroyed Jerusalem. Are not

1 This is likely to be a reference to the Cistercian abbot Caesarius von Heisterbach, but this passage cannot be found in his most famous work, the *Dialogus miraculorum*.
2 Ps 77.30f.
3 The 'man of God' is not named in 3 Kgs 13. He was told by God not to eat bread or drink water, nor to return by the same way.
4 Lk 16.22.
5 Nebuzaradan was the captain of the guard left by Nebuchadnezzar in Jerusalem. 'Prince of cooks' is a translation of the Greek *archimageiros*, but in the context it is more likely to mean 'prince of killers' (*mageiros* = 'butcher'), 4 Kgs 25.8f. The Vulgate has 'chief of the soldiers'.

the great dangers in gluttony obvious? And we can add the testimony of Scripture. For Solomon says:[6] 'Woe to the land, whose princes eat in the morning!' Also:[7] 'All the labour of man is for his mouth, but his soul shall not be filled.' The daughter of gluttony is drunkenness, because the vice of gluttony begets excess, which is the worst of plagues. What could be more disgusting than this vice? What is more ruinous than that through which virtue is slowly worn away, and, as the quest for victory languishes, the thirst for glory sleeps and turns to ignominy, and strength of mind and body alike is extinguished? For Basil says: 'When we serve the belly and throat, we are cattle, and striving to resemble beasts who are inclined to such behaviour, and whom nature has taught to look on the earth and obey their bellies.' Similarly Boethius says in *De Consolatione* Bk. IV:[8] 'He who abandons virtue ceases to be a man, for since he cannot aspire to a divine nature, all that is left to him is to turn into a beast.' And the Lord says in the Gospel:[9] 'See that your hearts be not overcharged with surfeiting and drunkenness.' How many people would have attained to wonderful wisdom and sound counsel had not gluttony and a passion for wine hindered them! How perilous it is for the father of a family or the ruler of a state to become heated with wine, for thus his wrath is kindled, his discernment is clouded, and his thirst for pleasure is aroused, so that his judgement is dulled and his lust embroils him in all manner of unspeakable acts! Thus Ovid says:[10]

Wine inclines the heart to love if you take an abundance.

Ah, what a dreadful vice is drunkenness! Through it virginity, which is the sister of the angels, the possession of all good things and the assurance of eternal joys, is lost. When Noah was heated with wine he bared his body and uncovered his private parts to his sons. Lot, a most chaste man, fell asleep through drinking too much wine when he fled to the mountain and lay in carnal union with his daughters as if they were his wives.[11] We read of men heated with wine who

6 Cf. Eccles 10.16.
7 Eccles 6.7.
8 IV.3.25.
9 Cf. Lk 21.34.
10 *si plurima sumas*: *Remedia Amoris*, 805: Ovid, however, says *nisi plurima sumas* (unless you take too much).
11 Gn 19.30ff.

179. Of gluttony and drunkenness

became so wrathful that, though they had been such friends that, if sober, each would have exposed himself to danger for the other, they stabbed each other to death. Herod Antipas would not have decapitated St John if there had been no surfeiting and drunkenness at his feast.[12] Balthasar, King of Babylon, would not have lost his life and kingdom if he had been sober on the night in which King Cyrus and King Darius slew him, together with his people, overcome as he was with wine.[13] For this reason the Apostle gives us the following advice concerning sobriety: 'Be sober and watch.'[14] Let us therefore pray to the Lord that we so preserve our sobriety on earth that we may be invited to the celestial banquet in heaven. Amen.

12 Mt 14.
13 This is Belshazzar, Dn 5.
14 1 Pt 5.8.

180. Of fidelity

Paul, who wrote the history of the Lombards, tells[1] of a certain knight named Onulphus of Pavia who gave such proof of his fidelity to his master, King Portaticus, that he exposed himself to death in order to save his life. For after the murder of Godobert, King of the Lombards, by Genebaldus, Duke of Ravenna, and the first betrayer of a royal crown, Grimoaldus, Duke of Beneventum, had by force and cunning succeeded to Godobert's throne, and King Godobert's brother Portaticus had been forced to flee to Hungary. The aforesaid knight Onulphus then effected a reconciliation between Portaticus and King Grimoaldus, so that he could leave Hungary, where he could not stay for fear of Grimoaldus, and seek pardon at the king's feet, and so be able to live in decent comfort, even if deprived of the royal status which was his by right. But a few days after this reconciliation had taken place, King Grimoaldus, trusting too readily some slanderous talk, ordered Portaticus, with whom he had made peace, to be put to death the very next day, and commanded that he be given sufficient wine to make him so drunk that he would have no chance of resisting. But Portaticus's knight Onulphus was well aware of the plot, and taking his squire he went to Portaticus's house, left his squire there hidden under the covers of Portaticus's bed; then, uttering threats and reproaches, and cuffing him as if he were his squire, he got Portaticus away to his own house. Although the king had a set a watch, or guard, outside the front door of Portaticus's house, they thought Portaticus was Onulphus's squire, not his lord. That same night, about cockcrow, Onulphus lowered a rope down the city wall against which his house stood, and let his master down. Portaticus

1 Paul the Deacon, *History of the Longobards* V.2–4.

180. Of fidelity

then caught up some horses that were at pasture and fled to the city of Asti, and from there hastened to the King of France.

Next morning Onulphus and his squire were detained by the king and interrogated as to the method and means by which they had enabled their master Portaticus to escape. They told him the simple truth, whereupon the king said to his counsellors: 'What punishment do they deserve for acting contrary to our royal will?' One of them said they should be put to death, another that they should be flayed alive, and another declared that they should be secretly crucified. But the king replied: 'By Him who gave me life, it is not death they deserve, but all possible honour, because they have proved so faithful to their master!' So King Grimoaldus loaded them with honours and gifts, while the traitor Genebaldus, Duke of Carignano,[2] was miserably, but justly, executed by the hand of the squire of his erstwhile king Godobert, whom he had robbed of his crown and life, on the feast of St John the Baptist, at Turin.

Moralization. Dear friends, this knight Onolphus represents the good Christian, who is faithful to his lord King Portaticus, i.e., the soul, in all things; whether working, keeping watch or sleeping, he directs all his actions towards the service of his lord, so that whatever the soul demands of him when inspired to do some good work, his body makes every effort to carry out and complete without weariness, in accordance with the prescriptions of the Ten Commandments and other precepts of the Church; so that, when the heart within him is persisting in vigils and prayer, and diligently and devoutly entreating the Lord's forgiveness for his sins, his body without begs that it may complete this work to its merit and not be overcome with weariness. This knight gave such proof of fidelity to his lord that he exposed himself to dangers on his behalf; for, as the Apostle says, the holy martyrs and others devoted to Christ were put to the test for the salvation of their lord, i.e., soul. Some were cut in pieces, some killed with the sword, and in addition underwent many different kinds of torture of which we read in the legends of the saints, in order to reconcile their lord, who had committed an offence through mortal sin, to Duke Grimoaldus, i.e., Jesus Christ, so that he might be free to leave Hungary, where he could not live through fear of Grimoaldus. Hungary signifies this world, which is full

---

2 *Canimentium dux*: the place cannot be identified with any certainty. Genebaldus (*Geribaldus*: Oest.) is earlier called Duke of Ravenna.

of trials and tribulations, and in which the soul wanders at peril and trembles with fear of death at the last. Therefore the knight, i.e., the body, busies himself to bring his lord, i.e., soul, to this Duke Grimoaldus from the Hungary of this world, and at once endeavours to win him pardon at the feet of the king through his humility, though he had often behaved arrogantly towards him, and deserved justice rather than mercy. But when the reconciliation is effected man often falls back into sin, and so King Grimoaldus, who is our Father and the Heavenly King, determined to condemn Portaticus, who is our soul, to death next day, in accordance with justice and equity; but mercy, who was well acquainted with the affair, prevented this, and concealed the body, i.e., the faithful knight, under the bed of repentance and atonement to do penance, until Grimoaldus, the King and Heavenly Father, let Portaticus down the wall of tribulation and mercifully concealed his sin; and Portaticus, catching up some horses at pasture, i.e., through the merits of other saints and the elect, got to the city of Asti. This city is the one of which John says in Revelation:[3] 'I saw the holy city of Jerusalem coming down from heaven etc.' And from there he hastened to the king of France. France signifies the court of the saints and angels of highest heaven, where the King, crowned with the diadem of everlasting glory, is seated in gladness and in the fullness of all joy. But next morning the body and soul, absolved of the sin they had committed, are brought to trial, and accused by the devil, and interrogated as to the method and means by which their lord, i.e., soul, was freed from the pains of eternal death and escaped his bonds. Then King Grimoaldus, Judge of the living and the dead, will ask his counsellors, i.e., justice and equity and mercy and kindness, what punishment they deserve. Justice then declares that they should be punished with a sentence of death, i.e., be damned eternally for the sin they committed. On the other side, devils will stand there accusing them and will cry out that the judge should justly sentence them to be flayed alive. But because their sin has been annulled through confession and the atonement of penance, the kindly duke will sentence them to enter life with the elect for the extreme fidelity they displayed one to another, and will deliver them from death, and say: 'They are worthy of all honour for being so faithful to their lord!' And he will crown them with a crown of glory and eternal joy, to which etc.

3 Cf. Rv 21.2.

181. Of adultery

We read that a certain king had a lion, a lioness and a leopard he loved dearly. Now in the lion's absence the lioness committed adultery with the leopard, and to prevent the lion from smelling the stench of her infidelity on her, she would regularly wash herself in a spring near the king's castle. But having seen this happen repeatedly, on one particular occasion when the lioness had been unfaithful the king had the spring closed up. And when the lion returned and smelt the stench of infidelity, like a judge carrying out his verdict, he killed the lioness before everyone.[1]

Allegorically interpreted, this king is the heavenly father; the lion is our Lord Jesus Christ, i.e., the lion of the tribe of Judah. The lioness is man's soul, which often commits adultery with the leopard, i.e., the devil. And when she has committed this adultery, she runs to confession and is saved; but if she sins without confession and contrition, she cannot escape the vengeance of the lion, and He will damn her with the just sentence that will be given to all reprobates:[2] 'Go, you cursed, into everlasting fire etc.' From which may He defend us, who lives and reigns without end, God, blessed for all ages to come. Amen.

---

1 Cf. the story of the unfaithful stork, no. 82.
2 Cf. Mt 25.41.

Bibliography

Editions and translations of the *Gesta Romanorum*

Gesta Romanorum, Wynkyn de Worde, London, c.1510–15, facsimile edition, Exeter: Exeter University Press, 1974

'*Gesta Romanorum*'. *Entertaining Stories Invented by the Monks as a Fire-Side Recreation and Commonly Applied in Their Discourses from the Pulpit*, trans. Charles Swan, London: Routledge, 1824

Gesta Romanorum, ed. Adelbert Keller, Stuttgart and Tübingen: Cotta, 1842

Gesta Romanorum, trans. Johann Gottfried Theodor Graesse, Dresden: n.p., 1842; rev. edn Hans Eckart Rubesamen, Munich: Heyne, 1962; partially reprinted Paderborn: Salzwasser, 2013

Le Violier des Histoires Rommaines, ed. and rev. Pierre-Gustave Brunet, Paris: Jannet, 1858

Gesta Romanorum, ed. Hermann Oesterley, Berlin: Weidmann, 1872

The Early English Versions of the 'Gesta Romanorum', ed. Sidney J. H. Herrtage, EETS, 33, London: Oxford University Press, 1879

Die 'Gesta Romanorum' nach der Innsbrucker Handschrift vom Jahre 1342 und vier Münchener Handschriften, ed. Wilhelm Dick, Erlanger Beiträge zur englischen Philologie, 7, Erlangen and Leipzig: Junge, 1890

Gesta Romanorum, trans. Winfried Trillitzsch, Leipzig: Insel, 1973

'*Gesta Romanorum*'. *Lateinisch/Deutsch*, trans. and ed. Rainer Nickel, Universal-Bibliothek, 717(3), Stuttgart: Reclam, 1991

Le Violier des Histoires Rommaines, ed. Geoffroy Hope, Textes Littéraires Français, 548, Geneva: Droz, 2008

Secondary literature

Archibald, Elizabeth, *Apollonius of Tyre: Medieval and Renaissance Themes and Variations*, Cambridge: Brewer, 1991

Bourne, Ella, 'Classical Elements in the *Gesta Romanorum*', in Christabel Forsythe Fiske (ed.), *Vassar Mediaeval Studies*, New Haven, CT: Yale University Press, 1923, pp. 345–76

Bright, Philippa, 'Anglo-Latin Collections of the *Gesta Romanorum* and their Role in the Cure of Souls', in Juanita Feros Ruys (ed.), *What Nature Does Not Teach. Didactic Literature in the Medieval and Early Modern Periods*, Disputatio, 15, Turnhout: Brépols, 2008, pp. 401–24

Dicke, Gerd and Grubmüller, Klaus, *Die Fabeln des Mittelalters und der frühen Neuzeit. Ein Katalog der deutschen Versionen und ihrer lateinischen Entsprechungen*, Münstersche Mittelalter-Schriften, 60, Munich: Fink, 1987

Farmer, D. H., *The Oxford Dictionary of Saints*, Oxford: Oxford University Press, 1978

Gerdes, Udo, '*Gesta Romanorum*', in Kurt Ruh et al. (eds), *Die deutsche Literatur des Mittelalters. Verfasserlexikon*, 13 vols, Berlin/New York: de Gruyter, 1978–2007, Vol. III (1981), cols 25–34 and Vol. XI (2004), col. 526

Gerhardt, Christoph, *Die Metamorphosen des Pelikans. Exempel und Auslegung in mittelalterlicher Literatur. Mit Beispielen aus der bildenden Kunst und einem Bildanhang*, Trierer Studien zur Literatur, 1, Frankfurt: Lang, 1979

Gibbon, Edward, *The History of the Decline and Fall of the Roman Empire*, Vol. V: *Justinian and the Roman Law*, London: The Folio Society, 1987

Hamer, Richard (ed.), *Gilte Legende*, Vol. I, EETS, 327, Oxford: Oxford University Press, 2006

Hommers, Peter, '*Gesta Romanorum* deutsch. Untersuchungen zur Überlieferung und Redaktionengliederung', unpublished PhD thesis, University of Munich, 1968

Hope, Geoffroy, 'Tales of Literacy and Authority in the *Violier* (1521): The French *Gesta Romanorum*', *Bibliothèque d'Humanisme et Renaissance*, 59 (1997), pp. 353–63

Krepinsky, Max, 'Quelques remarques relatives à l'histoire des *Gesta Romanorum*', *Le Moyen Age*, 24 (1911), pp. 307–18, 346–67

Krug, Rebecca, 'Shakespeare's Medieval Morality: *The Merchant of Venice* and the *Gesta Romanorum*', in Curtis Perry and John Watkins (eds), *Shakespeare and the Middle Ages*, Oxford: Oxford University Press, 2009, pp. 241–61

Maccoll, D. S., 'Grania in Church: of the Clever Daughter', *The Burlington Magazine*, 8 (November 1905), pp. 80–5

Makaryk, Irena R (ed.), *Encyclopedia of Contemporary Literary Theory. Approaches, Scholars, Terms*, Toronto: Toronto University Press, 1993

Marchalonis, Shirley, 'Medieval Symbols and the *Gesta Romanorum*', *Chaucer Review*, 8 (1974), pp. 311–19

Mary Immaculate, Sr, 'The Four Daughters of God in the *Gesta Romanorum* and the *Court of Sapience*', *Publications of the Modern Language Association*, 57 (1942), pp. 951–65

Murdoch, Brian, *Gregorius. An Incestuous Saint in Medieval Europe and*

Beyond, Oxford: Oxford University Press, 2012

Ohly, Friedrich (trans. David A. Wells), 'The Spiritual Sense of Words in the Middle Ages', *Forum for Modern Language Studies*, 41 (2005), pp. 18–42

Otto, A., *Sprichwörter der Römer* [1890], Hildesheim: Olms, 1971

Palmer, Nigel F., 'Das *Exempelwerk der englischen Bettelmönche*: Ein Gegenstück zu den *Gesta Romanorum*?', in Walter Haug and Burghart Wachinger (eds), *Exempel und Exempelsammlungen*, Fortuna vitrea, 2, Tübingen: Niemeyer, 1991, pp. 137–72

Plessow, Oliver, *Mittelalterliche Schachzabelbücher zwischen Spielsymbolik und Wertevermittlung – Der Schachtraktat des Jacobus de Cessolis im Kontext seiner spätmittelalterlichen Rezeption*, Münster: Rhema, 2007

Richmond, Velma Bourgeois, *The Legend of Guy of Warwick*, Garland Studies in Medieval Literature, 14, New York: Garland, 1996

Röll, Walter, 'Zur Überlieferungsgeschichte der *Gesta Romanorum*', *Mittellateinisches Jahrbuch*, 21 (1986), pp. 208–29

Röll, Walter, 'Nachlese zur Überlieferung der *Gesta Romanorum*', *Beiträge zur Geschichte der deutschen Sprache und Literatur*, 121 (1999), pp. 103–8

Sanders, Corinne J., *Rape and Ravishment in the Literature of Medieval England*, Cambridge: Boydell and Brewer, 2001

Schneider, Johannes, 'Das Fortleben der römischen Kaiser in den *Gesta Romanorum*', *Klio*, 52 (1970), pp. 395–409

Schumacher, Meinolf, *Ärzte mit der Zunge. Leckende Hunde in der europäischen Literatur. Von der patristischen Exegese des Lazarus-Gleichnisses (Lk. 16) bis zum 'Romanzero' Heinrich Heines*, Aisthesis Essay, 16, Bielefeld: Aisthesis, 2003

Speed, Diane, 'Middle English Romance and the *Gesta Romanorum*', in Rosalind Field (ed.), *Tradition and Transformation in Medieval Romance*, Cambridge: Brewer, 1999, pp. 45–56

Sprandel, Rolf, 'Die *Gesta Romanorum* als Quelle der spätmittelalterlichen Mentalitätengeschichte', *Saeculum*, 33 (1982), pp. 312–22

Tubach, Frederic C., *Index Exemplorum. A Handbook of Medieval Religious Tales*, FF Communications, 204, Helsinki: Finnish Academy of Sciences, 1969

Wawrzyniak, Udo, '*Gesta Romanorum*', in Rolf Wilhelm Brednich et al. (eds), *Enzyklopädie des Märchens. Handwörterbuch zur historischen und vergleichenden Erzählforschung*, 14 vols, Berlin/New York: de Gruyter, 1977–2014, Vol. V (1987), cols 1201–12

Weiske, Brigitte, 'Die *Gesta Romanorum* und das *Solsequium* Hugos von Trimberg', in Walter Haug and Burghart Wachinger (eds), *Exempel und Exempelsammlungen*, Fortuna vitrea, 2, Tübingen: Niemeyer, 1991, pp. 173–207

Weiske, Brigitte, *Gesta Romanorum*, 2 vols, Fortuna vitrea, 3–4, Tübingen: Niemeyer, 1992

Index

In an attempt to maximize its usefulness to readers, this necessarily selective index contains material of the following kinds:
1. Names of figures, places or natural phenomena (animals, plants, etc.) mentioned in the *Gesta* stories, as long as they are also interpreted in the accompanying moralizations – passing references within the narratives are not recorded. Identifiable historical figures are referred to as such; the role or status of unidentifiable or plainly fictional figures is quoted, where possible, from the *Gesta*.
2. Historical figures, including authors, discussed in the footnotes and introduction (some of these also appear, in (semi-)fictional form, in the *Gesta*).
3. Names of authors to whom stories (as distinct from individual quotations) are attributed in the stories themselves.

Abibas ('poor man') 154–6
Achilles 416
Adonias ('king') 287–8
Aesop 127 n.1, 199 n.1, 258 n.1
Agael (normally Aglaes, wife of Euphemianus) 39–40, 42–3
Agapitus (normally Agapius, son of Eustace) 275–82
agate 104 and n.2
Aglae (daughter of Vespasian) 162–4
Agrigentines 122
Albert ('knight') 411–15
Albert of Stade 366 n.1
Alboin, King of the Lombards 139 n.2
Alexander ('king') 157–8, 240, 429–30
Alexander the Great xvi, xix, 22–4, 26 n.2, 28 and n.1, 91–2, 96–9, 103, 350, 368, 372
Alexius, St 39 n.1, 40–4
Androcles xvii, 258 n.1
Anselm of Canterbury 363 n.13
ape 301–4, 421
Apollo 387, 439, 449
Apollonius of Tyre xviii, 111, 380–408
Aquinas, St Thomas 140 n.4
Arabian Nights 306 n.1
Arcadius, Byzantine Emperor 41 and n.5, 43–4
Argus 283–4
Ariadne 162 n.1
Arion 371
Aristotle 28 and n.1, 29, 96–9, 118, 127 n.1

Armenia 366–7
Arrius 94–5
Asmodeus ('king') 145
asses 199, 302, 304
Assuerus, King of Persia 479–80
Asti 491–2
Augustine, St, of Hippo 73 and n.1, 74, 155, 156 n.3, 343 and n.1, 368 and nn.1–2
Augustinians 54
Aulus Gellius 258 and n.1, 323 n.1, 371 and n.1

Baghdad, 'knight of' 455–8
Barlaam 359 n.1, 444 n.1, 447 and n.2
basilisk 350
bear 247–8
Bernard (of Clairvaux), St 166 and n.4, 453
boar 217–18
Boccaccio, Giovanni xiii, 271 n.2, 272 n.3, 299 n.1, 455 n.1
Boethius, Anicius Manlius Severinus 434 and n.1, 438 and n.8
Browning, Robert 262 n.1

Caesar, Julius, *see* Julius
Caesarius von Heisterbach 487 and n.1
Calatinus (normally Collatinus, husband of Lucretia) 343–4
Cambyses (II, King of Persia) 87 n.1
carbuncle 266–7
Carmelites 54
Celestinus ('son of King Alexander') 429–32
Chaucer, Geoffrey xiii, 94 n.1, 351 n.3
Cicero, Marcus Tullius 94 n.1, 160 n.2, 268 n.1
Claudius ('king') 157–8

Cleonitus ('prince') 378
cockerel 54, 89 n.1, 175–6
Codrus, King of Athens 111 and n.1
Collatinus, *see* Calatinus
Conan ('King of the Hungarians') 124
Conrad, Holy Roman Emperor 66–9
Constantius ('King of Britain') 239
Coriolanus 347 n.1
cow 283–4, 319–20 (calf)
cranes 475–6
crows 118–19, 321–2 and n.1

Darius (the Great?), King 306–7, 309–10
de Leempt, Gerhardus (printer) xv
Demaratus, King of Sparta 70 and n.3, 71 and n.5, 72
Denmark, 'King of' 120–1
Diocletian, Roman Emperor 17, 246
Diomedes ('pirate') 368–9
Dionysius Cato 122, 450 n.4
Dionysius I, tyrant of Sicily xvi, 129 and n.2
dogs 3, 5, 30–1, 32 and n.3, 49, 51, 81–2, 84–6, 98–9, 106, 150, 153, 185, 199 and n.1, 267, 272, 318–19, 340, 355–8, 363
dolphin 371
Dominicans xiv–xv, 32 n.3, 431
Domitian, Roman Emperor 254–7
Dorians 111
Dorotheus ('emperor') 37–8
dove 106
dragon 247–8, 289–90, 366–7, 447–8, 461, 466
Duns Scotus, John xiv

eagle 104–5, 361, 363–4
Egypt, 'knight of' 455–8

Index

elements, the four 58 and n.33, 180–1
elephant 291–2
Erasmus of Rotterdam xix
Esther 479–80
Euphemianus, senator 39–43
Eustace, St (originally Placidus) xvii, 60 n.2, 274–82
Exempelwerk der englischen Bettelmönche xv

Fabius (Quintus Fabius Cunctator) 128
falcon 150, 153, 220–1
fish 55–6, 143, 222–3
Florentina 159–61
Focus ('artisan') 141–4
Fortunatus 306 n.1
fox 32, 185, 363
France 491–2
Franciscans xiv–xv, xx, 54, 431
Frederick, Holy Roman Emperor 130–1 (Frederick II), 295, 297
Frontinus, Sextus Julius xviii
Fulgentius ('king') 353–4

Gallus, Roman Emperor 177–9
Ganter 247–9
Genebaldus ('Duke of Ravenna') 490–1
Gervase of Tilbury 409 and n.1, 411 and n.1, 426 and n.1
gnat 361, 363–4
Godobert ('King of the Lombards') 490–2
Gordian, Roman Emperor 175
Gorgo, Queen of Sparta 71 n.5
Gorgonius ('king') 285–6
Gower, John xiii, 122 n.1, 272 n.3, 301 n.1
Gran, Heinrich (printer) xxiii
Graziaplena ('princess') 196–7
Gregory the Great, Pope xviii, 161 n.6, 203–15

Grimoaldus ('king' or 'duke') 491–2
Guido ('poor man') 48–59, 301–5
Guy of Warwick 459–67

Hadrian, Roman Emperor 280
Haman 479–80
hares 32, 67, 69, 357
Hartmann von Aue 243 n.1
Helen of Troy 160 n.2, 416
Henry ('emperor Conrad's son-in-law') 66–9
Henry the Elder ('King of England') 424–5
Henry II, Holy Roman Emperor 106
Henry VI, King of England xxii
Heraclius, Byzantine Emperor 351–2
Herodotus of Helicarnassus 71 n.6, 87 n.1, 228 n.2, 371 n.1
Hoccleve, Thomas 306 n.1, 436 n.1
Hofmannsthal, Hugo von xiii
Holcot, Robert xiii, xvi, 4 n.4, 7 n.20
Honorius, Roman Emperor 41 and n.5, 43–4
horses 58–9, 103 (Bucephalus), 147, 150, 152–3, 167–70, 180–1, 239, 295, 297, 318–19, 366–7, 375–7, 412–15, 429–31, 440, 453, 479–80, 482, 484
Hugo von Trimberg xiii
Hungary 124, 490–2

Innocent I, Pope 41 and n.6, 42–4
Innocent III, Pope 436 n.1
Innsbruck, Universitätsbibliothek, cod. lat. 310 xiii

Jacobus de Voragine, *The Golden Legend* 105 n.8, 139 n.2, 272 n.3, 359 n.1, 444 n.1, 447 n.1,
Jacobus de Cessolis xvi, 436 n.1

Jakeway, Richard (printer and publisher) xxiii
Jerusalem, 'King of' xxii–xxiii, 132
Jonathan ('keeper of Trajan's boar') 217–18
Jonathan ('youngest son of King Darius') 306–11
Josephus, Flavius 127 and n.1, 421 and n.1
Jovinian, Roman Emperor xvii, 147–53
Julian the Hospitaller, St 60 and n.1, 61–2
Julius (author) 118
Julius (Caesar) ('king' or 'emperor') 11, 107–8, 244–5
Julius Caesar (Gnaeus Julius Caesar) 63 and n.1, 64 and n.3, 65, 241 and n.1
Jupiter 89–90
Justinus, Marcus Junianius 70 and n.1, 449 and n.1

Ketelaer, Nicolaus (printer) xv

La Fontaine, Jean de 321–2 and n.1
lamb 100, 421
lamprey 98–9
Leo, Byzantine Emperor 19–21
Leonidas I, King of Sparta 76 n.5
leopard 493
Leopold (count) 66–7
Lessing, Gotthold Ephraim xiii
Ligurius ('knight'), *see* Lycurgus
lion (or lioness) xvii, 32, 42, 92, 107, 163–4, 185, 247–8, 258 and n.1, 259, 277, 279–82, 301–4, 313 and n.3, 363, 421, 493
Livy, Titus Livius Patavinus 128 n.1, 343 n.3
Lydgate, John 179 n.2, 459 n.1
Lucretia, the rape of 343, 344 n.4
Lycurgus, lawgiver of Sparta 449 and n.2, 450–2

Macrobius, Ambrosius Theodosius xviii, 109 and n.2, 323 and nn.1–2
Mann, Thomas xiii, 203 n.1
Marcus Anilius 114
Marcus Curtius 114 n.1
Marcus ('king') 203, 213
Martinus Polonus (Martin of Opava) 419 n.1
Maxentius, Roman Emperor 239
Maximian, Roman Emperor 171, 173, 328
Medro ('king') 349
Mercury 283–4
mice 447
Mordecai 479–80

nightingale 312–13, 443–4
North, Queen of the 28–9

Onolphus ('knight', of Pavia) 490–1
ostrich egg 443, 445
Otto, Holy Roman Emperor 30–1, 426
Ovid (Publius Ovidius Naso) 122 n.2, 154 n.1, 416, 441 and nn.13–14, 488 and n.10

Pallas (son of Evander) 419–20
Panchatantra 447 n.2
Papirius ('wise boy') 323–4
Paris (abductor of Helen) 416
Parnell, Thomas 202 n.3
partridge 102–3
Paul the Deacon (Paulus Diaconus) 124 and n.1, 140 n.3, 490 and n.1
Pepin (King) 293–4
Peratinus 94
Perillus ('worker in bronze') 122–3
Persia, 'King of' 349
  see also Assuerus; Cambyses; Xerxes

Peter, St 433–4
Petrarch (Francesco Petrarca) 439 n.9
Petrus (Peter) Alfonsi xvi, 84 and n.1, 262 and n.1, 299 n.1, 314 n.1, 316 n.1, 345 n.1, 417 n.1, 444 n.1, 455 and n.2
Phalaris, tyrant of Acragas 122 and n.1
Philip (II) of Macedon 372 and n.1
pig 24, 185, 363
Placidus, see Eustace
Plebeus ('tyrant') 460, 462–4, 466 and n.11, 467
Pliny the Elder (Gaius Plinius Secundus) xviii, 55, 103 n.6, 104 and nn.1–2, 115 n.1, 122 n.1, 235 n.1, 373 and n.1, 474 and n.1
Polemius ('king') 233
Pompeius Trogus 70 n.1, 449
Pompey ('king') 3 and n.2, 4–5, 220–1
Pompey (Pompey the Great) 3 n.2, 63 and nn.1–2, 64 and n.3, 65
Pomponius Mela 103 n.6
Portaticus ('king') 490–2
Prudentius, Aurelius 160 n.3

Robinson, Richard (printer) xxiii
Rosamund (princess, eventual wife of Abibas) 154–6
Rosamund (princess, sister of Graziaplena) 196–7
Rosamund (wife of Alboin) 139 n.2
Rosimila (Romilda) xvii, 124

Sachs, Hans xiii
Secretum Secretorum 28 n.1
Seneca the elder (Marcus Annaeus Seneca) xvii–xviii, xx, xxvi n.24, 8 n.1, 11 n.2, 37 n.1, 156 n.3, 231 and n.1, 246 and n.1, 341, 440, 441 n.11
Seneca the younger (Lucius Annaeus Seneca, 'the Philosopher') xviii, 93 and n.1, 351 n.3
Sepher Toldoth Yeschu 262 n.1
serpents xxii, 98–9 ('viper'), 104–5 ('pervas'), 236, 244–5, 247, 248 ('worms'), 261–2, 289–90, 301–4, 353–4, 375–7, 380–1 n.3 ('viper'), 447 ('vipers'), 471–3, 477–8 ('Jacorlus')
Sextus (son of Tarquinius, assailant of Lucretia) 343, 344 and n.4
Shakespeare, William xiii, xxiii, 13 n.3 (*Othello*), 272 n.3 (*Merchant of Venice*), 379–408 (*Pericles*)
sheep 429–31
Sisamnes (judge) 87 n.1
snakes, see serpents
Socrates (a type of wise man) 157–8, 366–7
Solinus, Gaius Julius 103 and n.6, 441 and n.12
stag 60–1, 274, 281
storks 216
swallow 99
Symphosius 402 n.24
Syria, king and princess of 22–3

Tarquinius (Lucius Tarquinius Superbus) 343–4
Theodosius, Roman Emperor 41 n.5, 260–1
Theosbytus (normally Theopistus, son of Eustace) 275–82
Theospita, see Thesbyta
theriac 74 and n.1, 477 n.1, 478
Thesbyta (normally Theospita, wife of Eustace) 275–82
Tiberius, Roman Emperor 115, 127, 222–3, 250, 252

Titus, Roman Emperor 8, 141–4
toad xxii, 236, 244–5, 247, 248
   ('worms'), 260–1
Trajan, Roman Emperor 217–18,
   274, 280
trees 118–19, 447–8, 477–8
Troy 416
Tyrius ('English knight') 459–66

Ulysses 416
unicorn 447

Valentine ('Bishop of Arles') 422
Valerius Maximus xviii, xxv n.16,
   94 and n.1, 112 and n.1, 125
   and n.2, 128 and n.1, 129 and
   n.1, 235 n.1, 268 n.1, 372 and
   n.1
Vashti (wife of Assuerus) 479–80
Vespasian, Roman Emperor 26 and
   n.2, 162–4
Vincent of Beauvais (Vincentius
   Bellovacensis) xix, 35 n.2

Violier des Histoires Rommaines, Le
   xxviii, 47 n.3, 242 n.4
Virgil (Publius Virgilius Maro)
   141, 143, 439 n.9, 478 and n.7
Vitae Patrum 435

weasel 461, 466
wolf 32, 276–7, 279, 281–2, 340
Wynkyn de Worde (printer) xxiii,
   xxvii, 11 n.1, 17 n.1, 154 n.1,
   157 n.1, 189 n.1

Xerxes (the Great?), King of
   Persia 70–1

Zaleucus, lawgiver of Locri 125
   and n.3, 126
Zedekiah ('knight') 353–4
Zell, Ulrich (printer) xv, xxiii
Zelongus ('emperor'), *see* Zaleucus
Zeuxis 160 n.2